Russia and Courtly Europe

In this new book on early modern diplomacy, Jan Hennings explores the relationship between European powers and Russia beyond the conventional East–West divide from the Peace of Westphalia to the reign of Peter the Great. He examines how, at a moment of new departures in both Europe and Russia, the norms shaping diplomatic practice emerged from the complex relations and direct encounters within the world of princely courts rather than from incompatible political cultures. He makes clear the connections between dynastic representation, politics, and foreign relations and shows that Russia, despite its perceived isolation and cultural distinctiveness, participated in the developments and transformations that were taking place more broadly in diplomacy. The central themes of this study are the interlocking manifestations of social hierarchy, monarchical honour, and sovereign status in both text and ritual. Related issues of diplomatic customs, institutional structures, personnel, negotiation practice, international law, and the question of cultural transfer also figure prominently.

Jan Hennings is Assistant Professor of History at Central European University, Budapest.

New Studies in European History

The aim of this series in early modern and modern European history is to publish outstanding works of research, addressed to important themes across a wide geographical range, from southern and central Europe, to Scandinavia and Russia, from the time of the Renaissance to the present. As it develops the series will comprise focused works of wide contextual range and intellectual ambition.

A full list of titles published in the series can be found at: www.cambridge.org/newstudiesineuropeanhistory

Russia and Courtly Europe

Ritual and the Culture of Diplomacy, 1648–1725

Jan Hennings

Central European University

CAMBRIDGE
UNIVERSITY PRESS

CAMBRIDGE
UNIVERSITY PRESS

University Printing House, Cambridge CB2 8BS, United Kingdom

Cambridge University Press is part of the University of Cambridge.

It furthers the University's mission by disseminating knowledge in the pursuit of education, learning, and research at the highest international levels of excellence.

www.cambridge.org
Information on this title: www.cambridge.org/9781107050594

First published 2016

Printed in the United Kingdom by Clays, St Ives plc

A catalogue record for this publication is available from the British Library.

Library of Congress Cataloging-in-Publication Data
Hennings, Jan, author.
Russia and courtly Europe : ritual and the culture of diplomacy, 1648–1725 / Jan Hennings (University of Oxford).
Cambridge : Cambridge University Press, 2016. | Series: New studies in European history | Includes bibliographical references.
LCCN 2016036669 | ISBN 9781107050594 (hardback)
LCSH: Europe – Foreign relations – Russia. | Russia – Foreign relations – Europe. | Diplomacy – History – 17th century. | Diplomacy – History – 18th century. | Europe – Kings and rulers – History. | Russia – Kings and rulers – History. | Europe – Court and courtiers – History. | Russia – Court and courtiers – History. | Political customs and rites – Europe – History. | Political customs and rites – Russia – History.
LCC D34.R9 H46 2016 | DDC 327.470409/032–dc23
LC record available at https://lccn.loc.gov/2016036669

ISBN 978-1-107-05059-4 Hardback

Contents

Illustrations

Acknowledgements

Russia and Courtly Europe started life as a doctoral project. I thank my supervisor at Clare College, Cambridge, Hubertus Jahn, and my co-supervisor at the University of Münster, Barbara Stollberg-Rilinger, for their continued support and intellectual guidance during and long after the PhD. I consider myself very lucky to have benefited from their combined expertise of Russian and early modern history, a combination that was crucial for the way in which this book has evolved. Christopher Clark and Simon Dixon have accompanied my work from the *viva voce* examination at Cambridge to the early stages of the book manuscript, and I am thankful for both their detailed critique and encouraging feedback in the process of turning the dissertation into a monograph. I also thank Cambridge University Press' three anonymous readers for their thorough and constructive assessments of the book manuscript. A special debt must be paid to the Cottrell-Dormer family who kindly welcomed me at Rousham House and allowed me to use the manuscripts held in their private archive. I also wish to acknowledge and thank the members of staff of the archives and libraries that I visited in Moscow (AVPRI, RGADA, RGB, and GPIB), Vienna (HHStA and ÖNB), Paris (BnF, AN, BM, BA, and AAE), London (TNA and BL), Cambridge (Cambridge UL), Oxford (Bodleian Library), and Berlin (UB Humboldt-Universität and Staatsbibliothek). Those who have commented on versions of this book in its entirety, or on parts of it, will know how much I appreciate their criticism: I am grateful to the late Isabel de Madariaga, Jereon Duindam, André Krischer, Hamish Scott, Ol'ga G. Ageeva, Judith Loades, Tony Lentin, Tracey Sowerby, William O'Reilly, Robyn D. Radway, Joachim Klein, Mark Hanin, Ambrogio Caiani, Eftychia Bathrellou, and my colleagues at Central European University, Charles Shaw, Alexei Miller, and Alfred J. Rieber. My gratitude also extends to those who have generously shared their knowledge with me and given valuable advice at various stages of my work. In particular, I thank Petr I. Prudovskii, Tim Blanning, the late Lindsey Hughes, Nikolai M. Rogozhin, Aleksandr Lavrov, Lyndal Roper, Christian Windler, David Parrott, Andreas Pečar, Christina

Brauner, Dmitri Gouzevitch, Andrei G. Tiul'pin, Reinhard Frötschner, Christine Roll, Iskra Schwarcz, Jan Plamper, Frithjof Benjamin Schenk, Ingrid Schierle, Roland Cvetkovski, Till Hennings, Niels Fabian May, Christian Steppan, Henriette Korthals Altes, Yulia Karpova, Olaf Schmidt, Antje Girndt, the members of the Study Group on Eighteenth-Century Russia, the members of both the former Leibniz-Projekt 'Vormoderne Verfahren' and the Sonderforschungsbereich 496 at the University of Münster, and the members of the research network the 'Textual Ambassador' for insightful conversations as well as for practical support. I am indebted to Clare College for granting me the G. R. Elton Scholarship and to the Studienstiftung des deutschen Volkes, the ZEIT-Stiftung Ebelin und Gerd Bucerius, and the Kurt Hahn Trust for supporting my doctoral studies. A Junior Research Fellowship at St John's College in Oxford provided the space for me to grow, complete my research, and revise the manuscript for publication. I thank Taylor & Francis Group for giving permission to include materials from my article, 'The semiotics of diplomatic dialogue: pomp and circumstance in Tsar Peter I's visit to Vienna in 1698', *International History Review*, 30 (2008), 515–44, in the Introduction and Chapter 4 of this book. Finally, I wish to express my deep gratitude to my family and my friends, and to Robyn, without whose support this book could not have been written.

Notes on Transliteration, Spelling, and Dates

The transliteration of Russian words and names follows the Library of Congress system apart from names that have become familiar in other spelling (such as Peter I or Catherine II). All translations from Russian, German, and French sources are my own, unless otherwise indicated. The spelling has been retained as it appears in the original sources. Unless otherwise specified in the text, dates are given according to the Old Style Calendar then in use in both Russia and Britain, except in Chapter 4 where dates follow the New Style which was used in most parts of continental Europe. The beginning of the year is uniformly taken as 1 January. Where in doubt, it is assumed that resident diplomats followed the style in use at the court where they resided.

Abbreviations

AAE	Archives du Ministère des Affaires Etrangères
ADB	*Allgemeine Deutsche Biographie*
AN	Archives nationales
AVPRI	Arkhiv vneshnei politiki Rossiiskoi imperii
ÄZA	Ältere Zeremonialacten
BA	Bibliothèque de l'Arsenal
BM	Bibliothèque Mazarine
BnF	Bibliothèque nationale de France
Bodl. Libr.	Bodleian Library
CP	Correspondance politique
d.	*delo* (file)
fol(s).	folio(s)
f.	*fond* (collection)
HHStA	Haus- Hof- und Staatsarchiv
IPO	*Instrumentum Pacis Osnabrugensis*
l., ll.	*list, listy* (folio, folios)
MD	Mémoires et documents
NS	New Style (Gregorian Calendar)
ob	*oborot* (verso)
op.	*opis'* (inventory)
OS	Old Style (Julian Calendar)
otd.	*otdel* (section)
PDS	*Pamiatniki diplomaticheskikh snoshenii drevnei Rossii s derzhavami inostrannymi*
PiB	*Pis'ma i bumagi imperatora Petra Velikogo*
PSZRI	*Polnoe sobranie zakonov Rossiiskoi imperii*
RGADA	Rossiiskii gosudarstvennyi arkhiv drevnikh aktov
rubr.	rubric
SIRIO	*Sbornik Imperatorskogo Russkogo istoricheskogo obshchestva*
SP	State Papers
TNA	The National Archives
v	verso
ZA Prot	Zeremonialprotokolle

Introduction

In July 1721, the Russian ambassador Prince Vasilii L. Dolgorukov called on the home of the French secretary of state for foreign affairs, Cardinal Guillaume Dubois, to congratulate him on his recent promotion to the cardinalate. The diplomat's visit ended on Dubois' doorstep before it even began, however, owing to the cardinal's fastidious refusal to grant Dolgorukov or any foreign representative the customary right to the place of honour – 'the right hand' – in his house, a refusal which caused much commotion among the diplomatic corps in Paris.[1] Dubois explained to Dolgorukov that 'the subordination to the hierarchies and ranks, that form the constitution of a state, belong to the customs and conventions which foreign representatives are bound to follow; otherwise they would act against the law of nations because they would violate the public order'.[2] Defending his actions, the cardinal alluded to well-documented precedents from the preceding century, conferring on his decision the power of historical example and reminding the ambassador that 'there are not two courts where the ceremonial would be the same in all circumstances'.[3] The Russian diplomat deduced that Dubois was irked by the prospect of forfeiting his rank as state secretary if he should surrender the honour position in the ritual. Dolgorukov reverted to his sovereign, Tsar Peter I, for advice on how to proceed in this 'considerable business'.[4]

This episode serves as more than a testament to the wider anthropological assumption that ritual is inherent to human action.[5] It is also

[1] Dolgorukov to Peter I, 24 July 1721, AVPRI, f. 93, op. 93/1 (1721), d. 7, ll. 217ob–19ob.

[2] Dolgorukov to Peter I, 11 August 1721, AVPRI, f. 93, op. 93/1 (1721), d. 7, l. 248.

[3] Dubois referred to an edition of A. de Wicquefort, *L'ambassadeur et ses fonctions* (The Hague, 1681), pp. 542ff. Dolgorukov to Peter I, 11 August 1721, AVPRI, f. 93, op. 93/1 (1721), d. 7, ll. 248, 249ob.

[4] Dolgorukov to Peter I, 4 August 1721, AVPRI, f. 93, op. 93/1 (1721), d. 7., ll. 239–40ob.

[5] W. James, *The ceremonial animal: a new portrait of anthropology* (Oxford, 2003), p. 7. The anthropological literature on ritual is too voluminous to be discussed here. For an overview, see C. M. Bell, *Ritual theory, ritual practice*, 2nd edn. (Oxford, 2009). An up-to-date historical introduction is B. Stollberg-Rilinger, *Rituale* (Frankfurt a. M., 2013).

emblematic of early modern political culture more broadly, which was punctuated with similar instances of incessant manipulation and disputes over punctilios of ceremony. Honour, as displayed in face-to-face interaction, and how it was documented, pervaded almost all areas of early modern life. Political and social practices relied on the presence of the protagonists for the demonstration of rank and prestige which, in a thoroughly hierarchical society, controlled access to privilege, power, and political participation. The representation of status was inseparable from politics and policy because such rituals did not merely reflect existing social structures and power relations but also produced these structures, or, as witnessed by Dubois: they constituted the public order.[6]

This nexus between personal presence, status performance, symbolic practice, and political representation encompassed the world of dynastic courts, and their elites, as much as life in the city, in the university, in local government, across large polities, and in the colonies of the New World.[7] Ceremonies and subtleties of honour were also important generators of both the social order and political legitimacy in early modern Russia, as a long and distinguished tradition in the study of political

[6] B. Stollberg-Rilinger, 'Symbolische Kommunikation in der Vormoderne: Begriffe – Forschungsperspektiven – Thesen', *Zeitschrift für Historische Forschung*, 31 (2004), 489–527. For the theoretical underpinnings of the concept of face-to-face society (*Anwesenheitsgesellschaft*), see R. Schlögl, 'Kommunikation und Vergesellschaftung unter Anwesenden: Formen des Sozialen und ihre Transformation in der Frühen Neuzeit', *Geschichte und Gesellschaft*, 34 (2008), 155–224.

[7] The present book owes many of its insights to recent German-language research that has recovered the links between symbols and politics and shaped new approaches to the pre-modern world, mainly at the Münster-based Collaborative Research Centre 'Symbolic Communication and Social Value Systems from the Middle Ages to the French Revolution', and notably in B. Stollberg-Rilinger's work on the Holy Roman Empire. See her *The emperor's old clothes: constitutional history and the symbolic language of the Holy Roman Empire*, trans. T. Dunlap (New York, Oxford, 2015). See also D. Cannadine, 'Introduction: divine rites of kings', in *Rituals of royalty: power and ceremonial in traditional societies*, ed. D. Cannadine, S. R. F. Price (Cambridge, 1987), pp. 1–19; M. J. Braddick, 'Administrative performance: the representation of political authority in early modern England', in *Negotiating power in early modern society: order, hierarchy and subordination in Britain and Ireland*, ed. M. J. Braddick, J. Walter (Cambridge, 2001), pp. 166–87. For courts, J. Duindam, *Vienna and Versailles: the courts of Europe's dynastic rivals, 1550–1780* (Cambridge, 2003), ch. 6; G. Sternberg, *Status interaction during the reign of Louis XIV* (Oxford, 2014). For universities, see M. Füssel, *Gelehrtenkultur als symbolische Praxis: Rang, Ritual und Konflikt an der Universität der frühen Neuzeit* (Darmstadt, 2006). For towns, T. Weller, *Theatrum Praecedentiae: zeremonieller Rang und gesellschaftliche Ordnung in der frühneuzeitlichen Stadt, Leipzig 1500–1800* (Darmstadt, 2006); A. Krischer, *Reichsstädte in der Fürstengesellschaft. Zum politischen Zeichengebrauch in der Frühen Neuzeit* (Darmstadt, 2006), and P. Seed, *Ceremonies of possession in Europe's conquest of the New World, 1492–1640* (Cambridge, 1995), for colonies.

rituals and the role of rank and precedence (*mestnichestvo*) in Russian history has shown.[8]

The principles that governed life at home also held true abroad. Even for the most courtly and haughty ambassador, whether European or Russian, the display of honour in direct contact was more than an expression of vain formality, personal pride, or self-worth. It was a constitutive component of a state's sovereignty and legitimacy, and as such was precious and well-protected capital in relations between states. Early modern diplomats, then, faced a dilemma. How did diplomacy establish effective communication between rulers over long distances if their political culture necessitated ritual and bodily presence? Complex structures of diplomatic representation resulted from this paradox, including convoluted hierarchies, a large variety of roles, innumerable distinctions, and projections of power that through the continual mise-en-scène of sovereign dignity and rank maintained the international order.

This book is about Russia's place in that order. It explores Russian foreign relations through the lens of ritual and court culture in the crucial phase before Russia's rise as a so-called great power in the eighteenth century. Russia (or Muscovy, as it was known to foreign visitors until the eighteenth century) usually escapes traditional accounts of diplomatic history in the search for the origins of modern foreign relations. Russia might not have participated in the achievements of Renaissance diplomacy with its classic ideal of the resident diplomat, and, lying on the edge of Europe, it took some time to contribute to the rise of modern

[8] For an overview, see M. S. Flier, 'Political ideas and rituals', in *The Cambridge history of Russia*, ed. M. Perrie, D. C. B. Lieven, R. G. Suny, 3 vols. (Cambridge, 2006), I, pp. 387–408. For Muscovy, R. O. Crummey, 'Court spectacles in seventeenth-century Russia: illusion and reality', in *Essays in Honor of A. A. Zimin*, ed. D. C. Waugh (Columbus, 1985), pp. 130–58; N. S. Kollmann, 'Ritual and social drama at the Muscovite court', *Slavic Review*, 45 (1986), 486–502; P. A. Bushkovitch, 'The epiphany ceremony of the Russian court in the sixteenth and seventeenth centuries', *Russian Review*, 49 (1990), 1–17; M. S. Flier, 'Breaking the code: the image of the tsar in the Muscovite Palm Sunday ritual', in *Medieval Russian culture*, ed. M. S. Flier, D. B. Rowland (Berkeley, CA, 1994), pp. 213–42; D. Miller, 'Creating legitimacy: ritual, ideology, and power in sixteenth-century Russia', *Russian History/Histoire Russe*, 21 (1994), 289–315; N. S. Kollmann, *By honor bound: state and society in early modern Russia* (Ithaca, NY, 1999); S. Bogatyrev, *The sovereign and his counsellors: ritualised consultations in Muscovite political culture, 1350s–1570s* (Helsinki, 2000); A. Berelowitch, *La hiérarchie des égaux: la noblesse russe d'Ancien Régime (XVIe–XVIIe siècles)* (Paris, 2001); D. B. Rowland, 'Architecture, image, and ritual in the throne rooms of Muscovy, 1550–1650: a preliminary survey', in *Rude & barbarous kingdom revisited: essays in Russian history and culture in honor of Robert O. Crummey*, ed. C. S. L. Dunning, R. E. Martin, D. B. Rowland (Bloomington, IN, 2008), pp. 53–71. For imperial Russia, see R. Wortman, *Scenarios of power: myth and ceremony in Russian monarchy*, 2 vols. (Princeton, NJ, 1995/2000); E. A. Zitser, *The transfigured kingdom: sacred parody and charismatic authority at the court of Peter the Great* (Ithaca, NY, 2004).

diplomacy by integrating itself as member of the European states-system rather reluctantly.[9] But the gulf at the beginning of the early modern period between the new diplomacy of southern and western Europe and the continent's eastern fringes requires qualification, as from the later Middle Ages Muscovite diplomatic practice, and also that of both Poland-Lithuania and the Ottoman Empire, was evolving in processes not at all dissimilar to the ways in which connections between ritual, communication, negotiation, and military conflict shaped Renaissance diplomacy.[10]

A seemingly distant world, Russia of course remained a remote and exotic land for early modern Europeans.[11] Yet, diplomacy is also always concerned with crossing cultural boundaries over large distances, some more penetrable than others. The last two decades have seen a renaissance of diplomatic history under the label of the 'new diplomatic history' which has shifted the perspective away from the study of great – essentially European – affairs, and the modern state-focused notion of international relations, to a broader appreciation of cross-cultural exchange, individual actors, and the complexity of early modern polities in the evolution of diplomatic practice.[12]

[9] The *locus classicus* is G. Mattingly, *Renaissance diplomacy* (New York, NY, 2009, originally published in 1955), and M. S. Anderson, *The rise of modern diplomacy, 1450–1919* (London, 1993). Russia's place in early modern international relations will be discussed in Chapter 1. For a balanced critique of Mattingly, see M. Mallett, 'Italian renaissance diplomacy', *Diplomacy and Statecraft*, 12 (2001), 61–70. See also C. Fletcher, *Diplomacy in Renaissance Rome: the rise of the resident ambassador* (Cambridge, 2015), for a recent nuanced assessment of resident diplomacy.

[10] Ibid., esp. chs. 3 and 5; I. Lazzarini, *Communication and conflict: Italian diplomacy in the early Renaissance, 1350–1520* (Oxford, 2015). For Muscovy, R. M. Croskey, *Muscovite diplomatic practice in the reign of Ivan III* (New York, London, 1987). See also the materials in the composite work by G. Labuda, W. Michowicz, eds., *The history of Polish diplomacy X–XX c.* (Warsaw, 2005), and A. S. Kaminski, *Republic vs. autocracy: Poland-Lithuania and Russia, 1686–1697* (Cambridge, MA, 1993). A similar argument has been put forward by D. Goffman, 'Negotiating with the renaissance state: the Ottoman empire and the new diplomacy', in *Early modern Ottomans: remapping the empire*, ed. V. Aksan, D. Goffman (Cambridge, 2007), pp. 61–74.

[11] M. Poe, 'A distant world: Russian relations with Europe before Peter the Great', in *The world engages Russia*, ed. C. Whittaker (Cambridge, MA, 2003), pp. 2–23.

[12] See T. Sowerby's forthcoming survey of the field, 'Approaches to early modern diplomacy', *History Compass* (2016). Only a selection of representative examples from the growing body of literature can be included here. Most contain useful overviews with ample references to further individual case studies: D. Frigo, ed., *Politics and diplomacy in early modern Italy: the structure of diplomatic practice, 1450–1800*, trans. A. Belton (Cambridge, 2000); C. Windler, 'Diplomatic history as a field for cultural analysis: Muslim-Christian relations in Tunis, 1700–1840', *Historical Journal*, 44 (2001), 79–106; T. Osborne, *Dynasty and diplomacy in the court of Savoy: political culture and the Thirty Years' War* (Cambridge, 2002); H. Kugeler, C. Sepp, G. Wolf, eds., *Internationale Beziehungen in der Frühen Neuzeit: Ansätze und Perspektiven* (Hamburg, 2006); L. Bély, *L'art de la paix en Europe: naissance de la diplomatie moderne, XVIe–XVIIIe siècle* (Paris, 2007); J. Watkins, 'Toward a new diplomatic history of medieval and early modern

In diplomacy, then, the geopolitical distance between Russian and European rulers gradually gave way to physical proximity, as diplomatic representatives journeyed through vast expanses of land or across seas, slowly approaching the centre of the realm to face the monarch in his chambers. From the moment of crossing the border to the first public audience with the sovereign and beyond, the actions of diplomatic dignitaries were governed by an elaborate ceremonial. The prince invested his diplomat with surrogate authority, and each of his actions, however arbitrary or 'symbolic', acquired the importance of a political synonym that could initiate and alter relationships, for better or for worse. Ritual provided the structure for the diplomat's interactions with his host from the frontier to the capital, assuming ever-greater grandeur and complication as he approached the centre of power.[13]

Europe', *Journal of Medieval and Early Modern Studies*, 38 (2008), 1–14; H. v. Thiessen, C. Windler, eds., *Akteure der Aussenbeziehungen: Netzwerke und Interkulturalität im historischen Wandel* (Cologne, 2010). T. Hampton, *Fictions of embassy: literature and diplomacy in early modern Europe* (Ithaca, NY, 2009); J. Black, *A history of diplomacy* (London, 2010); R. Adams, R. Cox, eds., *Diplomacy and Early Modern Culture* (Basingstoke, 2011); C. Brauner, *Kompanien, Könige und caboceers. Interkulturelle Diplomatie an Gold- und Sklavenküste, 17.-18. Jahrhundert* (Cologne, 2015); P. Burschel, C. Vogel, eds., *Die Audienz: ritualisierter Kulturkontakt in der Frühen Neuzeit* (Cologne, 2014); D. Riches, *Protestant cosmopolitanism and diplomatic culture: Brandenburg-Swedish relations in the seventeenth century* (Leiden, Boston, 2013), esp. the introduction for a useful summary of the new diplomatic history; M. van Gelder, T. Krstić, 'Cross-confessional diplomacy and diplomatic intermediaries in the early modern Mediterranean', *Journal of Early Modern History*, 19 (2015).

[13] The best introduction is A. Krischer, 'Souveränität als sozialer Status: zur Funktion des diplomatischen Zeremoniells in der Frühen Neuzeit', in *Diplomatisches Zeremoniell in Europa und im Mittleren Osten in der Frühen Neuzeit*, ed. R. Kauz, J. P. Niederkorn, G. Rota (Vienna, 2009), pp. 1–32. See also W. J. Roosen, 'Early modern diplomatic ceremonial: a system's approach', *Journal of Modern History*, 52 (1980), 452–76; L. Wolff, 'A Duel for ceremonial precedence: the Papal Nuncio versus the Russian ambassador at Warsaw, 1775–1785', *International History Review*, 7 (1985), 235–44; L. Bély, 'Souveraineté et souverain: La question du cérémonial dans les relations internationales à l'époque moderne', *Annuaire-Bulletin de la Société de l'Histoire de France* (1993), 27–43. For Russia, see, among others, C. Garnier, '"Wer meinen Herrn ehrt, den ehre ich billig auch". Symbolische Kommunikationsformen bei Gesandtenempfängen am Moskauer Hof im 16. und 17. Jahrhundert', *Jahrbuch für Kommunikationsgeschichte*, 7 (2005), 27–51; C. Roll, 'Europäische Gesandtschaften am Zarenhof: Zeremoniell und Politik', in *Zarensilber: Augsburger Silber aus dem Kreml*, ed. C. Emmendörffer, C. Trepesch (Munich, 2008), pp. 30–55; M.-K. Schaub, 'Comment régler des incidents protocolaires? Diplomates russes et françaises au XVIIe siècle', in *L'incident diplomatique (XVIe–XVIIIe siècle)*, ed. L. Bély, G. Poumarède (Paris, 2010), pp. 323–36; R. Schilling, 'Kommunikation und Herrschaft im Moment der Ankunft: Ein Empfang in Moskau (1603) und eine Audienz in Versailles (1686)', in *Die Ankunft des Anderen: Repräsentationen sozialer und politischer Ordnungen in Empfangszeremonien*, ed. S. Baller et al. (Frankfurt a. M., 2008), pp. 135–51. The most comprehensive, in-depth study on the subject focuses on the eighteenth century: O. G. Ageeva, *Diplomaticheskii tseremonial imperatorskoi Rossii. XVIII vek.* (Moscow, 2012).

Some interpretations locate these ritual procedures in the sphere of spectacle, propaganda, ideology, and myth, describing them as an 'original expression of [Russian] national culture'.[14] Leonid A. Iuzefovich sees a reason for this distinctive Russianness in the fact that the emerging Muscovite state believed itself to be exposed to numerous cultural influences and desired to assert its own place in the international arena after it had gained independence from the Mongols.[15] One main occupation in the study of diplomatic ritual has been indeed the search for clues of Russian national identity and the cultural origins of Muscovite diplomacy. While the spectrum ranges from Western to Asian or Mongol; to Byzantine, Old-Russian, Polish-Lithuanian; or a mixture of all those strands, the ramification remains the same, that Russian ceremonial exhibited a double-layered foreignness: it emerged from foreign influences and remained deeply foreign to European diplomatic culture.[16] Russia distinguished itself from other cultures by receiving various traditions and moulding them into an expression of self-consciousness which was genuinely Russian: by implication, this saw a radical break under Peter I when Russian diplomacy became essentially European. Conversely, the tsars' sense of magnificence demonstrated at secular and religious solemnities, as well their claim to imperial superiority, is often seen as a symbol of Muscovy's exotic Orthodox ritualism which caused amazement and wonder among visitors to the Russian court. As one scholar put it, an obstacle to Peter

[14] L. A. Iuzefovich, '*Kak v posol'skikh obychaiakh vedetsia': Russkii posol'skii obychai kontsa XV – nachala XVII v.* (Moscow, 1988), p. 12.

[15] Ibid., pp. 9, 11f. See also the revised version: *Put' posla: russkii posol'skii obychai. Obikhod. Etiket. Tseremonial. Konets XV – pervaia polovina XVII v* (St Petersburg, 2007), p. 13.

[16] N. I. Veselovskii, 'Tatarskoe vliianie na russkii posol'skii tseremonial v moskovskii period russkoi istorii', in *Otchet o sostoianii i deiatel'nosti Imperatorskogo S.-Peterburgskogo universiteta za 1910*, ed. I. A. Ivanovskii (St Petersburg, 1911), pp. 1–19; V. I. Savva, *Moskovskie tsari i vizantiiskie vasilevsy: o vliianii Vizantii na obrazovanie idei tsarskoi vlasti moskovskikh gosudarei* (Khar'kov, 1901, reprint, The Hague, Paris, 1969), pp. 191, 268–70; Also representative for pre-revolutionary historiography: V. Leshkov, *O drevnei russkoi diplomatii* (Moscow, 1847), pp. 57ff., passim. L. A. Iuzefovich, 'Russkii posol'skii obychai xvi veka', *Voprosy istorii*, 8 (1977), 114–26; Iuzefovich, *Put'* posla, pp. 5–13; I. Semenov, *U istokov kremlevskogo protokola: istoriia vozniknoveniia rossiiskogo posol'skogo tseremoniala i nravy Kremlia v XV–XVII vekakh* (Moscow, 2005), pp. 197ff. For a Soviet account that stresses western but accommodates certain Byzantine and indigenous Slavic influences, see V. P. Potemkin et al., eds., *Istoriia diplomatii*, 2nd rev. edn., 5 vols. (Moscow, 1959–1979), I, pp. 303–15. It is interesting to note that the first edition of this work (published in 1941) had argued that Russian ceremonial was a faithful copy of its Western counterpart. The later 'Stalinist' revision added some Byzantine and original Slavic origins. This point is noted in G. Scheidegger, *Perverses Abendland, barbarisches Russland: Begegnungen des 16. und 17. Jahrhunderts im Schatten kultureller Missverständnisse* (Zurich, 1993), p. 30.

I's contacts with the West, Russian diplomatic practice before Peter I 'had become frozen in an elaborate ritual whose many formalities and details admitted of little modification; it seemed all too often that protocol, rather than negotiation, had become its chief preoccupation'.[17] Such interpretations address the important aspect of the uses of ceremony in the display of national cultural and ideological legacies, but they obfuscate complex patterns of political interaction in early modern diplomacy. This was a period – aptly characterised by Hillard von Thiessen as 'diplomacy of the *type ancien*' – when international relations were still a personal affair between rulers embedded in multilayered networks of diplomatic actors rather than the domain of representatives of national governments; a period when the idea of the nation as a political actor was still unborn and the socio-hierarchical environment of princely courts provided the dominant model for diplomats acting on a distinct combination of protocol and political practice.[18]

This book builds on the new diplomatic history and grapples with the old but persistent juxtaposition of Russia and Europe or, in its more encompassing version, Russia and the West. A core theme in Russian historiography, shaped by eighteenth- and nineteenth-century intellectual debates, Cold War rivalries, and strict chronological divisions, this distinction may have appeared just as strange to early modern contemporaries as their obsessive concern with ceremony appears to us.[19] This book firmly places 'Russia and the West' within the diplomacy of the *type ancien* and consciously avoids essentialising diplomatic cultures as specifically Russian or European. But this is not an easy task. The particular challenge lies in being unable to resolve these antitheses in anything other than the language of antithesis. Oppositions like this have defined both thought and language of generations of diplomatic historians.[20] Methodological reorientation, selection of different source materials, and analytical rigour will not make them go away. It appears impossible, even futile, to escape the firmly rooted

[17] A. Bohlen, 'Changes in Russian diplomacy under Peter the Great', *Cahiers du Monde Russe et Soviétique*, 7 (1966), 341–58, here on p. 343.

[18] H. v. Thiessen, 'Diplomatie vom *type ancien*. Überlegungen zu einem Idealtypus des frühneuzeitlichen Gesandtschaftswesens', in *Akteure der Außenbeziehungen*, ed. H. v. Thiessen, C. Windler, pp. 471–503.

[19] See Daniel Rowland's compelling discussion of the Russia/West dichotomy in early modern history: Rowland, 'Architecture', p. 62. For a recent debate about the Petrine and Russia/West divide and its wider implications for early modern Russian historiography, see Bushkovitch, 'Change and culture in early modern Russia' and N. S. Kollmann, 'A deeper early modern: a response to Paul Bushkovitch', *Kritika: Explorations in Russian and Eurasian History*, 16 (2015), 291–329.

[20] I. B. Neumann, *Uses of the Other: 'the East' in European identity formation* (Manchester, 1999), esp. ch. 3, for Russia; R. N. Lebow, *A cultural theory of international relations* (Cambridge, 2008), p. 10.

vocabularies of a tradition that the present work interrogates across both Russian and diplomatic history.[21] As a result, I will use these oppositions liberally throughout this comparative venture, not in order to imply that such distinctions determined early modern foreign relations in any way but to remind the reader that despite existing discourses of otherness and mutually ascribed stereotypes, the concrete practice of face-to-face encounter may well contradict and challenge the assumptions that we draw from a deeply ingrained notion of cultural difference.[22]

The book's chief aim, then, is to locate Russia in a context of wider, transcultural developments in early modern diplomacy by understanding diplomatic representation from within the practice and documentation of ritual itself, rather than by tracing the cultural origins of power imagery and myth and reifying idiosyncratic ceremonial traditions. It confronts the widely published ethnographical literature about 'the rude and barbarous kingdom' with the routines and ruptures of diplomatic encounters, bringing into sharp relief the differences and interdependencies between discourse and practice.[23] A basic assumption in the history of international relations has been the supremacy of the territorially bounded, sovereign nation state and that, in turn, diplomatic culture emerged from national traditions.[24] The book breaks away from this convention. It transcends the national paradigm and argues that diplomatic culture was itself a product of continuous cultural exchange.[25]

[21] The general implications of this problem have been elaborated in D. Chakrabarty, *Provincializing Europe: postcolonial thought and historical difference* (Princeton, NJ, Oxford, 2000), esp. pp. 4f. and passim in the introduction.

[22] I believe that a more radical approach – to drop such juxtapositions and vocabularies all together – would either lead to the use of awkward language or sweeping attempts at correlating political entities in novel ways, ultimately replacing one problem with another. A similar challenge presents the use of commonly established terms such as 'international', 'states-system', 'great power', or even 'diplomacy', which had not assumed their contemporary meaning before the eighteenth or the end of the eighteenth century. I will continue to use these terms for the sake of consistency although I am keenly aware – and it is indeed the purpose of this book to raise the awareness – that their modern connotations more often than not belie the distinct nature of early modern foreign relations. For 'diplomacy' and 'great power', see H. M. Scott, 'Diplomatic culture in Old Regime Europe', in *Cultures of power in Europe during the long eighteenth century: essays in honour of T. C. W. Blanning*, ed. H. M. Scott, B. Simms (Cambridge, 2007), pp. 58–85, here on pp. 58f.; H. M. Scott, *The emergence of the eastern powers*, 1756–1775 (Cambridge, 2001), pp. 7–10. For 'international', see Lebow, *A cultural theory*, p. 10.

[23] L. E. Berry, R. O. Crummey, eds., *Rude & barbarous kingdom: Russia in the accounts of sixteenth-century English voyagers* (Madison, WI, 1968).

[24] For a survey of international political thought that considers international relations beyond the idea of state sovereignty and aptly puts the nation state in historical perspective, see E. Keene, *International political thought: a historical introduction* (Cambridge, 2005), pp. 1–22.

[25] I follow Clifford Geertz's classic notion that 'culture, here, is not cults and customs, but the structure of meaning through which men give shape to their experience, and politics is

The practice of diplomacy provided an arena in which representatives of different or overlapping norm systems negotiated the meaning of body language, of words and symbols that provided procedures to engage in diplomatic dialogue. Therefore, the book focuses on the negotiation of diplomatic norms in direct interaction, both verbal and non-verbal, rather than locating the evolution of diplomatic practice in the indigenous customs or ideologies of political communities whose confrontations resulted in an involuntary clash of pre-existing and incompatible values.[26] It adopts a comparative perspective in order to clarify how dynastic competition impeded or expedited the standardisation of rules and procedures of diplomacy beyond national boundaries and to show to what degree Russia participated in this process. It argues that shared concepts of honour, prestige, and courtly representation involved Russian, Habsburg, English, French, and other European diplomats in a similar rivalry over the resources of glory and status. Disagreements arising from irreconcilable claims to status signified mutual understanding of what was politically at stake. Concrete ceremonial practice differed within Europe from court to court, as well as between Europe and Russia. And yet, in this arena of diplomacy, conflict, more often than not, was a sign of common discernment rather than an expression of cultural misunderstanding.

It is not the purpose of this book to give a comprehensive account of late Muscovite as well as Petrine diplomacy and foreign relations. The entire work combines, in chronological order, an exploration of Russia's images in various types of seventeenth- and eighteenth-century literatures with a series of case studies of Russian–European encounters from the Peace of Westphalia (1648) to the end of Peter I's reign (1725). The convergence of increased diplomatic activity in Russia since the 1650s and new developments in diplomacy in the century after the Thirty Years' War offers good grounds for comparing Russian–European practices from the second half of the seventeenth century until the early eighteenth century.[27]

not coups and constitutions, but one of the principal arenas in which such structures publicly unfold'. C. Geertz, *The Interpretation of Cultures* (New York, 1973, reprint, 2000), p. 312. See also his definition of 'culture' in ibid., p. 5.

[26] Such an approach to early modern diplomacy, which emphasises the negotiation of norms and the flexibility of intercultural practices as opposed to the notion of a cultural clash, has been advanced by Christian Windler in his pioneering work on French consuls in the Maghreb: C. Windler, *La diplomatie comme expérience de l'Autre: consuls français au Maghreb (1700–1840)* (Geneva, 2002), esp. pp. 29ff; 549ff. For a recent inspiring discussion of cultural commensurability and its production through, amongst others, diplomatic encounters and intercultural communication, see S. Subrahmanyam, *Courtly encounters: translating courtliness and violence in early modern Eurasia* (Cambridge, MA, 2012).

[27] See B. N. Floria, *Russkoe gosudarstvo i ego zapadnye sosedi: 1655–1661 gg.* (Moscow, 2010), pp. 10ff., for Russian diplomacy. For post-1648 diplomacy, see Chapter 1 below.

Any analysis of Russian diplomatic practice that treats Peter I's reign as a volte-face risks contrasting ritual behaviour as anachronistic and fundamentally 'Muscovite' with a European, bureaucratic, and more rational diplomacy introduced by Peter I. In order to redress the balance between such continuities and discontinuities, the present study examines Russian diplomatic practice across the conventional Petrine divide.[28] What follows is a prelude that bears out the connections between ritual, hierarchy, sovereignty, concepts of majesty, and social status, examining how the mindset of early modern court society, with its deeply ingrained sense of dynastic supremacy, impacted on foreign relations in the age of the baroque, a period that is also known to have witnessed the gradual emergence of the European states-system.

Chapter 1 briefly traces Russia's place in the international order through its prevailing image as an exotic outsider, as promoted in early modern ethnography, international law, diplomatic theory, contemporary state descriptions and historiography. It then shifts the perspective to introduce new materials and discuss the reasons for the integration of Russian rulers into the precedence system by contemporary scholars of *ius praecedentiae* (precedence law) and *Zeremonialwissenschaft* (ceremonial science). This angle provides some first counterpoints against Muscovy's diplomatic outlier status proliferating in the literature more common to students of Russian history, as these authors consciously incorporated Orthodox Russia into the ceremonial sphere of sovereigns well before the rise of Peter I, despite their pronounced reservations about Russian culture and customs.

The following four chapters peel away the layers of discourse by analysing diplomatic face-to-face encounters in order to confront the discursive image of Russia with the reality of diplomatic practice. These chapters move away from abstract norms regulating conflicts over dynastic supremacy and political power status and explore the tsars' place in concrete ritual junctures at prominent Western courts (Vienna, Versailles, and London) as well as the treatment of diplomatic dignitaries in Moscow and St Petersburg. Ceremonial records, memoirs, diplomatic reports and correspondences, as well as courtly media, form the basis for these chapters. Locating Russia in the wider picture of early modern court culture and its bearing on diplomacy requires a comparative approach that brings Russian and Western language materials into a dialogue beyond mere

[28] See also R. E. Martin, 'The Petrine divide and the periodization of early modern Russian history', *Slavic Review*, 69 (2010), 410–25; D. Ostrowski, 'The end of Muscovy: the case for circa 1800', *Slavic Review*, 69 (2010), 426–38; and Nancy Kollmann's balanced response: N. S. Kollmann, 'Comment: divides and ends – the problem of periodization', *Slavic Review*, 69 (2010), 439–47.

juxtaposition. This book uses both published and unpublished materials from libraries and archives in Great Britain, France, and Austria, as well as their equivalents from the Russian archives as an empirical basis for comparing diplomatic interactions closely with regard to the ways in which the production of these texts was enmeshed with ceremonial practice itself (and vice versa).[29] Such comparisons neither lead to the postulation of a single unified diplomatic sphere, nor do they lay bare the cultural bedrocks of fundamentally different practices. Instead, they permit to explore differences, similarities, and variances across diplomatic cultures beyond the assumptions about cultural incompatibility which prevail in much of Western early modern discourse about Russia and its historiographic legacy. A comparative study of ritual practices – court personnel, ceremonial procedure, argument strategies in asserting precedence, the codification of precedents, diplomatic ranks, etc., helps to understand how convergences and variations across diplomatic cultures could evolve within shared patterns of communication.

Chapter 2 opens with an overview of the administration of diplomatic procedure, focusing on Russia and covering, in a comparative perspective, basic aspects of institutional structures, personnel, the formation of diplomatic ranks, as well as the documentation of ceremony. This chapter clarifies central terms used in French, English, German, and Russian in order to trace the multidirectional transfer of ceremonial practice between European courts and to discern the specificities of Russia's participation in this process.

Chapter 3 begins with a survey of the routine of an embassy at the Russian court as a foil to the actual conflicts and ruptures that emerged from disagreements over ritual procedures. Based on English ambassadors' dispatches, Russian embassy reports, and the documentation of diplomats' sojourns in Moscow, this chapter reconstructs, as an example for Muscovite diplomacy, how both the English and Russians battled over the norms that underpinned their political exchanges in the second half of the seventeenth century and how this process influenced the negotiation of trade privileges, the main concern of Russian–English diplomacy in both the Commonwealth and Restoration periods.

Chapter 4 examines the role of ceremonies in politics during both Peter I's Grand Embassy at the court of Leopold I in Vienna in 1698 and the negotiations of an alliance treaty between Russia, Prussia, and France in Paris in 1717. These two milestones of Russia's relations with the Holy Roman Empire and Franco-Russian diplomacy highlight both the beginning and an advanced stage of an important transition period in Russian

[29] The sources will be introduced and discussed in Chapter 2.

diplomatic practice. At the same time they exemplify many important features of diplomatic dialogue in the early modern period: the mechanisms of ceremonial, its inherent difficulties and tactics to surmount these through strategies such as incognito or the pretended absence of ceremony, European court's insecurity in dealing with Russia, its recognition as a Christian power, and the ambivalent role of the tsar as a diplomat. This chapter continues to investigate the relationship between negotiation and court pageantry, yet its specific focus is on the participants' and the public's role in the rituals.

The final chapter returns to the court of the tsar, tracing changes and continuities of diplomatic practice under Peter I. It shows that, while the reforms he introduced did not completely eradicate Muscovite practice, they rather adapted the pre-existing norms that his predecessors had negotiated in diplomatic relations with other powers. Even if these transformations signalled a clear change in Russian diplomacy, the underlying norms that imbued political practice with notions of honour and hierarchy fundamentally remained the same, as can be seen in the related legal and ceremonial consequences resulting from the 1708 arrest of Andrei A. Matveev, Peter I's ambassador in London. The book concludes by exploring a precedent that rises the apogee of Russian claims to status. It examines Peter I's justifications for styling himself as *imperator* in 1721, suggesting that the tsar's powerful ceremonial coup which reorganised what Dubois called the 'public order', adopting the imperial title, was a new departure based on the continuation of old practice.

Geometry of Power: Court Society and Diplomacy

Historians almost universally accept that *gloria* and honour pervaded all areas of early modern life, especially that of court society: 'This was a culture in which status counted for everything.'[30] An allegorical frontispiece to a popular eighteenth-century handbook of ceremony and decorum (Figure I.1) illustrates contemporary efforts to measure and codify such intangible values as prestige and honour. Geometria leans against a ball-headed obelisk, the symbol of the *gloria principis*.[31] She gauges the honour of princes with units of '*Titulaturen, Courtoisien, References, Compliments, Ceremonien*', labelled on a measuring rod extending vertically along the

[30] T. C. W. Blanning, *The pursuit of glory: Europe, 1648–1815* (London, 2008), p. 113.

[31] For a discussion of the image, see M. Vec, *Zeremonialwissenschaft im Fürstenstaat: Studien zur juristischen und politischen Theorie absolutistischer Herrschaftsrepräsentation* (Frankfurt a. M., 1998), pp. 167f., based on G. Frühsorge, 'Vom Hof des Kaisers zum "Kaiserhof": Über das Ende des Ceremoniells als gesellschaftliches Ordnungsmuster', *Euphorion*, 78 (1984), 237–65, here pp. 249f.

Figure I.1 Geometria and Justitia watching the social order. Frontispiece to J. B. v. Rohr (1729).

monument. Across from Geometria stands Justitia, with a noticeably tense posture. No blindfold blocks her view. In her right hand Justitia bears a sword, and in her left hand she carries a scale with the words *suum cuique* engraved across the top. Justitia cautiously observes Geometria's work. With vigilant eyes and a raised sword, she watches to ensure that 'to each his own' honour is being distributed in a *just* manner, according to social status.

In the vocabulary of diplomatic historians, 'status' is a familiar term, often reappearing as 'great power status'. The term encapsulates a central theme of diplomatic history, namely 'a state's standing within the international hierarchy'.[32] According to Hamish Scott, 'a "great power" was simply one that could be recognised to be relatively much stronger and therefore to dominate its lesser rivals'.[33] Indeed, the history of diplomatic relations has traditionally been an account of the rise of European nation states competing for great power status. This process eventually led to the formation of the pentarchy (France, Austria, Britain, Prussia, and Russia) that, since the Seven Years' War (1756–1763), dominated international politics through the nineteenth century.[34] Great power status measured the ability of a state to mobilise its material resources and establish itself as a military power that was recognised as a full player in this balance of power.[35]

Status and its manifestations in hierarchy, rank, and prestige are common themes of this book but in a very different sense of the word. Here, it is important to introduce a distinction between 'great power status' in the sense of military domination in the states-system, on the one hand, and the form of status that expressed monarchical rank and international standing in the age of court society, on the other. The measurability of might was an issue that remained ambiguous throughout the early modern period. Taking account of military strength alone was not sufficient

[32] Scott, *Emergence*, p. 8. [33] Ibid.

[34] The founding text of diplomatic history which created this master narrative is L. v. Ranke, 'Die großen Mächte', *Historisch-Politische Zeitschrift*, 2 (1833), 1–51. Its legacy is continued and developed further by distinguished recent historians of early modern international relations, see for example D. Mckay, H. M. Scott, *The rise of the great powers 1648–1815* (London, 1983), and H. M. Scott, *The birth of a great power system, 1740–1815* (Harlow, 2006), for an updated survey. For a discussion, see Scott, 'Diplomatic culture', pp. 58ff. See also F. H. Hinsley, *Power and the pursuit of peace: theory and practice in the history of relations between states* (Cambridge, 1963), pp. 4f. (on Ranke) and ch. 8.

[35] Classic overviews are H. Duchhardt, *Balance of Power und Pentarchie: internationale Beziehungen 1700–1785* (Paderborn, 1997); C. Gantet, *Guerre, paix et construction des états, 1618–1714* (Paris, 2003); K. Malettke, *Hegemonie – Multipolares System – Gleichgewicht: Internationale Beziehungen 1648/1659–1713/1714* (Paderborn, 2012), and, for Russia, A. N. Sakharov, ed., *Istoriia vneshnei politiki Rossii: konets XV v.–1917 g.*, 5 vols. (Moscow, 1995–1999).

to assess the power of a monarch, or the standing of a court in the international hierarchy.[36] To be sure, military victory generated prestige, but members of court society also mobilised different kinds of resources: status crucially depended on the recognition by others, granted through ceremonies, titles, compliments, etc. – Geometria's measuring units.

While it is easy to agree that honour, status, and prestige played an important role in the fragmented societies of early modern Europe, it is difficult to specify precisely how glory and international prestige were defined, how they were interconnected, and why they mattered.[37] Were they simply rewards for effective state organisation and successful warfare? Were they themselves the organising pattern or the motivating reason for military and political undertakings? What was the link between early modern court culture – whose tropes are epitomised by Geometria's units of measure – and foreign relations in the early modern period? This section takes some steps towards developing the connection between the princely court, ritual, and international politics before the ensuing chapters will turn to mutual perceptions and encounters between Russia and courtly Europe.

Ritual and Recognition

The independence and equality of sovereign states are today formally protected by international law as principles governing the conduct of international relations.[38] Diplomatic protocol, by symbolising the principles, harmoniously represents the political process in its reduced form.[39]

Conflicts over protocol during difficult negotiations still occur in the modern age.[40] Nevertheless, seventeenth- and eighteenth-century practice, as presented in diplomatic dispatches, comes across to the modern observer as a curious and never-ending dispute about lavish ceremonies

[36] H. Klueting, *Die Lehre von der Macht der Staaten: das aussenpolitische Machtproblem in der 'politischen Wissenschaft' und in der praktischen Politik im 18. Jahrhundert* (Berlin, 1986), p. 15. See also a more recent synthesis of the subject: J. Black, *Great powers and the quest for hegemony: the world order since 1500* (London, 2008), pp. 67ff.

[37] An answer to this question has been attempted by Lebow, *Cultural theory*, who invokes the ancient Greeks and stresses the universal human need for self-esteem, recognition, and personhood.

[38] R. H. Steinberg, 'Who is sovereign?', *Stanford Journal of International Law*, 40 (2004), 329–49.

[39] J. R. Wood, J. Serres, *Diplomatic ceremonial and protocol: principles, procedures and practices* (London, 1970), pp. 17ff.

[40] For an interesting example from the Cold War, see S. Schattenberg, '"Gespräch zweier Taubstummer?" Die Kultur der Außenpolitik Chruščevs und Adenauers Moskaureise 1955', *Osteuropa*, 7 (2007), 27–46.

arranged for visiting dignitaries.[41] In early modern diplomatic culture, the relationship between ceremonial symbols and mechanisms of power was closer and of greater importance than it is today. Whereas today, protocol is used to anticipate and pre-empt controversies over status, in early modernity it was expressly designed to signify the relative status of an honoured guest and his sovereign host.[42]

Diplomatic practice was inextricably linked with the code of conduct prevalent among the aristocratic elite at princely courts.[43] In a hierarchical society where honour and prestige were basic values, social respect was the currency used to secure the coveted places at the top along with the power that came with those positions.[44] Prestige generated privilege that could neither be bought with money nor acquired through education. Prestige was the symbolic capital that the aristocracy derived from its reputation, the age of a dynasty, titles, the proximity to the ruling prince, and other means which were difficult to manifest beyond their symbolic representation.[45]

This feature of court life confronted the contemporaries with a major problem: prestige is an elusive thing. It does not itself create a tangible value and only exists in the moment of its display. Yet, the symbolic recognition of prestige and honour constituted the right to privilege and

[41] Especially in Russia, see B. Conrad-Lütt, 'Hochachtung und Mißtrauen: Aus den Berichten der Diplomaten des Moskauer Staates', in *Deutsche und Deutschland aus russischer Sicht, 11.–17. Jahrhundert (1)*, ed. D. Herrmann (Munich, 1989), pp. 149–78.

[42] Bély, 'Cérémonial'; Roosen, 'Ceremonial'.

[43] Thiessen, 'Diplomatie vom *type ancien*', p. 485f. A concise introduction is, L. Frey, M. Frey, *The history of diplomatic immunity* (Columbus, 1999), pp. 207–17. For the nobility, see H. M. Scott, *The European nobilities in the seventeenth and eighteenth centuries*, 2 vols. (London, New York, 1995). For a survey of the growing literature on dynastic courts, see J. Duindam, 'Early modern court studies: an overview and a proposal', in *Historiographie an europäischen Höfen (16. – 18. Jahrhundert): Studien zum Hof als Produktionsort von Geschichtsschreibung und historischer Repräsentation*, ed. M. Völkel, A. Strohmeyer (Berlin, 2009), pp. 37–60. For the Russian court, see L. A. J. Hughes, 'Russia: the courts of Moscow and St. Petersburg c. 1547–1725', in *The princely courts of Europe: ritual, politics and culture under the Ancient Régime 1500–1750*, ed. J. Adamson (London, 1999), pp. 295–313; P. Keenan, *St Petersburg and the Russian court, 1703–1761* (Basingstoke, 2013), eps. pp. 6–8. See also P. Bushkovitch, *Peter the Great: the struggle for power, 1671–1725* (Cambridge, 2001), that emphasises the strong role of the court in politics and heavily draws on foreign diplomats' correspondences. See also P. V. Sedov, *Zakat Moskovskogo tsarstva: tsarskii dvor kontsa XVII veka* (St Petersburg, 2006), for Tsar Fedor Alekseevich's reign.

[44] Krischer, 'Souveränität als sozialer Status'.

[45] The implicit reference is to Bourdieu's concept of interchangeable forms of capital: P. Bourdieu, *The logic of practice*, trans. R. Nice (Cambridge, 1992, reprint, 1999), pp. 112–21, passim. For an exemplary study that discusses and fruitfully applies Bourdieu's distinction of economic (material resources), cultural (books, cultural knowledge, academic titles), social (networks), and symbolic capital (prestige based on an act of recognition) to the aristocratic elite at the imperial court, see A. Pečar, *Die Ökonomie der Ehre: der höfische Adel am Kaiserhof Karls VI. (1711–1740)* (Darmstadt, 2003).

allowed its carrier to assert authority over others within a community of shared expectations.[46] The distribution and redistribution of power that accompanied the gain in or loss of prestige was expressed in elaborate and expensive ceremonies and entertainments at the court.[47]

In the light of the modern state, and ideological debates surrounding it, courtly pageantry has often been misunderstood as irrational and superfluous, a mere show to gratify a ruler's taste for extravagance. The ideal of secular and effective rulership that worked independently of its pompous representation formed a leitmotif of nineteenth-century scholarship. This ideal exposed the moral failures of absolutistic rulers who abused the state's financial resources for the luxurious needs of court society.[48] As such, ceremonial conflict emerges as a non-political, irrational, and irrelevant formalism, counterproductive to the business of politics.[49]

At the early modern court, however, rational behaviour was understood to be what helped to preserve or increase, by symbolic means, one's potential for power within the hierarchy.[50] The essence of state power,

[46] See the classic definition of honour by J. Pitt-Rivers, 'Honour and social status', in *Honour and shame: the values of Mediterranean society*, ed. J. G. Péristiany (London, 1966), pp. 21–77. Honour understood as 'a right to respect' is also emphasised by F. H. Stewart, *Honor* (Chicago, London, 1994). The Russian court's precedence system (*mestnichestvo*) is a good example for the inextricable relationship between a noble's place in court ritual and service appointments in military, diplomacy, and administration, see Kollmann, *By honor bound*, esp. pp. 1–30, and Kollmann, 'Social drama', esp. p. 487.

[47] The classic is, N. Elias, *Die höfische Gesellschaft: Untersuchungen zur Soziologie des Königtums und der Aristokratie mit einer Einleitung: Soziologie und Geschichtswissenschaft* (Neuwied, Berlin, 1969). Although the correlation between power potential (*Machtchancen*) and ceremony has not been questioned, Elias' narrow focus on the monarch has come under attack. J. F. v. Kruedener, *Die Rolle des Hofes im Absolutismus* (Stuttgart, 1973) and H. C. Ehalt, *Ausdrucksformen absolutistischer Herrschaft: der Wiener Hof im 17. und 18. Jahrhundert* (Munich, 1980) largely adopt Elias' approach in theory. See Pečar, *Ökonomie der Ehre*, pp. 296–301, for a study that challenges the monarch-centred perspective. On whether Elias' findings are generally transferrable to other European courts, see A. Winterling, *Der Hof der Kurfürsten von Köln, 1688–1794: eine Fallstudie zur Bedeutung 'absolutistischer' Hofhaltung* (Bonn, 1986), pp. 151–70. For a fundamental critique, see J. Duindam, *Myths of power: Norbert Elias and the early modern European court* (Amsterdam, 1994), esp. pp. 192–95.

[48] See Barbara Stollberg-Rilinger's assessment of Johann Gustav Droysen's and Ranke's derogatory comments about the coronation of Elector Frederick III into Frederick I, King in Prussia: B. Stollberg-Rilinger, 'Honores Regii: die Königswürde im zeremoniellen Zeichensystem der Frühen Neuzeit', in *Dreihundert Jahre preussische Königskrönung: eine Tagungsdokumentation*, ed. J. Kunisch (Berlin, 2002), pp. 1–26. For a discussion of the '*Verschwendungsargument*', see Ehalt, *Ausdrucksformen*, pp. 16–19; Kruedener, *Rolle des Hofes*, pp. 18–24.

[49] P.-M. Hahn, U. Schütte, 'Thesen zur Rekonstruktion höfischer Zeichensysteme in der Frühen Neuzeit', *Mitteilungen der Residenzen-Kommission der Akademie der Wissenschaften zu Göttingen*, 13 (2003), 19–47.

[50] Elias, *Höfische Gesellschaft*, p. 141, points out that this particular form of 'court rationality' only appears to be irrational in the light of the modern understanding of rational behaviour which is essentially based on economic optimisation and the increase of financial means of power.

in a more modern sense, is usually restricted to, for instance, military forces, availability of material resources, and the number of subjects ruled. But struggles over ceremonies were no less struggles for power. The ability to win the respect of others within a hierarchical community affected power relationships. Ceremonial victory or defeat secured the position of a ruler within this hierarchy. In the age of court society, they were treated as both sign and substance of the latter's authority, his potential to lay claim to privileges before others beneath him and, importantly, to participate in the political process. As Gottfried W. Leibniz acknowledged in 1701 (when pondering on the nature of kingship on the occasion of the coronation of the first Prussian king, Frederick I), a monarch had to cement his authority through ceremonial honours in order to gain the esteem of other sovereigns and exercise his rights and demand his privileges effectively, irrespective of any mismatch between his claimed status and 'hard power'.[51]

A monarch did not *eo ipso* embody the independence and power of a state. Sovereignty was a matter of constant recognition of his or her status in the social order. For that, military might alone was not enough. Sovereignty was not conceived of in the abstract. Because it meant less the independence of the state than the social status of the ruler, it was signified by the ceremonial treatment of his persona.[52] Only by establishing his claims to status ceremonially could a claimant hope to join the group of independent polities and lay claim to the corresponding privileges. Gaining the *honores regii*, for example, as did Frederick III in 1701 by putting a crown on his head, was an indispensable step towards firmly establishing the elector's *ius legationis*, his right to receive and send ambassadors, and ultimately, to participate in diplomatic dialogue.[53]

Thus, honour and prestige were important determinants of sovereign status in early modern international relations. The diplomat's reception at the frontier, his progress towards the capital, his solemn entry, and his public audience with the monarch were meticulously choreographed to ensure that the respect shown to a diplomat, thus indirectly to his

[51] G. W. Leibniz, 'Anhang, betreffend dasjenige, was nach heutigen Völker-Recht zu einem König erfordert wird', in *Leibnitz's deutsche Schriften*, ed. G. E. Guhrauer, 2 vols. (1838/1840), II, pp. 303–12. For a discussion, see Stollberg-Rilinger, 'Honores regii', pp. 5ff.

[52] This point is elaborated in Krischer, 'Souveränität als sozialer Status'.

[53] Stollberg-Rilinger, 'Honores regii'. See also C. Clark, 'When culture meets power: the Prussian coronation of 1701', in *Cultures of power*, ed. H. M. Scott, B. Simms, pp. 14–35, for an interpretation of the coronation ritual. See also C. Clark, *Iron kingdom: the rise and downfall of Prussia, 1600–1947* (London, 2006), pp. 67ff. For a discussion of the *ius legationis*, see H. Kugeler, '"Le parfait ambassadeur." The theory and practice of diplomacy in the century following the Peace of Westphalia' (unpublished DPhil dissertation, University of Oxford, 2006), pp. 130ff.

sovereign, accorded with his sovereign's rank.[54] Far from being merely preoccupied with outward appearance – resulting in a seemingly irrational waste of money – the choreography applied a 'rational' set of ritual rules that ranked each sovereign within the 'society of princes'.[55]

Contemporary Definitions of Diplomatic Ceremonial

The pecking order of states, then, was based on a deep-seated understanding of royal dignity and dynastic supremacy. European rulers saw themselves as being part of a social hierarchy that had existed since the Middle Ages. It continued to structure political practice even beyond the Peace of Westphalia (1648) which is known to have introduced the principles of sovereignty and the equality of states.[56] The social structure of the *res publica christiana* sprang from God, the one font of honour, and extended from the pope, the emperor, kings, grand dukes, etc. through the ranks of society down to those with academic titles somewhere at the bottom. This was initially perceived as a universal and God-given hierarchy. Jurists held disputations in which claims to precedence were scrutinised from all angles of their discipline, the *ius praecedentiae*.[57] Although the *superbia* that one ruler claimed over another derived from a higher dignity that was imbued with legalistic properties, dignity was not laid down in a legal text; it had to be made manifest and established by ceremonial precedent, the outcome of meetings at which political relationships were represented in spatial and temporal metaphors derived from the human body (top and bottom, left and right), space (near and

[54] For early modern Russia, Flier, 'Political ideas'; Garnier, 'Symbolische Kommunikationsformen'; Iuzefovich, *Put' posla*.

[55] The term is from L. Bély, *La société des princes: XVIe-XVIIIe siècle* (Paris, 1999). Bély applies his concept of the *société des princes* to early modern diplomacy in L. Bély, *L'art de la paix en Europe*. See also his *Espions et ambassadeurs au temps de Louis XIV* (Paris, 1990), esp. pp. 748f., on ceremony. This kind of 'rationality' was not restricted to relations between dynastic courts. For cities, see, for example, Krischer, *Reichsstädte*, pp. 211f., passim. For the role of courts in the relationship between politics and ceremony, see also T. Osborne, 'The surrogate war between the Savoys and the Medici: sovereignty and precedence in early modern Italy', *International History Review*, 29 (2007), 1–21.

[56] Thiessen, 'Diplomatie vom *type ancien*', pp. 474f., 479f. For the Peace of Westphalia see also the works by Heinz Duchhardt, for example, H. Duchhardt, 'Imperium und Regna im Zeitalter Ludwigs XIV.', *Historische Zeitschrift*, 232 (1981), 555–81, with a focus on 1648 and the issue of dynastic prestige.

[57] Here and for the following paragraphs, B. Stollberg-Rilinger, 'Die Wissenschaft der feinen Unterschiede: das Präzedenzrecht und die europäischen Monarchien vom 16. bis zum 18. Jahhundert', *Majestas*, 10 (2002), 1–26. See also M. Vec, 'Zeremonialrecht', in *Handwörterbuch zur deutschen Rechtsgeschichte*, ed. A. Erler, E. Kaufmann, 5 vols. (Berlin, 1998), V, pp. 1673–77.

far), time (acceleration and delay), etc.[58] Who wore a hat, who doffed one, and at what moment? Who was given the place of honour at the right hand? Who stood (or, under certain circumstances, sat) at what distance from the monarch? In which rooms did the participants meet? Who had to wait for whom, and for how long? Such were the symbolic manifestations of a monarch's status, his 'international prestige'.

The legal fiction of hierarchy, however, did not prevent European rulers from engaging in endless squabbles about their position in it. The idea of a static and linear hierarchy that shaped the medieval *res publica christiana* seemed increasingly obsolete. It did not reflect the political reality of the ever-shifting power relations within the emerging states-system of Europe.[59] This is not to say that the hierarchy stopped shaping the behaviour of princes and courtier diplomats towards each other. The period of the formation of the states-system saw, in fact, an increased occupation with ceremonies and conflicts over rank following the Peace of Westphalia.[60]

While the notion of dynastic supremacy and its ceremonial manifestation persisted, a change occurred in the way in which the hierarchy was justified in the light of the emerging principles of equality and independence. 'If one compares the political treatises that were written on such matters sixty or seventy years ago with those of today, then they differ from one another like the day from the night,' wrote ceremonial expert Julius B. von Rohr in 1729.[61] A decade earlier, another prominent scholar of ceremonies, Johann C. Lünig, had acknowledged that precedence was not rooted in the mythical idea of an irrevocable hierarchy. Rather, it was supported by 'preponderant might [. . .] that may be embellished with all kinds of ostentatious motives like age and wealth, possession of the true faith, knowledgeability of the peoples ruled, etc., but which lose their vital force [. . .] when preponderant might ceases to exist'.[62] One hastens to add, as the anthropologist Julian Pitt-Rivers put it, 'on the field of honour might is right'.[63] Indeed, blood and aristocratic privilege did not lose fully their legal status until the congresses of Vienna (1815) and Aachen (1818) put an end to quarrels over

[58] Stollberg-Rilinger, 'Zeremoniell', p. 396f. See also Iu. M. Lotman, *Universe of the mind: a semiotic theory of culture* (London, 2001), esp. pp. 131–33, for a semiotic explanation.

[59] Stollberg-Rilinger, 'Präzedenzrecht'.

[60] As observed by J. B. v. Rohr, *Einleitung zur Ceremoniel-Wissenschaft der grossen Herren*, ed. M. Schlechte (Leipzig, 1990, reprint of the 1733 edn.), p. 17.

[61] Ibid., p. 18.

[62] J. C. Lünig, *Theatrum Ceremoniale Historico-Politicum, oder Historisch- und politischer Schau-Platz aller Ceremonien*, 2 vols. (Leipzig, 1719/20), I, p. 8. See also Stollberg-Rilinger, 'Präzedenzrecht', p. 142.

[63] Pitt-Rivers, 'Honour and social status', p. 25.

precedence.[64] Already by the early eighteenth century, the distinctions and gradual ceremonial differences between sovereigns were no longer exclusively drawn from an objective and universal order of rank. They were treated as the result of mutual recognition of prestige and honour and used to grant favours or symbolise the state of diplomatic relations. The high demand for advice on how to position oneself as a courtier diplomat in this intricate web of reciprocal status relations gave birth to a new genre: *Zeremonialwissenschaft* superseded *ius praecedentiae* as the master discipline and emerged as an 'applied science' of the subject of rank and precedence.[65]

In the 1723 revision of a work first published in 1715, Gottfried Stieve described ceremonial as a set of actions that include the way people stand, sit, look, and dress. He defined diplomatic ceremonial as an 'order introduced [...] under sovereigns or persons that equal them, according to which they have to respect each other, their ambassadors, or envoys in meetings, so that no one is rewarded too much or too little'.[66] Again, one is reminded of Justitia's *suum cuique*. Stieve distinguished ceremonial from compliments originating in courtesy: diplomatic ceremonial was legally binding.[67] The gestures and body language described by Stieve pertained to the type Rohr called *Staats-Ceremoniel* which was distinct from other forms of ceremony: 'The state ceremonial prescribes rulers or their representatives a certain mode of decorum, so that they preserve or increase their honour and esteem before their subjects and servants, princely kin and other rulers of their kind.'[68] According to Rohr's definition, the ceremonial dictated the monarch's behaviour on two levels. It was directed towards the inner circle of the court, on the one hand,

[64] J. C. Barker, *The abuse of diplomatic privileges and immunities: a necessary evil?* (Aldershot, 1996), p. 26. E. H. Markel, *Die Entwicklung der diplomatischen Rangstufen* (Erlangen, 1951), pp. 71, 76. For the decline of diplomatic ceremonial, see also L. Frey, M. Frey, 'The reign of the charlatans is over: the French revolutionary attack on diplomatic practice', *Journal of Modern History*, 65 (1993), 706–44.

[65] Stollberg-Rilinger, 'Präzedenzrecht'; T. Weller, '*Kein Schauplatz der Eitelkeiten*: das frühneuzeitliche *Theatrum Praecedentiae* zwischen gelehrtem Diskurs und sozialer Praxis', *Metaphorik.de*, 14 (2008), 379–403. Available from www.metaphorik.de/sites/www.metaphorik.de/files/journal-pdf/14_2008_weller.pdf, last access 6 February 2016. Zeremonialwissenschaft has been studied extensively by Vec, *Zeremonialwissenschaft*. See also V. Bauer, *Hofökonomie: der Diskurs über den Fürstenhof in Zeremonialwissenschaft, Hausväterliteratur und Kameralismus* (Cologne, 1997).

[66] G. Stieve, *Europäisches Hoff-Ceremoniel. Andere vermehrte Auflage* (Leipzig, 1723), p. 2.

[67] Ibid., pp. 2ff. For a discussion, see Duindam, *Myths of power*, pp. 102–07; Krischer, *Reichsstädte*, pp. 26–28; Pečar, *Ökonomie der Ehre*, pp. 142–44.

[68] Rohr, *Ceremoniel-Wissenschaft der grossen Herren*, p. 1. For other forms of ceremony, see J. B. v. Rohr, *Einleitung zur Ceremoniel-Wissenschaft der Privat-Personen*, ed. F. Frühsorge (Weinheim, 1990, reprint of the 1728 edn.). Compare Peter Burke's seminal work on ceremonial presentations at the court of Louis XIV: P. Burke, *The fabrication of Louis XIV* (New Haven, London, 1992).

and towards foreign powers in diplomatic contexts, on the other. These, among others, were the means by which an ambassador represented the relative status and, by implication, the power of his sovereign.

The Court and the Public

In the pre-modern state, such rituals depended not only on the physical presence of the principals but also on the attendance of an audience who, by serving as a witness, confirmed the status displayed.[69] To take up, and defend, a position in a community of competing sovereigns, a monarch had to ensure that his status was regularly represented, in public, before the court, at home as well as abroad.[70] Therefore, ceremonial norms required both a common symbolic language and an audience that could translate, understand, and communicate in this language.[71] However, if diplomatic ceremonial was confined to personal contact between the participants of the ritual and depended on the presence of a direct witness, then information on intercourtly relations could only be conveyed within the immediate range of the court. The question is how monarchs at distant courts received word of the solemn events at which diplomats could increase their prestige or risk diminishing it. First, diplomats cautiously observed ceremonial occasions in the court where they resided and maintained close contact with their rulers through regular diplomatic reports. Second, the scholarly discourse on precedence and rank provided a rich source of information. Some of the works were written with a view to providing a collection of precedents upon which ceremonial conflicts could be solved.[72] Third and finally, occasional print publications such as brochures and courtly newspapers supplied the aristocracy with access to ceremonial news, so that all foreign courts had a relatively good

[69] The basic introduction remains, J. Habermas, *The structural transformation of the public sphere: an inquiry into a category of bourgeois society*, trans. T. Burger, 2nd edn. (Cambridge, 1992), pp. 5–14. Cf. U. Daniel, 'Überlegungen zum höfischen Fest der Barockzeit', *Niedersächsisches Jahrbuch für Landesgeschichte*, 72 (2000), 45–66, who rightly points out that the representation of power was staged not only before the subjects of a monarch but before the wider circle of European court society. Similar already, Rohr, *Ceremoniel-Wissenschaft der grossen Herren*, p. 1. J. Paulmann, *Pomp und Politik: Monarchenbegegnungen in Europa zwischen Ancien Régime und Erstem Weltkrieg* (Paderborn, 2000), pp. 47–55, discusses Habermas' public sphere in the context of early modern diplomatic encounters. For a comparative study that applies Habermas' notion on the early modern court, see T. C. W. Blanning, *The culture of power and the power of culture: old regime Europe 1660–1789* (Oxford, 2003), esp. pp. 5–14.

[70] See B. Stollberg-Rilinger, 'Höfische Öffentlichkeit: zur zeremoniellen Selbstdarstellung des brandenburgischen Hofes vor dem Europäischen Publikum', *Forschungen zur Brandenburgischen und Preussischen Geschichte*, NF 7 (1997), 145–76.

[71] Pečar, *Ökonomie der Ehre*, pp. 207ff. [72] Stollberg-Rilinger, 'Präzedenzrecht'.

knowledge about the treatment of diplomats.[73] Nobility and diplomacy shared the same print media in circulating information on prestige and social relations within the social realm of the aristocracy itself as well as between courts as centres of power.[74]

As mentioned at the beginning of this book, political actors placed such emphasis on ceremonies because these occasions not only *depicted* the relations between states but they also helped to *create* the political order in which monarchs acted in bids to achieve their aims.[75] Provided that this order only existed in its ritual display (and the media that recorded it), ritual was a key to the control of the political order and was itself more a source than a mere projection of power.[76] Diplomats paid detailed attention to public ceremonies because modifications, however slight, would be interpreted as a precedent that enabled witnesses to challenge, and perhaps diminish, his sovereign's prestige, signifying a loss of power. Whether or not a successfully asserted claim to precedence invested a prince with real power in the fundamental Weberian sense is not the issue here.[77] Nor should the historian infer from symbolic victories the ability of the victor to dominate the vanquished, as if there were an essentialist link between ceremony and might.[78] The question is why rulers and statesmen ascribed such importance to the issue of 'international prestige' and symbolic competition. Living by the paradigm of court society was exactly that: to think and act in categories of honour and hierarchy in which the representation of one's position implied the right to privilege and the power it generated.

The more prestige the place held in the hierarchy of states, the more ceremonies became the focus, as well as the expression, of political competition.[79] Thus, although ceremonies were usually agreed beforehand,

[73] R. Schlögl, 'Politik beobachten. Öffentlichkeit und Medien in der Frühen Neuzeit', *Zeitschrift für Historische Forschung*, 25 (2008), 581–616.

[74] A. Gestrich, *Absolutismus und Öffentlichkeit: politische Kommunikation in Deutschland zu Beginn des 18. Jahrhunderts* (Göttingen, 1994), pp. 78–91, and Daniel, 'Überlegungen', pp. 48–53.

[75] See Stollberg-Rilinger, 'Symbolische Kommunikation', p. 503.

[76] Cannadine, 'Introduction', p. 19.

[77] See Max Weber's celebrated definition: '"Power" [*Macht*] is the probability that one actor within a social relationship will be in a position to carry out his own will despite resistance, regardless of the basis on which this probability rests', in M. Weber, *Economy and society: an outline of interpretive sociology*, ed. G. Roth, C. Wittich (Berkeley, 1978), p. 53.

[78] For an attempt at nineteenth- and twentieth-century international relations, compare J. D. Singer, M. Small, 'The composition and status ordering of the international system: 1815–1940', *World politics*, 18 (1966), 236–82.

[79] The same principle gave structure to the constitution of the Holy Roman Empire, see B. Stollberg-Rilinger, 'Die zeremonielle Inszenierung des Reiches, oder: Was leistet der kulturalistische Ansatz für die Reichsverfassungsgeschichte?', in *Imperium Romanum – irregulare corpus – Teutscher Reichs-Staat: das Alte Reich im Verständnis der Zeitgenossen und der Historiographie*, ed. M. Schnettger (Mainz, 2002), pp. 233–46.

they were often interrupted, even with violence, as a means of enforcing disputed claims to status. Perhaps the most famous example occurred in London in 1661 when the long-lasting antagonism between France and Spain exploded into a fight between the ambassadors of Louis XIV (r. 1643–1715) and Philip IV (r. 1621–1665). Louis XIV's ambassador, the comte d'Estrades, had lost the struggle for the *place d'honneur* at a ceremonial parade in London. As a consequence, he threatened to declare war on Spain unless Philip IV, in the future, conceded Louis XIV's claim to precedence (which he did).[80] Louis XIV expected the public acknowledgement of his claims to bring 'definite advantages in negotiations and general political position',[81] even though the Austrian Habsburgs continued to give precedence to the Spanish ambassador, and popes treated the French and Spanish ambassadors as equals.[82] Similar disputes over ceremonies were given as one of the reasons why Russia, in 1700, declared war on Sweden.[83] The refusal of King Charles XII (r. 1697–1718) to offer reparation for the ceremonial insult to Peter I at Riga in 1697 may have been less a pretext for war than one important reason for it.[84] In short, disagreements about ceremonies did not simply interrupt the business of international politics: they were themselves political struggles. The following chapters now take a closer look at Russia's role in these struggles.

[80] For a brief discussion of the incident, see W. J. Roosen, *The age of Louis XIV: the rise of modern diplomacy* (Cambridge, MA, 1976), pp. 181f. For French claims to precedence in Europe, see M. Rohrschneider, 'Das französische Präzedenzstreben im Zeitalter Ludwigs XIV.: Diplomatische Praxis – zeitgenössische französische Publizistik – Rezeption in der frühen deutschen Zeremonialwissenschaft', *Francia. Forschungen zur westeuropäischen Geschichte*, 36 (2009), 135–79.

[81] Concludes W. J. Roosen, 'The functioning of ambassadors under Louis XIV', *French Historical Studies*, 6 (1970), 311–32, here p. 331.

[82] Roosen, 'Ceremonial', p. 463.

[83] For the contemporary elaboration, see P. P. Shafirov, *A discourse concerning the just causes of the war between Sweden and Russia: 1700–1721* (Dobbs Ferry, NY, 1973), pp. 23–34, 274–90.

[84] Cf. L. A. J. Hughes, *Russia in the age of Peter the Great* (New Haven, London, 2000), pp. 28f.

1 Barbarous Ceremonies? Russia's Places in Early Modern Diplomacy

Russia: A Blind Spot in the System?

A few years after the Great Northern War (1700–1721), Christian Gottfried Hoffmann delivered a lecture at the Alma Mater Viadrina, Brandenburg's principal university located in Frankfurt (Oder), on what is in today's terms best described as international relations. To this purpose, Hoffmann, who came to Frankfurt as a professor of law in 1723, had drafted a short treatise about 'the present state of Europe' which set out a detailed curriculum for the study of the relations between states.[1] His *Erkäntniß des gegenwärtigen Zustandes von Europa* marks a cornerstone of the foundation of international relations as an academic discipline.[2] It came at a time when many European rulers were making strenuous efforts towards the professionalisation of their diplomatic corps.[3] In France, the newly founded Académie politique (1712) served as a school for ambassadors, although it disappeared with the retirement of its founder, Colbert de Torcy, Louis XIV's minister of foreign affairs. After a brief revival, the school was dissolved by Cardinal Dubois in 1720. King George I (r. 1714–1727) established the Regius Professorships of Modern History at Oxford and Cambridge in 1724 in order that future diplomats should receive training in historical studies. Little came of it in the beginning, as the professors took it as a prestigious sinecure rather than a laborious post that involved them in

[1] C. G. Hoffmann, *Entwurff einer Einleitung zu dem Erkäntniß des gegenwärtigen Zustandes von Europa. Worinnen hierzu nöthigen Wissenschaften überhaupt geurtheilet, Insonderheit aber der Ursprung von denen wichtigsten Krieges= und Friedens=Angelegenheiten dieser Zeit vorgestellet und zu dem Grunde eines Collegii Privati geleget wird* (Leipzig, 1720). For Hoffmann, see *ABD*, XII, pp. 574f.

[2] H. Duchhardt, 'Die Formationsphase der Wissenschaft von den internationalen Beziehungen: Christian Gottfried Hofmanns Entwurff einer Einleitung zu dem Erkänntniß des gegenwärtigen Zustandes von Europa von 1720', in *Formen internationaler Beziehungen in der Frühen Neuzeit: Frankreich und das Alte Reich im europäischen Staatensystem. Festschrift für Klaus Malettke zum 65. Geburtstag*, ed. S. Externbrink, J. Ulbert (Berlin, 2001), pp. 37–42.

[3] For diplomatic training, see Kugeler, 'Theory', ch. 4; Bély, *Espions*, pp. 322–30.

teaching.[4] In Russia, Peter I requested plans and study proposals for a diplomatic school as early as 1715, but the institution that resulted from them was very short-lived.[5]

Despite the obvious awareness of the need for trained personnel, the subjects required for the study of international relations were not represented in the curricula of universities where students were usually steeped in the abstract sciences, law, or ancient history. Hoffmann was deeply dissatisfied with the widespread belief that foreign policy should remain a secret art, or that rulers' political decisions should not undergo the scrutiny of academics. Those who occupied the corridors of power spoke dismissively of academic studies and prided themselves on their arcane knowledge.[6] Hoffmann, on the other hand, sought to establish international relations as a taught university subject. Earlier scholars of the 'sciences of state' (*Staatswissenschaft*) at German universities had studied natural law and the general histories and constitutions of European states in order to present individual countries synoptically and map out the political Europe of their time.[7] But the effect of their works on Hoffmann was to stimulate a desire in him to impart to students the present state of world affairs by explaining the relations *between* polities.[8] According to his design, students hoping to represent their future masters in public affairs (*publicis negotiis*) should qualify in a course that would enhance their understanding of the world after graduation. Hoffmann was familiar with the abundance of sources in a variety of academic fields that were available for the study of foreign affairs. He acknowledged a lack of a methodology that would bring the highly disparate disciplines and materials together. In contrast to the scholars mentioned earlier, he envisaged an interdisciplinary course that started with a general introduction to the nature of the *notitia rerum publicarum* (together with geography, genealogy, heraldry, history, aspects of public and international law, domestic law and customs of the various nations, and the study of political journals). The course required further specialisations in the study of both the government and

[4] J. Black, *European international relations, 1648–1815* (Basingstoke, 2002), p. 32. For the origins of the Regius Professorships, see R. J. Evans, *Cosmopolitan islanders: British historians and the European continent* (Cambridge, 2009), pp. 59ff.

[5] Grabar, *International law*, pp. 52f. [6] Hoffmann, *Entwurff*, pp. 3f.

[7] See H. E. Bödeker, '"Europe" in the discourse of the sciences of state in 18th century Germany', *Cromohs*, 8 (2003), 1–14, available from www.cromohs.unifi.it/8_2003/bodeker.html, last access 6 February 2016. For an overview of *Staatswissenschaften*, its authors and relations to public law, see M. Stolleis, *Geschichte des öffentlichen Rechts in Deutschland*, 3 vols. (München, 1988), I, chs. 5, 8. See also J. Brückner, *Staatswissenschaften, Kameralismus und Naturrecht: ein Beitrag zur Geschichte der politischen Wissenschaft in Deutschland des späten 17. und frühen 18. Jahrhunderts* (Munich, 1977).

[8] Hoffmann, *Entwurff*, p. 4.

constitution of the pontificate, major peace treaties as well as the economy, power and military forces of individual states and conflicts between them. Even by today's standards of interdisciplinary learning, Hoffmann's syllabus covered a wide spectrum of topics.

His draft discloses a rationale typical of the period that saw the emergence of the states-system with its increased interconnectedness of states. Behind it was the premise that students would have to orient themselves in an intricate web of European politics in which there was no polity that was not bound to another through particular pacts and treaties.[9] In his concept of Europe as a political unit, held together by mutual ties between states it embraced, Hoffmann anticipated the well-known metaphors with which his contemporaries described the emerging European states-system. Jean de la Sarraz du Franquesnay, for instance, called Europe a 'general republic', explaining that 'the various states of Europe form a whole whose parts correspond to each other, almost like different lines drawn from a common centre to the circumference. [...] All the powers of Europe are one political body'.[10] Of course, the concept of Europe as a political entity with a corporate structure, joined together through culture and the imagined union of the Christian faith, had already attracted the eye of the duc de Sully, and, later, the abbé de Saint-Pierre, in their celebrated utopias of an eternally pacified states-system.[11] In Hoffmann's day, Europe had indeed reached a considerable degree of unity.[12] Yet, this was not achieved through the ideal of a perpetual peace administered from above by a council of European states. This unity was the result of a system of treaties and diplomatic interaction that kept the ever-hostile states in balance and held the belligerent ambitions of individual rulers in check.[13]

Moreover, the *république génerale* was no longer a medieval *res publica christiana*.[14] A mechanistic but still hierarchical understanding of the

[9] Ibid., p. 12.

[10] J. de la Sarraz du Franquesnay, *Le ministre public dans les cours étrangères: ses fonctions et ses prérogatives* (Amsterdam, 1731), pp. 111f.

[11] C.-I. Castel, abbé de Saint-Pierre, *A project for settling an everlasting peace in Europe. First proposed by Henry IV. of France, and approved of by Queen Elizabeth, ... and now discussed at large, and made practicable by the Abbot St. Pierre* (London, 1714); M. de Béthune, duc de Sully, *Sully's grand design of Henry IV. From the Memoirs as translated by Charlotte Lennox. With an introduction by David Ogg* (London, 1921).

[12] H. Mohnhaupt, '"Europa" und "ius publicum" im 17. und 18. Jahrhundert', in *Aspekte europäischer Rechtsgeschichte. Festgabe für Helmut Coing zum 70. Geburtstag*, ed. C. Bergfeld (Frankfurt a. M., 1982), pp. 207–32.

[13] For the 'belligerent disposition' of rulers and war as the ultimate goal of government in the early modern period, see J. Kunisch, *Fürst, Gesellschaft, Krieg: Studien zur bellizistischen Disposition des absoluten Fürstenstaates* (Cologne, 1992).

[14] For the *res publica christiana*, see the chapter on medieval diplomacy in Mattingly, *Renaissance diplomacy*, pp. 17–54.

international order gradually replaced the medieval notion of a Europe united in a universal monarchy, walled off from enemies by the bond of religion. States were seen to be interconnected like cogwheels in a machine whereby political action and the will of a ruler could neither be subjected to overarching institutions representing the many nor to consensual regulations that would reach beyond the singular and ever-shifting alliances between the few.[15] The system of states was perceived to be the total of individual actions. The rules of the system were the result of the actions and responses of individual sovereigns.[16]

It was the century after the Peace of Westphalia that saw the emergence of this states-system, largely owing its new diplomatic forms and intensified relations to the development of permanent embassies at foreign courts.[17] Ever since the Peace of Nijmegen (1678/79) and by the Peace of Utrecht (1713/14) at the latest, diplomats realised that they both created and witnessed a new diplomacy in the making.[18] 'Today, negotiations are conducted very differently', noted the French diplomat Antoine Pecquet in 1737.[19] 'The Corps of the Foreign Ministers in a Country forms a kind of independent society, whose members live among themselves in an intimacy proportionate to how well their Sovereigns get along.'[20] Not quite the modern professional group of career diplomats representing national governments, the diplomatic corps still reflected the social world of the *société des princes* in that ambassadors and lower-ranking representatives re-enacted the kind of court life that their sovereigns pursued at home with all the characteristics of the court society.[21] Favouritism, personal networks, mixed cross-border loyalties, patronage relationships, and a high degree of professionalism in representing both

[15] For the 'machine' metaphor, see B. Stollberg-Rilinger, *Der Staat als Maschine: zur politischen Metaphorik des absoluten Fürstenstaats* (Berlin, 1986).

[16] H. Kleinschmidt, 'Systeme und Ordnungen in der Geschichte der internationalen Beziehungen', *Archiv für Kulturgeschichte*, 82 (2000), 433–54. See also the introduction to J. Siegelberg, K. Schlichte, eds., *Strukturwandel internationaler Beziehungen: zum Verhältnis von Staat und internationalem System seit dem Westfälischen Frieden* (Wiesbaden, 2000), pp. 11–56.

[17] For the conceptual background of the Westphalian System as it appears today and how it changed over the years, see J. A. Caporaso, 'Changes in the Westphalian order: territory, public authority, and sovereignty', *International Studies Review*, 2 (2000), 1–28. For the limits of 1648 as a paradigm for the study of diplomatic history, see H. Duchhardt, '"Westphalian System". Zur Problematik einer Denkfigur', *Historische Zeitschrift*, 269 (1999), 305–15.

[18] Kugeler, 'Theory', p. 9. See also Thiessen, 'Diplomatie vom *type ancien*', p. 474.

[19] A. Pecquet, *Discourse on the art of negotiation*, trans. A. Gruzinska, M. D. Sirkis (New York, NY, 2005, first published in 1737 in French), p. 7.

[20] Ibid., p. 73.

[21] L. Bély, 'La négociation comme idéal et comme art: un modèle westphalian?', in *L'Europe des traités de Westphalie: esprit de la diplomatie et diplomatie de l'esprit*, ed. L. Bély, I. Richefort (Paris, 2000), pp. 604–12, esp. p. 607.

personal status and sovereign dignity in various roles were the diplomat's fields of competence mostly obtained by birth and privilege.[22] To borrow a term from the semiotician Iurii Lotman, diplomatic culture provided the 'semiosphere' in which gradually standardised ways of symbolic interaction communicated shared goals and expectations, preserved common privileges, and created the political order in which foreign representatives positioned themselves.[23] By the mid-eighteenth century, the idea of Europe as a political unit had become commonplace:

> Europe forms a political system in which the nations inhabiting this part of the world are bound together by their relations and various interests into a single body. It is no longer, as in former times, a confused heap of detached parts, each of which had but little concern for the lot of the others. . . . The constant attention of sovereigns to all that goes on, the custom of resident ministers, the continual negotiations that take place, make modern Europe a sort of republic, whose members – each independent, but all bound together by a common interest – unite for the maintenance of order and the preservation of liberty. This is what has given rise to the well-known principle of the balance of power, by which is meant an arrangement of affairs so that no state shall be in a position to have absolute mastery and dominate over the others.[24]

Since then, the traditional narrative of modern diplomacy has presented the relations between states in the terms that were a product of these relations themselves: the European states-system and the balance of power.[25]

The question, then, is: was Russia a part of the 'republic'? How strong were its connections with other European states? Would Hoffmann have

[22] Thiessen, 'Diplomatie vom *type ancien*', pp. 487–93. For patronage, see T. Haug, *Ungleiche Außenbeziehungen und grenzüberschreitende Patronage: die französische Krone und die geistlichen Kurfürsten (1648–1679)* (Cologne, 2015). See also M. Köhler, *Strategie und Symbolik: Verhandeln auf dem Kongress von Nimwegen* (Cologne, 2011), with an emphasis on the role of peace congresses in the development of diplomatic practice. See also Bély, *Espions*, chs. V, VI, for congresses.

[23] For Lotman's 'semiosphere', see Iu. M. Lotman, 'Über die Semiosphäre', *Zeitschrift für Semiotik*, 12 (1990), 287–305. See also Scott, 'Diplomatic culture', and P. W. Schroeder, *The transformation of European politics, 1763–1848* (Oxford, 1994), pp. xiif., on the notion of 'shared practice'.

[24] E. de Vattel, *Le droit des gens, ou Principes de la loi naturelle, appliqués à la conduite et aux affaires des nations et des souverains*, 3 vols. (Paris, 1820, first published 1758), I, p. 532. English translation from Hinsley, *Power*, p. 166.

[25] See, for example, E. Luard, *The balance of power: the system of international relations, 1648–1815* (Basingstoke, 1992); Malettke, *Hegemonie*, and Duchhardt, *Balance of Power*, for the eighteenth century. For an affirmative but critical approach to 'system' and 'balance of power', see Black, *European international relations*, pp. 1ff. For an overview of more recent literature, which cannot be discussed here, see Externbrink, 'Internationale Politik in der Frühen Neuzeit. Stand und Perspektiven der Forschung zu Diplomatie und Staatensystem', in *Geschichte der Politik: Alte und neue Wege (Historische Zeitschrift, Beiheft, 44)*, ed. H.-C. Kraus, T. Nicklas (Munich, 2007), pp. 15–39.

lectured on Russia? Presumably he could not have ignored Peter I's major diplomatic advances in western Europe nor the war the tsar had fought against Sweden: indeed, the Great Northern War has been described as a 'first European World War' because of its diplomatic–political entanglements with the concurrent War of the Spanish Succession (1701–1714).[26] How far, if at all, would a professor at a European university have delved back in time to include Russia in a lecture on the 'present state of Europe'? The question is not new. As a distinguished historian of eastern Europe wrote, 'For more than five hundred years the cardinal problem in defining Europe has centred on the inclusion or exclusion of Russia.'[27]

Closed-ended questions do not always elicit clear answers, and so the problem of the inclusion or exclusion of Russia resulted in very ambiguous responses. John Milton, in 1682, acknowledged Russia 'as being the most northern Region of *Europe* reputed civil'.[28] Sully, on the other hand, in his *Grand design*, first published as part of his memoirs in 1638, had counted the tsar among the 'infidel princes of Europe' who ruled over barbarians. They have 'introduced so many superstitious practices in their worship, that there scarce remains any conformity with us among them; besides, they belong to Asia at least as much as to Europe. We may indeed almost consider them as a barbarous country, and place them in the same class with Turkey, though for these five hundred years, we have ranked them among the Christian powers'.[29] Positioned on two continents, and breaking away from Europe along the fault line of religion, Russia was an uncertain candidate for membership in the general council as envisioned by Sully. The author cautioned that the tsar 'ought to be treated like the Sultan of Turkey, deprived of his possessions in Europe, and confined to Asia' should he refuse 'to conform to any of the Christian doctrines of religion' and decline 'to enter into the association after it is proposed to him'.[30] Not until the publication of Saint-Pierre's *Paix Perpetuelle*, the first edition of which appeared three years after Peter I's victory at Poltava (1709), did Russia emerge as a reckoned political force in Europe's early

[26] K. Zernack, 'Das Zeitalter der nordischen Kriege von 1558 bis 1809 als frühneuzeitliche Geschichtsepoche', *Zeitschrift für Historische Forschung*, 1 (1974), 55–79, here on p. 69.

[27] N. Davies, *Europe: a history* (Oxford, 1996), p. 10, as quoted and discussed in S. Dixon, *The modernisation of Russia 1676–1825* (Cambridge, 1999), p. 27.

[28] J. Milton, *A Brief History of Moscovia and other less-known countries lying eastward of Russia as far as Cathay. Gather'd from the writings of several eye witnesses* (London, 1682), author's preface.

[29] Sully, *Grand design*, pp. 32f., 41f. On the 'grand design', see D. Ogg's introduction, pp. 3–13.

[30] Ibid., p. 33.

modern utopias of peace.[31] In the preface of the 1714 English translation, Saint-Pierre ranks 'Muscovy' among 'the eighteen Principal Christian Sovereignties, which should each of them have a Voice in the general Diet of Europe'. He shared Sully's reservations about the Russian monarch: 'I well know that the Christianity of his Dominions is very different from that of ours', but he insists that 'they hope for Salvation through *Jesus Christ*; therefore they are *Christians*'.[32] For him 'the *European Society* cannot well omit to make with him [the tsar] a Treaty of Commerce and everlasting Peace. [...] But to speak the Truth, this Treaty would be more secure both for him and the whole Union, if he had a Voice in the Congress, and were look'd upon as a Member of the Union'.[33] The surest answer is given by Voltaire. In the first chapter to the *Age of Louis XIV* (1751), the *philosophe* leaves no doubt about Russia's outlier role in the history of the European 'republic' before the reign of Peter I (while, of course, celebrating the tsar's enlightened reforms and Europeanising efforts in his later works):

> For a long time past the Christian part of Europe – Russia excepted – might be considered as a great republic divided into several states, some of which were monarchial, others mixed, some aristocratic, and others popular; but all corresponding with one another; all having the same basis of religion, though divided into several sects, and acknowledging the same principles of public and political equity, which were unknown to the other parts of the world.[34]

A clearly and increasingly exclusive notion of 'Europe' marked the epistemes of the 'enlightened' age which historians continued to carry through time, implying a concept that distinguishes a priori between two Europes: the centre-states, whose inner relations progressed into a modern states-system, and the periphery that failed to synchronise its diplomacy with these developments.[35] As a result, many scholars have placed

[31] Dixon, *Modernisation*, p. 28. For a discussion of Russia's place in this type of literature, see É. Schnakenbourg, *La France, le Nord et l'Europe au début du XVIIIe siècle* (Paris, 2008), p. 460.

[32] Saint-Pierre, *Project*, p. 105.

[33] Ibid. Note that in a later French edition, Saint-Pierre commented on Sully's remarks on Russia and showed that Henry IV (in whose name Sully was writing) would have accepted the tsar to associate himself with the union had he ever wished to do so, see C.-I. Castel, abbé de Saint-Pierre, *Projet de traité pour rendre la paix perpétuelle entre les souverains chrétiens* (Utrecht, 1717), p. 415.

[34] Voltaire, *The works of Voltaire: a contemporary version*, trans. W. F. Fleming, 22 vols. (New York, 1901), XII (*Age of Louis XIV*), p. 13. For Voltaire and the Enlightenment's impact on the image of Russia, see L. Wolff, *Inventing Eastern Europe: the map of civilization on the mind of the Enlightenment* (Stanford, 1994), ch. 5.

[35] Anderson, *Modern diplomacy*, pp. 27f. Similar E. V. Anisimov, 'The imperial heritage of Peter the Great in the foreign policy of his early successors', in *Imperial Russian foreign policy*, ed. H. Ragsdale, V. N. Ponomarev (Cambridge, New York 1993), pp. 21–35. This

pre-Petrine Russia outside the amalgam of states.[36] In the Rankean classification of great powers, the tsar, or grand duke of Moscow, was relegated to a negligible outsider position: isolated and impoverished, Russia was not able to use its military and economic resources for diplomatic aims and fell behind other powers. Hamish Scott has shown that it was not until the end of the Seven Years' War (1756–1763) that Russia rose from obscurity to the status of a great power to be accepted as an equal operator in the system.[37] Largely because of the prevailing influence of Ranke's concept, the study of foreign policy has indeed continued to concentrate on the tsars' attempts at surmounting their marginal existence within the system of great powers, which automatically limited the focus to the eighteenth century, starting with Peter the Great's reforms.[38]

view is even more pronounced in M. S. Anderson, *The origins of the modern European state system, 1494–1618* (London, 1998), esp. the section on 'Eastern Europe lags behind', pp. 55ff. For a critique, see Watkins, 'New diplomatic history', pp. 2f. On the notion of periphery, Frigo, Belton, eds., *Diplomatic practice*, pp. 3f. See also J. Darwin, *After Tamerlane: the global history of empire since 1405* (London, 2008), pp. 21, 67, for Russia. For a discussion of the development of Eurocentrism, see fn. 185.

36 A recent exception is P. Dukes, G. P. Herd, J. T. Kotilaine, *Stuarts and Romanovs: the rise and fall of a special relationship* (Dundee, 2009). See also A. Watson, 'Russia and the European states system', in *The expansion of international society*, ed. H. Bull, A. Watson (Oxford, New York, 1984), pp. 61–74. A. L. Khoroshkevich, see A. L. Khoroshkevich, *Russkoe gosudarstvo v sisteme mezhdunarodnykh otnoshenii kontsa XV-nachala XVI v.* (Moscow, 1980), and A. L. Khoroshkevich, *Rossiia v sisteme mezhdunarodnykh otnoshenii serediny XVI veka* (Moscow, 2003), trace Russia's place in the 'international system' already before the seventeenth century.

37 Scott, *Emergence*. Similar already, V. N. Aleksandrenko, *Russkie diplomaticheskie agenty v Londone v XVIII v.*, 2 vols. (Warsaw, 1897), I, p. 17. Cf. Black, *European international relations*, p. 40. Black ascribes Russia great power status as early as 1648 (together with Austria, France, Spain, Turkey; Britain and Prussia entered the category in the period that followed) but acknowledges that the West only began to perceive Russia as a major power from 1709 onwards. See also J. Black, 'Russia's rise as a European power, 1650–1750', in *Russia and Europe*, ed. P. Dukes (London, 1991), pp. 69–83.

38 See, for example, J. Kunisch, 'Der Aufstieg neuer Großmächte im 18. Jahrhundert und die Aufteilung der Machtspären in Ostmitteleuropa', in *Das europäische Staatensystem im Wandel. Strukturelle Bedingeungen und bewegende Kräfte seit der Frühen Neuzeit*, ed. P. Krüger (Munich, 1996), pp. 89–105; W. Mediger, *Moskaus Weg nach Europa: der Aufstieg Russlands zum europäischen Machtstaat im Zeitalter Friedrichs des Grossen* (Braunschweig, 1952); W. Mediger, *Mecklenburg, Russland und England-Hannover 1706–1721: ein Beitrag zur Geschichte des Nordischen Krieges*, 2 vols. (Hildesheim, 1967). A notable review of Walter Mediger's seminal work speaks volumes about the traditional, and generally accepted, view of Russia's place in early modern diplomacy (and Peter I's role in it): A. Lossky, 'Moskaus Weg nach Europa: der Aufstieg Russlands zum Europäischen Machtstaat im Zeitalter Friedrich des Grossen [Review]', *American Historical Review*, 58 (1953), 920–22. See also Mediger's view of the differences between Muscovy and the Petrine empire in his chapter on 'The spiritual and mental backgrounds of Russian foreign policy until the accession to the throne of Elisabeth 1500–1741', in Mediger, *Aufstieg*, ch. 3. See also M. Hellmann, 'Die Friedensschlüsse von Nystad (1721) und Teschen (1779) als Etappen des Vordringens Russlands nach Europa', *Historisches Jahrbuch*, 97/98 (1978),

The emperors and empresses of Russia entered the world of diplomacy in the eighteenth century, as they began to absorb European culture, rooted in the legacy of Louis XIV's France, and to perturb Western statesmen in their attempts to re-balance the powers of Europe.[39]

It is difficult to disagree with these conclusions; they are correct within the heuristic limits of the great-power approach with its explicit modernising pattern and focus on the European states-system. But the Eurocentric perspective that inheres in this approach presents a major problem when studying early modern Russian diplomacy in that it generates little interest in states that do not fit the pattern because of their ambivalent status and cultural difference. In other words, the concept of the states-system does not provide the nomenclature for what it conveniently labels as outsiders. Just as culturally diverse as the European system of states was from within, it emerges an indivisible whole when confronted with cultural outliers that are lumped together as 'the other', the barbarous.[40] The concept of a closed states-system dictates a member/non-member antagonism by which exclusion or inclusion – and, with it, historical relevance – is determined by perceived cultural difference. The diplomacy of polities, which because of their perceived otherness are thought to lie outside the system, and its diplomatic culture, remain poorly researched. Diplomacy before Peter I is often labelled as 'primitive' and 'incompatible' with modern European international relations. Where it is difficult to place Russia in the system, where Russian diplomacy eludes the familiar categories of description, its foreign policy and diplomatic apparatus are conveniently contextualised in the pervasive discourse of barbarism.[41] Based on the assumption that early

270–88, and M. Schulze-Wessel, 'Systembegriff und Europapolitik der russischen Diplomatie im 18. Jahrhundert', *Historische Zeitschrift*, 266 (1998), 649–69.

39 Scott, 'Diplomatic culture', p. 62.

40 For an excellent survey of European attitudes to what was considered 'barbarous', see J. Osterhammel, *Die Entzauberung Asiens: Europa und die asiatischen Reiche im 18. Jahrhundert* (Munich, 1998), pp. 242ff. See also I. B. Neumann, J. M. Welsh, 'The Other in European self-definition: an addendum to the literature on international society', *Review of International Studies*, 17 (1991), 327–48; G. Delanty, *Formations of European modernity: a historical and political sociology of Europe* (Basingstoke, 2013), esp. pp. 4–10. See also Marshall Poe's perspicacious remark on Russia's outsider status as an Asian country: 'But Russia isn't Asian, because no place is really Asian. The concept itself is a useless artifact of the clumsy, homogenizing European imperial gaze. Europeans proved very adept at making fine distinctions within their own civilizational house – a product, perhaps, of being profoundly and politically multiethnic. Yet they failed completely to capture the diversity of the world they came to dominate. Nowhere is this truer than in Asia. What in the world do Iran, Sri Lanka, and Vietnam have in common? Not much, except they were all uncomfortably lumped into the same bulbous civilizational category. They were all somehow "Asiatic" '. M. Poe, *The Russian moment in world history* (Princeton, Oxford, 2003), p. 8.

41 E. Kobzareva, 'Vestfal'skaia mirnaia sistema i Rossiia', *Otechestvennaia istoriia*, 4 (1999), 146–52, esp. p. 147.

modern Europeans considered Russia a remote, xenophobic, and despotic country as described in foreign travellers' accounts,[42] Russian diplomatic culture, too, was classified as oriental, obscure, and strangely ritualistic.[43] In particular, the tsars' rigid ritual representation and mounting status-claims are taken to be a token of Russia's exotic heritage and outsider status.[44] Russia stood alongside the Ottoman or Persian powers because it lacked economic wealth, military presence, and political involvement in the Westphalian system and was instead concerned with the outward appearance of protocol and ceremonies rather than with the substance of political affairs.[45]

However, assessing Russian early modern diplomacy by the standards of modern state rationality, which infers international (great power) status of a polity from its economic capability and military potential, can only serve as an obstacle to a better understanding of the tsars' place in early modern international politics and of their, and other monarchs', persistence on ceremonial forms in foreign relations. Indeed, even Hoffmann, in his 1720 curriculum for the study of international relations, still placed special emphasis on the *ius ceremoniale*, that is, the conflicting claims manifest in the display of honour and dignity. For a student of 'the present state of Europe', it was important not only to learn about the ways in which various polities were interconnected but also to be able to distinguish between rightfully justified assertions of honours, on the one hand, and the unscrupulous fabrication of status that was often founded on sophistry rather than true dignity, on the other. The 'science of disputes over precedence and ceremonial' (*Wissenschaft von denen Praecedenz-Streitigkeiten und des Ceremoniells*) formed part of *ius ceremoniale* and occupied a central place in Hoffmann's projected university course.[46] The question, then, whether or not Russia was included in the European states-system must be opened up and reformulated by mediating between the prevailing contemporary norms underpinning what Norbert Elias termed 'courtly rationality' and those that have written themselves into diplomatic history since the Enlightenment. Rather than trying to trace Russia in the 'republic' or the European states-

42 For travel literature see Marshall Poe's seminal work, *A people born to slavery: Russia in early modern European ethnography, 1476–1748* (Ithaca, NY, London, 2000). See also S. Mund, *Orbis russiarum: genèse et développement de la représentation du monde 'russe' en Occident à la Renaissance* (Geneva, 2003), for sixteenth- and seventeenth-century writings on Russia.

43 Matsuki, 'A diplomatic custom in Muscovy'.

44 For example, Anderson, *Modern diplomacy*, p. 61. Similar, Lebow, *A cultural theory*, p. 10, and R. Bonney, *The European dynastic states*, 1494–1660 (Oxford, 1991), pp. 272–84.

45 For a useful summary of the classic geopolitical approach, see, Anisimov, 'Foreign policy', p. 31.

46 Hoffmann, *Entwurff*, pp. 7–13, passim.

system, it is important to ask where its place was in early modern 'diplomacy of the *type ancien*'.

Discourses of Russian Barbarism

To pose the question another way: where was Russia's place in early modern ceremonies of diplomacy? The subject matter of the here selected seventeenth- and eighteenth-century writers consisted of what Hoffmann regarded as an indispensable element in the study of international relations, namely, diplomatic practice more generally and the 'science of precedence-quarrels' in particular.

The following sections discuss the central themes that determined Russia's position in the discourse of honour and rank. They also examine the sources at the heart of this discourse to reveal the kind of Russia-related information to which scholars of ceremony and precedence had access. Finally, they analyse how these scholars interpreted and appropriated the information on and the stereotypes of Russia to the needs of their specific subject matter. The ubiquitous discourse of barbarism, a European speciality,[47] in which Russia undoubtedly figured prominently, suggests that *Zeremonialwissenschaft*, too, used the same kind of 'otherisation' in order to remove the tsars from the European *société des princes*. However, the opposite was the case. Seventeenth- and eighteenth-century experts on ceremonial aspects of diplomacy attempted to present a more or less sober calculation of the tsars' status vis-à-vis other European princes. While they grappled with uncertainties about Russian culture and its European appearance, they showed a clear tendency to rank the tsars among the powerful sovereigns in the monarchical society. Before the discussion turns to these authors, it is helpful to recall, as a counterweight, the origins of Russia's prevailing image as a barbarous country.

In Samuel von Pufendorf's *An introduction to the history of the principal kingdoms and states of Europe*, Russia appears as a country within the borders of Europe.[48] Yet, the character and quality of its people set it apart from civilised nations. Writing under the protection of the Swedish king – Russia's feared neighbour on its north-western border – Pufendorf stated that

> nothing very praise-worthy can be said [of the Russian people]. For among them there is no such Education as among most other European Nations. [...] They are

[47] Keene, *Political thought*, ch. 1, passim.

[48] S. v. Pufendorf, *An introduction to the history of the principal kingdoms and states of Europe by Samuel Puffendorf. Made English from the Original* (London, 1695), ch. 11. Note that Pufendorf also published a separate work on decidedly 'non-European' states: S. v. Pufendorf, *The history of the kingdoms and states of Asia, Africa and America. Both ancient and modern*, 6th edn. (London, 1736).

also jealous, cruel and bloody-minded; insupportably proud in prosperity, and dejected and cowardly in adversity. [...] Nevertheless they have such an Opinion of their own Abilities and Merits, that you can scarce ever pay them sufficient Respect.[49]

Pufendorf's unfavourable assessment echoes a long-standing literary tradition. Since the first diplomatic contacts with Western courts at the beginning of the early modern period, Russia had been the object of curiosity and cultural demarcation. The perception of Russia came in different modes. In Elizabethan England, it could take the form of a literary image of the strange but comic 'frozen Muscovite' who had arrived in the West (as in Shakespeare's *Love's Labour's Lost*).[50] Shortly after a Russian embassy had departed from France in 1668, Raymond Poisson, a comic actor and author at the Hôtel de Bourgogne in Paris, portrayed Russian ambassadors as *Les faux Moscovites* in his one-act farce by the same name.[51] Sculptured representations of Russian, Moroccan, and Siamese ambassadors conveyed their exotic image to the Parisian public. The personal painter to Louis XIV, Antoine Benoist, was granted, in 1688, the privilege to cast and exhibit wax figures and portraits 'not only of distinguished persons of Europe but also of the amb[assadors] extraord[inaries] of Siam, Morocco, Muscovy, Algeria, the Doge of Genoa, the court of the Grand Seigneur [the Ottoman sultan] and other foreign courts'.[52] Clearly, Russia's place on the map of cultural representation was near non-European societies like those of Siam, Morocco, or the Ottoman Empire (see Figure 1.1).[53] Moscow was certainly

[49] Pufendorf, *Introduction*, p. 363.

[50] For the image of Russia in Shakespeare's plays, see J. W. Draper, 'Shakespeare and Muscovy', *The Slavonic and East European Review*, 33 (1954), 217–21; K. H. Ruffmann, *Das Russlandbild im England Shakespeares* (Göttingen, 1952). See also D. W. Palmer, *Writing Russia in the age of Shakespeare* (Aldershot, 2004). The image of Russia in Elizabethan theatre was partly shaped by the activities of the Muscovy Company: R. Wilson, 'Visible bullets: Tamburlaine the Great and Ivan the Terrible', *English Literary History*, 62 (1995), 47–68.

[51] C. R. Jensen, J. S. Powell, '"A mess of Russian left us but of late": diplomatic blunder, literary satire, and the Muscovite ambassador's 1668 visit to Paris theatres', *Theatre Research International*, 24 (1999), 131–44. For the 1668 embassy, see Chapter 2, fn. 129.

[52] BnF, MS f 10654, fols. 68–69. The privilege was renewed and granted to his son, Gabriel Benoist, in 1717, see E. Vaudin, *Notice sur Antoine Benoist de Joigny peintre et sculpteur en cire de Louis XIV* (Paris, 1887), pp. 41–42. For a discussion of European images of Russia with special attention to the French perspective, see Schnakenbourg, *La France*, pp. 449–62.

[53] See, for example, A. Heidenfeld, *Asiatischer Schauplatz / Das ist / Ausfuehrliche Beschreibung Der tuerkischen / Persianischen/ Moskowitischen und Chinischen Beherrscheren sampt Deren Inwohnern Sitten* (Frankfurt a. M., 1678). On this work, see S. Rauschenbach, 'Albert Heidenfeld: Asiatischer Schauplatz', *Welt und Wissen auf der Bühne: Theatrum-Literatur der Frühen Neuzeit.* Available from www.theatra.de/repertorium/ed000094.pdf, last access 6 February 2016.

Figure 1.1 Public audience of Ambassador Petr I. Potemkin at Versailles in 1681.

Note the displays of Siamese and Moroccan embassies at the top of the engraving. While such representations reveal relatively little accurate information about the ceremonial treatment of Russian diplomats, they illustrate how the French court sought to express a perceived cultural connection between Muscovite embassies and other diplomatic missions from 'exotic' countries not least to convey the vast geographic reach of the French monarch's power.

not perceived to lie in the cultural vicinity of Vienna, Versailles, or London.[54]

Russians were regarded on a level with the peoples who inhabited the newly explored lands in the age of discovery and European expansion.[55] Russia also figured as the cruel enemy on the borders of Europe: an anti-Russian propaganda machine spread the printed word about the atrocities committed by Ivan IV's (r. 1533–1584) army in the wars against Poland-Lithuania.[56] Furthermore, Russia became the focus of early ethnographic interest. Numerous travellers, including those cosmographic writers, who journeyed to Russia without ever leaving the comfort of their desk at home,[57] described Russian mores, government, and religion as something distinctly foreign to their own.[58]

All these images were variations on a single theme: 'The Russians are a People who differ from all other Nations of the world, in most of their Actions.'[59] Among the vast amount of travel literature, Marshall Poe has identified the three authors who were instrumental in forming

[54] W. Schmale, *Geschichte und Zukunft der europäischen Identität* (Stuttgart, 2008), esp. pp. 93f. for Russia.

[55] E. Klug, 'Das "Asiatische" Rußland. Über die Entstehung eines europäischen Vorurteils', *Historische Zeitschrift*, 245 (1987), 265–89, pp. 268f; M.-L. Pelus, 'Un des aspects de la naissance d'une conscience européenne: la Russie vue d'Europe occidentale au XVIe siècle', in *La Conscience européenne au XVe et au XVIe siècle*, ed. Ecole Normale Supérieur de Jeunes Filles (Paris, 1982), pp. 309–28, esp. p. 309. See also M. S. Anderson, *Britain's discovery of Russia, 1553–1815* (London, 1958); P. Dukes, *The making of Russian absolutism 1613–1801* (London, New York, 1982), pp. 1f.

[56] A. Kappeler, *Ivan Groznyj im Spiegel der ausländischen Druckschriften seiner Zeit: ein Beitrag zur Geschichte des westlichen Russlandbildes* (Bern, 1972). According to Philip Longworth, Russia's exclusion from Europe was mainly the result of Polish diplomacy which 'opposed any lasting reconciliation between Muscovy and the powers of central and western Europe, especially the papacy'. P. Longworth, 'Muscovy and the "Antemurale Christianitatis"', in *Mesto Rossii v Evrope: materialy mezhdunarodnoi konferentsii*, ed. G. Szvák (Budapest, 1999), pp. 82–87, here on p. 83. For an alternative view (challenged by Longworth), which emphasises the return of Russia to Europe in the mid-fifteenth century, after the Tatar invasion, see E. Winter, *Russland und das Papsttum*, 3 vols. (Berlin, 1960–1972), I, p. 179.

[57] Neither Milton nor Pufendorf had ever been to Russia. For the characteristics of 'derivative items such as cosmographical vignettes and books written by stay-at-home scholars', see M. Poe, 'Introduction', in *Early explorations of Russia*, ed. M. Poe, 14 vols. (London, New York, 2003–2004), I, pp. 2ff.

[58] The travel accounts have been studied extensively by Poe, *A people born to slavery*. See also E. Binello, *Muscovite politics and culture in the sixteenth and seventeenth centuries through the eyes of foreign travellers* (London, 1996). Scheidegger, *Perverses Abendland*, insightfully complements the picture by describing the Russian conception of Europe. See also G. Scheidegger, 'Das Eigene im Bild vom Anderen. Quellenkritische Überlegungen zur russisch-abendländischen Begegnung im 16. und 17. Jahrhundert', *Jahrbücher für Geschichte Osteuropas*, 35 (1987), 339–55.

[59] S. Collins, *The present state of Russia in a letter to a friend at London/written by an eminent person residing at the great czars court at Mosco for the space of nine years* (London, 1671), p. 66. See also Scheidegger, *Perverses Abendland*, p. 33.

early modern European images of Russia: Sigismund von Herberstein (1486–1566), Antonio Possevino (1533/34–1611), and Adam Olearius (1603–1671).[60] Their legacy has not ceased to nourish our clichés about Russians (and those of Russians about themselves) to this day.[61]

Herberstein was sent to Russia as a Habsburg diplomat under Emperor Maximilian I (r. 1493–1519) and King Ferdinand I (r. 1526–1564) in 1517/18 and 1526/27, respectively, to mediate a peace between Russia and Poland with a view to forming a united attack against the Ottomans. More than twenty years later, in 1549, he published an account of his journey, the celebrated *Rerum moscoviticarum commentarii*. This first full-blown account of Muscovite life soon rose to an 'international bestseller'.[62] By the end of the seventeenth century, it had appeared in thirty-one editions in Latin, German, Italian, Polish, English, Dutch, and French.[63] Herberstein depicted Russia as an inferior country ruled by a tyrant whose government had forced the whole population into a slavish existence. His confidence in these 'wild people', who referred to themselves as 'their prince's *kholop*, that is, sold slave', was low. For him, however, it remained undecided 'whether such a people must have such oppressive rulers or whether the oppressive rulers have made the people so stupid'.[64]

[60] Poe, 'Introduction', p. 20. For an example of how these clichés – rehashed during the Cold War – still serve as an inspiring source of debate, see V. A. Kivelson, 'On words, sources, and historical method: which truth about Muscovy?', *Kritika: Explorations in Russian and Eurasian History*, 3 (2002), 487–99, in response to M. Poe, 'The Truth about Muscovy', *Kritika: Explorations in Russian and Eurasian History*, 3 (2002), 473–86. For a full bibliography of early modern descriptions of Russia, see M. Poe, *Foreign descriptions of Muscovy: an analytic bibliography of primary and secondary sources* (Columbus, OH, 1995). A revised edition is available from http://ir.uiowa.edu/cgi/viewcontent.cgi?article=1008&context=history_pubs, last access 6 February 2016.

[61] As can be seen from recent literary representations of Eastern Europe which were read at the *Literaturfestival* Berlin 2010, J. Thumfart, 'Zurzeit liegt Osteuropa im Orient', *Zeit Online*, 22 September 2010, available from www.zeit.de/kultur/literatur/2010-09/literaturfestival-berlin-osteuropa, last access 6 February 2016. The travel accounts had a similar effect on modern historiography, see C. J. Halperin, 'Sixteenth-century foreign travel accounts to Muscovy: a methodological excursus', *Sixteenth-Century Journal*, 6 (1975), 89–111, for a discussion.

[62] F. Kämpfer et al., eds., *Sigismund von Herberstein: Rerum Moscoviticarum Commentarii. Synoptische Edition der lateinischen und der deutschen Fassung letzter Hand. Basel 1556 und Wien 1557* (Munich, 2007), p. 7 (introduction).

[63] For a list of Herberstein editions, see M. Poe, *Early exploration of Russia*, 12 vols. (London, New York, 2003), II, p. 3. The literature on Herberstein is too large to be cited here in detail. For the diplomatic context of his travels, see G. Pferschy, ed., *Siegmund von Herberstein: Kaiserlicher Gesandter und Begründer der Russlandkunde und die europäische Diplomatie* (Graz, 1989). For the recent literature, see the contributions and the bibliography in R. Frötschner, F. Kämpfer, eds., *450 Jahre Sigismund von Herbersteins Rerum Moscoviticarum Commentarii: 1549–1999* (Wiesbaden, 2002).

[64] Kämpfer et al., ed., *Rerum Moscoviticarum*, pp. 388, 175, 73f. English translation from B. Picard, ed., *Herberstein, Sigmund: description of Moscow and Muscovy, 1557* (London,

Possevino at least admired the modesty and simplicity of the Russian people, their steadfastness in their faith. A papal legate and the first Jesuit to travel to Moscow, Possevino was sent to the court of Ivan IV in 1581 to negotiate a truce between Russia and Poland-Lithuania. Pope Gregory XIII (1502–1585) was hoping to build momentum for the establishment of diplomatic relations with the tsar in order to unite the Catholic and Orthodox worlds against the Turks.[65] Although Possevino was convinced that the Muscovites had much in common with the Scythians and Tatars, he nurtured the hope that through their devotion and profound belief in the word of Christ, they could be lured back to the true Orthodox faith, that is, the Catholic Church.[66] Yet, his experience in Russia taught him a lesson when, according to his memoir, Ivan IV almost attacked him in a fit of anger that resulted from their discussion of the pope's claim to universal authority.[67] While Possevino's mediation facilitated a peace settlement which ended the Livonian war, his attempt at bringing the two churches together failed. He acquitted himself of any disappointment by explaining the insurmountable difficulties in introducing the true faith into this country. The Russians, like

> the peoples of the northern expanse, especially those who have not been freed from savagery by the influence of the true religion, possess highly suspicious temperaments because they know that they are lacking in natural ability. They strive to acquire by deceit and violence (and, in the case of the Muscovites, by stubbornness as well) what they cannot obtain through zeal or compromise.[68]

In the end, depressed by his unsuccessful efforts, Possevino suggested that a Catholic priest should not even attempt to 'instil a doubt concerning the schism into the minds of a people who are quite primitive, and perhaps even saved by their very simplicity'.[69]

Another traveller, whose writings exerted a tremendous influence on how early modern Europeans viewed Russia, was Olearius. As a man of letters, he was appointed secretary to the ambassadors Philipp Crusius and Otto Brüggemann, a jurisconsult and a merchant, who embarked on a journey to establish commercial ties with Russia and Persia on behalf of Frederick III, the duke of Holstein-Gottorp (r. 1616–1659). After returning to

1969), pp. 43, 54. For Herberstein's concept of despotism in view of Russia and its influence on later generations, see Poe, *A people born to slavery*.

[65] A. Possevino, *The Moscovia of Antonio Possevino*, trans. H. F. Graham (Pittsburgh, 1977, reprint, 2003), p. ix.

[66] Ibid., pp. 53ff., 61.

[67] Ibid., p. 72. For the religious debate between Possevino and Ivan IV over the superiority of the Roman Catholic dogma, see I. de Madariaga, *Ivan the Terrible: first tsar of Russia* (New Haven, London, 2005), pp. 345ff.

[68] Possevino, *The Moscovia of Antonio Possevino*, p. 26. [69] Ibid., p. 56.

Gottorp in 1639, Olearius enjoyed a life as a scholar at Frederick III's court and put pen to paper to compose an extensive narrative about his travels. His *Ausführliche Beschreibung der kundbaren Reyss nach Muscow und Persien* first appeared in 1647 and saw numerous editions and translations. Olearius' views on Russia were in the same vein as his predecessors', and he largely confirmed the notion of a tyrannical state that was based on the natural inclination of its inhabitants to give themselves over to bondage and servitude.[70] It is safe to say that he expressed what came to the mind of many Europeans when they thought of Russia: 'If a man consider the natures and manner of life of the *Muscovites*, he will be forc'd to avow, there cannot any thing be more barbarous than that people.'[71]

These views of the three most influential authors could be extended by numerous virtually identical quotations that encapsulate European imaginaries of Russia as a 'rude and barbarous kingdom'.[72] The similarity of these judgements about Russian culture is no surprise. A striking feature of accounts of Russia is their authors' 'systematic plagiarism'.[73] Not only did almost all writers – irrespective of whether they had been to Russia or observed its people from an armchair perspective – borrow from Herberstein, Possevino, and Olearius. These authors also copied from each other, with Herberstein's 'citation index' being particularly impressive in this respect.[74] The entrenchment of a 'barbarous other' was

70 Poe, 'Distant world', p. 9.

71 A. Olearius, *The voyages and travells of the ambassadors sent by Frederick, Duke of Holstein, to the Great Duke of Muscovy and the King of Persia begun in the year M.DC.XXXIII. and finish'd in M.DC.XXXIX, trans. J. Davies* (London, 1669), p. 57. István Vásáry sees the reason for Russia's 'barbarous' image in Europe in the long Tatar domination over Russia, I. Vásáry, 'Why was Muscovite Russia considered "Barbarian" by contemporary Europe?', in *Mesto Rossii v Evrope*, ed. Szvák, pp. 97–102.

72 Many of these authors were diplomats, and their testimonies about Russian life and diplomatic practice will reappear at various points in the following chapters. For a collection of English-language accounts, see Berry, Crummey, eds., *Rude & barbarous kingdom*. For French accounts, see also M. Mervaud, J.-C. Roberti, *Une infinie brutalité: l'image de la Russie dans la France des XVIe et XVIIe siècles* (Paris, 1991). See M. S. Anderson, 'English views of Russia in the 17th century', *Slavonic and East European Review*, 33 (1954), 140–60, for seventeenth-century English accounts. For the late Petrine era, see M. S. Anderson, 'English views of Russia in the Age of Peter the Great', *American Slavic and East European Review*, 13 (1954), 200–14; L. A. J. Hughes, 'Russia in 1689: court politics in Foy de la Neuville's Relation curieuse et nouvelle de Moscovie', in *New perspectives on Muscovite history: selected papers from the Fourth World Congress for Soviet and East European Studies, Harrogate, 1990*, ed. L. A. J. Hughes (London, 1993), 177–87.

73 This point is elaborated in Poe, 'Introduction', pp. 15, 18ff.

74 S. H. Baron, 'Herberstein's image of Russia and its transmission through later writings', in *Siegmund von Herberstein: Kaiserlicher Gesandter und Begründer der Russlandkunde und die europäische Diplomatie*, ed. G. Pferschy (Graz, 1989), pp. 245–79; W. Leitsch, 'Herberstein's impact on the reports about Muscovy in the sixteenth and seventeenth

inevitable and informed virtually all attempts to make sense of what to Europeans seemed to be an entirely foreign culture: Russia.[75]

This image was appropriated even by Russians themselves in order to contrast Peter I's achievements with the allegedly miserable state in which the country had found itself before his reforms. In a diplomatic context, this picture was well suited to establishing a glorious image of Peter I in contrast to seemingly old-fashioned Muscovite practices.

For example, Petr P. Shafirov, one of Tsar Peter I's chief diplomats and author of the first Russian treatise on international law, wrote towards the end of the Great Northern War that the tsar had brought honour and recognition to Russia. The tsar's achievements shone even brighter against the fact that 'some decades ago the Russian people and state were discussed and described in other European States as were Indians and Persians and other peoples that have no relations with Europe save a little bit of trade. [Russia] was not part of European affairs, in either peace or war, and was hardly ever included in the community of European peoples'.[76] These words are taken from the *Discourse*'s dedication to the tsarevich, Petr Petrovich. They reminded the reader that only with his father did Russia start to become seriously involved in European affairs, as the Russian ruler grew in status as both an attractive ally and a terrifying enemy. Such a claim is, of course, less a description of pre-Petrine reality than part of the panegyric tone with which its author played up to his master, Peter I, who had revised the manuscript personally.[77]

Russia, according to Shafirov, had yet to become a civilised Christian nation if it was to be part of the European states-system, and it requires no explanation that the text points to Peter I as the one who ushered it into the *société des princes*. In the conclusion of the treatise, written by Feofan Prokopovich (1681–1736), Peter I's ideological mastermind, and added to

centuries: some choice observations on the technique of borrowing', *Forschungen zur Osteuropäischen Geschichte*, 24 (1978), 163–77.

75 This was noted with great hostility by the seventeenth-century pan-Slavist Iurii Krizhanich (1618–1683), a Croatian Jesuit who went to Russia to promote the reconciliation of the Roman Catholic with the Russian Orthodox churches and wrote an account in which he expressed deep resentment against foreigners who lived at the tsar's expense but portrayed Russia in such a negative light: J. M. Letiche, B. Dmytryshyn, eds., *Russian statecraft: the Politika of Iurii Krizhanich* (Oxford, 1985), pp. 109–12, 16–24, 44f., passim. See also Matsuki, 'A diplomatic custom in Muscovy', p. 25.

76 Shafirov, *Discourse*, p. 2 (Russian version). This work has been described as the first treatise on international law in Russian by W. E. Butler, 'On the origins of international legal science in Russia', *Journal of the History of International Law/Revue d'Histoire du droit international*, 4 (2002), 1–41.

77 Evidenced by the underlining in the original manuscript, which stem from Peter I's own hand, RGADA, f. 156, op. 1, d. 173.

Shafirov's manuscript,[78] the theme was picked up once again. Prokopovich remarked (directly referencing Pufendorf) that 'there is no Comparison to be made between those Times and Conjunctures and the present', referring to the difference between Muscovite Russia and the newly born Petrine empire.[79] He pointed out that the country once portrayed by Pufendorf as 'but a blind nation' had now developed into a powerful and respected state.[80]

To juxtapose past and present in this way means to accept preconceived ideas that typified Muscovite culture as profoundly alien to Europeans. These stereotypes surfaced in the early writings of Western travellers, were borrowed and then passed on by numerous authors, spread through state descriptions like that of Pufendorf, and from there, with the basic tint of early enlightened criticism, returned to Petrine Russia where they were welcomed as a device to justify reform and war. But the legacy of Herberstein, Possevino, Olearius, and other similar authors did not stop there.

In the same vein as Shafirov (and Peter I and Prokopovich), the eminent nineteenth-century Russian legal scholar Fedor Fedorovich Martens acknowledged that 'it would be erroneous to consider Muscovy as a member of international exchange and to maintain that the Russian people and its government already at that time understood the necessity of international communication with western powers. [...] Such relations started only in the time of Tsar Peter the Great and only in the time of Catherine II received a firm basis'.[81] Indeed, modern classic legal scholarship in Russia wedded the study of international law to the question of civilisational belonging, dating the beginning of Russia's participation in international affairs to Peter I's efforts of Europeanising the country.[82] From that perspective, it seems only logical to describe early modern Russian foreign relations prior to the tsar's reforms, especially ceremonial behaviour, as incompatible with new 'European' ways.[83] Already in 1957, Günther Stökl, the then-leading German

[78] The manuscript in RGADA, f. 156, op. 1, d. 173, suggests that the conclusion ('*zakliuchenie chitateliu*') was added by Prokopovich.

[79] Shafirov, *Discourse*, pp. 73f. (Russian version) and 344 (English translation). [80] Ibid.

[81] F. F. Martens, *Sovremennoe mezhdunarodnoe pravo tsivilizovannykh narodov*, 5th edn., 2 vols. (St Petersburg, 1904), I, pp. 157f. Translation from L. Mälksoo, 'The history of international legal theory in Russia: a civilizational dialogue with Europe', *European Journal of International Law*, 19 (2008), 211–32, here on p. 221. For Martens, see V. V. Pustogarov, *Our Martens: F.F. Martens, international lawyer and architect of peace*, trans. W. E. Butler (London, 2000).

[82] L. Mälksoo, *Russian approaches to international law* (Oxford, 2015), p. 71.

[83] See the discussion of Russia's places in the states-system above. See also, J. H. Billington, 'The projection of power', in *Gifts to the Tsars, 1500–1700: Treasures from the Kremlin*, ed. B. Shifman, G. Walton (New York, 2001), pp. 11–19. For a balanced discussion that

historian of pre-Petrine Russia, suggested that 'it is unjustifiable to discuss Russia and Europe as two exponents of entirely different, antagonistic worlds, and that it is important to identify Russia's position in Europe in its specific historical context'.[84] The following sections will trace this position in the context of *ius praecedentiae* and *Zeremonialwissenschaft* and provide a few counterpoints to prevailing interpretations of Russian magnificence and emphasis on ritual as evidence of its cultural otherness.

Ceremonial Counterpoints

The authors, whose task was to identify and describe the position of rulers within the pecking order of polities, saw Russia in a different historical context than that of barbarism and otherness or even that of a 'states-system'. Their context was that of the workings of dynastic prestige, rank, and precedence. What follows is a close examination of texts by contemporary German, French, and English authors who concerned themselves with the political order of early modern Europe. The aim is not to verify whether these writers were right or wrong in their assessment of dynastic hierarchies, but to present their views on Russia's place in it.

A common feature of the legal and scholarly literature on rank is a textual structure that in itself exemplifies the social order as depicted by the author. The formal composition of the text inevitably follows the ceremonial rules it frames. In other words, when form and content coalesce, the structure works as an implicit yet very powerful argument. Many authors carefully chose the order, in which they portrayed sovereigns and their qualities, to establish a hierarchical framework that they could then fill with subtle legal and historical justifications. It may be assumed that a ruler to whom a book or treatise was dedicated would receive a more favourable assessment than others. One of the authors who employed such a literary strategy was Balthasar Sigismund von Stosch. He published a sizeable tome on the order of precedence of all monarchs

raises the issue of cultural incompatibility of 'occidental' and Russian norms underpinning diplomatic practice, see Schaub, 'Diplomates russe et français', esp. pp. 335f., and M.-K. Schaub, 'Avoir l'oreille du roi: l'ambassade de Pierre Potemkin et Siméon Roumiantsev en France en 1668', in *Paroles de négociateurs: l'entretien dans la pratique diplomatique de la fin du Moyen âge à la fin du XIXe siècle*, ed. S. Andretta et al. (Rome, 2010), pp. 213–29. On cultural differences in ritual more generally, see Berelowitch, *La hiérarchie des égaux*, for Muscovy, and D. Zakharine, *Von Angesicht zu Angesicht: der Wandel direkter Kommunikation in der ost- und westeuropäischen Neuzeit* (Konstanz, 2005), for a broad East–West comparison.

[84] G. Stökl, 'Rußland und Europa vor Peter dem Großen', *Historische Zeitschrift*, 184 (1957), 531–54, here on p. 532.

and republics of Europe in 1677,[85] in the Silesian city of Breslau (Wrocław), which – under Habsburg rule since 1526 – had been a centre of German baroque literature.[86] Stosch, a Catholic, faithfully dedicated the book to the Holy Roman Emperor Leopold I (r. 1658–1705).[87] Who if not the emperor delivered the most authoritative judgement, for he 'outshines other potentates like phosphorus', Stosch suggestively asked, and in the same breath bestowed the book on Leopold I, 'the highest ruler in the whole of Christendom'.[88] Not only did this dedication buttress the pre-eminence of the imperial court, it also invested all other claims brought forward in the book with the impeccable authority of the emperor. A succession of ornate metaphors follows to bear out the glory of Leopold I. 'It is indisputable', Stosch wrote, 'that the imperial majesty is a fountain of all highness from which spring and flow the streams of all dignity. Other potentates are only kings of private persons, the imperial majesty is a king of kings'.[89]

Stosch showed an understanding of ceremonial that was also shared by legal experts and the scholars of the later generation of the eighteenth century. He explained the need to display status and dignity in the relations between rulers and ruled. Ceremonies created and depicted the necessary hierarchies within society at large. Power was so abstract a concept, and so impalpable by nature, that it had to be made visible to be understood and respected by the dull-witted masses: 'Royal authority must reveal itself to the rabble by certain tokens.'[90] Or in Johann C. Lünig's words, written almost half a century later: 'Because most human beings, but in particular common men, are of such nature that sensual sensation and imagination is more plausible to them than wit and reason, and that they are hence easier convinced by the things which tickle the senses and appear before the eyes than by the most concise and perspicuous arguments.'[91] The common people did not possess enough reason to grasp the reality of power, and ceremonial distinctions needed to appeal to the senses so that the supreme authority was met with due obedience in its specific social context. Decorum and dress reinforced

[85] B. S. v. Stosch, *Von dem Praecedentz= Oder Vorder=Recht aller Potentaten und Respubliquen in Europa: Samt einer sonderbaren Zugabe von der Hoheit des Ertz-Hertzoglichen Hauses Oesterreich* (Breßlau, 1677).

[86] E. Sagarra, P. N. Skrine, *A companion to German literature: from 1500 to the present* (Oxford, 1999), ch. 2.

[87] Although the book stresses the greatness of the emperor, its focus is not the emperor himself but the subject of rank and ceremony. For the rich panegyric literature written for Leopold I, see M. Goloubeva, *The glorification of Emperor Leopold I in image, spectacle and text* (Mainz, 2000).

[88] Stosch, *Vorder=Recht*, pp. a2f. [89] Ibid., p. a3. [90] Ibid., p. 894.

[91] Lünig, *Theatrum Ceremoniale*, I, p. 5.

distinctions among mankind, and to ignore this natural hierarchy would ultimately result in a 'most unequal equality' that violated the given order of things and resulted in uncontrollable chaos.[92]

Whether the contemporary distinction between an ignorant populace and wise rulers fully explains the functioning of rank and ceremony is debatable. It is safe to say, however, that the specific anthropology behind this view rather represents particularly neo-stoic discourse than it describes actual ceremonial procedures at court because these mainly addressed members of court society rather than the common people.[93] Rulers had to demonstrate dignity to their peers in order to consolidate the hierarchical framework that pervaded not only the society they ruled but also, and especially so, the relations between the states they embodied. Since the Reformation, Protestant writers had been trying to instil the idea into monarchs that ambition and reputation, pageantry and spectacle symbolised the failures of human nature and stood in stark opposition to Christian values.[94] Contrary to the writings, which expounded such values, Stosch exposed a different view on the function of ceremony and splendour. 'God himself is aligned with both honour and glory; from hence sprouts the conflict, pervading all of Europe, over precedence among distinguished potentates.'[95] If the disciples of Jesus wrangled with each other over pre-eminence, if the Eastern and Western Christian churches as well as their two imperial representatives on earth fought over precedence, then ceremonial struggles seemed only natural for princes.[96]

The first secular ruler who follows the pope in Stosch's order of precedence is the *dominus Mundi*, the Holy Roman Emperor.[97] Stosch repeatedly ridiculed rulers of lower rank to emphasise the superior status of an emperor as opposed to monarchs of royal dignity: 'Because the king of France is called a *Rex Asinorum*, a king of donkeys, that in Spain a *Rex hominum*, a king of men, that in England a *Rex Diabolorum*, a king of devils, that in Poland a *Rex Dominorum*, a king of lords, we call our *Imperatorem Regem Regum*, a king of all kings.'[98] Before he moved on to

[92] Stosch, *Vorder=Recht*, p. 892.
[93] For a discussion, see Pečar, *Ökonomie der Ehre*, pp. 146–49; Duindam, *Vienna and Versailles*, p. 194. See also A. Gestrich, 'Höfisches Zeremoniell und sinnliches Volk. Die Rechtfertigung des Hofzeremoniells im 17. und frühen 18. Jahrhundert', in *Zeremoniell als höfische Ästhetik in Spätmittelalter und Früher Neizeit*, ed. J. J. Berns, T. Rahn (Tübingen, 1995), pp. 57–73. See also G. Oestreich, *Neostoicism and the early modern state*, ed. B. Oestreich, H. G. Koenigsberger, trans. D. McLintock (Cambridge, 1982), esp. pp. 258–73.
[94] For a discussion of Protestant anti-ceremonial writings, see Vec, *Zeremonialwissenschaft*, pp. 337ff.
[95] Stosch, *Vorder=Recht*, p. 2. [96] Ibid. [97] Ibid., p. 121. [98] Ibid., p. 123.

discuss the precedence of kings, electors, counts, barons, etc., Stosch included another monarch of imperial dignity: the Orthodox tsar. 'After the Roman emperor follows [...] justly the grand duke in Moscow, or the Muscovite emperor [*Moscowitische Keyser*]. [...] Although [he] owns many lands in Asia he is counted among the European princes because he possesses most in Europe.'[99]

As a basic rule, the absolute tolerates nothing that comes with a claim to absoluteness. This was a key element of imperial self-conception. The fact that Stosch spoke of two emperors before dealing with kings inferior to them might come as a surprise in the eyes of those who relegated the tsar beyond the community of European sovereigns. Here, the tsar is aligned with other European rulers as opposed to the Ottoman sultan or the emperor of China who are absent from Stosch's list. The tsar is to be taken seriously within the society of princes as both donor of and threat to another ruler's honour. He is a veritable competitor in the order of precedence. On what basis did Stosch make such an unexpected statement? Stosch cited a number of reasons why other monarchs yielded precedence to the tsar. The Russian prince ruled over a multitude of lands, possessed wealth so great that it almost exceeded that of other European princes, and he had established an '*Imperium Despoticum*' over his subjects that invested him with unlimited and uncontested power. Although he possessed many lands in Asia, most of his domains were situated in Europe, and he thus belonged to the circle of European princes.[100] What is more, the Russian ruler derived his superior dignity from his ancient Roman counterpart, Caesar, because in the Russian language the word 'tsar' meant 'Caesar', that is, emperor, according to Stosch. The tsar's revenues were incalculable. He disposed of not only all the produce of his inexhaustible resources but also the riches of the noblest men in his realm. He earned large sums from import duties, notably in the trading town of Archangel and drew large incomes from the prosperous trade with Turkey and Persia. The tsar wore a crown that was three times as valuable as those of the pope, the Holy Roman Emperor, and the kings of Spain and France. Some of the diamonds stitched onto his ceremonial attire reached the size of hazelnuts, so heavy they were that one began to wonder how he could bear the weight of them all simultaneously. All in all, the tsar was granted precedence on the grounds of his wealth and authority. To underline these facts, Stosch devoted a few pages to the elaborate coronation ritual that displayed the

[99] Ibid., p. 127.

[100] Similarly ambivalent on Russia's position between Europe and Asia: F. W. v. Winterfeld, *Teutsche und Ceremonial-Politica*, 3 vols. (Frankfurt a. M., Leipzig, 1700), I, p. 73.

grandeur of the tsar's authority, but in which the tsar was also reminded by the Orthodox patriarch to propagate the Christian faith and to show the love for God in all his doings.[101]

The Christian religion was in fact the common tie that united the tsars with Western sovereigns and set them apart from Oriental rulers notwithstanding all reservations about Russian cultural peculiarities.[102] The tsar's subjects, Stosch argued, may have conceived of themselves as slaves (*chlopos* [*sic*]).[103] They may have been contemptuous of the fine arts, they may not have been allowed to leave the country under pain of death, Russian women may have felt happiness only when beaten by their husbands, and many may have expressed their doubts as to whether the Russian nation can be called Christian for its cruel streak and barbarous customs. But 'despite this, they are justly counted among those of the Greek religion and respected by Christians', he reminded the sceptical reader.[104] After a digression on the origins of Russian Orthodoxy and the sources of the Russian Bible, he praised the practice of forbidding believers to bring their Bibles to church, pointing out the commonality between the Orthodox and Catholic Churches. Orthodox Russians thought, as did faithful Catholics, that young men and virtuous women ought to be spared the abominable and impure stories that abounded in the Old Testament.[105] It is important to note that Stosch did not present these judgements as his own deductions and opinion. He treated Russia as a polity that needed to be placed in the princely hierarchy on the grounds of widely accepted facts. He thus chose a mode of description in which conclusions about the tsar's status were delivered as a digest of generally available information that encapsulated the consensus on the subject matter. How far did other authors share Stosch's views?

In 1706, Zacharias Zwantzig (?–1716), under the pseudonym Ehrenhart Zweyburg, published a monograph on the order of rank that encompassed not only Europe but all 'important potentates and grandees in the world'.[106] Zwantzig had studied at Wittenberg University and, after having risen through the ranks of the then-electoral administration, served on the

[101] Stosch, *Vorder=Recht*, pp. 127–32.

[102] Compare F.-D. Liechtenhan, 'Le Russe, ennemi héréditaire de la chrétienté?: La diffusion de l'image de Moscovie en Europe occidentale au XVIe et XVIIe siècles', *Revue Historique*, 285 (1991), 77–103 and Neumann, *Uses of the Other*, pp. 67–74; Schnakenbourg, *La France*, pp. 458f.

[103] For the sociopolitical meaning of the Russian word for slave, '*kholop*', see M. Poe, 'What did Russians mean when they called themselves "slaves of the tsar"?', *Slavic Review*, 57 (1998), 585–608.

[104] Stosch, *Vorder=Recht*, p. 133. [105] Ibid., pp. 132–37.

[106] Z. Zwantzig, *Theatrum Praecedentiae oder Eines Theils Illustrer Rang-Streit* (Berlin, 1706), title page.

Prussian Aulic Council at the royal court of Berlin. In this position, he had access to the archives and acted as adviser on various court affairs, including the reception of foreign ambassadors.[107]

Zwantzig was also aware of the ordering force of textual composition. But unlike Stosch, he warned the reader that the content of his book should not be treated as an authority on a fixed order of states or be seen as a treatise that would set precedents itself. The order in which princes and republics appeared in the book emerged from a random collection of disputes over status and did not represent the ever-contested hierarchy of states, though it featured the usual ranking of monarchs that conformed to some form of a hierarchical structure.[108] The Holy Roman Emperor, to whom the book was dedicated, comes first, followed by kings, electors, 'barbarous' and Asian sovereigns, dukes, republics, and so forth.[109] The author worried that the way he structured the chapters might offend many princes if they took their position in the book as the equivalent to where they stood in the hierarchy. Scholarly literature on ceremonial matters exhibited ceremonial quality itself, for better or for worse. Zwantzig resembled the English historiographer James Howell in his awareness. Howell wrote, '[W]hat a ticklish and tremendous Task it is to treat of *Kings*, who have power of Life and Death; Ther must be as much *Caution* as *Care* usd therin; It is as *perilous* as it is *painful:* It is as walking upon the Ridg of a high House, or dancing upon a Rope, where unless one be well counterpoizd, he is in danger to break his Neck'.[110]

Whereas Stosch, whose work had appeared some thirty years earlier, had still treated the order of precedence as a given and static hierarchy, Zwantzig acknowledged that in practice the pursuit of glory and prestige kept the hierarchical order in a state of constant flux. He admitted that

> 'because the quality and persona of great sovereigns is sacred and stands in holy veneration, their dignity [...] and magnificence is to be respected as a sacred object as well'.

Yet, he did not make a secret of the fact that

> 'since these high potentates, emperors, kings, princes [...] have become so punctilious on the question of rank [...], the ensuing struggles for precedence will never find a definite conclusion nor be decided'.

107 For a biographical sketch and Zwantzig's work as a publicist and author of works on ceremony, see Vec, *Zeremonialwissenschaft*, pp. 33–42.

108 Other authors were equally cautious. For a discussion of the relationship between text and ceremonial, see Vec, *Zeremonialwissenschaft*, pp. 245ff.

109 Zwantzig, *Theatrum Praecedentiae*, 'An den Leser'.

110 J. Howell, *Proedria vasilike a discourse concerning the precedency of kings* (London, 1664), 'To the discerning reader'.

He added that these ceremonial battles had to some extent become *Formalia Inutilia* which, in reality, did more harm to sovereigns than they contributed to their grandeur. Many conventions and negotiations got bogged down in untimely zealousness and unmeritorious claims to rank, which earned many noble families much jealousy and hatred.[111] It is no wonder Zwantzig did not wish to be cited as an advocate of glory and prestige. Rather, he preferred to keep out of such quarrels and was concerned to present his book as a work that simply reflected the reality of a volatile hierarchy of political communities. Like many other works of the genre, which emerged after the turn of the eighteenth century, it was designed as a guide to a difficult, if impenetrable, subject, and not as a representation of a God-given order.[112] One chapter, amidst detailed accounts of precedence disputes between European kingdoms, republics, and principalities, is devoted to Russia.

Zwantzig began with a *tour d'horizon* of Russian medieval history in order to determine the status of the tsar.[113] His narrative reads as follows: In the beginning, Russians were a Scythian nation situated between Asia and Europe, living in isolated barbarism and hardly known to Europeans. After the Russians had ended their pagan existence by adopting the Greek religion under Grand Prince Vladimir I, who married Anna, sister of the Byzantine emperor Basil II, they started to become better known to European monarchs, whose friendship they pursued. This proved difficult during the ensuing appanage period. The grand princes, weakened through the continual partition of their lands, struggled to acquire the status they sought from foreign monarchs. Then came the Tatars. Deprived of their sovereignty, the grand princes lost all the respect they had yet been able to gain abroad while western powers went on to accumulate wealth, might, and grandeur. Diplomatic contact with European monarchs was interrupted. After more than 200 years of Mongol domination, Ivan III (r. 1462–1505) shook off the Tatar yoke; put an end to Russia's tributary existence; married Zoe Palaiologina, niece of the last Byzantine emperor; and established himself as the sovereign grand prince of Muscovy. Ivan III's son, Vasilii III (r. 1505–1533), defended the sovereignty his father had wrestled from the Tatars, continued the policy of centralising political power by incorporating many of the various independent principalities into one united state, and annexed a number of territories from Poland-Lithuania. Inspired by his success, Vasilii III also sought to acquire increased political prestige to reflect his achievements and his new standing in the world. But, Zwantzig

[111] Zwantzig, *Theatrum Praecedentiae*, 'An den Leser'.
[112] Weller, '*Kein Schauplatz*', esp. p. 406.
[113] Zwantzig, *Theatrum Praecedentiae*, pp. 52–56.

wrote, '[A]lthough the Russian nation is an innately haughty and boastful nation, this grand prince [. . .] did not know what title [. . .] he should assume for himself and his successors, as the previous title Welikiknesa [*sic*] or *Magnus Princeps* seemed to him all too inferior'.[114] Finally, the tsar decided to endorse his correspondence with the pope, the Holy Roman Emperor, various kings, the sultan, and the grand master of the Order of Teutonic Knights as 'tsar' which – contrary to Stosch's interpretation – meant 'king' in Russian. Vasilii III's son, who passed into history as Ivan IV and appeared in Zwantzig's account as a 'brave, sagacious, and hearty soldier', imbued the new title 'tsar' with immense glory to show that his honour and power was on a par with the greatest monarchs. He incorporated the khanates of Kazan and Astrakhan into his realm, was a friend of Emperor Maximilian II (r. 1564–1576), and, according to Zwantzig, adopted the double-headed eagle on a new state seal that showed three crowns symbolising the territories of Moscow, Kazan, and Astrakhan.[115]

Without explaining why, Zwantzig asserted that Russian rulers came to believe that their title surpassed the status of other rulers. They demanded that their diplomats be treated with higher honours and particular marks of distinction so that the superiority of their dynasty be recognised. Zwantzig explained why Russian diplomats could in fact occasionally enjoy such privileged position, not because they were in receipt of favours bestowed by more powerful rulers on an insignificant cultural outlier but because of reciprocal agreement:

> Even when various royal, imperial, and electoral courts receive the Muscovite ambassadors and envoys with special and most highly distinguished honours, this does not happen because Europe and the Christian potentates pay more respect to the Muscovite tsar and [. . .] to his representatives than to other high-ranking and great princes. Rather, because the Muscovites are accustomed to treat ministers and envoys sent by European states and monarchs with special honours, [these rulers] are bound to establish and guarantee the same manner of treatment [to the tsar] according to the *jure gentium*, as is stipulated by the *Jura Legationum inter Potentesparia*.[116]

Reciprocity was the gauge of equality. But why should sovereigns worry about precedence if they treated themselves as equals? Elsewhere in his

[114] Ibid., p. 53.

[115] Zwantzig, *Theatrum Praecedentiae*, 53f. The adoption by Ivan III (not, as Zwantzig writes, by his grandson, Ivan IV) of the double-headed eagle in the 1490s resulted from the diplomatic relations with Emperor Maximilian I to whom Ivan III sought to stress his sovereignty by using a state seal that was in no way inferior to that of the Holy Roman Emperor. See G. Alef, 'The adoption of the Muscovite two-headed eagle: a discordant view', *Speculum*, 41 (1966), 1–21.

[116] Zwantzig, *Theatrum Praecedentiae*, p. 54.

discussion, Zwantzig alluded to the fact that kings had begun to treat each other on an equal footing, 'because they no longer want to compare the extent of their mutual rank'. Ceremony and rank continued to matter among sovereigns, but little status distinction was derived from sovereign honours as such. 'The royal dignity and sovereignty may be younger or older than that of another king, [it] shall grant the same character, honour, prerogative, and grandeur.'[117] Zwantzig's elaboration on the overlapping forces of state parity and status hierarchies reveals what Reinhart Koselleck famously called the 'simultaneity of the non-simultaneous' present in the diplomatic practice of the age.[118] On the one hand, the concept of equality among sovereign powers had gradually been gaining ground in the early modern period. On the other hand, the age-old practice of distinguishing and ranking monarchs continued to produce ceremonial conflicts, which not least motivated authors such as Zwantzig to explain and systematise the subject of ceremony and rank.

The same underlying contradiction appears to inhere in Zwantzig's assessment of Russia's position. According to this author, the Russian state was still very young when it embarked on a new sovereign existence, having vegetated in a state of powerlessness and dependence until the late fifteenth century. Although the incorporation of Kazan and Astrakhan into the realm of the Russian ruler signified a huge success and prompted the grand duke to arrogate to himself the dignity of an emperor (here, Zwantzig refers to 'tsar' as 'emperor') in the sixteenth century, the ancient kingdoms of Europe, some of whose rulers dated their titles back to the second century, were not required to yield precedence to the tsar. All European kings had been in ancient possession of royal dignity long before Moscow rose to imperial status. Zwantzig made another important observation: Europeans refused to let Russian diplomatic representatives go first during public assemblies and negotiations. In order to spare his diplomats the shame of being denied the appropriate rank, that is, his own status, the tsar forbade them to appear at gatherings of foreign diplomats. Such strict measures are commonly construed as a token of 'despotic diplomacy',

[117] Ibid., p. 12. On page 11, Zwantzig lists former reasons that once had accounted for the precedence of one king over another: antiquity of the kingdom, papal honours, customs and precedent, power, number, and wealth of a king's lands. The reason why Zwantzig argues in favour of equality lies in the fact that he was taking the view of the king of Prussia. As the most recent and thus lowest-ranking ruler to be crowned king, Frederick I used every possible argument to emphasise his parity with other monarchs. For the tensions between rank and sovereignty, see Krischer, 'Souveränität als sozialer Status'. See also Stollberg-Rilinger, 'Honores regii'.

[118] R. Koselleck, *Vergangene Zukunft: zur Semantik geschichtlicher Zeiten* (Frankfurt a. M., 1989), pp. 132f., passim.

characteristic of Orthodox prejudice and ignorance of Western practices, and the fear that Russian diplomats risked being tainted by too close a contact with the Latin West. Zwantzig's account shows, however, that this was a strategy common both to Europe and to Russia designed to prevent ceremonial conflicts and avoid jeopardising one's own rank. The author ascribed to Russia a place within the princely society and ranked the tsar, in accordance with the *ius gentium*, among the crowned heads and sovereign states of Europe, lisiting the following practices: first, Russian rulers were crowned and anointed; second, all European powers accepted the tsar's letter of credence and addressed him by his sovereign title; third, European kings granted the tsar the title 'majesty' and the place of honour to their ambassadors during personal visits. The tsars were also given preferential treatment over sovereign but non-crowned princes of the Holy Roman Empire.[119]

Stosch and Zwantzig addressed topics that recur through many writings dealing with Russia's standing as a sovereign power. The English jurist and philosopher John Selden (1584–1654) concerned himself with the meaning of *Titles of honor*, a remarkable and influential scholarly undertaking that earned him wide recognition in peerage law, genealogy, and heraldry.[120] The book is composed of two parts. The first is dedicated to the titles of Christian and non-Christian sovereigns; the second deals with the titles of princes without a crown, that is, dukes, counts, marquises, earls, and so on. It begins with a historical survey of the origins of monarchical rule, followed by a chapter discussing the two highest titles that signal sovereignty in the Western world, that is, 'king' and 'emperor', two categories to which the Russian rulers undoubtedly belonged, although the variance of their titles caused some confusion, as the heading of the book's second chapter suggests: '*Difference of* King *and* Emperor, *and much of them. the great* Duke *or Emperor of* Muscouy *or* Russia.'[121]

Compared to Stosch, Selden revealed an almost 'relativist' approach to the subject matter. The Englishman acknowledged that an emperor had supremacy but made it clear that he had no power over kings, 'for what might not a King (absolute in regard of any superior) do, which the Emperor could? [. . .] Therefore, as the name of *Emperor* was (notwithstanding some particular differences) lawfully giuen as well to him of the East, as of the West, and

[119] Zwantzig, *Theatrum Praecedentiae*, pp. 54–55.

[120] J. Selden, *Titles of honor* (London, 1614). See D. S. Berkowitz, *John Selden's formative years: politics and society in early seventeenth-century England* (Washington, DC, 1988), p. 34, passim.

[121] Selden, *Titles of honor*, table of contents following the preface.

allowed so by the VVestern part; in like form it is or may be without difficultie applied to, or vsed by any which is truly a King'.[122] The same was true, according to Selden, for Russian rulers who used the title of king *or* emperor since Vasilii III had begun to name himself 'tsar'. The Russian prince was often called 'Emperor of Russia' as interpreters had erred in their interpretation of the word 'tsar' as 'Caesar'. The Russian title should be translated as king because the tsars used another term, *Kessar*, to address the emperor of the Holy Roman Empire. As to the status of the tsar, Selden reported that Vasilii III compared himself with the emperor and thus placed himself above other rulers. Selden remained neutral on this issue – 'with his precedence, I medle not' – and carefully abstained from a definite statement about the rank of the Russian ruler: 'But', he added, 'I see not reason why he might not vse either the name of *King* or *Emperor* out of his own autority, as well as the [Holy Roman] Emperor. [...] Other Princes giue him somtimes the title of *Emperor*, somtimes *Great Duke* and *King*'.[123]

Russia also attracted the attention of Christoph Hermann von Schweder. Appointed by King Frederick I (r. 1688/1701–1713) as a trainee in the judicial service, he completed his *Theatrum historicum praetensionum* at a Prussian local court in Stargard, Pomerania, surrounded by the traces of a ravaging plague that the Great Northern War had brought to the north-eastern regions of Germany.[124] Published in 1712, the year that saw the opening of the peace conference at Utrecht, which concluded the War of the Spanish Succession, his work brought together all territorial claims raised by one European country over the lands of another.[125]

The work comprises two books. The first is reserved for the claims of the Holy Roman Emperor. In the second, titled 'Of the claims and quarrels of the kings now living in Europe', Schweder approached the claims of all other European rulers in alphabetical order so as to avoid committing himself to the heavily contested rank system. His list starts with the kings of Bohemia and Hungary and the House of Austria, continuing with the kings of Denmark and Norway, England, France, Poland, Portugal, Prussia, Sweden, and Spain. At the bottom of the list is the monarch whose title begins, in Schweder's spelling, with the last

[122] Ibid., p. 27. [123] Ibid., pp. 27–28.

[124] C. H. Schweder, *Theatrum historicum paetensionum et controversiarum illustrium in Europa, oder Historischer Schauplatz der Ansprüche und Streitigkeiten hoher Potentaten und anderer regierenden Herrschafften in Europa* (Leipzig, 1712). For Schweder, see J. F. Jugler, *Beyträge zur juristischen Biographie. Oder, genauere litterarische und critische Nachrichten von dem Leben und den Schriften verstorbener Rechtsgelehrten auch Staatsmänner, welche sich in Europa berühmt gemacht haben*, 6 vols. (Leipzig, 1773–1780), V, pp. 122–30.

[125] See A. Wolf, 'Geographie und Jurisprudenz – Historia und Genealogie. Zum "Theatrum praetensionum ... in Europa"', *Ius Commune*, 14 (1987), 225–45. See also Vec, *Zeremonialwissenschaft*, pp. 256f.

letter in the alphabet: the Russian *Zaar in Moskovien* (at the time a deviant version of the more common 'czar'). Schweder discussed the long-lasting struggles of the Russian tsars with Poland-Lithuania, Sweden, and Denmark (over possessions in Lithuania, Ingria, Karelia, Livonia, Lapland, and the island of Novaia Zemlia) as well as the question of tribute still demanded by the Crimean Tatars, which had always been a thorn in the side of the Russian prince.[126]

While Schweder had declared that he would exclude ceremonial conflicts, as these went beyond the scope of his work and had already received detailed treatment in Zwantzig's publication,[127] a few paragraphs on struggles over symbolic issues were added by Adam Friedrich Glafey. Glafey edited a revised edition of the *Theatrum Praetensionum* and dedicated it to Emperor Charles VI (r. 1711–1740), six years after a new political situation had been brought about by the Peace of Nystad (1721) and Peter I's adoption of the title *imperator*. In a legal treatise that discussed the territorial claims of the Russian tsar, the corresponding symbolic manifestations of titles could not be omitted. They worked as justifications on the basis of which the tsars asserted their rights over certain territories. Glafey explained for the same reasons, which had been adduced by Zwantzig, that the Russian rulers not only laid claim to both Greece and to the imperial dignity, they also derived their rights over Polish and Lithuanian possessions from the ancient title *tsar i velikii kniaz velikiia, malyia i belyia Rossii* whereby 'small' and 'white' Russia referred to 'Russian' territories that had formerly passed to Poland-Lithuania.[128] Glafey faithfully dismantled and refuted each point allegedly raised by the Russians to assert imperial superiority, which must have pleased Charles VI who had suffered an embarrassing setback after being forced by Peter I to deliver up the Tsarevich Aleksei, to whom he had granted asylum.[129] Glafey downplayed the status of Peter I. His contemporaries distinguished sharply between legally binding solemnities and polite favours, both of which derived their symbolism from the same pool of gestures, behaviour, speech, and titles, but had different consequences and produced a different degree of liability. If the tsar was hailed by other nations as an emperor, then this was a form of politeness, often born out of the pressing circumstances during negotiations; it carried no legal

[126] Schweder, *Theatrum historicum praetensionum*, pp. 332–34. [127] Ibid., 'Vorbericht'.

[128] A. F. Glafey, ed., *Christoph Hermann Schweders Theatrum historicum praetensionum et controversiarum illustrium, oder Historischer Schauplatz der Ansprüche und Streitigkeiten hoher Potentaten und anderer regierenden Herrschafften in Europa* (Leipzig, 1727), pp. 560–68.

[129] For the tsarevich's flight to Vienna, see P. Bushkovitch, 'Power and the historian: the case of Tsarevich Aleksei 1716–1718 and N. G. Ustrialov 1845–1859', *Proceedings of the American Philosophical Society*, 141 (1997), 177–212.

weight. With a statement less balanced than that of John Selden, he concluded that the Russian nation could not aspire to the dignity of the Holy Roman Empire and the prestige of its princes, its reputation among other states, its brave and glorious achievements in culture, science and commerce, and the number of its population. The tsar could not be on a par with the Holy Roman Emperor. Peter I and his predecessors were perceived as a threat in the symbolic competition, as veritable competitors against whom the emperor had to stand comparison in the struggle for honour. Therefore, Glafey did not exclude Russia from the European *Theatrum*.

Nor did Gottfried Stieve, librarian and professor of history, ethics, and state-science at the academy for young nobles (*Ritterakademie*) in Liegnitz.[130] Stieve recognised the natural hierarchical order which, according to him, placed a horse above a donkey, diamonds above pebbles. Nevertheless, he explained that European monarchs received an equal sovereign dignity from God. No sovereign was subject to another's will and was dependent on God's grace alone. Yet despite this mutually acknowledged equality, they continued to squabble about the right to preeminence. While some laid claim to superiority, others were content to be acknowledged as equals.[131] According to Stieve, the ceremonial order could be traced back to the seating order of diplomats in the papal chapel. The master of ceremonies at the Roman Curia, Paris de Grassis, in 1504, had produced a list of monarchs which many authorities in the seventeenth and eighteenth centuries regularly adduced as the prototype of the European order of precedence. Few princes adhered to the alleged papal regulation, especially if they did not see their self-proclaimed rank reflected in this *urtext* of ceremonial norms.[132] Philipp Stenzig has shown that while various drafts of such an *ordo regum* circulated for internal usage at the Curia, the papal court abstained, in fact, from releasing an officially binding seating plan for diplomats in order to obviate ceremonial conflicts.[133]

[130] For Stieve, see J. H. Zedler, *Grosses vollständiges Universal Lexicon aller Wissenschafften und Künste, welche bisshero durch menschlichen Verstand und Witz erfunden und verbessert worden*, 64 + 4 suppl. vols. (Halle, Leipzig, 1732–1754), XL, p. 37.

[131] G. Stieve, *Europäisches Hoff-Ceremoniel, worinnen Nachricht gegeben wird, was für eine Beschaffenheit es habe mit der Prärogativ, und dem daraus fliessenden Ceremoniel* (Leipzig, 1715), pp. 3–4.

[132] Ibid., pp. 8–10. See also J. B. v. Rohr, *Einleitung zur Ceremoniel-Wissenschaft der Grossen Herren*, p. 340.

[133] De Grassis' list can be found in his Tractatus de oratoribus of 1508 and in an entry of his diary of 1504, see P. Stenzig, *Botschafterzeremoniell am Papsthof der Renaissance: Der Tractatus de oratoribus des Paris de Grassi – Edition und Kommentar*, 2 vols. (Frankfurt a. M., 2014), I, pp. 244f., for the list, and pp. 548–75, for a discussion. For the ambassadorial ceremonial at the Curia, see P. Stenzig, 'Nunquam antea in usu. Das diplomatische Protokoll an der Kurie', in *Das Ursprüngliche und das Neue: Zur Dynamik*

Russia had no place in Stieve's version of the papal ranking order. The fact that the author pointed to this absence shows that he would have expected the tsar to be included in this list of Christian sovereigns; neither Sweden nor Denmark had found their way into the ranking. They had been purposefully omitted or simply been forgotten according to Stieve.[134] For Russia the case was simpler. The pope did not assign the tsar a place in the ranking of Christian sovereigns as the Russian ruler was not a member of the Catholic Church over which he presided. The tsar belonged to the Orthodox world in which he occupied the highest position.[135] Lünig, who also wondered about the absence of Russia in the papal list, gave the obvious explanation that the tsar had no connections with the Catholic Church.[136]

The rest of Stieve's account resembles that of the other authors. He mentioned the weakness of Russia during the appanage period and under Tatar rule; explained its regained strength and international prestige under Ivan III, Vasilii III, and Ivan IV; and recounted the story of how the tsars arrogated to themselves imperial state symbols. The meaning of 'tsar' required special discussion. By way of (pseudo-)etymological analysis Stieve concluded that 'tsar' meant king, although this conflicted with the claim to imperial equality. In conclusion, it was a matter of a ruler's individual decision whether to grant superior honour to the tsar as the French king had done in 1654, or, like the Holy Roman Emperor, to refuse such acknowledgement. For Stieve, it was not clear at the time whether the tsar's claim to imperial dignity was justified. He had little doubt that it would only be a matter of time before the age-old claim was vindicated in view of Peter I's growing success in taking Russia's prestige to another level through his travels, wars, and alliances.[137]

Stieve's prediction soon became a reality. Johann Ehrenfried Zschackwitz, professor of history and law at Halle,[138] wrote in 1734 that Russia played a part in all European affairs, especially after many powers had accepted Peter I's adoption of the imperial title. Zschackwitz ascribed to Peter I the

ritueller Prozesse in Geschichte und Gegenwart, ed. B. Dücker, G. Schwedler (Münster, 2008), pp. 207–25. See also N. Staubach, '"Honor Dei" oder "Bapsts Gepreng" Zur Reorganisation des Papstzeremoniells in der Renaissance', in *Rom und das Reich vor der Reformation*, ed. N. Staubach (Frankfurt a. M., 2004), pp. 91–136, 116f., and Fletcher, *Diplomacy*, pp. 59–80.

[134] The list includes in the order of their rank: 'the emperor, the king of the Romans, the kings of France, Spain, Aragon, Portugal, England, Sicily, Scotland, Hungary, Navarre, Cyprus, Bohemia, and Poland'. Stieve, *Hoff-Ceremoniel* (1715), p. 8.

[135] Ibid., p. 29. For the relations between Russia and the papacy, see Winter, *Russland und das Papsttum'*, I.

[136] Lünig, *Theatrum Ceremoniale*, I, pp. 8f.

[137] Stieve, *Hoff-Ceremoniel* (1715), pp. 31ff., 130f.

[138] For Zschackwitz, see *ADB*, XL, pp. 444f.

conventional leading role in reforming Russia and bringing it closer to Europe. Yet his conclusion did not blind him to the diplomatic achievements of pre-Petrine tsars, particularly Ivan IV, who, Zschackwitz claimed, was unjustifiably called a tyrant and had managed to involve Russia in European foreign politics long before.[139] Zschackwitz was also the editor of the *Neu-eröffneter Welt- und Staatsspiegel* that, like the Leipzig-based *Die europäische Fama*, regularly published articles by Heinrich von Huyssen whom Peter I had hired to improve Russia's image in European periodicals.[140]

With the exception of Selden and Howell, all of the authors discussed so far in order to trace Russia's position in what had been 'the present state of Europe' were German. Jean Rousset de Missy, a French contemporary historian and publicist, who wrote a major history of Peter the Great's reign and contributed two volumes on diplomatic ceremonial to the celebrated *Corps universel diplomatique du droit des gens*,[141] enthused about the thoroughness and erudition of German *Zeremonialwissenschaft*. At the same time, he regretted that these authors were not very well known outside the Holy Roman Empire.[142] Almost a hundred years after the Peace of Westphalia, Rousset observed that the issue of rank had not ceased to trouble rulers and their representatives: princes ceded cities and provinces but they still did not let go of a rank they thought was due to them even if one displayed all the skill and talent of the greatest negotiator.[143] He intended to put this chaos of conflicting claims in order but at the same time averred that his work was only descriptive and did neither anticipate nor determine the structure of the hierarchy itself.[144] Here, too, descriptions of the ranking system contained the trace of ceremonial logic.

Rousset started with the pope and continued with the Holy Roman Emperor, asking why the latter took precedence over the sultan. The Ottoman ruler acknowledged the Holy Roman Emperor as the highest head of Christendom but, in return, merely received the attribute of highest ruler of the Turkish nation and sovereign of Asia, Greece, and the Orient. Next came the 'tsar or emperor of all the Russias'. After the imperial rulers, there followed kings and other sovereigns down the hierarchy. There is no need to present Rousset's detailed discussion here.

[139] J. E. Zschackwitz, *Einleitung zu denen vornehmsten Rechts-Ansprüchen derer gecrönten hohen Häupter und anderer Souverainen in Europa*, 3 vols. (Frankfurt a. M., Leipzig 1734), III, pp. 349–51.
[140] See S. Korzun, *Heinrich von Huyssen (1666–1739): Prinzenerzieher, Diplomat und Publizist in den Diensten Zar Peters I., des Großen* (Wiesbaden, 2013), pp. 63f.
[141] J. Rousset de Missy, *Le cérémonial diplomatique des cours de l'Europe* (= *Corps universel diplomatique du droit des gens*, suppl. vols. 4–5), 2 vols. (Amsterdam, The Hague, 1739).
[142] J. Rousset de Missy, *Mémoires sur le rang et la préséance entre les Souverains de l'Europe et entre leurs ministres représentans* (Amsterdam, 1746), 'Aux lecteurs'.
[143] Ibid. [144] Ibid. See also Vec, *Zeremonialwissenschaft*, p. 250.

So strong was his faith in German scholarship that he largely adopted the accounts of the *Zeremonialwissenschaftler*, in particular that of Zwantzig. It suffices to note that Rousset, like the other authors, dated the beginning of Russia's serious involvement in European affairs back to the rise of its international prestige in the late fifteenth and sixteenth centuries. Before that, Russia had languished in slavish dependence upon the Mongol Empire and had no place in European diplomacy.[145] True, in another work on ceremony, Rousset described the way in which Russian ambassadors were received at the French court in a section entitled 'Reception of Oriental ambassadors'.[146] He pointed out that there were no established rules that organised the stay of 'Oriental' ambassadors at European courts, and each case was decided individually. Presumably, his account was based on the notes of the French *introducteur des ambassadeurs*,[147] Nicolas de Sainctot. Rousset's descriptions are strikingly similar to those of Sainctot and similarly ambivalent towards Russia. Sainctot wrote: 'I give no set rules for the reception of Muscovite ambassadors, nor for oriental ambassadors.'[148] While the associative nearness between 'Oriental' and 'Muscovite' in the *introducteur*'s papers may have prompted Rousset to include Russia in the said section, it must be pointed out that Sainctot's juxtaposition clearly discriminates between oriental and Muscovite diplomats. To assume that in practice the French court merged the Muscovites and the Ottomans into one cultural group as Europe's composite 'other' would be misleading, although the rarity of Russian embassies in France and the fact that Sainctot mentions the Russians and Ottomans in one breath speaks to Muscovy's ambiguous status, not as an outsider but as a cultural outlier that the logic of diplomatic protocol had integrated into the European precedence system.

During the eighteenth century, diplomatic ceremonial gradually became the subject of enlightened critique.[149] Rousset was convinced that 'both order and rank are based on the same laws as is nature'. But he commented that 'nature had not come into being before the Creator destroyed chaos and confusion, putting each and every element in its place and all things in a set order that still subsists today'.[150] The

[145] Rousset de Missy, *Mémoires sur le rang*, pp. 45–57.
[146] Rousset de Missy, *Cérémonial diplomatique*, I, p. 93.
[147] See Chapter 2, for the office of *introducteur des ambassadeurs*.
[148] BA, MS 4232, vol. II, fol. 1. The copy of the second volume of Sainctot's memoires held by the Bibliothèque de l'Arsenal is entitled '*Reception des ambassad. Orientaux et princes etrangers*'. The chapter headings for the text quoted here is '*Reception des Ambassadeurs Moscouvites et des ambassadeurs Orientaux*'. Compare the copy in BnF, MS f 14118, where these headings are missing.
[149] Vec, *Zeremonialwissenschaft*, pp. 366ff.
[150] Rousset de Missy, *Mémoires sur le rang*, p. 4.

principles of equality and independence of states had started to undermine the medieval idea of a universal hierarchy by the time he published his work. The *Zeremonialwissenschaftler* had also come to understand that differences in rank were not based on objective, naturally given criteria. These were understood to mediate between equal sovereigns who used them to bestow special honours upon their peers in return for equivalent favours.[151] In Rousset's eyes, the conflict between social hierarchy, on the one hand, and the equality of states, on the other, continued to complicate the issue: 'All sovereigns recognise the need for this order; they themselves establish it among their subjects. But they do not think the same when one talks about establishing it among themselves.'[152]

Other authors, in particular publicists and learned diplomats, understood that rank and status were not simply rooted in an undisputed hierarchy but in long established traditions sanctioned only by the arbitrary will of sovereigns or the consensus between them. They acknowledged the necessity of ceremonial as a diplomatic language with which a diplomat defended 'an acquired right certified by long-standing usage'.[153] The foremost duty of an ambassador was to uphold these rights. 'It [was] not for the representative to diminish them in any way, because it is an attribute of each Sovereignty, and consequently it is not an asset that the Representative, who is only the image of the Sovereign, can dispose of in any manner.'[154] The higher the claims were, the more difficult it became to assert them successfully.

Maintaining the rights of the tsars must have been an especially challenging task, if one believes Jacob Friedrich von Bielfeld. The honours the Russian rulers had been receiving since the end of the fifteenth century were immense: 'As the tsars' power grew and as European nations needed their support or their trade, they granted them very high-ranking titles and honours.'[155] And yet, as much as diplomats were expected to defend the status of their masters, they were also reminded that 'personal modesty is not incompatible with the dignity that a representative's personality must have'.[156] Through its glorification of reason and its contempt for human passion the Enlightenment had unmasked the 'pursuit of glory' as the human desire to elevate oneself in order to achieve greater if undeserved recognition among others, which led to undue and costly ostentation and affectation.[157] The publicists had grown more critical about pomp and

151 Stollberg-Rilinger, 'Präzedenzrecht'.
152 Rousset de Missy, *Mémoires sur le rang*, p. 4.
153 Pecquet, *Discourse on the art of negotiation*, p. 42. 154 Ibid., p. 72.
155 J. v. Bielfeld, *Institutions politiques*, 2 vols. (The Hague, 1760), II, p. 237.
156 Pecquet, *Discourse on the art of negotiation*, p. 26.
157 B. Stollberg-Rilinger, 'Zeremoniell als politisches Verfahren: Rangordnung und Rangstreit als Strukturmerkmale des frühneuzeitlichen Reichstages', in *Neue Studien zur Frühneuzeitlichen Reichsgeschichte* (*Zeitschrift für Historische Forschung*, Beiheft 19),

éclat, in particular its excessive use in diplomatic relations.[158] While they did not despise court culture as such and accepted ceremonial as a necessary tool in diplomatic dialogue, they condemned its unwarranted use which often resulted in the breakdown of negotiations. Such was the Janus nature of early modern diplomacy: the *double aspect du cérémonial*.[159]

Some wondered if the order of rank could be abolished completely since the principle of the equality of states had gained enough ground to render the international hierarchy superfluous. Precedence based on titles; coat of arms; or the size, wealth, and population of a country had no foundation in reason. It was full of sham, an illusion of the human mind that seemed incompatible with international law.[160] Russian examples were cited in this context to illustrate the frivolity of ceremonial exaggerations. Ivan IV, for instance, allegedly ordered that a hat be nailed to the head of an Italian envoy, as the latter refused to take it off in the presence of the tsar.[161] However, this story – well known from folk tales across central and eastern Europe[162] – did not serve so much the purpose of marking the cultural difference between Europe and a barbarous other as to expose the obscene nature of ceremony and ostentation in general. Other rulers, whose Europeanity cannot be denied, were equally subject to ridicule. The story is reported that Philip III of Spain died from the ill consequences of court etiquette. Sitting in an overly heated room, he prompted the Marquis de Pobar to put out the fire. The marquis refused. To touch and remove the brazier did not conform to the rules of etiquette

ed. J. Kunisch (Berlin, 1997), pp. 91–132, here p. 128. See also Bauer, *Hofökonomie: der Diskurs über den Fürstenhof in Zeremonialwissenschaft, Hausväterliteratur und Kameralismus* (Vienna, Cologne, Weimar, 1997); Vec, *Zeremonialwissenschaft*, pp. 162ff., for the influence of court criticism. For the repercussions of enlightened thought and its emphasis on reason, see, for example, Bielfeld, *Institutions politiques*, pp. 235f.; Lünig, *Theatrum Ceremoniale*, I, p. 1; Rohr, *Einleitung zur Ceremoniel-Wissenschaft der Grossen Herren*, pp. 3f.

158 Bielfeld, *Institutions politiques*, II, p. 170; La Sarraz du Franquesnay, *Ministre public*, p. 137; A. de Wicquefort, *The embassador and his functions*, trans. M. Digby (London, 1716, reprint, Leicester 1997), I, p. 352.

159 Bielfeld, *Institutions politiques*, II, p. 234. Cited in Kugeler, 'Theory', p. 148.

160 J. C. Hennings, 'Betrachtungen über die Etiquette mit Anwendung auf die Präcedenz der Gesandten und Monarchen durch Beyspiele aus der Geschichte', in J. C. Hennings, *Verjährte Vorurtheile in verschiedenen Abhandlungen bestritten* (Riga, 1778), pp. 1 111, 55f., 89, passim.

161 Ibid., p. 39.

162 H. Haumann, 'Dracula und die Vampire Osteuropas. Zur Entstehung eines Mythos', *Zeitschrift für Siebenbürgische Landeskunde*, 28 (2005), 1–17. There are striking parallels between the tales about Ivan IV and those about Vlad Tepes, the Wallachian prince known as Dracula who was reputed to have nailed a hat to a Turkish ambassador's head when he refused to take it off. See M. Perrie, *The image of Ivan the Terrible in Russian folklore* (Cambridge, 1987), pp. 96ff.

for a man of his standing. No other gentleman was present to accomplish the task. The king did not move for fear of compromising his honour before Pobar. In order to preserve his status, he decided to remain seated and ordered that a gentleman of the chamber be found to extinguish the fire. But the servant arrived too late, and the king died from excessive body heat.[163]

Seventeenth-century diplomatic manuals had already shown a similar pattern of critique towards the 'whim of precedence', the 'fancy' of it, and the 'uncanny adventures' that emerged from diplomats' curious tactics to elevate themselves above others.[164] Conrad von Hoevelen pointed out that it was right and proper to insist on one's entitlements and privileges, but he lamented the vain struggle for status that often cost much more than the results of negotiations were actually worth. The Russians in their 'discourteous peasant pride' deigned to indulge in this 'foul greed for honour'.[165] They were not alone, however. On the contrary, they shared these qualities with Europeans. Hoevelen's comparisons show that their undue zealousness regarding ceremonial norms did not distinguish Russians from, say, their French or Spanish colleagues whose manners were equally corrupted by ceremonial brawls.[166] Another example for such foolish behaviour was the Diet of the Holy Roman Empire where precedence issues led to constant rows and delays: it seemed to be common practice that diplomats – 'obstinate and haughty fools', driven by 'their fantastic conceitedness' – preferred to make their farewells before commencing business than to yield precedence and grant the more honourable place to others.[167] The resplendent attire of Russian diplomats dressed in fur and jewellery may have struck Hoevelen as foreign and crude.[168] Such a statement must be put in perspective, however, as there was no single European counterpart that defined Russian dress as specifically non-European. The Germans did not come off well either in that they did not even appear to have had a genuine costume and dressed themselves like Frenchmen *à la mode*; some millions of 'our good German ducats and *Reichstaler* had been diverted into the French labyrinthine abyss'.[169] This seemed even more outrageous than the manners of the Russians, as 'nothing in the French language, history, or dress has permanence. [. . .] How strange it must be to see a Dutchman or Swiss in Polish habit, a Muscovite in Spanish accoutrement, a German

163 Hennings, 'Etiquette', p. 9.
164 C. v. Hoevelen, *Candorins Vollkommener Teutsche Gesandte* (Frankfurt a. M., 1679), p. 286.
165 Ibid., p. 249. 166 Ibid., p. 224.
167 Ibid., p. 249. For the Holy Roman Empire, see Stollberg-Rilinger, *Old clothes*.
168 Hoevelen, *Teutsche Gesandte*, p. 82. 169 Ibid., p. 87.

in Turkish decoration, an Englishman in Swabian garnishment, a Portuguese in Laplandish jewellery'.[170] Hoevelen wished that diplomats adhered to their native costume. In short, for Hoevelen as for others, Russian magnificence and ritualism was part of the same continuum ranging between the constructing of the necessary ceremonial order, at one end, and the voracious appetite for honour that seemed to have infected all civilised nations in their pursuit of glory, at the other.

Ceremonial Discourse and Its Sources: Who Were the Barbarians?

Like the travel writers, scholars of diplomatic ceremonial, too, borrowed heavily from one another and from other sources. Information on Russia was scarce; a proper historiographical work was not available.[171] Consequently, they had to rely on the travel accounts. Yet, as has become clear, not one of the discussed scholars classified Russia as a barbarous country outside the circle of European monarchs on the basis of these accounts. The same is true for the practitioners of court ceremony and diplomatic protocol. In 1733, the English master of ceremonies, Sir Clement Cottrell copied, compiled, and bound his predecessors' notes into a volume titled 'Papers Relating to matters of Ceremony of Forreign Courts'.[172] Sir Charles and Sir Charles Lodowick Cottrell had been managing diplomatic ceremonies at the court of St James from 1641 to 1710 and also collected English diplomats' reports about diplomatic ceremonial in foreign countries.[173] Sir Clement was interested in the details of ceremonial arrangements, the defrayment of diplomats' expenses, and the bestowal of presents, all marking the technical distinctions in the diplomatic practice of the states described, namely France, Prussia, Pisa, Genoa, Venice, and Florence, including brief entries on Denmark and Sweden. This compilation also contains 'A perfect Relation of The Reception Audience, and Dispatch, of All Ambassadors from Forreign Princes, sent unto The Emperour of

170 Ibid.

171 Zschackwitz, *Einleitung*, I, p. 362. Despite Zschackwitz's claim regarding Russian history, Russian contemporary affairs frequently appeared in the early modern press and increasingly so in the eighteenth century, see A. Blome, '"Die Zeitungen sind der Grund, die Anweisungen und Richtschnur aller Klugheit ...": Zu den Grundlagen der Rußlandhistoriographie im 17. und 18. Jahrhundert', in *Die Kenntnis Rußlands im deutschsprachigen Raum im 18. Jahrhundert: Wissenschaft und Publizistik über das Russische Reich*, ed. D. Dahlmann (Bonn, 2006), pp. 25–41; M. Welke, 'Rußland in der deutschen Publizistik des 17. Jahrhunderts (1613–89)', *Forschungen zur osteuropäischen Geschichte*, 23 (1976), 105–276, for the seventeenth century.

172 Rousham, MC 15.

173 For a discussion of the functions of the master of ceremonies, see Chapter 2.

All Russia etc.'[174] It may be a coincidence that Russia appears here among various European powers while others, for example, the Viennese court, are missing. However, it is striking that the account of Russia is not distinct in any way from the accounts of other states. It is written in the same procedural language with no specific concern for cultural peculiarities and curiosities. Differences between other countries' ceremonies are only of technical relevance and can also be found between, for example, Prussia and France. There is no mention of behaviour patterns associated by Europeans with Asia, not the slightest hint of rude or ostentatious behaviour, closed-minded and obscurantist traditionalism, or Asiatic indulgence. The fact that diplomats in Russia were constantly under guard is interpreted as a security measure rather than the attempt to treat ambassadors like prisoners. Even the heavy drinking of 'their double and treble distill'd waters'[175] is not used as a point of departure to mark the usual stereotypes encountered in the travel literature. The papers of the master of ceremonies exhibit a similar mode of description as that of the *Zeremonialwissenschaftler* who largely filtered the discourse of barbarism from their accounts of Russian diplomatic ceremonies. This is all the more surprising as most of the publicists and theorists do reserve long chapters for decidedly 'barbarous' states in Asia and along the north coast of Africa. Russia did not belong there. Ceremonial logic compelled European courts to find a place for an outlying Christian ruler within their hierarchy. At least in the case of Russia, the learned descriptions of ceremonies demonstrate that ritual practice of face-to-face encounters outweighed centre–periphery relationships or discursive attributions such as marginal, different, or barbarous. If not the Russians, who, then, in the eyes of the doyens of 'ceremonial science', were the barbarians?

Zschackwitz clearly distinguished between European courts and those that did not belong to the *société des princes*. Countries like Persia, China, Japan, Ethiopia, Morocco, Tatar Crimea, and Siam entertained occasional relations with European states, mostly in matters of trade. France, England, and Russia are mentioned among the European countries that

[174] Rousham, MC 15, pp. 140–50. The original document from the second half of the seventeenth century has been preserved in Rousham, MC Box 4. A published version can be found in J. Hennings, '"A perfect Relation of The Reception, Audience, and Dispatch, of All Ambassadors from Foreign Princes, sent unto The Emperour of All Russia": *Pristav, Master of ceremonies* und die Dokumentation des frühneuzeitlichen Gesandtschaftsrituals in vergleichender Perspektive', in *Interkulturelle Ritualpraxis in der Vormoderne: Diplomatische Interaktion an den östlichen Grenzen der Fürstengesellschaft (Zeitschrift für Historische Forschung, Beiheft, 52)*, ed. C. Garnier, C. Vogel (Berlin, 2016), pp. 71–94.

[175] Rousham, MC 15, p. 146.

sent ambassadors to China, for instance.[176] In these foreign countries ('foreign' in Zschackwitz's terms means non-European), European diplomats were usually received with due honours, but they did not seem to care too much, as they felt no competition, whether among themselves or when faced with the splendour of their 'barbarous' hosts. These countries were not in the running for glory and prestige. To be received by the Chinese emperor with extraordinary ceremonies would not have impressed one's fellow monarch back home in Europe, who was also one's nearest rival.[177] Hence, Louis XIV could copy Siamese court ceremonial at Versailles and style himself as an omnipotent Asian emperor with extraordinary ceremonies in order to impress the diplomats sent by Narai (r. 1656–1688), the king of Siam, in 1685/86.[178] He did not risk to deal a blow against the European courtly public who watched increased splendour and ceremonial dignity with great suspicion on behalf of their own courts. The king of Siam was not believed to be a contributor of or threat to one's own honour. To receive Russian diplomats, on the other hand, with such elevated claims to Louis XIV's status would have been impossible, as the reception of Russians could be cited as a precedent in status quarrels with other European monarchs, as had happened in the case of the elector of Brandenburg, Frederick III, for example.[179] In exchange for support in the war against the Ottomans, the latter negotiated a treaty with Russian diplomats, stipulating that his own representatives should receive the *honores regii* with which he hoped to buttress his claim to the honour of a crowned head in view of his impending coronation.[180]

Unusual ceremonies, which surpassed the established norm short of undermining it to the benefit of one's competitors, could also be given to the Ottoman sultan. The papers of Louis-Nicolas de Breteuil, *introducteur des ambassadeurs* from 1699 to 1715, include a copy of notes on the

176 Zschackwitz, *Einleitung*, III, p. 386. For the ceremonial context of embassies to the Ottoman Empire and north Africa, see D. Kolodziejczyk, 'Semiotics of behavior in early modern diplomacy: Polish embassies in Istanbul and Bahcesaray', *Journal of Early Modern History*, 7 (2003), 245–56. See also Windler, 'Diplomatic history'; Windler, *Diplomatie comme expérience de l'Autre*. For Sino-Russian relations, see P. C. Perdue, *China marches West: the Qing conquest of central Eurasia* (Cambridge, MA, 2010).

177 Zschackwitz, *Einleitung*, III, pp. 385–94. See also Stosch, *Vorder=Recht*, pp. 311ff.; Zwantzig, *Theatrum Praecedentiae*, pp. 84–100.

178 For the stay of the ambassadors of Siam at Versailles, see R. S. Love, 'Rituals of majesty: France, Siam, and court spectacle in royal image-building at Versailles in 1685 and 1686', *Canadian Journal of History*, 31 (1996), 171–98.

179 Further examples will be examined in Chapter 3.

180 See A. N. Sakharov, *Istoriia vneshnei politiki Rossii*, II, p. 19. See P. Prudovskii, 'K voprosu formirovaniia diplomaticheskogo protokola: Rossiia i Brandenburg v seredine XVII veka', *Vestnik arkhivista*, 85 (2005), 252–59, for the beginnings of relations between Russia and Brandenburg as well as their ceremonial manifestations.

reception of the sultan's envoy in 1669. These reports mentioned that 'the curious extravagance of the audience that the king granted to the Turkish envoy yesterday made me go and attend the occasion. I do not believe that there has ever been given an audience with such pomp and solemnity in France'.[181] The reception of the Russian ambassador Petr I. Potemkin in 1668 did not exhibit such ceremonial extravagance, evoking much less 'curiosity', since, as Marie-Karine Schaub pointed out, the Russians adhered to strict formalism in matters of protocol.[182] Similarly, Zwantzig reports that 'Persian barbarians', that is, the ambassadors of the Shah, were welcomed with unprecedentedly lavish rituals at the courts of Gottorp, Rome, Portugal, and Moscow. Here, again, Russia is aligned with European states as opposed to a 'barbarous' Persia.[183]

What, then, did the word 'European' imply? Neither did it describe the cultural exclusivity of rulers or their subjects nor did it refer to national characteristics or mentalities.[184] Had this been the case, Russia surely would have been ranked among the barbarous states as it appears in the accounts of Western travellers. Early modern international relations exhibited what global historian Jürgen Osterhammel called 'inclusive Eurocentrism' in that Europe figured as the political space in which courts recognised each other in the language of ceremonial, contending for the symbolic resources of status and rank.[185] Russia's participation in diplomacy and its membership in the precedence system were not determined by the Europeanisation of its culture. Dynastic recognition extended beyond geographical assumptions that underpinned the Europe/Asia divide, and the attendant discourses about civilisation and barbarism, provided that a perceived cultural outsider participated in common diplomatic practices and fitted into the heritage notion of the Christian commonwealth. This inclusivity had limits. 'Europe' also implied that not every 'barbarous' monarch outside the European

[181] BA, MS 3859, vol. I, fol. 241. (The first volume of Breteuil's papers contains copies of notes by his predecessors with marginal notes by Breteuil.) A selection of Breteuil's papers has been published in E. Lever, *Baron de Breteuil: mémoires* (Paris, 1992).

[182] BA, MS 3859, vol. I, fols. 199–240; BnF, MS naf 3133, fol. 107; Schaub, 'L'ambassade', p. 215, *passim*.

[183] Zwantzig, Theatrum Praecedentiae, p. 82.

[184] On '*l'espace européen*' in early modern international relations, see L. Bély, *Les relations internationales en Europe: (XVIIe – XVIIIe siècles)* (Paris, 1992), pp. 53–55.

[185] Osterhammel, *Entzauberung Asiens*, pp. 380ff. For a discussion of 'inclusive Eurocentrism' as a hallmark of early modern descriptions of foreign cultures, and the concept's gradual changes to an 'exclusive Eurocentrism' during the eighteenth century, see C. Brauner, 'Ein Schlüssel für zwei Truhen: Diplomatie als interkulturelle Praxis am Beispiel einer westafrikanischen Gesandtschaft nach Frankreich (1670/71)', *Historische Anthropologie*, 21 (2013), 199–226, here on p. 212, and Brauner, *Kompanien*, pp. 88, 159f., 555, *passim*.

community of sovereigns was recognised in the complex web of reciprocal exchanges of honour and prestige. Orthodox Russia, it appears, was included.

What were the sources of *ius praecedentiae* and *Zeremonialwissenschaft* that allowed authors to count Russia among the princely hierarchy of Europe despite its generally accepted image of a barbarous kingdom? Paradoxically, ceremonial scholars drew their information from the same sources that had created the image of Moscow's oddity and Asian barbarism. For example, Zwantzig's account is predominantly based on Herberstein and Olearius as well as on the work of the Swedish diplomat Petrus Petreius (1570–1622) and chroniclers like Alexander Guagnini (1538–1614), both of whom, in turn, borrowed heavily from their German forerunners.[186] Zschackwitz quoted the same authors.[187] Stosch cited Herberstein as a witness to the elaborate ceremonies during a diplomatic reception in Moscow. However, Stosch did not use these descriptions in order to emphasise the exotic nature of courtly pomp in the sense in which Western diplomats' experiences in Moscow are normally interpreted.[188] He did not describe the interior of the palace and the accoutrements of the tsar with the ethnographic excitement of a foreigner. On the contrary, he construed them as familiar tokens of honour, employing them in support of the high status-claims brought forward by the Russian monarchs.[189] Stosch and his contemporaries bypassed the discourse of barbarism and simply read these descriptions as political texts that informed them about the position of the tsar in the order of precedence. The fact that Olearius was regularly cited is even more puzzling. While his *Ausführliche Beschreibung* was used as an authoritative starting-point to calculate Russia's rank among the European monarchical society, the same account is quoted in Zwantzig's chapter on the 'character and rank of great barbarous potentates' as proof of the exoticism of Persians.[190]

[186] See Zwantzig, *Theatrum Praecedentiae*, pp. 52–56. Picard, ed., *Herberstein*, p. 4 editor's preface). A. Guagnini, *Sarmatiae Europeae descriptio, quae regnum Poloniae, Lituaniam, Samogitiam, Russiam, Massouiam, Prussiam, Pomeraniam, Liuoniam, et Moschouiae, Tartariaeque partem complectitur* (Spirae, 1581), pp. 78–105; P. *Petreius, Historien und Bericht von dem Grossfürstenthumb Muschkow* (Lipsae, 1620, reprint, 2003).

[187] Zschackwitz, *Einleitung*, III, pp. 348–51.

[188] Eighteenth-century *philosophes*, who used Muscovite ceremonies and Russia's backward image as implicit criticism against courtly pomp, provided the basis for such interpretations. Compare, for example, Voltaire's remark on the 1663 English embassy to Russia (see Chapter 3 for the embassy): 'But on public days the [Russian] court displayed all the splendor of a Persian monarch. The earl of Carlisle says he could see nothing but gold and precious stones on the robes of the Czar and his courtiers.' Voltaire, *The works of Voltaire: a contemporary version*, trans. W. F. Fleming, 22 vols. (New York, 1901), XVIII (*History of the Russian empire under Peter the Great*), p. 29.

[189] Stosch, *Vorder=Recht*, pp. 129ff.

[190] Zwantzig, *Theatrum Praecedentiae*, pp. 84f.

To return to the initial question: Was Russia part of the 'republic' of Europe? Would Hoffmann have told his students about seventeenth-century tsars in his lecture on *The present state of Europe*? All things considered, there is a notable lack of differentiation between Russia and the West when contemporaries determined the tsars' ceremonial status. The negative image of Russian culture and society abounding in the travel accounts had little effect on the inclusion of the tsars in the circle of European sovereigns. *Zeremonialwissenschaft* did not calculate the tsars' status in terms of cultural or civilisational belonging. They included the Russian sovereign as a Christian monarch according to the norms that emerged from the exchanges within the semiotic web spun by diplomats and rulers between dynastic courts. Granted, many authors cited here were contemporaries of Peter I and wrote under the impression of the reforms he had achieved by the time they published their works. Nevertheless, it is striking that their writings did not follow the widespread view that Peter I's reign constituted a clear break with the Muscovite past. They did not, as Shafirov did, portray Petrine Russia as a turning point that marked the beginning of Russian–European relations. Rather, they continued the tradition already manifest in works by, for example, Stosch or Selden, which predate Peter I's reign and included his predecessors in the race for glory and prestige. As Marshall Poe put it, European polities were 'Russia's closest neighbours'.[191]

Discussing Russian diplomacy – Muscovite or Petrine – in the context of the states-system, civilisation, cultural belonging, and difference is of little help in creating a new narrative that reaches beyond the level of reflection of the travel writers or Petrine propagandists. Plain notions of Russian barbarism are obstructive to understanding the complex diplomatic interactions between the tsars and other monarchs. What needs to be the focus instead are the rituals and other symbolic interactions themselves, their social logic and diplomatic functions, not their dismissive cultural representations; otherwise the image of Russia as a barbarous country and its modern ideological outgrowth graft themselves upon the prosaic reality of diplomatic procedure which might otherwise reveal fresh insights into the workings of diplomacy in the early modern world. In a way, this suggests a return to the beginnings of international relations as an academic discipline and to take seriously Hoffmann's advice to study precedence quarrels and ceremonial conflicts. The following chapters do this by exploring diplomatic practice and direct encounters between Russia and courtly Europe.

[191] Poe, 'Distant world', p. 5. See also Neumann, *Uses of the Other*, p. 67.

2 Facts and Fictions

The Organisation of Diplomatic Practice

The Ambassadorial Chancellery

Like any proceedings at the early modern court, diplomatic ceremonies required careful administration. The ritual routine was supported by a large apparatus, various household staffs, and a refined system of record-taking.[1] In Muscovite Russia, foreign affairs were administered by one of the numerous *prikazy* (chancelleries).[2] Founded under Ivan IV in 1549, the *Posol'skii prikaz* (ambassadorial or foreign affairs chancellery) grew to become one of the largest and most prestigious chancelleries in the Muscovite state.[3] Thanks to the wealth of sources preserved in the archives of the *Posol'skii prikaz*, its institutional history is not only an ideal mirror of the continuities but also all the ruptures in the history of the Russian state, reflecting the process of increasing centralisation under Ivan IV, the changes during the *smuta*, the recovery under the first Romanovs, and the increased activity in foreign policy in the second half of the seventeenth century. The *Posol'skii prikaz* became more and more important during the reigns of Aleksei Mikhailovich (r. 1645–1676) and Fedor Alekseevich (r. 1676–1682), as increased diplomatic advances to draw Western powers into an anti-Ottoman alliance and the protracted

[1] For an exemplary comparative overview of the courts of Versailles and Vienna, see Duindam, *Vienna and Versailles*, pp. 181–219.

[2] For the chancelleries (with ample bibliographical references on the subject and an interesting application of Max Weber's ideas on a bureaucracy), see P. B. Brown, 'How Muscovy governed: seventeenth-century Russian central administration', *Russian History*, 36 (2009), 459–529. There is no consent as to how many chancelleries there were in total. Up to ninety-six have been counted. See B. Plavsic, 'Seventeenth-century chanceries and their staffs', in *Russian officialdom: the bureaucratization of Russian society from the seventeenth to the twentieth century*, ed. W. M. Pintner, D. K. Rowney, H. A. Bennett (London, 1980), pp. 19–45, 21, fn. 3.

[3] For a classic and still influential study of the ambassadorial chancellery, see S. A. Belokurov, *O Posol'skom prikaze* (Moscow, 1906). See also B. Meissner, 'Die zaristische Diplomatie. A. Der Gesandtschafts-Prikas (Posol'skij Prikas)', *Jahrbücher für Geschichte Osteuropas*, 4 (1956), 237–45. Although the founding date is widely accepted in Russian historiography, it is still subject of debate, see Sakharov, *Istoriia vneshnei politiki Rossii*, I, p. 349.

peace negotiations with Poland-Lithuania triggered a rapid growth of the chancellery.[4] The *Posol'skii prikaz* kept the state seal, and it oversaw all relations of the Russian government with foreign polities, including diplomatic interactions with the Cossacks, the Kalmyk Khanate, the Nogai Horde, and the Tatars.[5] In this role, it organised embassies to other courts as well as the reception of diplomats in Moscow. The chancellery was also responsible for foreigners in Russia.[6]

The *Posol'skii prikaz* was much more than just an organ of foreign policy in the strict sense. Since the beginning of the seventeenth century, when the old *tsarskii arkhiv* merged with the records of the ambassadorial chancellery, it had been managing the central archive of the Russian state.[7] Another of its tasks was the acquisition of news about events in western Europe.[8] The Russian court had been gathering information about the hierarchy of European states since the beginning of the sixteenth century, presumably from Italian sources.[9] The *Posol'skii prikaz* continued collecting pamphlets and brochures, as well as periodical newspapers, translated the relevant items

[4] N. M. Rogozhin, *U gosudarevykh del byt' ukazano* (Moscow, 2002), pp. 14–29; N. M. Rogozhin, *Posol'skii prikaz: kolybel' rossiiskoi diplomatii* (Moscow, 2003), pp. 38ff. See V. I. Savva, *O posol'skom prikaze v XVI veke* (Kharkov, 1917), and N. M. Rogozhin, *Posol'skie knigi Rossii kontsa XV – nachala XVII vv.* (Moscow, 1994), for the sixteenth century. For the *smuta*, see D. V. Liseitsev, *Posol'skii prikaz v epokhu smuty*, 2 vols. (Moscow, 2003).

[5] For Cossacks, see B. J. Boeck, *Imperial boundaries: Cossack communities and empire building in the age of Peter the Great* (Cambridge, 2009). See also, M. Khodarkovsky, *Where two worlds met: the Russian state and the Kalmyk nomads*, 1600–1771 (Ithaca, NY, London, 1992); M. Khodarkovsky, *Russia's steppe frontier: the making of a colonial empire*, 1500–1800 (Bloomington, IN, 2002).

[6] For foreigners from western Europe, see S. P. Orlenko, *Vykhodtsy iz Zapadnoi Evropy v Rossii XVII veka. Pravovoi status i real'noe polozhenie* (Moscow, 2004).

[7] S. O. Shmidt, ed., *Opisi Tsarskogo arkhiva XVI veka i arkhiva Posol'skogo prikaza 1614 goda* (Moscow, 1960), p. 6. See also S. O. Shmidt, ed., *Opis' arkhiva Posol'skogo prikaza 1626* goda, 2 vols. (Moscow, 1977); S. O. Shmidt, ed., *Opis' archiva Posol'kogo prikaza 1673 goda* (Moscow, 1990).

[8] Moscow's knowledge of international affairs in the sixteenth century has been described as low, see K. Rasmussen, 'On the information level of the Muscovite Posol'skii prikaz in the sixteenth century', *Forschungen zur osteuropäischen Geschichte*, 24 (1978), 88–99. Cf. Rogozhin's positive assessment of Moscow's awareness of international events, based on Russian diplomatic reports: N. M. Rogozhin, *Obzor posol'skikh knig iz fondov-kollektsii, khraniashchikhsia v TsGADA (konetz XV – nachalo XVIII v.)* (Moscow, 1990), p. 14. For a similar view on the seventeenth century, see M. A. Alpatov, 'Chto znal Posol'skii prikaz o Zapadnoi Evrope vo vtoroi polovine XVII v.', in *Istoriia i istoriki. Istoriografiia vseobshchei istorii*, ed. M. A. Alpatov (Moscow, 1966), pp. 89–129. For Moscow's expertise on the Holy Roman Empire, see C. Roll, 'Hatten die Moskowiter einen Begriff vom Reich? Beobachtungen zu den Kenntnissen und Vorstellungen von der politischen Ordnung des Alten Reichs am vorpetrinischen Zarenhof', in *Imperium romanum*, ed. Schnettger, pp. 135–65.

[9] N. A. Kazakova, '"Evropeiskoi strany koroli"', in *Issledovaniia po otechestvennomu istochnikovedeniiu: sbornik statei, posviashchennykh 75-letiiu professora S. N. Valka*, ed. S. S. Volk et al. (Moscow, Leningrad, 1964), pp. 418–26.

into Russian, and compiled sets of handwritten bulletins. These so-called *Vesti-Kuranty* were read out to the tsar and his inner circle and represented an early modern version of a press digest which, importantly, also contained detailed information about ceremonial occasions. This included, for example, notification of the Truce of Andrusovo (1667) in the *Europaeische Mitwochentliche Zeitung* (Hamburg) which elaborated on the ceremonial of the peace ratification and confirms both the interest of European readers in Russian diplomatic ceremony and the tsars' concern about their ceremonial image in Europe.[10] Long before the first Russian newspaper *Vedomosti* appeared in print at the behest of Tsar Peter I in 1703, an elaborate news-system had been informing the tsar about European affairs.[11]

In the second half of the seventeenth century, the chancellery began to design elaborate books for the family of the tsar.[12] Many unique and lavishly illustrated manuscripts appeared between 1672 and 1675; for example, *The seven liberal arts* [*Sedm svobodnykh uchenii*], the *Book about the election of Tsar Mikhail Fedorovich*, and the *Vasiliologion* (a history of European, Greek, Roman, Assyrian, and Persian emperors). Among these works the *Tsarskii tituliarnik* (book of royal titles) stands out.[13] The *tituliarnik* was issued by Aleksei Mikhailovich in 1672 and produced under the direction of his favourite and head of the *Posol'skii prikaz*, Artamon S. Matveev (1625–1682). Produced by artists from the chancellery and the Moscow armoury, the book is an ornate collection of secular portraits of Russian tsars

[10] I. Maier, A. M. Moldovana, eds., *Vesti-Kuranty: 1656 g., 1660–1662 gg., 1664–1670 gg.: Chast' 1: Russkie teksty* (Moscow, 2009), pp. 247f., for the contemporary Russian translation. For the original German, see I. Maier, ed., *Vesti-Kuranty: 1656 g., 1660–1662 gg., 1664–1670 gg.: Chast' 2: Inostrannye originaly k russkim tekstam* (Moscow, 2008), pp. 310f. Earlier published versions of the *Vesti-Kuranty* include: S. I. Kotkov, ed., *Vesti-Kuranty: 1600–1639 gg.* (Moscow, 1972); S. I. Kotkov, ed., *Vesti-Kuranty: 1642–1644 gg.* (Moscow, 1976); S. I. Kotkov, ed., *Vesti-Kuranty: 1645–1646, 1648 gg.* (Moscow, 1980); S. I. Kotkov, ed., *Vesti-Kuranty: 1648–1650 gg.* (Moscow, 1983); V. P. Vomperskii, ed., *Vesti-Kuranty: 1651–1652 gg., 1654–1656 gg., 1658–1660 gg.* (Moscow, 1996). Ingrid Maier is the authority on the *Vesti-Kuranty* and has published extensively on them. For a useful survey, see I. Maier, 'Presseberichte am Zarenhof im 17. Jahrhundert. Ein Beitrag zur Vorgeschichte der gedruckten Zeitung in Russland', *Jahrbuch für Kommunikationsgeschichte*, 6 (2004), 103–29.

[11] I. Maier, D. C. Waugh, 'How well was Muscovy connected with the world?', in *Imperienvergleich. Beispiele und Ansätze aus osteuropäischer Perspektive. Festschrift für Andreas Kappeler*, ed. G. Hausmann, A. Rustemeyer (Wiesbaden, 2009), pp. 17–28, put the *Vesti-Kuranty* in the context of the European postal system.

[12] For the production of manuscripts in the chancellery and its 'editorial activities', see I. M. Kudriatsev, '"Izdatel'skaia" deiatel'nost' Posol'skogo prikaza (k istorii russkoi rukopisnoi knigi vo vtoroi polovine XVII veka)', *Kniga: issledovaniia i materialy*, 8 (1963), 179–244. For print culture in seventeenth-century Russia, see S. Franklin, 'Printing Moscow: significances of the Frontispiece to the 1663 Bible', *Slavonic and East European Review*, 88 (2010), 73–95.

[13] See I. M. Eskina, ed., *Tsarskii tituliarnik*, 2 vols. (Moscow, 2007), I, for an excellent reproduction of the manuscript, and vol. II, for text, commentaries, and analysis.

and other Christian as well as Muslim rulers, featuring many heraldic displays and seals of Russian sovereigns. This work was also called the 'Great book of the state' (*Bol'shaia gosudarstvennaia kniga*), as it narrated the history of the tsars' diplomatic relations with other monarchs by citing the titles they used in diplomatic correspondence. The extended heading of the book reveals its content and purpose:

> Book, in it a collection that shows the roots of the Russian great sovereigns the tsars and grand princes, and how [they] wrote in letters to neighbouring great Christian and Muslim sovereigns in past years, until the year 1672, and with what seals the letters are stamped, and how to the ancestors of the Russian great sovereigns the tsars and to the great sovereign the tsar and grand prince Mikhail Fedorovich [...] and to his son, to the great sovereign the tsar and grand prince Aleksei Mikhailovich [...] the neighbouring great Christian and Muslim sovereigns write their names and titles, and the state portraits and coats of arms of them.[14]

While its historical nature has earned the *tituliarnik* the fame of being one of the first Russian historiographical works, its purpose was a clearly ceremonial one: to illustrate the continuity of the Romanov dynasty and reserve Russia a place among the powerful rulers in the world (see Figure 2.1).[15]

At the time of the *tituliarnik*'s appearance, another artistic undertaking introduced a novelty to the Russian court under the aegis of the *Posol'skii prikaz*. The first but short-lived Russian theatre was established under Matveev between 1672 and 1676.[16] Jacob Reutenfels, who visited Moscow in 1671–1673, reported that Tsar Aleksei had learned from foreigners that ambassadors frequently attended theatre performances at European courts. The *Vesti-Kuranty* also contained descriptions of theatrical and musical entertainments staged for court society and invited diplomats. While Russian embassies usually travelled with trumpeters and kettle-drummers who played their instruments on solemn occasions, an established theatre provided an even more efficient vehicle for stimulating the exchange of honour and prestige in diplomatic contact.[17]

[14] Ibid., II, p. 6. For the wider artistic context of the *tituliarnik*, see L. A. J. Hughes, 'The Moscow armoury and innovations in seventeenth-century Muscovite art', *Canadian-American Slavic Studies*, 13 (1979), 204–23, esp. p. 208.

[15] Cf. E. V. Chistiakova, N. M. Rogozhin, *'Oko vsei velikoi Rossii': ob istorii russkoi diplomaticheskoi sluzhby XVI–XVII vekov* (Moscow, 1989), p. 32. It has also been suggested that the *tituliarnik* served as a diplomatic manual for the preparation of diplomatic missions in the *Posol'skii prikaz*; see Grabar, *International law*, pp. 28f.

[16] C. R. Jensen, *Musical cultures in seventeenth-century Russia* (Bloomington, 2009) ch. 6; E. Opochinin, *Russkii teatr, ego nachalo u razvitie: istoricheskii ocherk* (Moscow, 2005), pp. 10–20.

[17] For these aspects of 'musical diplomacy', see C. R. Jensen, 'Music for the tsar: a preliminary study of the music of the Muscovite court theater', *The Musical Quarterly*, 79 (1995), 368–401, esp. pp. 385ff. Some interesting connections between the establishment of the first Moscow theatre and diplomacy are brought out by Jensen, Powell, 'Faux Moscovites'.

Figure 2.1 *Tsarskii tituliarnik* (1672). In order of appearance: Tsar Aleksei Mikhailovich, King Louis XIV, Holy Roman Emperor Leopold I, Elector of Brandenburg Frederick William.

Given that foreign relations were handled by the *Posol'skii prikaz*, the organisation and documentation of ambassadorial ceremonies were major duties within its remit. Virtually every service provided to diplomats was connected to the question of prestige, from solemn receptions to the provision of food and accommodation. The chancellery was also in charge of providing means of communication between a foreign embassy and the boiars who led the negotiations. Thus, various staff positions evolved over the centuries to meet the demands of such diverse tasks.

The second half of the seventeenth century saw the formation of specific categories of chancellery personnel. Until 1667, the *Posol'skii prikaz* was headed by *dumnye liudi*, that is, 'bureaucratic specialists' who held ranks in the duma as *dumnye d'iaki*. A *dumnyi dvorianin, okol'nichii*, or boiar oversaw its affairs thereafter.[18] The position entitled them to sit in the duma from where they conveyed decisions to the respective department in their chancellery. They were supported by up to four assistants with the rank of *prikaznyi* or *posol'skii d'iak* who, in the latter half of the seventeenth century, could rise to *dumnyi d'iak*.[19] The latter concerned themselves with all major affairs of the chancellery. It was incumbent on them to supervise the office work and record-keeping.

After the Truce of Andrusovo, which secured for Russia Left-bank Ukraine, Kiev, and the provinces of Smolensk and Severia, the *Posol'skii prikaz* enjoyed an even higher status and became a state institution in its own right with greater independence from the duma. The directors of the chancellery were rewarded with higher honours, rose to the rank of boiar, and were granted a new title that reflected their responsibilities as both keeper of the state seal and chief diplomat (*tsarstvennyia bol'shiia pechati i gosudarstvennykh velikikh posol'skikh del oberegatel'*).[20] Afanasii L. Ordin-Nashchokin (1605–1680) recognised the importance of the chancellery when he was appointed to its head in reward for his successful negotiations at Andrusovo. He wrote to the tsar that the ambassadorial

18 Rogozhin, *Posol'skii prikaz*, p. 39. The term 'bureaucratic specialists' was coined by Robert O. Crummey and refers to a group of non-aristocratic, professional bureaucrats who had earned their duma rank in reward for a long and successful service as career officials in one of the chancelleries. See R. O. Crummey, *Aristocrats and servitors: the boyar elite in Russia, 1613–1689* (Princeton, NJ, 1983), pp. 23, 36f., 39, 58f. For a still useful introduction into the complicated world of Muscovite court ranks (with insightful comments on the relation between prestige and tangible benefits), see V. A. Evreinov, *Grazhdanskoe chinoproizvodstvo v Rossii: istoricheskii ocherk* (St Petersburg, 1888). For their English translations, see Hughes, *Age of Peter the Great*, p. 5.

19 The attribute *posol'skii* distinguished them from their peers in other chancelleries, see F. P. Sergeev, *Russkaia diplomaticheskaia terminologiia XI–XVII vv.* (Kishinev, 1971), p. 104.

20 Rogozhin, *Posol'skii prikaz*, pp. 39f. Title quoted in Belokurov, *O Posol'skom prikaze*, p. 43. The title was used through the seventeenth century, see *ukazy* from 17 September 1682 and 19 October 1682, in *Sobranie gosudarstvennykh gramot i dogovorov khaniashchikhsia v Gosudarstvennoi kollegii inostrannykh del*, 5 vols. (Moscow, 1813–1894), IV, p. 464, and *PSZRI*, II, no. 1134 (17 September 1685), p. 687. For an overview of the directors of the foreign chancellery with biographical sketches and accounts of their individual activities and achievements, see Rogozhin, *U gosudarevykh del byt' ukazano*, pp. 75–233.

chancellery was 'the eye of the entire great Russia [*oko vsei velikoi Rossii*]' that watched over the honour and the well-being of the state.[21] This statement can be taken quite literally as far as honour is concerned, as the chancellery was also the arbiter of diplomatic ceremonies. The increased importance of the chancellery and its wide-ranging activities enhanced the prestige of the individual who conducted its business and who soon rose to become the 'second man' in the state, enjoying close intimacy with the tsar. The *Posol'skii prikaz* produced three formidable statesmen whom historians have described as the seventeenth-century Westernisers and forbearers of Peter I's reforms. Apart from Ordin-Nashchokin, Matveev and Prince Vasilii V. Golitsyn (1643–1714) also left their personal imprint on the direction of Russian foreign policy: while Ordin-Nashchokin favoured rapprochement with Poland to form an alliance against Sweden, Golitsyn focused on a broad anti-Ottoman alliance in combination with the Poles. Matveev concentrated on Kiev and eastern Ukraine which inevitably led to a clash with Poland.[22]

The daily work and administration of the *Posol'skii prikaz* was managed by a number of undersecretaries (*pod'iachie*). Up to thirty undersecretaries worked at the chancellery at any one time, and in the 1670s the number could even rise to fifty. The higher-ranking *pod'iachie* (there were four categories divided by seniority) presided over one of the sections (*povyt'ia*) of the chancellery (three for Europe and two for Asia on average) and conducted specific functions such as running the postal service or matters concerning foreign merchants. They handled the paperwork, submitted drafts to the *d'iaki*, and produced the official documents that were then countersigned by their superiors. One of the undersecretaries, Grigorii K. Kotoshikhin (1630–1667), has earned considerable fame among historians for his description of the Russian state and diplomatic practice.[23] This work has been found to give a faithful

[21] Quoted in Belokurov, *O Posol'skom prikaze*, 43.

[22] Crummey, *Aristocrats*, pp. 58f.; For brief comparative accounts, see also Belokurov, *O Posol'skom prikaze*, pp. 42–47; Bushkovitch, *Peter the Great*, pp. 51ff., 55ff. For Ordin-Nashchokin, see in particular N. M. Rogozhin, 'Russian Richelieu: Ordin-Nashchokin', *International Affairs*, 46 (2000), 185–93; B. N. Floria, *Vneshnepoliticheskaia programma A. L. Ordina-Nashchokina i popytki ee osushchestvleniia* (Moscow, 2013). For Matveev, L. A. J. Hughes, 'Matveev, Artamon Sergeevich (1625–1682)', in *Modern Encyclopodia of Russian and Soviet History*, ed. J. L. Wieczynski et al., 59 vols and supplements (Gulf Breeze, FL, 1976–1996), XXI, pp. 142–44. For Golitsyn, L. A. J. Hughes, *Russia and the West: the life of a seventeenth-century westernizer, Prince Vasily Vasil'evich Golitsyn (1643–1714)* (Newtonville, MA, 1984), and, more recently, A. V. Man'ko, *Velikikh posol'skikh del oberegatel': politicheskaia biografiia kniazia* V. V. Golitsyna (Moscow, 2007).

[23] G. K. Kotoshikhin, *O Rossii v tsarstvovanie Alekseia Mikhailovicha: text and commentary*, ed. A. E. Pennington (Oxford, 1980). For Kotoshikhin, see ibid., pp. 2–11 (introduction by A. E. Pennington). The first English translation has become available recently:

account of Russian state administration, although one needs to be aware that it was written at the behest of the Swedish government that protected Kotoshikhin after he went into voluntary exile, arriving at Stockholm in 1666, and so it cannot be said to be entirely unbiased.[24] Nevertheless, as will become clear later, Kotoshikhin's detailed descriptions of diplomatic protocol prove to be a crucial source of information.

The chancellery also employed specialists whose expertise was indispensable in diplomacy. Andrei V. Beliakov has counted 84 translators, for both Western and Oriental languages, and 185 interpreters for the period between 1645 and 1682. The translators alone mastered an impressive range of languages: English, French, German, Latin, Hungarian, Polish, Danish, Dutch, Swedish, modern Greek, classical Greek, Arabic, Georgian, Belorussian, Wallachian, Persian, Mongolian, Turkish, Kalmyk, and Tatar. The interpreters spoke even more languages, thirty-three in total, some with a command of both Western and Oriental tongues at the same time, including Hebrew, Italian, Spanish, Armenian, Bukharan, Bashkir, and others.[25] Another important position in diplomatic dialogue was occupied by the gold painters (*zoloto-pistsy*) who decorated letters and other important documents with gold and silver paint to signify the rank held by the addressee.[26] The elaborate book projects mentioned above also required the hiring of bookbinders, artists, icon-painters, cartographers, and jewellers. The theatrical activities of Aleksei's court necessitated that actors, musicians as well as stage designers and costume-makers appeared on the payroll of the ambassadorial chancellery.[27] Last but not least, there were the guardians or watchmen (*storozhi*) who fulfilled various tasks in safeguarding the chancellery or providing basic services like cutting firewood or buying ink for the scribes. The *pristavy* represented another category of guards. As police officers or bailiffs (*sudebnye pristavy*) they performed a range of functions in judicial affairs.[28]

G. K. Kotoshikhin, *Russia in the reign of Aleksei Mikhailovich*, trans. B. P. Uroff, ed. M. Poe (Berlin, Warsaw, 2014).

24 A. V. Beliakov, 'Sluzhashchie Posol'skogo prikaza vtoroi treti XVII veka' (unpublished doctoral dissertation, Russian Academy of Sciences, Moscow, 2002), 285, passim, confirms Kotoshikhin's overall accuracy through correlation with other sources, although he acknowledges that not all individual claims by Kotoshikhin can be proven.

25 Beliakov, 'Sluzhashchie', 105, 109, 117f., 148, 154.

26 For a relatively well-preserved example, see TNA, SP 102/49. For decorated letters and their use in diplomacy, see M. Jansson, *Art and diplomacy: seventeenth-century decorated royal letters to Russia and the Far East* (Leiden, Boston, 2015).

27 Beliakov, 'Sluzhashchie', pp. 22, 172–83.

28 Ibid., pp. 183–87. Rogozhin, *Posol'skii prikaz*, p. 48, writes that the *pristav* appears in the chancellery as a permanent member of staff as late as 1664.

Pristavy, Introducteurs des Ambassadeurs, and Masters of Ceremonies

The term *pristav* was also used for higher-ranking courtiers, *stol'niki, okol'nichie*, and boiars, for example, who were appointed by the tsar ad hoc to receive and accompany foreign diplomats at various stages on their way to the capital, rising in rank in accordance with increasing proximity to the court.[29] They supervised the ceremonial, transmitted diplomats' requests, conveyed messages from the chancellery, and assumed the role of the commissary of the diplomats' affairs. They also reported to the *Posol'skii prikaz* on the progress of the embassy and any unforeseen incidents. In short, they formed the personal link between an embassy and the court. Because the *pristav* had continued personal contact with the honourable guest, he stood in the epicentre of cultural encounter and potential conflict.[30] Some sources suggest that similar roles were performed by the *vstrechnik*, someone who greeted the diplomats at solemn receptions in Moscow.[31] The related term *tseremonshchik* appears in Russian descriptions of diplomatic receptions at western courts and refers to the office of the master of ceremonies.[32] Although such an office did not exist in Russia until the eighteenth century, the *pristav* administered comparable duties.[33] In a Russian embassy report of 1662, for example, Charles Cottrell is referred to as *pristav* in his role as master of ceremonies at the court of St James.[34] In western Europe, conversely, the *pristav* was known to ceremonial scholars and diplomatic theorists as the Russian equivalent of the master of ceremonies.[35]

The early modern court accommodated a large number of diplomatic dignitaries, and each represented his master with particular regard for hierarchy. Ceremonies involving claims to rank required shrewd planning and cautious manoeuvring. They were such an important part of court life

[29] Far away in Smolensk, for example, a '*zhilets*' was enough for the reception of diplomats whereas the rank of a *pristav* in Moscow could be expected to be much higher. See, for example, '*Nakaz zhiltsu Bogdanovu*,' (23 April 1662), in *PDS*, IV, cols. 333f.

[30] Herberstein already mentions the '*pristaw*' in his German version of his travel account (1557). The *pristav* appears as '*procurator*' in the earlier Latin version of the text (1556). See F. Kämpfer et al., eds., *Rerum Moscoviticarum*, p. 401, passim. Cf. Chistiakova, Rogozhin, '*Oko*', p. 28.

[31] Kotoshikhin, *O Rossii*, pp. 75, passim.

[32] See, for example, Paul Menzies' account of his reception at the papal court in 1673, *PDS*, IV, cols. 1041f., passim. For Menzies' diplomatic mission to Rome, see P. Dukes, 'Paul Menzies and his mission from Muscovy to Rome, 1672–1674', *The Innes Review*, 35 (1984), 88–95.

[33] Sergeev, *Diplomaticheskaia terminologiia*, pp. 122–24, compares the roles of the *vstrechnik* and the *tseremonshchik* and concludes that they fulfilled the same tasks at times.

[34] RGADA, f. 35, op. 1, d. 8, l. 193.

[35] Lünig, *Theatrum Ceremoniale*, II, p. 1320. Wicquefort, *Embassador*, p. 128.

that their organisation was entrusted to individuals with a specialised court office. In the late sixteenth century, the courts of France and Spain established the office of the *introducteur* (*conducteur*) *des ambassadeurs* whose exclusive duties were the reception of foreign diplomats, the organisation of their stay, and their presentation to the king.[36] In France, two *introducteurs* served on a semestrial basis in any given year, supported by a secretary. Although it was their task to bring order to the confusing world of ceremony, the rank of the office itself confronted them with ceremonial difficulties in their own professional realm. The title bestowed much prestige on its incumbent and inevitably drew him into competition with the grand master of ceremonies whose ceremonial functions overlapped with his own. An edict was issued in 1643 to separate their duties and preclude such quarrels.[37] But dispute persisted. In 1717, the reception of Tsar Peter I and his entourage in Paris still gave rise to ceremonial arguments among court officials.[38]

In England, the 'master of the ceremonies' was established by James I (r. 1603–1625) in 1603. In the description of Sir Lewis Lewkenor, the first person who held the office, his duty was 'to entertayne and receave sutch foreyn ambassadors as shal repayre into this realme to do his majesty honor and service' and to provide 'by all possible means all favor, assistance and address for their negotiations'.[39] Sir John Finet succeeded him in 1627 and remained in office until his death in 1641.[40] From then until 1818, the role of the master of ceremonies was performed by members of the Cottrell and, later, Cottrell-Dormer family. The master received orders from the lord chamberlain (not from the secretaries of state responsible for foreign affairs) and directed an assistant master and a marshal of ceremonies who supported his work.[41]

[36] The office has been studied extensively by A. Boppe, *Les Introducteurs des ambassadeurs. 1585–1900* (Paris, 1901); A. J. Loomie, 'The conducteur des ambassadeurs of seventeenth-century France and Spain', *Revue belge de philologie et d'histoire*, 52 (1975), 333–56.

[37] AN, KK 1431('Règlement du Roy pour les différents [. . .] entre les grands Mâitres et Mâitre des Cérémonie et les conducteurs des ambassadeurs'), fols. 60–62v. See also ibid. ('De charge fonction et Rang des introducteurs des ambassadeurs. Et fonction du grand Mâitre des Cérémonies'), fols. 48–52.

[38] BM, MS 2747, fols. 242–254v, esp. fols. 243v, 247. See the section 'Vienna 1698' in Chapter 4. For a list of conflicts between the *introducteur* and the master of ceremonies, see AN, K 1712, fols. 4v–5. See also Duindam, *Vienna and Versailles*, p. 207, for more examples.

[39] 'Master of the ceremonies' was the official title. For the origins of this office, see A. J. Loomie, *Ceremonies of Charles I: the notebooks of John Finet 1628–1641* (London, New York, 1987), pp. 20–25, quotations on p. 23.

[40] For Sir John Finet's career, see ibid., pp. 8–11.

[41] Rousham, MC box 1 ('Concerning the Reception of Ambassadours, Envoyés, etc. in the Court of England', ca. 1672–1674), p. 1.

Sir Charles Cottrell served from 1641 to 1649, followed Charles II (r. 1660–1685) into exile, and was confirmed in office in 1660.[42] In 1685, he retired in favour of his son Charles who had served as an assistant under his father.[43] On the day before the coronation of Charles II, Charles Cottrell received, in reward for his unfailing service during the Civil War, a chain of gold with a medal displaying an emblem of peace with King James I's motto '*Beati Pacifici*' on one side and an emblem of war with *Dieu et mon Droit* subscribed on the other.[44] The heavy gold chain reminded the master that diplomatic business in general and the reception of diplomats in particular was a tightrope between war and peace. When Cottrell took charge of diplomatic protocol at the beginning of the Restoration, he laid out in several points the 'Reasons to confirme the M[aster] of the Ceremonyies Claims'.[45] He held himself responsible for controlling access to the king, watching over the ranks of diplomats, and treating them equally to avoid complaints. Apart from preventing conflicts among diplomats, he observed the 'Policy which is used in other Countryis, & not to allow a greater freedom to theyr Ambassadors here then those of England in other places'. He was to make sure 'that the Order & Decency of the Court may be preserved', in other words, that the international order maintained at St James remained intact.[46]

In other parts of Europe, an *introducteur* did not exist. His duties were divided among various court offices or remained an integral part of the role of the general master of ceremonies whose functions included the

[42] For Charles Cottrell, see R. Clayton, 'Cotterell, Sir Charles (1615–1701)', *Oxford Dictionary of National Biography* (Oxford, 2004), available from www.oxforddnb.com/view/article/6397, last access 6 February 2016.

[43] Sir Balthazar Gerbier was granted a reversionary patent to succeed Finet upon his death. He did follow into office accordingly but never actually officiated. Charles Cottrell, the then-assistant, acted as master of ceremonies to Charles I when the king fell out with Parliament and set up his court in Oxford as well as through the Civil War. He received a patent of reversion in 1645 at Oxford to take over office after Gerbier. Gerbier's patent was revoked in 1660, and Cottrell was appointed as master by King Charles II. Sir Oliver Fleming served under the Commonwealth and Protectorate but obviously could not continue his post with the return of the monarchy. See the handwritten introductory notes to extracts of the unpublished note books of Charles Cottrell, compiled in 1830: TNA, LC 5/2 and Rousham, MC box 1 ('Concerning the Lord Chamberlains Office', 18 May 1683). See also R. Clayton, 'Diplomats and diplomacy in London, 1667 1672' (unpublished DPhil dissertation, University of Oxford, 1995), p. 189.

[44] Rousham, MC box 1 ('Concerning Master, Assistent, & Marshall of the Ceremonyes, & the first grant of the Medall', 1678). Lünig, *Theatrum Ceremoniale*, II, p. 1320, mentions the medal.

[45] Rousham, MC box 1 ('Reasons to confirme the Mr. of the Ceremonyies Claims', n. d.). A handwritten copy from 1830 dates the original to the year 1660, see TNA, LC 5/2, fol. 1.

[46] Rousham, MC box 1 ('Reasons to confirme the Mr. of the Ceremonyies Claims', n.d.).

supervision of domestic court ceremonies. Vienna, for example, did not have separate, specialised personnel to deal with diplomatic receptions. From 1652 onwards, a *Zeremonienamt* was under the direction of the *Obersthofmeister*. The reception of diplomats fell into the domain of the *Obersthofmarschall* who attended the ambassadors' solemn entry and escorted them to their public audience. However, many other court dignitaries were involved, so that it is impossible to identify the equivalent of an *introducteur*. Diplomats requested their public audience from the *Oberstkämmerer* or the *Obersthofmeister*, and a special commissary (*Audienzkommissar*) was occasionally appointed to conduct the audience. While Denmark, Sweden, and Prussia employed grand masters of ceremonies (*Oberzeremonienmeister*), who acted as *introducteurs* but were also responsible for other solemn functions at court, such an office was not created at the court of Vienna until the early nineteenth century.[47]

Russia had not seen an office of a master of ceremonies until the institution of the table of ranks in 1722.[48] The office of *ober-tseremoniimeister* was introduced as a civil rank (*shtatskii chin*) of the fifth class but remained vacant during the initial years (1722–1724) and between 1730 and 1741. In addition, a *tseremoniimeister* (civil rank, seventh class) and a *nadvornyi tseremoniimeister* (court rank, ninth class) were created, although the latter position was never filled in the eighteenth century.[49] The office of *ober-tseremoniimeister* had been unfilled until the Piedmontese Count Francesco (Frants Matveevich) Santi (1683–1768), who had served as an assistant to the herald (*gerol'dmeister*) under Peter I, took it up in 1725 (the patent was issued in 1726). Santi was suspected to have sided with Petr A. Tolstoi, who opposed Peter II's accession to the throne, and was sent to Siberia in 1727. Baron Georg von Habichtsthal (Gabikhstal'), a Swiss Calvinist, who had served as the representative of the duke of Mecklenburg at the Russian court between 1714 and 1721 and served in Prussia thereafter, was invited

[47] Lünig, *Theatrum Ceremoniale*, II, pp. 1318–22, lists the offices responsible for the treatment of diplomats at various European courts, including the republics and the papal court. For Vienna, see Duindam, *Vienna and Versailles*, pp. 193–97. See also J. Duindam, 'Ceremonial staffs and paperwork at two courts: France and the Habsburg monarchy ca. 1550–720', in *Hofgesellschaft und Höflinge an europäischen Fürstenhöfen in der Frühen Neuzeit (15.–18. Jh.)*, ed. K. Malettke, C. Grell (Münster, 2001), pp. 369–88; P. C. Hartmann, 'Zum Gesandtschaftszeremoniell an den Höfen von München, Wien, Madrid und Versailles im 18. Jahrhundert', in *Études d'histoire européene. Mélanges offerts à René et Suzanne Pillorget* (Angers, 1990), pp. 149–57. For the management of diplomatic protocol in the imperial cities, see Krischer, *Reichsstädte*, pp. 175ff.

[48] *PSZRI*, VI, no. 3890 (24 January 1722), pp. 486–89. For the table of ranks and the changes it brought about in the administration of the Russian court, see L. E. Shepelev, *Chinovnyi mir Rossii: XVIII-nachalo XX v.* (St Petersburg, 1999), pp. 131ff. Cf. Amburger's table of rank of 1722, in E. Amburger, *Geschichte der Behördenorganisation Russlands von Peter dem Grossen bis 1917* (Leiden, 1966), p. 56.

[49] *PSZRI*, XI, no. 8818 (14 November 1743), p. 946.

to take up the office in 1727. Habichtsthal died in 1730.[50] The functions of the *ober-tseremoniimeister* were soon transferred to the *ober-gofmarshal* and remained there until Santi's return from exile in 1742. During Santi's second tenure (1742–1764) the ceremonial offices at the Russian court were incorporated into the *Kollegiia inostrannykh del* (the successor institution to the *Posol'skii prikaz*) as a departmental unit called *tseremonial'naia chast'*. It had its own seal, secretaries, translators, and copyists. The *ober-tseremoniimeister* and his supporting staff concerned themselves with all major ceremonial events at the court: weddings, coronations, court mourning, diplomatic receptions, festive dinners, court solemnities, and entertainments. Towards the end of the eighteenth century, the then-*obertseremoniimeister* Petr S. Valuev (1743–1814) still complained that the specific functions of his office as distinct from those of the *tseremoniimeister* had never been laid down in particular, although these offices had been in existence for almost a century.[51] In comparison to the French court, the office under the direction of the *ober-tseremoniimeister* combined the roles of the *introducteur* and the *grand maître des cérémonies*. Although the diplomatic protocol was only one among a range of other responsibilities, the *ober-tseremoniimeister*, too, like his English equivalent, was to maintain the symbolic order at court. He reminded people attending the ceremonies that they ought not to violate the symbolic order. In order to do so, he was urged to wear his badge – the imperial state arms in black on a light blue ribbon – visible to everyone so that he be recognised in this capacity.[52]

Before the reforms of Peter I, the *pristav*, then, fulfilled tasks similar to those exercised by the *introducteur* in France or the master of ceremonies in England. As ritual functionaries, they are comparable. Yet a comparison reveals that their integration into the royal household and court life was very different. A master of ceremonies filled a permanent court office that came with the prestige of a court rank, relatively well-defined duties, and a fixed income. Supported by appointed staff, he monopolised skill, documentation, and planning expertise and handed this ritual know-how down to his successors, as did, for example, the Cottrells in England who inherited and held the office and its archive over many decades. The master of ceremonies possessed executive powers and acted within his own remit, which allowed for greater flexibility when responding to ceremonial conflicts. Not so the *pristav*. An ad hoc appointed *pristav* managed the stay and

[50] AVPRI, f. 23, op. 23/1, d. 2, for Habichtsthal's archive. For Habichtsthal and Santi, see Ageeva, *Diplomaticheskii tseremonial*, pp. 51–59, 63–72. See also O. G. Ageeva, *Evropeizatsiia russkogo dvora 1700–1796 gg.* (Moscow, 2006), ch. 2.

[51] AVPRI, f. 2, op. 2/6, d. 5552 ('Mnenie o dolzhnosti ober-tseremoniimeistera, tseremoniimeistera', n.d., *c.* 1795), l. 1.

[52] Ibid, ll. 2, 3ob–4.

communications of an embassy in all its practical aspects. He performed the symbolic allocations of rank and status and observed the distribution of honour in order to protect the prestige of the tsar in the international hierarchy. But he did not have both the ceremonial staff and expertise which qualified his peers in England or France for a separate court office. Ritual knowledge and planning rested with the scribes within the institutional structure of the *Posol'skii prikaz*. The clerks managed a huge ceremonial archive of precedents, composed detailed instructions in preparation for the reception of a foreign embassy, and passed their directives down to several *pristavy* who were expected to execute the instructions with painstaking accuracy and no room for deviation. While a master of ceremonies administered ritual, the *pristav* received strict orders from the administration.[53]

Ceremony and the Written Word

The machinery of diplomatic protocol produced a sea of documents, irrespective of the fact whether a court had a special functionary for diplomatic ceremonies, like France and England, or made ad hoc appointments for the arrangement of diplomatic receptions, as the Russian or Viennese courts did until the eighteenth and nineteenth centuries, respectively. The documents were prepared as a 'repository of ritual' for future consultation when ceremonial occasions had to be organised on the basis of past precedents.

The 'collection of rituals', that is, the documentation of performative acts was necessary to turn the fleeting message of ceremony into an enduring argument of supremacy. Not only were the rituals reflected in the record-keeping, ritual and text were contingent upon each other. The writing down of ceremonial events became part of the procedure of precedence in that the claims manifest in these writings extended to the future handling of rituals, whereby the written word created a social reality that could itself be subject to manipulation.[54] Descriptive as these highly repetitive texts may appear, their function was also

[53] I elaborate these points in comparative perspective in my 'A Perfect Relation', esp. pp. 76ff.

[54] A. Krischer, 'Können Rituale gesammelt werden? Vormoderne Aufschreibesysteme für symbolisches Handeln in außereuropäischen Gesellschaften', *TRANS. Internet-Zeitschrift für Kulturwissenschaften*, 15 (2004), available from www.inst.at/trans/15Nr/06_2/krischer15.htm, last access 6 February 2016. For the manipulative aspect of ceremonial documentation, see G. Sternberg, 'Manipulating information in the Ancien Régime: ceremonial records, aristocratic strategies, and the limits of the state perspective', *Journal of Modern History*, 85 (2013), 239–79, esp. pp. 278ff.; Sternberg, *Status interaction*, p. 23.

a performative one, at least when the descriptions of past events were cited to prove one's right to precedence.

No wonder that the French *introducteurs* and their assistants assiduously kept, copied, and continued diaries and occasional notes. Voluminous collections of descriptions of ceremonies have thus survived. They do not always display a systematic pattern in the record-keeping, except for a chronological or thematic order within the individual writings.[55] But they had a considerable impact on creating a 'ceremonial system', that is, a common symbolic code increasingly shared by various courts across Europe. They contributed to the circulation of ceremonial knowledge within the *société des princes* in that ceremonial scholars and publicists partly based their writings on the notes of the masters of ceremonies.[56]

One of the consequences of the emerging states-system and the development of resident diplomacy was an augmentation of ceremonial interaction between diplomats who populated European courts, both complicating the symbolic communication among sovereigns and increasing the scholarly interest in the subject.[57] This coincided with

55 Duindam, *Vienna and Versailles*, p. 192. In France, the memoirs are scattered around various libraries and archives in Paris. The most eminent body of sources comes from the Sainctot family (*maître des cérémonies* 1635–1691, *introducteurs* 1691–1752), in particular from Nicolas de Sainctot. See, for example, BnF, MS f 14117–14120: 'Mémoires de M. de Sainctot Introducteur des ambassadeurs'; BM, MS 2737–2751: 'Recueil de relations des cérémonies de la cour de France, copié pour M. Desgranges sur les originaux, appartenant au sieur de Sainctot, maître des cérémonies', or BnF, MS naf 3123–3133: 'Journal de M. de Villeras, secrètaire ordinaire du roy a la conduite des ambassadeurs 1699–1713'. See Duindam, *Vienna and Versailles*, p. 193, fn. 37, for a complete list of the materials (published and unpublished), and Sternberg, 'Manipulating information', pp. 241–47, for a discussion of the materials. For England, see James Howell's publication of Sir Finet's notebooks: J. Finet, *Finetti philoxenis* (London, 1656). The notes of the Cottrells and Cottrell-Dormers are at the private archive at Rousham, nr. Steeple Aston. None of Charles Cottrell's notes before his appointment in 1660 survived (if he took any). His notebook starts in the year of his appointment: Rousham, MC 6; MC 10, for Sir Charles-Lodowick Cottrell's (1686–1710) notes; MC 7, for Sir Clement Cottrell's (1710–1758) notes. Copies of extracts can be found in TNA, LC 5/2 (notes until 1710) and LC 5/3 (notes from 1710). For Prussia, see P.-M. Hahn, K. Kiesant, eds., *Johann von Besser (1654–1729): Schriften*, 3 vols. (Heidelberg, 2009), III: 'Ceremonial-Acta'.

56 For example, Rousset de Missy, *Cérémonial diplomatique*, I, in the 'avertissement', mentions the unpublished notes of Nicolas de Sainctot as one of the sources he used. Sainctot's writings were also known in England, Saxony, and Prussia; see Kugeler, 'Theory', p. 255. Wicquefort and Gregorio Leti (*Il ceremoniale historico e politico*, 6 vols. Amsterdam, 1685) cite Finet's notes from Howell's edition of 1656; see Loomie, *Notebooks*, p. 13.

57 See Rohr, *Einleitung zur Ceremoniel-Wissenschaft der Grossen Herren*, p. 17. The sending of resident diplomats is widely acknowledged to be the key aspect in the evolution of modern diplomacy. But, as Herbert Butterfield puts it, its development since its inception in fifteenth-century Italy remained considerably slow and did not gain momentum till the second half of the seventeenth century: H. Butterfield, 'Diplomacy', in *Studies in diplomatic history: essays in memory of David Bayne Horn*, ed. R. Hatton, M. S. Anderson (London, 1970), pp. 357–72, here on pp. 362ff.

the attempt to reform the princely household at the imperial court, whose ceremonial organisation had reached a state of debilitating complexity. Ferdinand III's (r. 1637–1657) response was to summon a court conference in 1651 to reform the hitherto flexible but confusing order of ceremonial norms. The conference opposed the idea of a central, monolithic set of regulations, given the unpredictability and variety of ceremonial occasions. But it proposed the documentation of ceremonies for future reference. Thus, from 1652 the *Oberhofmeisteramt* started to keep records, and with this began the systematic writing down of diplomatic ritual at the imperial court that lasted until the end of the Habsburg monarchy.[58]

The Russian court started the systematic collecting of diplomatic rituals as part of an extensive archive as early as the late fifteenth century. Diplomatic relations and their ritual documentation have been an inherent aspect of Russian state-building since the beginning of the centralisation of the Muscovite state. In fact, together with other diplomatic documents descriptions of ceremonies left one of the largest, rather complete and well-preserved, archival collections of the early modern Russian state. Written records of diplomatic relations were kept as individual documents, scrolls, or books. All papers, which accrued over the course of an embassy or the stay of a foreign diplomat at the Russian court, were collated, put in chronological order, and joined together into *stolbtsy*. After a mission was completed, the most important documents were reproduced, written into bound papers, and finally sewn together as ambassadorial books *(posol'skie knigi)*.[59] The *stolbtsy* were retained and served as reference materials, as they contained much information that did not go into the books, for example, on financial organisation, on correspondence between foreign diplomats and the chancellery, and on instructions to local *voevody* about the reception of an embassy. N. M. Rogozhin suggests that the *pod'iachie* under the supervision of a *dumnyi d'iak* managed this process of documentation. Today, 766 *posol'skie knigi* survive (including copies), 610 of which are devoted to relations with foreign powers,

[58] M. Hengerer, 'Die Zeremonialprotokolle und weitere Quellen zum Zeremoniell des Kaiserhofes im Wiener Haus-, Hof- und Staatsarchiv', in *Quellenkunde der Habsburgermonarchie (16.–18. Jahrhundert). Ein exemplarisches Handbuch*, ed. J. Pauser, M. Scheutz, T. Winkelbauer (Vienna, Munich, 2004), pp. 76–93.

[59] For a recently published example, see P. I. Prudovskii, *Rossiia i Prussiia v seredine XVII veka. Tom 1: Posol'skaia kniga po sviaziam Rossii s Brandenburgsko-Prusskim gosudarstvom 1649–1671 gg.* (Moscow, 2013). For another example available in English translation, see M. Jansson, N. M. Rogozhin, eds., *England and the North: the Russian embassy of 1613–1614*, trans. P. Bushkovitch (Philadelphia, 1994).

while the rest deal with relations between the Russian government and the peoples that were later incorporated into the Russian empire.[60]

The *posol'skie knigi* contain a wide range of documents.[61] They include, for example, major treaties and lists of presents given to monarchs, but also the chancellery's communications with other institutions involved in the preparation or reception of an embassy. The *knigi* also registered the letters of credence or credentials (*veriushchie*). These letters granted recognition to the diplomat in his official function, announced his diplomatic rank, and guaranteed that he enjoyed the customary diplomatic privileges. Once the ambassador had presented his credentials to the monarch, negotiations could begin.[62] Diplomats were given 'letters of friendship' (*liubitel'nye gramoty*). These passports announced the diplomats' peaceful intentions and asked for immediate safe conduct while they passed through other states. The tsar promised to treat diplomats from these states with equal respect.[63] In certain circumstances, documents called *opasnye* ('hazards') were issued to foreigners to guarantee free entry and exit to and from Russia. Russians received similar passes, the *proezzhye*, when staying abroad. In order to be supplied with food and accommodation on their way through Russia, diplomats and *pristavy* produced the so-called *ukaznye* with which they could claim a prescribed allocation of board and lodging from a local *voevoda*.

The main part of the *knigi* is made up of *nakazy* and *stateinye spiski*. A *nakaz* instructed a Russian diplomat and laid out – in a highly standardised and repetitive language – his mission, the route of the embassy, his code of conduct, a detailed list of presents, and above all the ceremonial rules he ought to follow. It even prescribed word by word the speeches he was to deliver to the monarch, which also included advice on when a diplomat was to remain silent. The instructions also laid down how to behave at dinner and what to do with one's servants when invited to dine at the monarch's table:

> [He] is strictly ordered that he behaves properly and cautiously at table and that he does not get drunk and say nasty words. And that he does not take his servants into the dining hall with him in order to avoid them getting drunk and excessive, and

[60] Unless stated otherwise, this and the following sections are based on Rogozhin, *Obzor*, pp. 3–15. An updated version of this excellent overview of the *posol'skie knigi* is now available from www.vostlit.info/Texts/Dokumenty/Russ/XVI/Posolbook/PosolBook.html, last access 6 February 2016.

[61] Rogozhin, *Obzor*, pp. 11ff.

[62] For the role of credentials in diplomatic contact, see Lünig, *Theatrum Ceremoniale*, I, p. 374; Stieve, *Hoff-Ceremoniel* (1723), pp. 235ff.; Wicquefort, *Embassador*, pp. 109ff. For a collection of credentials (copies) presented to English rulers between 1688 and 1736, see Rousham, MC 19 and MC 20.

[63] For the western European equivalent, see Wicquefort, *Embassador*, pp. 121ff.

that he orders them to sit in a different hall, in an orderly manner, and that he does not take revellers and fools to the court of the king.[64]

Each diplomatic mission received an individual *nakaz*, compiled by the clerks in the chancellery with minute attention to detail especially if it concerned the honour of the tsar. The clerks based the instructions on previous *nakyzy* which, in turn, derived from even older directions held in the chancellery's archive. A similar system was at work at the court of Vienna where the ceremonial records reproduced a chain of ritual events and predetermined the course of future ceremonies. The fact that one ceremony bore the pattern of another explains the highly self-referential character of ceremonial descriptions. Ritual forms were made permanent through frequent reiteration and documentation, a practice that served the ultimate aim of preserving and controlling the *Herkommen*, that is, the norms of the 'olden days'.[65] Russians referred to this process as *starina*, a term that denoted a system of precedents in which the norms of diplomatic practice were sanctioned by usage and tradition. So strict were the rules governing the behaviour of a Russian diplomat that a breach of diplomatic protocol was liable to be punished.[66] Ceremonial disputes were common, and to what extent the threat of punishment or even the death penalty materialised is uncertain.[67] However, Charles Cottrell reports that the messenger Dmitrii L. Simonovskii, in 1682, did not accept the king's letter presented to him by a state secretary, 'saying, he should loose his head, if he took it from any hands, but his Majesty's'.[68] The king refused to see the messenger on the ground that the latter had prompted him to raise and doff his hat during the audience, an unexpected 'brutishness' for which the master of ceremonies was scolded. The letter remained in the Russian's lodgings for a few days, untouched by Simonovskii or his servants, until he threatened to hang himself should the king continue to deny him an audience. The Russian finally prevailed and saw his request fulfilled.

[64] *Nakaz* to Andrei Vinius, messenger to England, France, and Spain (1672/3), *PDS*, IV, col. 816.

[65] The term abounds in the ceremonial records at the Viennese court.

[66] The Russian sources keep silent about such incidents but Western travellers report that *pristavy* were beaten with the knout if they failed to preserve the prescribed ceremonial. See Semenov, *U istokov kremlevskogo protokola*, pp. 207f.

[67] Although this is presented as an established fact by some scholars, see O. Krauske, *Die Entwickelung der ständigen Diplomatie vom fünfzehnten Jahrhundert bis zu den Beschlüssen von 1815 und 1818* (Leipzig, 1885), p. 143.

[68] Rousham, MC 6, fol. 175. Cottrell's account is printed in I. Vinogradoff, 'Russian missions to London, 1569–1687: seven accounts by the masters of the ceremonies', *Oxford Slavonic Papers, New Series*, 14 (1981), 36–72, here on pp. 63f.

In order to ensure that diplomats would act within the strict limits of the *starina* they were instructed to submit to the *Posol'skii prikaz* a final report upon the completion of their mission. This so-called *stateinyi spisok* was compiled by a member of the embassy's staff and authorised by the chief diplomat. It became a standard element of the *posol'skie knigi* from the second half of the sixteenth century. The first embassies to include such reports in their documentation were those of Fedor I. Umnoi-Kolychev to Lithuania and Poland and of Ivan M. Vorontsov to Sweden in the 1560's. In the preceding period, occasional letters had been sent to Moscow to keep the tsar up to date about a diplomat's mission.[69] The *stateinyi spisok* corresponded to the points raised in the *nakaz* and served as the proof of the embassy's strict adherence to its instructions. The diplomats amassed a wide range of information in the *spisok*, as they were ordered to report on everything they did and saw during the course of their stay abroad. Day by day in chronological order, they described the route of the embassy and its reception by foreign monarchs. They took extensive notes on negotiations, collected letters exchanged with foreign courts, reported about major events in international relations, and gathered information about the countries they visited.

It would be misleading, however, to assume that the *spiski* provided sufficient source material for the study of cultural stereotypes or customs of other countries.[70] They were not the Russian equivalent of Western travel accounts or of the 'highly filtered, deeply pondered' Venetian *relazioni*.[71] While a travel account is a composed literary form that often seeks to uncover the mysteries of the 'other' and thereby further exoticises the foreign land, a diplomatic report turns the focus on its author and his doings. The purpose of the *spiski* was exactly that: to provide a comprehensive picture of the diplomats' activities, and not to give a full-blown ethnographic account of foreign and exotic countries.[72] The *spiski* resembled their European counterparts in this respect. French and Austrian diplomatic reports, for instance, brought to the fore the affairs of the diplomats and their treatment by other powers. Even Herberstein's famous tales about his adventures in Russia were not an inherent part of the ongoing

[69] Khoroshkevich, *Rossiia v sisteme mezhdunarodnykh otnoshenii*, p. 14.

[70] Cf. N. M. Rogozhin, 'Mesto Rossii XVI–XVII vekov v Evrope po materialam posol'skikh knig', in *Mesto Rossii v Evrope*, ed. Szvák, pp. 88–96, esp. p. 94; N. M. Rogozhin, 'Obrazovanie i deiatel'nost' Posol'skogo prikaza', in *Rossiiskaia diplomatiia: Istoriia i sovremennost'. Materialy nauchno-prakticheskoi konferentsii, posviashchennoi 450-letiiu sozdaniia Posol'skogo prikaza*, ed. I. S. Ivanov et al. (Moscow, 2001), pp. 51–64, here on p. 60.

[71] G. Benzoni, 'Ranke's favourite source: the relazioni of the Venetian ambassadors', *The Courier*, 22 (1987), 11–26, quotation from p. 23.

[72] Scheidegger, *Perverses Abendland*, pp. 36–38.

diplomatic reporting to the emperor.[73] Similarly, the elaborate *relazioni*, known for their state descriptions and details about other cultures, have been compared to 'historical essays' which lack the immediacy of regular diplomatic correspondence.[74] Thus, one should take care not to confuse diplomatic communication with ethnographic observation or literary synthesis of a diplomat's experience. Historians in search of explanations for cultural misunderstandings will be disappointed when consulting the *stateinye spiski* as well as finding only uninspired and repetitive accounts of diplomatic ceremonies which occupy the greater part of Russian diplomatic correspondence.[75] The 'Muscovites' lack of curiosity about their environment and their marked indifference' is a long-standing image of Russia prior to the reign of Peter I, a theme which is often picked up by scholars.[76] One might assume that Russian diplomats, as opposed to perceptive European travellers, were blind to the life of a foreign people when their only concern was to count the number of steps they took or to note who doffed his hat and when. In reality, their accounts, with their deep apprehension about formalities, corresponded to widespread contemporary conventions of a specific genre, namely that of diplomatic reports, or 'relations' as they were then called.[77]

This is not to say that the Russian form of reporting was not distinct from its Western equivalent. In western Europe diplomats stood in direct contact with their masters during their mission. Herberstein, for instance, wrote a letter to the emperor every second or third day to report on the progress of his mission, sometimes up to three times a day.[78] An established postal system facilitated the exchange of information and enabled sovereigns to intervene in the affairs of their diplomats in good time, although the transmission of a decision or a particular piece of news could extend over days, and in some cases weeks, given the limited speed of communication.[79] A postal office was established in Münster

[73] See B. Picard, *Das Gesandtschaftswesen Ostmitteleuropas in der frühen Neuzeit: Beiträge zur Geschichte der Diplomatie in der ersten Hälfte des sechzehnten Jahrhunderts nach den Aufzeichnungen des Freiherrn Sigmund von Herberstein* (Graz, 1967), pp. 129–46, esp. pp. 144ff., for Austria with ample bibliographical references for other western European countries. Similarly, on the distinction between travel literature and diplomatic reports, see Schnakenbourg, *La France*, p. 463.

[74] Benzoni, 'Relazioni', p. 24, compared a *relazione* with the regular dispatches and missives written by the same ambassador.

[75] See, for example, Scheidegger, *Perverses Abendland*, p. 16.

[76] V. A. Kivelson, *Cartographies of Tsardom: the land and its meanings in seventeenth-century Russia* (Ithaca, NY, 2006), pp. 1f., for a challenging view.

[77] Conrad-Lütt, 'Hochachtung und Mißtrauen', 153.

[78] Picard, *Gesandtschaftswesen*, p. 131.

[79] See, for example, the role of the postal system during the peace negotiations at Münster and Osnabrück: W. Behringer, *Im Zeichen des Merkur: Reichspost und Kommunikationsrevolution in der Frühen Neuzeit* (Göttingen, 2003), pp. 227ff. Thiessen, 'Diplomatie vom type ancien',

at the behest of the Holy Roman Emperor in 1643 to provide services for the diplomats who negotiated the end of the Thirty Years' War. Their dispatches were delivered within five to six days to Dresden and more than four weeks to Madrid.[80] Moreover, a diplomat was expected to report to his sovereign on a regular basis, send letters to his court, and conclude his mission with a final written or oral report.[81]

The long route from Russia to western Europe and the late development of a reliable postal system made the practice of regular correspondence impossible. The late establishment of a foreign post system in Russia in the 1660s was motivated by the desire to obtain foreign news rather than by the practicality of direct diplomatic exchange.[82] Exchanges between the Russian government and its embassies abroad would eventually become part of the postal service, but this was not contemplated in the initial plans. Until a letter from an embassy arrived in Moscow by a courier via Archangel, negotiations might already have been concluded or have taken a different direction due to changing circumstances. Because the *Posol'skii prikaz* had little means of direct influence on an embassy's activities and negotiation, the tsar very much depended on the behaviour of the diplomats. In order that they acted to achieve a predictable outcome without compromising the sovereign status of the Russian ruler, their instructions were refined to the last detail with no tolerance of deviation. This situation ensured a minimal degree of control even if the chancellery could not intervene on the spot. All actions of the diplomat had to be predetermined in order to achieve the desirable outcome of an embassy. Hence, the *nakazy*'s and the *spiski*'s detailedness, their apparent inflexibility and strict formal design.

Upon the completion of their mission, diplomats sent a courier to Moscow via Archangel to provide the tsar with a summary of the results of the negotiations. The courier also reported on the contents of the monarch's letter to the tsar (*otvetnaia gramota*) and gave an approximate date of the embassy's arrival in Moscow. When the diplomats had reached the court of the tsar, the chancellery proceeded to hold oral enquiries (*rasprosnye rechi*) with them and their staff about the behaviour

p. 479, sees these new means of communication as a milestone in the development of early modern diplomacy.

80 F. Dickmann, *Der Westfälische Frieden* (Munster, 1959), p. 192.

81 For the information system in western Europe, see Roosen, *Rise of modern diplomacy*, ch. 6.

82 See Maier, Waugh, 'How well was Muscovy', pp. 31f. For the beginnings of the Russian postal system, see the fundamental study by I. P. Kozlovskii, *Pervye pochty i pervye pochtmeistery v Moskovskom gosudarstve*, 2 vols. (Warsaw, 1913), I, pp. 50ff. See also R. Cvetkovski, *Modernisierung durch Beschleunigung: Raum und Mobilität im Zarenreich* (Frankfurt a. M., 2006), pp. 89–132, for an interesting connection between the establishment of communication routes and the changing perception of time and space in Russia.

of the embassy's members, conflicts among them and details of the negotiations. These enquiries were documented, and they represent the continuation and at the same time the conclusion of the diplomats' *stateinyi spisok.*[83]

The *posol'skie knigi* also documented the stay of a foreign embassy in Moscow, from its arrival at the Russian border to its departure from the tsar's lands. It is safe to say that the collection of information about foreign diplomats in Russia form the mirror image to the *stateinye spiski.* They focus on the same issues that were reported by Russians from abroad and corresponded to the treatment the tsar's diplomats had experienced in other countries. The principle of reciprocity justified the special treatment of foreign diplomats in Russia. The instructions that were given to the *pristavy* about the reception of foreign diplomats were largely rooted in the way Russians were treated abroad and, in turn, drew their basis from the large pool of information gathered in the *spiski.* Thus, detailed descriptions of the defrayment of the costs of foreign representatives, their ceremonial receptions as well as notes and records of negotiations, have survived.

The Sovereign's Breath and Voice: Representation and Diplomatic Ranks

Any form of proxy agency required, as it still does today, an intricate system of mutual recognition. A representative is legitimate as long as he or she appears to represent someone else and as long as this relationship is confirmed by a third party. In order to reach a consensus on this, the negotiating parties have to match their expectations as to what the nature of their status and roles as substitutes are.[84] The study of early modern diplomacy shows that it took a long process until standardised procedures with clearly defined levels of relationships between ruler and diplomats were hammered out.

The key to the acceptance of a ruler's authority and its representation at foreign courts lay in his 'majesty' which, in Jean Bodin's words, stood for the independence of a polity: 'Sovereignty is the absolute and perpetual power of a commonwealth, which the Latins call *maiestas*.'[85] The justification of

[83] Rogozhin, *Obzor*, pp. 14f.

[84] See W. Sofsky, R. Paris, *Figurationen sozialer Macht: Autorität, Stellvertretung, Koalition* (Frankfurt a. M., 1994), pp. 160ff.

[85] J. Bodin, *On sovereignty: four chapters from the six books of the commonwealth*, trans. and ed. J. H. Franklin (Cambridge, 1992), p. 1. The connection between sovereignty and majesty as well as its implications for the ruler/ambassador relationship is excellently treated by A. Krischer, 'Das Gesandtschaftswesen und das vormoderne Völkerrecht', in *Rechtsformen*

Peter I's Law on Succession (*Pravda voli monarshei*, published in 1722) picks up the theme of majesty and superiority. Adducing Grotius' *On the law of war and peace* as the authoritative work on the matter, *Pravda voli monarshei* states that 'among all peoples, Slavic and others, the word *Majestät* or *majesty* is used of the supreme honour; it refers to the supreme authorities alone, and it denotes not only their higher dignity, than which, after God, there is none greater in the world, but also the supreme legislative, judicial and executive power'.[86]

The prince personified this majesty, and the diplomat embodied the prince. As James Howell, in 1664, put it:

> In the present Prince ther is real Majesty, in an Ambassador only a representative; In the Prince ther is the truth of the thing, in an Ambassador the effigies or shadow: Now as the shadow yeelds to the light, so an Ambassador must yeeld to a Prince; For although a Fiction operats as much as the truth of the thing, yet where Truth and Fiction aim at one thing, Truth is Prevalent.[87]

From the Middle Ages through the sixteenth century, the gap that separated 'truth' from 'fiction' was bridged by the assumed identity between monarch and diplomat, sustained by a constructed similarity between the sovereign and the office holder who represented him. Although the diplomat was not put on a par with his master, he had to appear as his coequal, descend from the higher nobility, and exhibit the same social attributes that would allow him to convey the majesty of the monarch.[88] Juan A. de Vera y Figueroa, in the French translation of his *El embaxador* (1620), called the diplomat a holy image, a *Hyerogliphe*, of his master.[89] To put it plainly, André Krischer described this relationship in classic semiotic terminology: the connection between the sovereign and his representative was an iconic one, embedded in the structural similarity between object and sign and manifest in social likeness and like demeanour which ultimately created the illusion of presence.[90] A person

Internationaler Politik. Theorie, Norm und Praxis vom 12. bis 18. Jahrhundert, ed. M. Jucker, M. Kintzinger, R. C. Schwinges (Berlin, 2011), pp. 197–240.

86 A. Lentin, *Peter the Great: his law on the Imperial succession in Russia, 1722. The official commentary (=Pravda voli monarshei vo opredelenii naslednika derzhavy svoei* (The justice of the monarch's right to appoint the heir to his throne) (Oxford, 1996), pp. 186f.

87 Howell, *Discourse*, pp. 187f.

88 Krauske, *Entwickelung*, pp. 220f. See also Krischer, 'Gesandtschaftswesen', p. 209.

89 J. A. de Vera y Figueroa, *Le parfait ambassadeur*, trans. N. Lancelot (Paris, 1642), pp. 14f., as quoted in Krischer, 'Gesandtschaftswesen', p. 209.

90 Ibid. See Charles S. Peirce fundamental definition of the iconic sign: 'An icon is a sign which refers to the Object that it denotes merely by virtue of characters of its own, and which it possesses, just the same, whether any such Object actually exists or not.' C. Hartshorne, P. Weiss, eds., *Collected papers of Charles Sanders Peirce*, 6 vols. (Cambridge, MA, 1974), II, p. 143. The same principle applied to diplomatic administration abroad where 'diplomatic institutions and their personnel formed the organic

negotiating on behalf of a monarch had to 'resemble' him and represent him directly. All diplomats embodied the persona of the prince, irrespective of whether they were called '*legatus, orator, nuntius, ablegatus, commissarius, procurator, mandatarius, agens,* or *ambaxator*'.[91] The various titles did not discriminate between different ranks according to levels of representation: 'for all these several termes do include one Function exercised in divers manners'.[92] If different honours were paid to individual diplomats, then this expressed the greater or lesser respect shown to their masters; it did not distinguish them in their diplomatic rank.[93]

Eventually, the random nature of diplomatic ranks was succeeded and restricted by the trend of making exclusive use of the title 'ambassador' for the diplomats of crowned heads.[94] By the middle of the sixteenth century, the difference between diplomats of two classes – ambassadors fully representing sovereign powers on the one hand, agents and residents on the other – had become fixed. The French diplomat Jean Hotman (1552–1636) explained that 'those are named agents which mannage the affaires of Princes, not soueraigne, and such as are much inferiour to Monarchs and great Common-wealths'.[95] However, this convention added complexity and occasion for dispute. The difficulty of deciding who enjoyed the exclusive right to send the higher rank became increasingly pressing and could lead to awkward solutions. In 1632 the English master of ceremonies, for instance, allowed the Hanseatic representative in England to be called 'ambassador' by his own attendants, but made clear that the court preferred to address him as 'deputy'.[96] Not only was it never really clear what distinguished diplomatic ranks from one another on a formal legal level. The power relations within

counterpart to the central authorities of the early modern government'. See C. Wieland, *Fürsten, Freunde, Diplomaten: die römisch-florentinischen Beziehungen unter Paul V. (1605–1621)* (Cologne, 2004), p. 153f.

91 Krauske, *Entwickelung*, p. 152; Fletcher, *Diplomacy*, p. 4, emphasises the absence of both clearly defined vocabularies and stable categories of diplomatic ranks at the beginning of the early modern period.

92 F. Thynne, *The perfect ambassadour treating of the antiquitie, priveledges, and behaviour of men belonging to that function* (London, 1652) ('Epistle'). See also D. E. Queller, *The office of ambassador in the Middle Ages* (Princeton, NJ, 1967), esp. pp. 25, 225.

93 See Markel, *Rangstufen*, p. 35.

94 This included the Republic of Venice that derived the privilege of sending ambassadors from its possession of the kingdom of Cyprus; see Lünig, *Theatrum Ceremoniale*, I, p. 13. See also Krischer, 'Gesandtschaftswesen', fn. 24.

95 J. Hotman, *The Ambassador* (London, 1603), n.p. 'Ambassador'.

96 Loomie, *Notebooks*, p. 129. The Hanse continued to use the ambassadorial ceremonial to underline its independence through the seventeenth century. See, for example, the report of the Venetian resident in England in 1662: 'Three ambassadors of the Hanse Towns have arrived at Court, made their entry and had their first audiences. At these functions they had a royal coach but did not speak to the king in the great hall, but in another where private audiences used to be given. They come on maritime business and to arrange certain privileges which those towns formerly enjoyed in London. They informed all the

the intricate system of feudal dependencies also raised the question as to whether republics or princes, whose sovereignty was curbed by feudal relations, had the right to employ ambassadors. Emperor Charles V (r. 1519–1556), for example, while travelling through an Italian city, ordered the titles '*ambasciatori*' to be removed from the doors of the houses of the diplomats sent by the dukes of Mantua and Ferrara. Inferiors such as princes without a crown, free cities, or republics could not be represented by an ambassador who ought to personify only the majesty of crowned heads. On the other hand, Charles V mentioned the '*ambassades si solempnelz*' of the German electors and called the couriers of his brother Ferdinand '*Ambassadeurs*' despite the fact that these princes according to feudal law were equally subject to the emperor as were Mantua and Ferrara.[97]

This inconsistent distribution of diplomatic ranks faded away in the course of the seventeenth century, as more and more political entities, whose status had hitherto been unclear, joined the circle of independent powers. Towards the end of the century, Abraham de Wicquefort wrote that 'there is not a more illustrious Mark of Sovereignty than the Right of sending and receiving Embassadors'.[98] While Wicquefort's statement summarised trends and ideas that had been voiced in numerous works since the sixteenth century,[99] it was the Peace of Westphalia's formative impact on diplomatic procedure that put the principle into practice.[100] The negotiations at Münster and Osnabrück brought together a great number of powers in order to end a long and exhausting war.[101] During

foreign ministers of their coming, but no one has called yet. Denmark, Sweden, Brandenburg and others will not see them without express orders from their masters, because they claim the title of Excellency, although these towns were once independent, formidable and united in one body, while now they are disunited and many are subject to other princes. I have not yet called and shall not without the Senate's direction, which I ask.' Giavarina to the Doge and Senate, 1. December 1662, 'Venice: December 1662', in *Calendar of state papers relating to English affairs in the archives of Venice*, vol. 33: 1661–1664 (1932), pp. 216–24, available from www.british-history.ac.uk/report.aspx?compid=90111, last access 6 February 2016.

97 Examples from Krauske, *Entwickelung*, 155f.; Krischer, 'Gesandtschaftswesen', p. 202. For republics, see T. Maissen, *Die Geburt der Republic: Staatsverständnis und Repräsentation in der frühneuzeitlichen Eidgenossenschaft* (Göttingen, 2006), esp. p. 104. See Krischer, 'Reichsstädte', for imperial cities.

98 Wicquefort, *Embassador*, p. 6.

99 See Hampton, *Fictions of embassy*, ch. 5.

100 Dickmann, *Der Westfälische Frieden*, p. 206. This point is elaborated in B. Stollberg-Rilinger, 'Völkerrechtlicher Status und zeremonielle Praxis auf dem Westfälischen Friedenskongreß', in *Rechtsformen internationaler Politik*, ed. Kintzinger, Jucker, Schwinges, pp. 147–64. For the role of the Peace of Westphalia in the *longue durée* of peace treaties, see R. Lesaffer, 'Peace treaties from Lodi to Westphalia', in *Peace treaties*, ed. Lesaffer, pp. 9–44; H. Duchhardt, 'Peace treaties from Westphalia to the revolutionary era', in ibid., pp. 45–58.

101 For a critical assessment of the impact of the Peace of Westphalia, see Black, *History of diplomacy*, pp. 63ff.

the negotiations, that is, face-to-face encounters of rulers in the persons of their diplomats, diplomacy had to undergo the test against the theory of sovereignty and provide answers to the question of who, in practice, was to be recognised as sovereign.[102] In particular, this concerned states and rulers who could lay claim neither to royal nor imperial majesty. In order for these powers to gain the equal rights in negotiations and enjoy the same diplomatic privileges as did the representatives of the established European monarchies, they had to press their claims for ambassadorial titles. 'Every little prince sends ambassadors', mocked La Fontaine in his fable *The frog that wished to be as big as the ox.*[103]

One polity that successfully asserted sovereignty despite the lack of royal majesty was the Dutch Republic. Until the peace congress, Spain had continuously refused to recognise the independence of the United Provinces, but now sought to entice the Dutch away from the alliance system of the French and readily acknowledged the ambassadorial rank of Dutch diplomats. The German electors followed suit and achieved the status of ambassador for their diplomats through the recognition by the Holy Roman Emperor, as did the Italian Princes. How was the status of an ambassador constituted? As a basic rule, legitimacy rested on the recognition by others. To confer one's own diplomat the title ambassador did not suffice. The rank had to be accepted by virtue of public witness, and this was done through the bestowal of ceremonial honours. The address of 'excellency', the privilege of receiving the first visit by other diplomats upon one's arrival at court, and the right to receive the *place d'honneur*, that is, to stand or sit to the right of the host, were the most common signs of honour that distinguished an ambassador from lesser diplomats (envoys, residents, agents, etc.) and thereby created his rank.[104] It is here where the constitutive function of ritual in social and political relationships is most obvious.

Despite the electors' and Italian princes' ceremonial achievements in gaining ambassadorial status at Münster and Osnabrück, the *ius legationis*, that is, the right to send diplomats of the first rank, was still frequently denied in subsequent years to states without a crown and, consequently, received in-depth treatment in the works of Wicquefort, Leibniz, Howell,

[102] Cf. A. Osiander, 'Sovereignty, international relations, and the Westphalian myth', *International Organization*, 55 (2001), 251–87, for a challenging view of the standard interpretation that the peace settled the principle of sovereignty and autonomy of all actors involved. See also D. Croxton, 'The Peace of Westphalia of 1648 and the origins of sovereignty', *International History Review*, 21 (1999), 569–91, for a balanced discussion.

[103] Hampton, *Fictions of embassy*, p. 115.

[104] Dickmann, *Der Westfälische Frieden*, p. 208.

and others.[105] The idea that the honours granted to an ambassador were the marks of distinction reserved for kings remained a predominant feature of a diplomatic culture which was quintessentially the culture of the *société des princes*. The ceremonial that created the rank of an ambassador was also known as the *honores regii*.[106] Each time the electorates of the empire wanted to send ambassadors, they needed to win a ceremonial struggle in order to gain the rights to which they had already been entitled by international law through the treaties of Osnabrück and Münster. For Saxony, Brandenburg, and Hanover this problem only subsided with the adoption of the royal crowns of Poland, Prussia, and Great Britain, respectively, in the years before and after 1700.[107]

Contrary to previous developments, the conflicts over ceremonies and diplomatic ranks ceased, however, to centre exclusively on questions of birth, ancestry, or the personal eminence of the diplomat. At the core of these struggles now lay his legal position within an increasingly standardised system of diplomatic ranks. As an ambassador occupied an official position and the perception of him as the living image of his sovereigns grew obsolete, it could equally also happen that an aristocrat of an inferior diplomatic rank had to yield precedence to a higher-ranking bourgeois ambassador.[108] The diplomat of noble birth remained, of course, the ideal and this explains the dominance of the aristocracy in diplomacy beyond the early modern period. Wicquefort wrote that 'if he derives it [birth] from an illustrious House, or a noble Family, it gives a great Lustre to the Embassy; and if it be accompany'd by natural Parts that set it off, these render the Embassador so much the more proper for this eminent Employ'.[109] But the point is that an ambassador and his master ceased to be connected through a relationship of resemblance. To recognise an ambassador, no longer consisted of the acknowledgement of similarity. Recognition became an act of interpretation. Sovereign and diplomat found themselves in an 'arbitrary' relationship, like the signifier relates to the signified.[110] To invoke semiotic terminology again, their relationship became, in Peirce's terms, 'symbolic': 'A *Symbol* is a sign which refers to the object that it denotes by virtue of law, usually an association of general ideas, which operates to cause the Symbol to be interpreted as referring to that object.'[111] Applied to early modern diplomacy, this

[105] For the debate of the *ius legationis* in diplomatic theory, see Kugeler, 'Theory', pp. 131–33.
[106] Stollberg-Rilinger, 'Honores regii'.
[107] Kugeler, 'Theory', p. 133. See also Stollberg-Rilinger, 'Höfische Öffentlichkeit', esp. pp. 173ff., for Prussia.
[108] Dickmann, *Der Westfälische Frieden*, p. 209.
[109] Wicquefort, *Embassador*, I, p. 47.
[110] Krischer, 'Gesandtschaftswesen', p. 209.
[111] Hartshorne, Weiss, eds., *Collected papers*, II, p. 143.

means that not structural homology but legal construal now authorised a diplomat as a direct representative of his sovereign's majesty. Yet, the law that defined diplomatic ranks did not comprise of a set of acts written down in legal texts. This law manifested itself in a diplomatic performance, a codified system of ceremonial norms.[112] By the eighteenth century, the dissociation of a diplomat's social persona from the office of ambassador was complete:

> In every Country greater honors are bestowed on the office of Ambassador than on any other office. Although a Prince has the power to give this eminent distinction to whomever he wishes, out of concerns for his own grandeur, he bestows it, however, only upon persons of high birth or persons decorated for great services. The very Prince to whom one might send as Ambassador a person of low origin or no renown might see that itself as a lack of respect, which would make the sending less pleasant, although one could not avoid bestowing upon such an Ambassador the same honors that he would receive if he were as well distinguished by birth or service, because these honors are bestowed upon the office and not upon the person.[113]

The rank of an ambassador, then, was a purely symbolic form in that envoys or plenipotentiaries, who did neither represent their sovereign directly nor receive the honours associated with him, could be entrusted with the same professional role and fulfil the same tasks in negotiations.[114] In other words, the logic of mediated presence by virtue of similarity gave way to the legal fiction of 'as if' – as if the sovereign were present in the person of his ambassador – which has provided the basis of diplomatic practice ever since.[115] The ruler/ambassador analogy did not lose its practical meaning, however. During negotiations ambassadors were still 'the emissititious Eyes of a Prince, they [were] his ears and hands, they [were] his very understanding and reason, they [were] his breath and voice'.[116] An ambassador still embodied the persona of his master, but not because he stood in a natural relationship to his master; his role was assigned to him by virtue of the legal doctrine of 'representative character': 'An ambassador is equipped with the *Charactere repraesentatitio* [. . .] which is why he is to be granted as much honour and respect during the entry [into the city], the visits, at the audience, and other occasions as if his high master were present himself.'[117]

[112] Krischer, 'Gesandtschaftswesen', p. 207f.

[113] Pecquet, *Discourse on the art of negotiation*, p. 74.

[114] Stieve, *Hoff-Ceremoniel* (1715), p. 256.

[115] Krischer, 'Gesandtschaftswesen', pp. 208f. For the modern context, see A. Vermeer-Künzli, 'As if: the legal fiction in diplomatic protection', *European Journal of International Law*, 18 (2007), 37–68.

[116] Howell, *Discourse*, p. 182. [117] Lünig, *Theatrum Ceremoniale*, I, p. 368.

By the end of the seventeenth century, the distinction between two orders of diplomatic ranks had become common: the ambassador (*ambassadeur, Botschafter, legatus*) belonged to the first order, the envoy (*envoyé, Abgesandter, ablegatus*) and residents to the second.[118] While these ranks were considered 'public Ministers on the Sovereigns Account that employs [them]' and enjoyed the 'Protection by the *Law of Nations*',[119] diplomats were given ambassadorial status only if they represented abroad in full the ceremonial honours to which their sovereign claimed to be entitled.[120] Only the ambassador, not the envoy or the resident, possessed 'representative character' that conveyed to foreign courts the international standing of his sovereign. Envoys were received with lesser honours; residents could not expect to be treated with any ceremonial, although at some courts they did enjoy equal treatment to envoys. The ambassadors of the Holy See – the nuncios – occupied a special position. While they were given precedence before all other powers at Catholic courts, the Protestants regarded the pope as just another Italian prince and ranked him among the dukes.[121] The list is incomplete. Not only were there further distinctions between diplomats ordinary or extraordinary within the emerging tripartite system. Diplomatic practice also saw the addition of numerous diplomatic titles whose public character remained a moot point or that did not enjoy official status at all. These, in addition to envoys, were often sent to fulfil special functions and circumvent ceremonial struggles since diplomats carrying such titles were devoid of representational qualities. They included agents, consuls, deputies, secretaries, commissioners, plenipotentiaries, and simple ministers, not to mention the various distinctions the Papal court reserved for its representatives abroad.[122]

It is true, the multitude of options available to rulers to appoint their diplomats in various functions complicated, on the face of it, relations

[118] Wicquefort, *Embassador*, I, pp. 33–44, devotes a chapter to the functions of the different ranks and their appropriate treatment. See also F. de Callières, *Art of diplomacy*, trans. from the French (London, 1716, reprint, Leicester, 1983), pp. 101–07; Lünig, *Theatrum Ceremoniale*, I, pp. 368–76; Stieve, *Hoff-Ceremoniel* (1715), pp. 189–263. Cf. Bielfeld, *Institutions politiques*, II, pp. 170f., who speaks of three orders but follows the tripartite distinction of ranks.

[119] Wicquefort, *Embassador*, I, p. 36.

[120] For the diplomatic rank system in general, see D. B. Horn, 'Rank and Emolument in the British Diplomatic Service 1689–1789', *Transactions of the Royal Historical Society, 5th Series*, 9 (1959), 19–49; Roosen, *Rise of modern diplomacy*, pp. 59–64. For the emergence of the system of ranks at the imperial court, see K. Müller, *Das kaiserliche Gesandtschaftswesen im Jahrhundert nach dem Westfälischen Frieden: (1648–1740)* (Bonn, 1976), pp. 116–24.

[121] Lünig, *Theatrum Ceremoniale*, I, pp. 369, 373.

[122] For ministers and plenipotentiaries, for example, see Pecquet, *Discourse on the art of negotiation*, p. 73.

between princes. The fact that diplomatic ranks had to be demarcated by convoluted ceremonial procedures (even the renunciation of ceremonies was a ritual act of indicating the absence of a public character) added yet further symbolic weight to the intricate social structures of court society. However, over time, diplomatic practice generated a rank system with staggered levels of representation that put diplomatic relations on a firm basis of widely recognised legal norms manifesting themselves in ritual performances. The diplomatic ceremonial was a 'symbolic language of the highest precision, political functionality, and legal relevance',[123] a language that condensed the distance between absent rulers in a culture of presence.

What about Russia? Did the Russian court categorise its diplomats in the same way? Russian diplomacy, too, distinguished between a number of different ranks which in the sixteenth century developed into three basic classes, each of which received distinct ceremonies: *posly, poslanniki,* and *gontsy*. Kotoshikhin devoted a chapter 'On Muscovite diplomats (*o moskovskikh poslekh*), who with which rank and honours is sent to neighbouring states as ambassadors (*v poslekh*), envoys (*v poslannikekh*), couriers (*v gontsekh*)'.[124] These titles could be complemented with numerous attributes, specifying the function of a diplomat or the importance of the mission (*polnomochnyi, velikii, bol'shoi, pervonachal'nyi, legkii, narochnyi, skoryi, chrezvychainyi,* etc.). The titles could also be replaced with more generic terms like *poslannyi* or *poslanets* (representative, literally 'he who has been sent').[125]

The various additions and synonyms could cause confusion or were indeed strategically muddled during the negotiation of ceremonies. Aleksei Vasil'ev, who was sent to the imperial court in 1689 asked the chancellor in Vienna that he be given the emperor's written answer to the tsar from his own hands. The emperor had offered this privilege to Russian diplomats of the first and second ranks (*posly* and *poslanniki*) as part of previous ceremonial adjustments in the hope that foreigners in Russia might gain the right to openly practice the Catholic faith in return. The chancellor indicated that Vasil'ev's request was impossible to fulfil since the tsar's letter classified him as *poslannyi*, and such rank was not included in the emperor's offer. Vasil'ev artfully argued his case, shoehorning his own rank into the established twofold division without due authority. He explained that the ranking system actually included four ranks: two distinctions within the first rank (1. *velikie i polnomochnye posly*;

[123] Stollberg-Rilinger, 'Völkerrechtlicher Status', p. 164.
[124] Kotoshikhin, *O Rossii*, pp. 54ff.
[125] For a linguistic analysis of the ranks with ample examples from the *stateinye spiski*, see Sergeev, *Diplomaticheskaia terminologiia*, pp. 56ff.

2. *velikie posly* or simply *posly*) and two within the second rank, that is, *poslanniki* and *poslannye* (the latter being the one to which he was appointed). This construct did not impress the chancellor. He knew that only *posly* and *poslanniki* had been specified when the emperor accepted the change in the ceremonial. On the way to the diplomat's residence, an imperial secretary advised Vasil'ev that he give a few presents to the chancellor and some other court officials in order to advance the matter. After gifts of sable and damask, tea and incense had been distributed, the Russian representative could proudly report back to Moscow that he received the letter from the emperor's own hands.[126] Despite Vasil'ev's contextual adjustments, this example suggests that Russian diplomacy was fully aware of the basic tripartite ranking system, including its symbolic implications.[127]

One might assume, on the face of it, that the similarity of diplomatic ranking reflected Western developments in Russian diplomatic practice. A whole series of arguments supports this impression. First, the conclusions reached in the previous chapter show that Russia was regarded by theorists and legal scholars as a country that competed for ceremonial resources like all other European powers. Second, in practice, too, diplomats of the tsar received the *honores regii* and never faced the need to vindicate the tsar's ducal title (*magnus dux moscoviae*) in view of his sovereignty. Viennese ceremonial recognised the tsar as a Christian prince and put him above the king of France on a par with the king of Spain, as the ceremonial records of the reception of Russian ambassadors at the imperial court in 1679 reveal.[128] The Russian ambassador Petr I. Potemkin may not have been satisfied with the small number of people that gathered on the streets to greet him on his entry into Paris in 1668. But he was assured by his French host that 'we would not carry out the ceremonies in any different fashion than for the ambassadors of the greatest princes of Europe'.[129] Louis XIV, in turn, was not short of

[126] *PDS*, VII, cols. 541–46; N. N. Bantysh-Kamenskii, *Obzor vneshnikh snoshenii Rossii (po 1800 god)*, 4 vols. (Moscow, 1894–1902), I, pp. 30f.

[127] For more examples, see Sergeev, *Diplomaticheskaia terminologiia*, p. 57.

[128] See the section on Peter I's Grand Embassy to Vienna in Chapter 4. The practice of the Viennese court was closely observed by the French court. In regard to the defrayment of a Russian embassy's expenses, the French suggested to follow the example of the Austrians. The French concluded, in 1687, that '*comme les Czars vouloient qu'on les traitant de mesme que le autres Princes Chretiens, sa M.*^{te} *Imp.*^{le} *souhaitoit qu'à l'avenir quand ces Princes envoyeroient une amb.*^{deur} *a Vienne, ce fuit a leurs depens*'. See, AAE, MD Russie, 3 ('Sur le cérémonial observé en France a l'egard des ministres envoyez par le Czars de la grande Russie', September 1716, NS), fol. 125v.

[129] BnF, MS f 10280 ('Journal du sieur de Catheux [...] touchant les Moscouvites arrivez en France en l'annéé 1668'), fol. 6. A similar observation can be found in Brienne's notes, BnF, MS naf 3133, fol. 107, confirming that the French king received the Russian

complaints either: 'His majesty had good reason to be unhappy that he [Potemkin] had been to Spain prior to coming to France because the kings of France had the right of precedence over the kings of Spain.' Potemkin replied wittily that 'he did not do so intentionally; rather, the sea and the winds were responsible'.[130] The Russian 1687 embassy to Paris, led by Prince Iakov F. Dolgorukov, was also received with a ceremonial that displayed all 'honours due to the representatives of crowned heads'.[131] The French court might have followed the example of the lavish reception of a Russian grand embassy to the Holy Roman Empire, led by Boris P. Sheremetev. Sheremetev's public entry into Vienna and his audience with Leopold I had taken place shortly before the arrival of Dolgorukov in Paris, and left long entries in French contemporary periodicals.[132] The 1687 embassy was not completely devoid of ceremonial quarrels, but, as in 1679, the Holy Roman Emperor received the Russians with a ceremonial that was reserved for European monarchs.[133]

diplomat with the same honours with which he also received all other crowned heads. See also the description of Potemkin's audience in the *Gazette de France*, no. 105 (1668), '*de Paris*, 7 September 1668 (NS)', pp. 937f. To be sure, a 1716 memoir reveals that '*on observa a son [Potemkin] egard le ceremonial etabli pour les ambassad.*[rs] *de Princes orientaux*'. But the author of this memoir contradicted himself when acknowledging that later embassies were treated like that of Potemkin and that it was decided (in regard to the defrayment of ambassadors' expenses), '*de ne les traiter que comme ceux des couronnes de l' Europe*'; see AAE, MD, Russie, 3 ('Sur le cérémonial observé en France a l'egard des ministres envoyez par le Czars de la grande Russie', September 1716, NS), fols. 120, 126. Potemkin did not mention his complaint in his *stateinyi spisok*; see D. S. Likhachev, ed., *Puteshestviia russkikh poslov XVI–XVII vv.: stateinye spiski* (Moscow, 1954), pp. 227–315, see pp. 251f., for Potemkin's solemn entry into Paris. The French account can also be found in BnF, MS f 14118, vol. II, fols. 41–75v. See also the copy by the *introducteur des ambassadeurs*, Baron du Breteuil: BA, MS 3859, vol. I, fol. 199. Extracts have been published in E. Galitzin, *La Russie du XVIIe siècle dans ses rapports avec l'Europe occidentale récit du voyage de Pierre Potemkin envoyé en ambassade par le tsar Alexis Mikhailovilch à Philippe IV d'Espagne et à Louis XIV en 1668* (Paris, 1855), pp. 420–33.

130 BnF, MS f 10280 ('Journal du sieur de Catheux [. . .] touchant les Moscouvites arrivez en France en l'annéé 1668'), fols. 1v–2.

131 *SIRIO*, XXXIV, pp. 15–19, here on p. 16. This view was also disseminated in the *Gazette de France*, no. 25 (16 August 1687, NS), pp. 435f. However, Dolgorukov felt himself badly treated by the French (despite being granted these honours) because of issues arising from the incorrect usage of the tsar's title. The ceremonial quarrels eventually led to a disruption of Franco-Russian relations. See C. B. O'Brien, 'Russian envoys at the court of Louis XIV, 1681–1687', *The Historian*, 4 (1941), 34–42.

132 *Mercure historique et politique*, vol. 2 (May 1687, NS), pp. 727–29; *Gazette de France*, no 17 (12 April 1687, NS), 'de Vienne, 23 March 1687 (NS)', pp. 209f.; no. 18 (19 April 1687, NS), 'de Vienne, 30 March 1687 (NS)', pp. 221–23. See also F. Grönebaum, *Frankreich in Ost- und Nordeuropa* (Wiesbaden, 1968), p. 107.

133 For Sheremetev's embassy, see C. Augustynowicz, '"Ablegations-negocien von keiner erhöblichkeit?": Wirken und Wirkung der Moskauer Grossgesandtschaft in Wien 1687', *Mitteilungen des Österreichischen Staatsarchivs*, 50 (2003), 43–63.

Third, Russia arguably was involved in the struggle that led to the Peace of Westphalia, which had such an enormous impact on the development of diplomatic practice. Contemporaries were aware of Russia's participation in the war: 'In these late, bad, and worst of times, where in all the Christian World hath been impbroyl'd with Warre [...] when Nation did rise against Nation, and Realme against Realme; The Swede against the German Emperour, the Pole against the Russian, the Spaniard against the French, the Hollander against the Spaniard, and France in most bloody and cruell Civill Warre with it selfe.'[134] However, despite Russia's involvement in the war, linked through its conflict with Poland-Lithuania over Smolensk in the 1630s and the continual assistance Russia provided to Sweden, the tsar did not send diplomats to Münster or Osnabrück. The Treaty of Osnabrück only mentions the tsar as an ally of Sweden, using the title '*magnus dux Muschoviae*'.[135] The tsar, who received word of the inclusion of his person in the treaty through the *Vesti-Kuranty*,[136] was outraged and complained to the Swedish king about the inferior title. The Swedish monarch replied laconically that his inclusion had only occurred by chance.[137]

Fourth, the treaties of Münster and Osnabrück are commonly accepted to have created a 'legally agreed-upon peace' that laid the foundation of the future European order, although they did not establish a 'fundamental law for Europe'.[138] The fact that there is mention of the Russian ruler in the treaties prompted legal historian Heinhard Steiger to emphasise that 'the Orthodox were also included with the grand prince of Moscow in the IPO [*Instrumentum Pacis Osnabrugensis*] and thereby joined the

[134] *VVee have brought our hogges to a faire market; with some remembrances of the estates and conditions of the Church, King, kingdome, Parliament, Armie, and citie of London. And the one, and onely way to cure all our miseries described* (London, 1648), fol. 2. Russia's role in the Thirty Years' War is usually neglected; see, for example, P. H. Wilson, *Europe's tragedy: a new history of the Thirty Years War* (London, 2010), p. 9. While Russia's involvement should not be exaggerated, Paul Dukes rightly corrects the picture: P. Dukes, 'The Thirty Years' War, the Smolensk War and the modernization of international relations in Europe', in *Modernizing Muscovy*, ed. Kotilaine, Poe, pp. 203–22. For a more detailed account of the relations between Sweden and Russia (that forms the basis of Duke's above article), see B. F. Porshnev, *Muscovy and Sweden in the Thirty Years' War, 1630 1635*, trans. B. Pearce (Cambridge, 1995).

[135] *IPO*, Art. XVII, 11. A full text version of the peace treaties in various European languages is available from www.pax-westphalica.de/, last access 6 February 2016.

[136] Kotkov, ed., *Vesti-Kuranty: 1648–1650 gg.*, p. 63.

[137] Stieve, *Hoff-Ceremoniel* (1715), p. 34.

[138] H. Steiger, 'Concrete peace and general order: the legal meaning of the treaties of 24 October 1648', in *1648: war an peace in Europe. Exhibition catalogue*, ed. H. Schilling, K. Bussmann, 3 vols. (Münster, Osnabrück, 1998), I, pp. 437–45, here on p. 437.

community of international law'.[139] This argument is wholly sustainable, and the facts that Russian diplomacy knew the same division of diplomatic ranks and was an actor on the stage of the European *theatrum praecedentiae* further support the idea of a de facto membership.

There is a caveat, however. Membership in the world of legal norms or the convergence of diplomatic vocabulary did not mean that Russians would always follow the same rules that their Western colleagues had established during the peace congress. André Krischer concluded that international law in the early modern period did not distinguish between diplomatic practice on the one hand and abstract norms sanctioned by positive law, on the other. Legal norms and diplomatic procedure were still inextricably connected; international law emerged from developing practice and not the other way around.[140] Consequently, participation in this process was essential in order for a diplomat to know and act according to gradually standardised rules.

The rank system in Russian diplomacy is a case in point. Russian diplomats were not among the parties that hammered out the doctrine of a 'representative character', its exclusive attribution to ambassadors and its ritual implications. True, *posly* and *poslanniki* received different ceremonial honours; but not, as Pecquet wrote of Western diplomats, 'because these honors are bestowed upon the office'.[141] In Russia, the ceremonial distinctions pointed in another direction. They continued to refer to the social status of individual diplomats, which also reflected the importance of the diplomatic mission as well as the prestige of the sovereign to whom they were sent.[142] Kotoshikhin, who had served as a diplomat at missions led by Ordin-Nashchokin, gave an overview of the practice of sending diplomats of different ranks up to the 1660s. *Posly* were recruited from the upper echelons of Muscovite society. Boiars of different ranks were sent to the English and Polish monarchs. The Swedish king, on the other hand, only received *okol'nichie* of the second rank (*drugoi stat'i rodov kotorye v boiarekh ne byvaet*), as did the Persian shah. *Stol'niki* and *dvoriane* with access to the duma were sent to the Danish king, to the German electors, and to the sultan. No *posly* were sent to the imperial court until 1679 on the grounds that the 'journey is long, [leads] through many different countries, and grand ambassadors will suffer much harm and losses on the way'.[143] This awareness on the part of the Russian government of the need to protect its ambassadors again underlines the high social status these representatives enjoyed. They

[139] Ibid., p. 443. This argument is picked up by Dukes, 'The Thirty Years' War', p. 220. Cf. Wilson, *Europe's tragedy*, p. 672.
[140] Krischer, 'Gesandtschaftswesen', pp. 197–201. [141] See fn. 113.
[142] Grabar, *International law*, pp. 56–59. [143] Kotoshikhin, *O Rossii*, p. 54.

were often confidants of the tsar, with the right to negotiate with foreign powers and propose draft treaties to the sovereign and his government. According to the importance of a diplomatic mission, three or more ambassadors were appointed to the head of a grand embassy (*velikoe posol'stvo*).[144] While all had the same diplomatic title, there was a division of labour among them. Ceremonial duties were reserved to the first ambassador, who was of very high social status. The others contributed the expertise they had gained in previous missions and were charged with specific tasks. The Venetian resident in England reported to the doge about the Russian embassy sent to London in 1662 that 'he [Prince Petr S. Prozorovskii, the first ambassador] is said to be a man of high birth and standing in his own country. [...] There are three of them, and after formalities they say the first is to treat for the resumption of trade, interrupted in the late disturbances, during which the Grand Duke would have nothing to do with the English. The second is to go to Venice and the third to Florence.'[145]

Embassies with lesser status were headed by a *poslannik. Dvoriane* (*srednikh rodov*) were sent as *poslanniki* to the Crimean khan and the Kalmyk ruler. *Poslanniki* that visited Christian states came from the group of honourable *dvoriane* (*dvoriane chestnykh*) or *d'iaki; gontsy* were recruited from *striapchie, d'iaki, zhil'tsy, podiachie*, and *nachal'nye liudi*. The *posly* and the *poslanniki* were accompanied by a predefined number of various distinguished persons as a function of their social prestige (*po chesti ikh*) that ultimately expressed their diplomatic rank (*dlia posol'skoi chesti*).[146] The ranks also found expression in a system of rewards that remunerated diplomats with cash, payment in kind, and the allocation of land before they embarked on their mission as well as with further remuneration afterwards. These rewards were granted independently of the success of an embassy and were measured according to the status of a diplomat.[147]

Throughout their entire stay at a foreign court, diplomats were supplied with food and accommodation by the host. This was unusual in western Europe where the entertainment of a foreign diplomat only extended over the first few days after his arrival.[148] Western courts usually

144 Rogozhin, *U gosudarevykh del byt' ukazano*, pp. 36f.

145 Giavarina to the Doge and Senate, 15 December 1662, 'Venice: December 1662', in *Calendar of state papers relating to English affairs in the archives of Venice*, vol. 33: 1661–1664 (1932), pp. 216–224, available from www.british-history.ac.uk/report.aspx?compid=90111, last access 6 February 2016.

146 Kotoshikhin, *O Rossii*, pp. 54f.

147 Kotoshikhin, *O Rossii*, pp. 60f.; *PSZRI*, II, no. 715 (16 January 1678), p. 149. See also Chistiakova, Rogozhin, '*Oko*', p. 30.

148 Roosen, *Rise of modern diplomacy*, pp. 116f. In England, for example, since the beginning of Charles I's reign, the defrayment of diplomats' expenses was restricted, upon

reciprocated at the request of the Russians, since their diplomats were treated in the same way in Russia.[149] Here too, the Russian government tried to keep costs under control and negotiated fixed sums with the states with whom it exchanged diplomats.[150]

In western Europe only ambassadors '*cum charactere*' conveyed the impression that their principle was present in person, enjoying the prerogatives and privileges due to their master. What stands out in comparison to this principle is that in Russia all representatives – *posly, poslanniki,* and *gontsy* – were endowed with the majesty of the tsar. The Russian distinction of diplomatic ranks did not go hand in hand with a system of graded levels of representation. The idea that a Russian representative stood for his sovereign extended over all ranks, but not in an 'as if' construct that ascribed a specific role and 'representative character' to the appointed person irrespective of his social status. The relationship between tsar and diplomat remained 'iconic', as it were.[151]

All Russian diplomats claimed to embody and demonstrate the sovereign dignity of the tsar, which, in the West, was reserved to those of the first rank. This claim lacked an awareness of both the abstract nature and the practical consequences of the concept of 'representative character'. The ritual implications of this difference led to an innumerable number of awkward ceremonial incidents. For example, in 1687, a *gonets,* who was instructed to announce the arrival of a Russian embassy in France, was turned away from the French court without achieving anything. He had

agreement with other courts, to the first three days after their arrival in order to limit the costs involved. See Rousham, Box 1 ('Concerning the Reception of Ambassadours, Envoyés, etc. in the Court of England', ca. 1672–1674), pp. 1–2.

149 See, for example, Catheux's account of Potemkin's embassy of 1668, BnF, MS f 10280, fol. 1: '*Elle [sa Maté] me commanda [. . .] le [Potemkin] faire defrayer partout par ce que le grand Duc de Moscouvie en use de mesme a l'esgard des ambassadeurs qui arrivent en ses Estats*'. For England, see Charles Cottrell's account of the reception of Petr Ivanovich Potemkin in England in 1681/82, Rousham, MC 6, p. 141: 'All amb[assadors], Envoys, or Messengers from Russia, being on the Kings account; from the time, they come into, his Majestys Kingdom; till their departure.' See also Vasilii T. Postnikov's arrival in England in 1687: Rousham, MC 6, fols. 302ff. Cottrell's accounts are printed in Vinogradoff, 'Russian missions', pp. 54–63, 64ff. The imperial court, however, in 1689, pressed the tsar to advise his diplomats that they live at their own expenses while staying in Vienna 'as it was custom in all Christian states', see *PDS*, VII, col. 540.

150 See the arrangements with the Danish court, *PSZRI*, II, no. 1088 (10 August 1684), pp. 636–38. The Russian government more and more tried to move away from payment in kind and preferred to advance foreign diplomats sums in cash, although the latter could still receive pre-determined amounts of bread, meat, fish, wine, etc. if they so wished. Similar arrangements were made with the Swedes in 1684, in a contract that complemented the Treaty of Cardis (1661), see *PSZRI*, II, no. 1076 (22 May 1684), p. 621. Stieve, *Hoff-Ceremoniel* (1715), pp. 222f., reports that the Russians and the Swedes agreed that their envoys ordinaries and residents had to provide for their own needs while envoys extraordinaries' expenses should be defrayed by the host.

151 See fn. 90.

demanded to be received by the king in person in order to make his announcement. The French tried for two days to convince the courier, who had asked for the privileges of ambassadors and envoys, of the impossibility of his brazen request until they sent him home without knowing why he had been sent.[152] Andrei A. Vinius, a translator of the Dutch language at the *Posol'skii prikaz*,[153] who was sent to the English, French, and Spanish kings in 1672 to ask if they would offer the Polish monarch help against the Turks, complained to the English master of ceremonies about the ceremonial honours he was given during his reception. Vinius came as a *poslannyi* and had no character that would entitle him to higher diplomatic honours.[154] Nevertheless, he demanded that he be conveyed in the king's coach, a privilege that the English had long refused to grant except to ambassadors. Envoys had begun to enjoy it more recently. Vinius, despite the fact that he was regarded as a messenger (or courier) by the English court, threatened that envoys from the English king would not be received in the tsar's coach in the future.[155] In France, on the other hand, Vinius was received as an *envoyé extraordinaire* although his diplomatic rank had not changed since his stay in England, which attests that Russian diplomacy had not yet adapted its rank system to western European practice, and diplomats were able to modify it ad hoc at their leisure.[156]

Language itself could cause problems despite the fact that the threefold ranking system found its equivalent expression in Russian terminology. The ceremonial implication of rank could deliberately be lost in translation if a diplomat decided to equivocate. Petr I. Potemkin exploited this situation by arrogating to himself a higher rank than he was actually given. In 1680–1682 he was sent to France, Spain, and England as an envoy (*poslannik*).[157] Upon his arrival at the court of the English king he informed the master of ceremonies 'that he was [an] Amb[assador], and equall to the greatest, that ever came from Russia, and that he should expect, the Reception of one'.[158] Charles Cottrell contested this claim

[152] *SIRIO*, XXXIV, p. 16.

[153] For Vinius, see K. Boterbloem, *Moderniser of Russia: Andrei Vinius*, 1641–1716 (Basingstoke, 2013), esp. ch. 4, for his diplomatic missions.

[154] See Tsar Aleksei's letter to Louis XIV from 11 October 1672, in *PDS*, IV, col. 806, where Vinius appears as '*poslannyi*'. Rogozhin, *Obzor*, p. 138, calls him *gonets*.

[155] Charles Cottrell had sent the coach of the Lord Chamberlain as he assumed that Vinius should be treated as a messenger rather than an envoy, Rousham, MC 6, p. 92. Cottrell's account is printed in Vinogradoff, 'Russian missions', pp. 52–54. For the privilege of being collected in the king's coach, see Rousham, Box 1 ('Concerning the Reception of Ambassadours, Envoyés, etc. in the Court of England', ca. 1672–1674), p. 2.

[156] BA, MS 3859, vol. I, fol. 267; BnF, MS f 14118, vol. II, fols. 76–77v.

[157] RGADA, f. 93, op. 1 (1680–1682), d. 7.

[158] Rousham, MC 6, p. 140. Cottrell's account is printed in Vinogradoff, 'Russian missions', pp. 54–63.

and pointed to the Latin version of the passport which Potemkin had been given by the tsar. In it, he figured as *ablegatus*, that is, envoy, and Cottrell insisted that his reception would have to be arranged accordingly, with less honours.[159] For Cottrell, Potemkin did not possess 'representative character'. Potemkin replied that he had been received as an ambassador in France and Spain and demanded the same treatment.[160] When Cottrell asked what the words for ambassador and envoy were in his language, Potemkin failed to produce an answer and simply repeated 'that he was equall to, the greatest amb[assador]'.[161] In the list of the embassy suite, that Potemkin had submitted to the court in Russian, his rank is confirmed as *poslannik*.[162] Nevertheless, the master of ceremonies accepted Potemkin's pretended rank under protest and only if the king yielded assent. He said that he would enquire into this matter as soon as he received the credentials and warned Potemkin of the consequences of the arrogation of a false rank. In the end, the Russian received the full ambassadorial honours, although even the credentials clearly qualified the diplomat as an envoy.[163] Potemkin could benefit from the higher rank as it was formerly connected to his personal status: as a lower *stol'nik* he could exploit his diplomatic rank for his own social standing back in Moscow.

For Russian diplomats, one of the key issues, that reflects the pre-Petrine conception of the diplomat-sovereign relationship, was the establishment of direct verbal or ritual communication with the hosting ruler. The *nakaz* prescribed that the first contact, which conveyed the tsar's greetings and requests, was to be established with the receiving monarch himself. Negotiation with his councillors ensued, but only once the presence of the tsar, in the person of his diplomats, was confirmed through the initial direct exchange with the sovereign host. This instruction involved the envoys *dvorianin* Ivan I. Baklanovskii and *d'iak* Ivan Mikhailov in a ceremonial dispute when they arrived in Vienna in 1654. They had been sent to ask for the continuation of the emperor's friendship with the tsar and to call upon him to deny his support to the Poles in the

[159] TNA, SP 91/3, fol. 327: 'Pass for safe conduct of the embassy, issued by the tsar to *Nostros Tzareae majestatis Ablegatos [. . .] Petrum Iwanowiz Potemkin et [. . .] Stephanum Polkoff*, Moscow, 14 September 1680'.

[160] Potemkin did indeed receive the ambassadorial ceremonial in France despite his inferior rank: AN, KK 1426, no. 25 ('Arrivée des ambassadeurs Moscouvites en France'), fol. 555, *passim*. See also *SIRIO*, XXXIV, pp. 1–10, and O'Brien, 'Russian envoys'.

[161] Rousham, MC 6, p. 141; Vinogradoff, 'Russian missions', p. 55. See also Rousham, MC 9 ('Pub[lic] Ministers from Russia 1681'), p. 1.

[162] TNA, SP 91/3, fol. 332 (list of the embassy's suite).

[163] TNA, SP 91/3, fol. 328 (credentials, 14 September 1680).

looming war with Russia.[164] Soon after their arrival at the imperial court, the diplomats were invited to meet the emperor's councillors to submit a letter that explained the nature of their mission. Once the letter had been passed on to the emperor, they would be invited to meet him personally. Baklanovskii and Mikhailov replied that 'we were sent by [...] his tsarist majesty to his brother the great sovereign his imperial majesty and not to his councillors'.[165] The court attempted to persuade the diplomats that their obstinate refusal to comply with the established rule was unreasonable, as all other ambassadors and envoys first presented themselves to court officials before being summoned for an audience with the emperor. 'Ambassadors and envoys of other states are no example for us', answered the Russian diplomats, 'we have orders from his tsarist majesty to see the eyes of his imperial majesty without delay [...] and that he take [the tsar's] letter from us and listen to us in person'.[166] The Russians deemed this initial ritual contact necessary so that the 'brotherly friendship and love deepened and grew' between the tsar and the emperor.[167] This principle applied to Russian diplomats of all ranks. It also explains why *gontsy*, *poslanniki*, and *posly* alike insisted that they receive a written answer addressed to the tsar in the presence of the ruler, which in the West was reserved to ambassadors during their departure audience, for only they represented their sovereigns directly.

In Russia, then, until the end of the seventeenth century, a ruler's authority could not be substituted by an imagined presence or an 'as if' existence as embodied by ambassadors in the West. For Russian diplomats, the idea that any diplomatic representative personified the majesty of the tsar and that diplomatic ranks merely displayed the status of the individual person and the significance of the diplomatic mission, remained consistent for some fifty years after the Peace of Westphalia. The first who realised the significance of the Western ranking system were the diplomats of Peter I. Andrei A. Matveev (1666–1728), the son of the former head of the *Posol'skii prikaz*, was travelling to Paris incognito in 1705 to negotiate a trade agreement with France. He gave an account in his *stateinyi spisok* of 'the ceremonial reception in France and the conduct of ministers of all characters'.[168] Prince Boris I. Kurakin, a key figure in Petrine diplomacy, submitted sixty-seven questions to his superiors in Moscow during the preparation of his diplomatic mission as minister plenipotentiary to London in 1710/11.[169] In his questionnaire he asked,

164 Bantysh-Kamenskii, *Obzor*, I, p. 20. 165 *PDS*, III, cols. 196f. 166 Ibid., col. 198.
167 Ibid.
168 Sharkova, I. S., ed., *Russkii diplomat vo Frantsii (zapiski Andreia Matveeva)* (Leningrad, 1972), pp. 142ff.
169 M. I. Semevskii, ed., *Arkhiv kniazia F. A. Kurakina*, 10 vols. (St Petersburg, 1891–1902), III, pp. 262–75.

for example, whether ministers who bore the title plenipotentiary but were without public character received a public audience. The answer was that one did not receive a public audience without the full character but could expect to be received in a private reception by the monarch.[170] More than a decade later, Kurakin, who had been promoted by Peter I in 1722 to coordinate the affairs of all accredited representatives abroad, wrote to his son Aleksandr B. Kurakin in the same year to advise him on 'how to behave at the French court in respect of ceremonial matters'.[171] His instructions pointed out that in France public ceremonies were only devised for diplomats 'with character', and that he, having been sent as a minister without character, should keep away from such events. His father was concerned that Aleksandr Kurakin would receive a correspondingly low place at such ceremonies, which was incompatible with his status as a 'distinguished person'.[172] On the arrival of foreign ambassadors at Versailles, Kurakin's son was obliged to pay the first visit, granting them the *place d'honneur*. To avoid this humiliation, his father recommended to him to visit the ambassadors when they were not at home.[173]

Differences and Similarities

The evolution of diplomatic ceremonial appears a truly transcultural process. It emerged as a set of shared norms and symbolic rules that translated sovereignty, hierarchy and equality as well as dynastic prestige into the reality of diplomatic face-to-face encounters, gradually aligning early modern polities in a complex precedence system. Different levels of representation made interpersonal contact between rulers possible to the effect that ambassadors carried the greatness of their masters to foreign courts and, with it, their sovereign majesty. It is striking that this political order was formed in constant exchange between members of the *société des princes*, giving rise to a diplomatic culture that also provided a model for the diplomacy of republics or city states. This diplomatic culture did not grow out of a clash of different national diplomacies as the history of individual national diplomatic institutions may suggest; nor was each court's diplomatic ritual the product of domestic ceremonial conventions. The rise of the international order in the early modern period was inextricably interwoven with the development of diplomatic practices

[170] Ibid., III, p. 270. [171] Ibid., III, pp. 78–81. [172] Ibid., III, p. 78.
[173] Ibid., III, p. 79. For further evidence on the changes of diplomatic ranks, see C. Steppan, *Akteure am fremden Hof: Politische Kommunikation und Repräsentation kaiserlicher Gesandter im Jahrzehnt des Wandels am russischen Hof* (1720–1730) (Göttingen, 2015), pp. 155f.

which mediated norms at a transcultural level from where they found their way into international law.[174]

There are in principle obvious similarities in the organisation of diplomatic ceremonial: ritual fulfilled the same functions, necessitated the employment of specialised staff, generated a system of documentation and produced identical diplomatic ranks and titles. It seems as though all diplomatic actors played their role in a single theatrical performance that was staged and reproduced at different places at different times. Yet, the comparison of diplomacy to theatre is distorted. First, there was no single screenplay followed by everyone: conflicts were fought out on stage while every ruler had his own ideas about his position in the plot; second, lifting the curtain of the *theatrum ceremoniale* reveals that the practice of protocol took various forms and influenced the procedure in different directions. Each court had a distinct approach to the organisation of diplomatic ceremonial.[175] Madame de Villars, the wife of a French ambassador in Spain, was irritated by the differences in protocol. She wrote in 1679 that 'there are so many manners and so many ceremonies to observe that he [the ambassador] must teach me about everything, from the least important to the most important things. Nothing here resembles the practice in France.'[176]

The case of Russia, in particular, illuminates the tensions between the outward similarity within the system and the discrepancy in a practical organisation that often led to conflicts between diplomats and foreign courts.[177] Consider, for instance, the administration and recording of ceremonial usage. This mattered because it represented a collection of prestige. It was Russia's (as much as other courts') stock of symbolic capital that served as a reserve of precedents for use against challenges to the honour of the tsar and, with it, the sovereign status of the Russian state. Like other European states, Russia developed a highly functional system to manage and keep track of diplomatic ceremonies. This perspective suggests that Russian diplomacy – despite the '"ceremonious stomacks" of Russian ambassadors' – was not all that different from its Western

174 See also Krischer, 'Gesandtschaftswesen', and Windler, 'Diplomatic history', esp. pp. 83f.

175 This is obvious from the description of individual courts and their ceremonies in Rousset de Missy, *Cérémonial diplomatique*. See also Volker Bauer's ideal-type categorisation of early modern courts: V. Bauer, *Die höfische Gesellschaft in Deutschland von der Mitte des 17. bis zum Ausgang des 18. Jahrhunderts: Versuch einer Typologie* (Tübingen, 1993), pp. 63–66.

176 A. de Courtois, ed., *Lettres de Madame de Villars à Madame de Coulanges (1679–1681), Nouv. éd.* (Paris, 1868), p. 84. English translation from Roosen, 'Ceremonial', p. 465.

177 Cf. T. V. Zonova, 'Komparativnyi analiz stanovleniia rossiiskoi i evropeiskoi professional'noi diplomaticheskoi sluzhby', in *Rossiiskaia diplomatiia*, ed. Ivanov et al., pp. 93–109.

counterpart.[178] In fact, the effort put by Russia into symbolic communication matches that of other European states and demonstrates the tsars' willingness to compete and engage in a constant dialogue with their neighbours. At the same time, Russia remained distinct in that it did not, for example, leave the responsibility of planning and executing ceremonial orders to individual office holders until after the reign of Peter I. At western courts, the organisation of ritual drew on the personal experience of individuals who arranged and administered the reception of foreign ambassadors. The masters of ceremonies, or *introducteurs*, acquired an expertise that endowed them with the authority to negotiate ceremonial conflicts independently and relate their action to domestic precedents, to the practice at foreign courts, and to the emerging literature on the subject. In Russia, it was the *Posol'skii prikaz* that kept a tight grip on the procedure. Its clerks based diplomatic ceremonies on the authority of the *posol'skie knigi* which, in turn, documented the institutional knowledge of Russia's foreign relations over many generations and allowed little deviation from the text. The huge distance between Russia and the countries to which it sent ambassadors resulted in the inflexibility of ceremonial instructions, as direct intervention from Moscow was impossible. This may make the behaviour of diplomats from Moscow appear even more rigid than that of their European peers. The upshot is that conflicts and misunderstandings within a common culture of honour arose from different levels of interconnectedness, different paces of standardisation and varying degrees of adaptation rather than from the inherently ceremonious nature of Russian diplomacy or its cultural-ideological incompatibility.

The ranking system of diplomats is another example of how integrated yet different Russia remained within early modern diplomacy. While the division of three diplomatic ranks can be found in Russian as well as European diplomacy, the resemblance of vocabulary does not reflect synchronic developments. In western Europe, the sovereign–diplomat relationship based on similarity was gradually superseded by standardised ceremonial rules and legal attribution, a process that reached its conclusion by 1648. In Russia the doctrine of representative character did not exist as an abstract concept. The status of all ranks remained directly linked to the honour of the tsar. The threefold ranking was not a system of different degrees of representation that defined the relationship between diplomats and the ruler. Rather, it expressed the social status of the representative and mirrored that of the host. The resulting ceremonial difficulties about ranking and its inherent privileges cannot be explained

[178] John Finet's remark quoted in Anderson, *Modern diplomacy*, p. 61.

by virtue of cultural or ideological differences between Russia and the West. They merely demonstrate that Russia was only beginning to participate fully in the process of standardisation in which increased contact between diplomatic dignitaries after the Peace of Westphalia and the following peace congresses set the agenda for a new era of diplomacy. Neither does this circumstance prove that Russian diplomatic practice was deadlocked in obsolete and non-European customs, while European diplomatic relations were already founded on the pillars of international law. In fact, international law, too, evolved from changing diplomatic customs, their gradual standardisation and formulation into a set of internationally accepted rules. While Russia joined this process early, Russian diplomacy continued to derive its ceremonial knowledge exclusively from the archive accumulated over the centuries by the *Posol'skii prikaz*. It was many years before change and adaptation percolated through the *posol'skie knigi* to actual practice which was always ahead of the scribes' note-taking. Early modern diplomatic ritual embraced ceremonies, legal procedure, various staffs, documentation systems, and numerous levels of representation. The question is not whether these were alike or incompatible but rather how they emerged from and remained a part of a transcultural process of direct interaction.

3 Through the Prism of Ritual

Anglo-Russian Encounters in the Seventeenth Century

Routine

Honour was a coveted symbolic commodity in early modern diplomacy and suffused international relations with conflict and competition. The core idea that rulers and their representatives craved ceremonial prestige as an important public sign of sovereign strength is the leitmotif of this chapter. Before entering the arena of recognition and prestige, it is helpful to imagine the routine of an embassy at the Russian court.[1]

When Moscow received word of an embassy approaching the Russian border, it sent out a *pristav* – usually a *voevoda* from the peripheral towns – to welcome the diplomat and his entourage and accompany them to Moscow. If the diplomats did not travel to Russia over land via Smolensk, then they came by sea via Archangel. In this case, they could not bring their own horses and were provided with a number from the tsar's stables. The *pristav* was in charge of arranging a comfortable and safe journey for the guests, including the provision of accommodation, food, and carriage. He also made sure that the diplomat made no contact with local Russians and foreigners in the towns where he passed. Even in Moscow, personal contact was prohibited until after the first public audience with the tsar. If diplomats complained about the insufficient quantity or the quality of food, the *pristav* had to write a report and provide arrangements to the satisfaction of the guests.

The embassy was led through the country in a multi-day journey to the *podkhozhii stan*, a temporary dwelling place in the north-west of Moscow (*na Khodynke*). There they stopped to negotiate the terms of the ceremonial that would usher them into the tsar's capital. Now, a new, higher-ranking, *pristav* acted as the commissary for all ensuing communications. Sometimes, more than one *pristav* was ordered to accompany an embassy throughout their stay.

[1] The following section is based on Belokurov, *O Posol'skom prikaze*, pp. 76ff. Iuzefovich, *Put' posla*, chs. 3–7. See also Kotoshikhin's description in Kotoshikhin, *O Rossii*, pp. 73-84.

The *pristavy* received instructions prescribing how to behave during the ceremonial, how to treat the diplomats, and what should be said in response to questions that one might expect from foreign diplomats. Everything in the instructions was laid out in minute detail to make sure that the correct procedure was not compromised by possible disputes with the diplomats. When the terms were settled, the embassy formed a lavish train with the diplomats amidst their noblemen and servicemen, proceeding through the Tverskie Vorota Belogo Goroda, further on Tverskaia Ulitsa until the Voskresenskie Vorota Kitai Goroda. Since the reign of Aleksei, the tsar sat in a palace room with a window designed to observe the entry of foreign embassies into Moscow. The Habsburg diplomat Carl V. Wickhart wrote that the *pristav* alerted him to the fact that the tsar had observed his entry from a special lookout.[2] The train went on to Red Square, passed the Kremlin, and turned left onto Il'inka, where the *posol'skii dvor* (ambassadorial court) had been erected in 1634. This route was fixed by a decree in 1636 and remained unchanged throughout the seventeenth century.[3] Until the erection of the ambassadorial court on Il'inka, there were no fixed buildings that served as accommodation for diplomats. Lodgings were available in different parts of town: on Ostozhenka, Prechistenka, Nikitskaia, Tverskaia, Vozdvizhenka, Rozhdestvenka, Dmitrovka, and Petrovka. Embassies from Poland, from the Nogai horde, and from the Crimean khanate had specially assigned accommodation. For others, it could vary.

Horses and carriages were sent to collect the diplomatic dignitaries from their temporary dwelling place outside Moscow, and people of different rank were summoned to attend their reception. The streets were filled with people, so that everything appeared 'populous and graceful'.[4] The diplomats were then brought to their assigned accommodation. The *pristav* reported to a *d'iak* of the ambassadorial chancellery to forward the news to the tsar. The tsar sent out a courtier to enquire with the foreign guests about the health of their master. This greeting

[2] C. V. Wickhart, *Moscowittische Reiss-Beschreibung* (Vienna, c. 1675/6), p. 65.

[3] Iuzefovich, *Put' posla*, p. 94. For contemporary visual impressions of the route, see F. v. Adelung, ed., *Sammlung von Ansichten, Gebräuchen, Bildnissen, Trachten usw. welche der Röm. Kaiserl. Gesandte Augustin Fryherr von Meyerberg auf seiner Reise und während seines Afenthalts in Russland in den Jahren 1661 und 1662 hat entworfen lassen* (St Petersburg, 1827), esp. p. 41 for the *posol'skii dvor*. See also F. v. Adelung, *Augustin Freiherr von Meyerberg und seine Reise nach Russland. Nebst einer von ihm auf dieser Reise veranstalteten Sammlung von Ansichten, Gebräuchen, Bildnissen u.s.w* (St Petersburg, 1827), for detailed descriptions of Meyerberg's illustrations.

[4] See, for example, the instruction to all *stol'niki, strapchie, and zhil'tsy* within 250 verst of Moscow to come to the capital and line up for the entry of Swedish diplomats in 1684, in *PSZRI*, II, no. 1061 (17 February 1684), pp. 575–76. See also *PSZRI*, I, no. 611 (19 November 1675), p. 1014, for the reception of a Dutch ambassador.

concluded the main ritual event before the first public audience with the monarch.

Diplomats were usually put under surveillance by a *strazh*. The *strazh* acted as a guard when the guests left their homes, as well as a kind of police, reporting on the diplomats' actions to the ambassadorial chancellery. Until the public audience, diplomats were not allowed to leave their house. Sometimes, even stricter measures were taken, especially when relations between rulers worsened.

Shortly after their arrival, the diplomats were invited to a public audience with the tsar. The number of days between the solemn entry and the public audience indicated the degree of honour bestowed on the guest. Diplomats were usually permitted two audiences. During the first audience, they presented their credentials to the tsar. The second audience followed the same symbolic pattern, but was adapted to the process of negotiations. The foreign representatives were instructed on how to proceed to the tsar's chambers. They then negotiated their position in the ceremonial, although the protocol left little room to accommodate their wishes. The court sent nobles, horses, and carriages to collect the diplomats and their entourage and brought them to the Kremlin, where they stopped at an assigned place, either before the Cathedral of the Archangel or between that cathedral and the Cathedral of the Annunciation. *Strel'tsy* stood in front of the palace to greet the diplomats. Christian diplomats took the stairs to the parvis of the Cathedral of the Annunciation. Taking this route, they proceeded to the *krasnoe kryl'tso*, a staircase that led the foreign guests into the palace. Diplomats from Muslim states were not allowed to go through the church porch and had to ascend one of the ceremonial staircases directly.[5] Before being admitted to an audience with the tsar, diplomats had to divest themselves of their weapons. On the way to the throne room, where the audience with the tsar was to be held, the diplomats met different persons whose social position depended on the diplomatic rank of the diplomat and the prestige of the monarch he represented. From the beginning of the seventeenth century, the audience took place in the Hall of Facets (*Granovitaia palata*).[6]

[5] Iuzefovich, *Put' posla*, pp. 145f. For the route diplomats took through the Moscow Kremlin, see also J. Hennings, 'Diplomacy, culture and space: the Muscovite court', in *Beyond Scylla and Charybdis. European Courts and Court Residences outside Habsburg and Valois/Bourbon Territories 1500–1700*, ed. B. B. Johannsen, K. A. Ottenheym (Odense, 2015), pp. 56–63.

[6] Iuzefovich, *Put' posla*, p. 154. For the role of the throne room in diplomatic receptions, see Rowland, 'Architecture', esp. pp. 66ff.; D. B. Rowland, 'Two cultures, one throne room: secular courtiers and Orthodox culture in the Golden Hall of the Moscow Kremlin', in *Orthodox Russia: belief and practice under the tsars*, ed. R. Greene, V. Kivelson (University Park, PA, 2003), pp. 33–57.

When a diplomatic dignitary entered the audience chamber, the tsar sat on his throne in the presence of several boiars. The credentials were handed over with varying tokens of deference paid by the diplomat to the tsar. The tsar asked about the health of the foreign representative's master and held out his hand to be kissed, although only diplomats of Christian faith enjoyed the privilege of kissing the tsar's hand. The list of presents was then read out, and the relevant items were placed before the ruler. This first face-to-face encounter between the Russian ruler and the foreign monarch in the person of his diplomat was concluded by a speech of the tsar in which he appointed his councils to prepare the negotiations. A solemn feast followed the public audience to regale the diplomat and his suite.

The preceding account depicts the ideal course of an embassy to the Russian court. Yet, disputes over ceremonies were so prevalent that breaches of protocol became more common than the faultless performance of the routine itself. Diplomatic protocol was a highly contested medium of international status that required strictly prescribed rules precisely because not everyone in the hierarchy was willing to follow them. The conflicts that arose when participants questioned established tradition in light of their political positions or dynastic interests are revelatory in numerous ways. Much can be learned about the purpose of diplomatic rituals, as well as their implications for the relations between polities, by looking closely at the ruptures in customary practice. Therefore, the present chapter concentrates on symbolic clashes that punctuated Anglo-Russian diplomacy in the second half of the seventeenth century.

The Embassies of Dokhturov and Colepeper (1645–1649)

On 6 January 1649, two days after the English House of Commons declared its independence from the king and the Lords, it convened a court and brought Charles I (r. 1625–1649) to trial. Less than four weeks later, on 30 January, King Charles I was led to the scaffold and decapitated at Whitehall. To deny the court its legitimacy, Charles had refused to plead his case against charges of high treason and the 'advancement and upholding of a personal interest of will, power, and pretended prerogative to himself and his family, against the public interest, common right, liberty, justice, and peace of the people of his nation'.[7] The sovereign was deposed and executed in the name of the English people.

[7] Charges against Charles I quoted in M. J. Braddick, *God's fury, England's fire: a new history of the English Civil Wars* (London, 2008), p. 571. For the trial, see C. Holmes, 'The trial and execution of Charles I', *Historical Journal*, 53 (2010), 289–316.

The monarchy was terminated, and England became a de facto republic. The Puritan Richard Baxter expressed what a large part of the ruling elite thought of the event, namely that it was an 'unspeakable Injury of the Christian Name and Protestant cause'.[8]

Most of Europe, Protestant or not, was appalled by the death of the king. Rulers were horror-stricken by the fate of one of their brother fellow monarchs.[9] The French court, itself troubled by the Fronde, recalled its ambassador from London in May and banned trade with England. A declaration was issued in Paris on 2 September 1649, stating that 'by our Royall Proclamation which we have caused to be published in all our Cities and Towns [. . .] We have strictly prohibited all English Wool and woolen Cloth, or any other commodities to be brought into this Kingdome'.[10] The king – 'conceiving [himself] bound both as a Christian and a King, by the bonds of Religion and Nature, and the long continued League between the Kingdomes' – announced to 'revenge the barbarous murder of the late King of *England*'.[11] Only eighteen days later, on 20 September, Tsar Aleksei Mikhailovich followed suit to demonstrate his solidarity with the English monarchy by cutting off commerce with the Commonwealth and expelling all English merchants affiliated with the Muscovy Company from Moscow.[12]

The tsar was fully informed about the Civil War by his *gonets* Gerasim S. Dokhturov, who had been sent in 1645/46 to the court of Charles I to announce Aleksei's accession to the throne.[13] Much to his surprise the emissary learned that the king was absent and could not receive him.

[8] Quoted in K. v. Greyerz, *England im Jahrhundert der Revolutionen 1603–1714* (Stuttgart, 1994), p. 189.

[9] For the individual reactions of European courts, see R. Bonney, 'The European Reaction to the Trial and Execution of Charles I', in *The Regicides and the Execution of the Charles I*, ed. J. Peacey (Basingstoke, 2001), pp. 247–79.

[10] *A declaration of the most Christian King, Lovis the XIIIth. [sic!] King of France and Navarre. Declaring the reasons wherefore his Majesty hath prohibited all trade with England* (London, 1649).

[11] Ibid.

[12] *A declaration, of His Imperiall Majestie, The most High and Mighty Potentate Alexea, Emperor of Russia, and great Duke of Muscovia, &c. Wherein is conteined his Detestation of the Murther of Charles the First, King of Great Britain and Ireland* (n. p., 1650). In the scholarship on the Civil War, the role of the tsar in the royalists' attempts to gain foreign help is usually underappreciated. For a discussion, see G. M. Phipps, 'The Russian embassy to London of 1645–46 and the abrogation of the Muscovy Company's charter', *Slavonic and East European Review*, 68 (1990), 257–76, here on p. 259, fn. 5.

[13] Dokhturov's *stateinyi spisok*, printed in Z. I. Roginskii, *Poezdka gontsa Gerasima Semenovicha Dokhturova v Angliiu v 1645–1646 gg.: iz istorii anglo-russkikh otnoshenii v period angliiskoi revoliutsii XVII veka* (Iaroslavl', 1959), p. 19, qualifies him as *gonets*. For an excellent study of Dokhturov's embassy, see Phipps, 'Russian embassy to London'.

Dokhturov's arrival caused confusion in the House of Lords about 'whether [he should be welcomed] in the Quality of an Ambassador or Messenger, or addressed to the King, Parliament, or both'.[14] The merchants in London were quick to realise the political impact of ceremonies and that their trade privileges in Moscow were under threat if the ceremonial did not meet the diplomat's expectations. The fact that there was no king who could give him an audience was irritating enough. They petitioned Parliament 'that the Reception and Entertainment of this Person (however qualified) may be of great Concernment [...] whereas, on the contrary, if he should apprehend any Disrespect, [...] and make Report thereof to the Emperor his Master at his Return Home, the same may prove of exceeding ill Consequence'. To that end, the merchants insisted that 'although His Majesty our King be absent, yet the Parliament hath had Regard unto the Dignity of his Master, in shewing fitting Respect to him, coming from so great an Emperor'.[15]

Dokhturov, however, refused to be received by Parliament. He had orders to see the king, and no one else. He also declined an invitation to a dinner that the parliamentarians proposed to arrange in his honour. Nevertheless, he agreed to host a reception of the master of ceremonies, Oliver Fleming, and Member of Parliament, the Earl of Stamford ('*boiarin Stanford*'), at his own lodgings, so as to avoid the impression of officially meeting the parliamentarians in lieu of their sovereign. Sitting at Dokhturov's dinner table in late May, Stamford mollified the emissary with the prospect that thousands of English soldiers stood ready for the tsar's command. Although Dokhturov made it clear that his master was not in need of help, and that his *nakaz* did not authorise him to negotiate such terms, the generous offer steered the discussion straight to the ceremonial details for a diplomatic reception. The diplomat was now willing to attend an audience in both chambers of Parliament.[16]

Preparations were made to receive the Russian representative with the distinctions of an ambassador by both Houses of Parliament on 13 June. The House of Commons made sure 'that there be a Chair, with Arms, set upon a Carpet, within this House, to receive him, together with great Cushions, and other sitting Accommodations, for the Reception of an Ambassador from so great a Prince'.[17] As Dokhturov entered Parliament,

[14] *Journal of the House of Lords Volume 7: 11 November 1645*, p. 696, available from www.british-history.ac.uk/report.aspx?compid=33443, last access 6 February 2016.

[15] Ibid. See also Phipps, 'Russian embassy to London', p. 263.

[16] Roginskii, *Poezdka*, pp. 37–41. See also Phipps, 'Russian embassy to London', pp. 266–70.

[17] *Journal of the House of Commons: volume 4: 1644–1646*, p. 574, available from www.british-history.ac.uk/report.aspx?compid=23716, and *Journal of the House of Lords:*

all English 'boiars' doffed their hats. The Speaker of the House of Lords, the Earl of Manchester, stood up from his chair in the middle of the hall, quite near the place where the king used to sit. All other present members followed suit and listened to the diplomat's speech. Dokhturov sat down to the right of the Speaker, who then rose again to give the diplomat a letter addressed to the tsar. The Speaker asked Dokhturov to convey to the tsar all the good wishes of the members of Parliament.[18]

If the presentation of the letter – embedded in an elaborate ritual – was meant to curry favour with the tsar on behalf of English trade, it proved a failure. It identified the Russian merchants as supporters of the parliamentarian forces who were fighting a war against the sovereign to whom the tsar's embassy had initially been sent.[19] All honours granted to the Dokhturov could not prevent Aleksei from calling off a grand embassy, which he had initially planned to send to England around that time.[20] The strategy of using ambassadorial ceremonies for a low-ranking representative was therefore unsuccessful. The lavish ritual arranged by Parliament did not compensate for the absence of the king, and it failed to convince the tsar of the benefits of continued trade relations with England. While the ceremonies did not achieve the desired success, it would be misleading to neglect their functionality in political dialogue and dismiss them as cumbersome details.[21] Why, if not for the tangible commercial benefits, which the English hoped to gain from the good relations between the two courts, did Parliament make such an effort to receive a minor *gonets* with ambassadorial splendour?

In addition to the ill-conceived letter to the tsar, another document worsened Anglo-Russian relations. Dokhturov's diplomatic report was complemented by a *rospis'*, an unofficial account of the embassy's experience in London. In it, Fedor Arkhipov, the *Posol'skii prikaz*'s interpreter, who travelled with the embassy as a secretary and presumably wrote the *stateinyi spisok*, reported about the ignorance of the English regarding religious practices and their acts of iconoclasm.[22] Dokhturov's observations about the Civil War and the desolate state of the monarchy in London must have tapped a raw nerve in the Russian tsar.

volume 8: 1645–1647, p. 369, available from www.british-history.ac.uk/report.aspx?compid=34049, last access 6 February 2016.

[18] Roginskii, *Poezdka*, pp. 41–45. [19] Phipps, 'Russian embassy to London', pp. 266ff.

[20] I. Lubimenko, 'Anglo-Russian relations during the first English revolution', *Transactions of the Royal Historical Society, fourth series*, 11 (1928), 39–59, p. 43.

[21] Cf. ibid., pp. 41f.

[22] Z. I. Roginskii, *London 1645–1646 godov: novye istochniki o poezdke gontsa Gerasima Semenovicha Dokhturova v Angliiu* (Iaroslavl', 1960), pp. 11f.

The early years of Aleksei's reign were rebellious times, a '*buntashnoe vremia*', as Kliuchevskii quotes contemporary sources.[23] The tsar had seen a popular uprising that set Moscow aflame in the year before Charles I's execution.[24] No wonder that Aleksei styled the 'Rebellion of England, as an universall Contagion being become epidemicall, [which] hath poysoned and infected most parts of Christendom'.[25] His decision to expel the English merchants from Russia in 1649 was based on the grounds that the English had 'committed an enormous evil deed' by killing their sovereign.[26]

The symbolism surrounding Aleksei's expulsion of the merchants was significant. Nevertheless, the Civil War was not the main reason for the rupture in commercial ties. Anglo-Russian trade relations had been deteriorating towards the mid-seventeenth century. The fellows of the Muscovy Company had managed to monopolise commerce with Russia on the basis of generous privileges granted to them by Ivan IV in 1555. They included, among others, duty-free trade, tax-free ownership of houses which the English merchants were granted in Moscow, Kholmogory, and Vologda, as well as restricted employment of locals. The foreigners were also promised legal protection in quarrels with Russians, and they were given jurisdiction over English residents.[27] Russia became a major supplier of tar, naval stores, timber, hemp, and rope. It also provided a profitable market for English goods due to high demand for weapons and other military commodities.[28]

The Company flourished in the sixteenth century and managed to renew its privileges several times thereafter. But it soon experienced massive pressure from protests by Russian merchants who perceived the activities of the English as a threat to their own business.[29] In a 1646 petition against foreign trade, Russian merchants argued that the

[23] V. O. Kliuchevskii, *Kurs russkoi istorii*, 9 vols. (Moscow, 1987–1990), III, p. 125.

[24] For the 1648 uprising, see P. Longworth, *Alexis, Tsar of all the Russias* (London, 1984), pp. 38–46.

[25] *Declaration, of His Imperiall Majestie.*

[26] *PSZRI*, I, no. 9 ('O vysylke Anglinskikh kuptsov iz Rossii i o priezde im tokmo k Arkhangel'sku, za mnogie nespravedlivye i vrednye ikh dlia torgovli Rossiiskoi postupki, osobenno zh za uchinennoe v Anglii ubiistvo Korolia Karla I', 1 June 1649), p. 167.

[27] For the initial privileges, see T. S. Willan, *The early history of the Russia Company 1553–1603* (Manchester, 1956), pp. 11ff.

[28] For an introduction to Russian seventeenth-century trade policy, see J. T. Kotilaine, 'Mercantilism in pre-Petrine Russia', in *Modernizing Muscovy*, ed. Kotilaine, Poe, pp. 143–73. See also R. Hellie, *The economy and material culture of Russia, 1600–1725* (Chicago, London, 1999), for Russian seventeenth-century economy.

[29] See M. S. Arel, 'Masters in their own house: the Russian merchant elite and complaints against the English in the first half of the seventeenth century', *Slavonic and East European Review*, 77 (1999), 401–47, for a critical assessment of the existing literature on the Muscovy Company.

privileges enjoyed by the English had been originally granted to their king.[30] They reminded the tsar that now 'all the English traders, are not loyal to Him [Charles I], but have been at war with him for four years'.[31] The situation for foreigners in Moscow grew tense, and anger against advantaged non-Russian merchants fuelled the overall atmosphere of social unrest. Thus, the exemption from paying custom duties was revoked from the English while Dokhturov was preparing to depart from London in June 1646. The tsar rescinded the exemption in order to secure his state revenues from foreign trade and to placate Russian merchants.[32] The execution of the English king served as a convenient pretext to completely scrap the privileges which for almost a century had placed the English in a special position in European trade relations with Moscow.[33] This mixture of general resentment and protectionism led the tsar to expel the English from the Russian capital altogether.[34] Besides murdering their king, the English were accused of failing to reciprocate their privileges by selling poor quality products in Russia and importing forbidden products such as tobacco.[35]

Apart from sending a sign of solidarity to Charles II by expelling from Russia the subjects who had turned against him, Tsar Aleksei went a step further. He proposed, in remarkably concrete terms, a meeting of all European princely powers in order to take action against the rebels under the united forces of what the French king had called the 'League between the Kingdomes':

> Now whereas it is the Office of Princes to execute Justice and Judgement, and to punish Vice and subdue Rebellion; Wee have thought it our Duty both to God and Man, to vindicate the cause of the late Murthered King of *Great Britaine*, and restore his exiled son to the possession of his Thrones, in Triumph and Majesty: And for as much as all Christian Princes are equally concerned in this Cause with Us; Wee have thought good to invite them to a generall Diet; Which wee desire may bee convoked at *Antwerp* [. . .]; where, upon the tenth of Aprill, in the yeare of Grace 1650. Plenepotentiaries may meet from all Emperours, Kings, and Princes that prosesse Christianity; where a generall and holy League being coucluded, and

30 For Russian merchants in the seventeenth century, see P. Bushkovitch, *The merchants of Moscow, 1580–1650* (Cambridge, 1980).

31 Quoted in Kotilaine, *Russia's foreign trade*, p. 106.

32 Phipps, 'Russian embassy to London', p. 272.

33 A useful survey is, Kotilaine, *Russia's foreign trade*, pp. 93–123.

34 See S. H. Baron, 'Die Ursprünge der *Nemeckaja Sloboda*', in *Deutsche und Deutschland*, ed. D. Herrmann, pp. 217–37, for a description of the situation of and hostilities against foreigners in mid-seventeenth-century Russia.

35 See *Declaration, of His Imperiall Majestie*. For the failed English attempt to establish the trade of tobacco in Russia, see M. P. Romaniello, 'Through the filter of tobacco: the limits of global trade in the early modern world', *Comparative Studies in Society and History*, 49 (2007), 914–37.

all ancient and private Quarrels lay'd aside, Wee may all agree to fight under one Banner; that there a set Modell may bee concluded on and drawn up, wherein every Prince shall beare a proportionable share, in raysing and maintaining a great numerous Army, in which the whole Forces of Christendom shall bee united in prosecution of this second holy Warre, wherewith wee will Invade that Kingdome both by Sea and Land.[36]

The tsar 'was pleased of [his] owne Royall benignity' and promised to raise 10,000 soldiers on horse and foot, as well as an artillery and all necessary equipment, paid out of his treasury.[37]

This declaration coincided with the dispatch of John Colepeper (1600–1660), Charles II's envoy, to Tsar Aleksei. Colepeper was sent to inform the tsar about the rebellion in England and to ask for financial assistance. Charles II had also sent a representative to Spain in order to raise money for the royal cause. While the Earl of Clarendon's efforts to obtain aid from the Spanish (beyond the moral support of Phillip IV) were futile,[38] Colepeper, on his mission to Moscow, successfully negotiated a loan of 20,000 roubles in grain and furs.[39]

His embassy consisted of a comparatively modest group of eighteen people and had little to offer the tsar.[40] Colepeper apologised to the tsar that he was not in the position to bring any presents from his master.[41] Instead, in order to solicit a loan of one hundred thousand roubles, he presented to Aleksei a letter in which Charles II appeals to the tsar's sympathy about the 'grief and evil business and murder' that his subjects had brought upon his father.[42]

Like Dokhturov's *stateinyi spisok*, Colepeper's report detailed the ceremonies of his reception at great length. He did not do this in order to complain about the curiousness or incongruity of the procedure but to record the honour he reaped from the Russian ceremonial. The recognition of his master's legitimate authority was crucial for the English

[36] *Declaration, of His Imperiall Majestie.* [37] Ibid.

[38] See P. Seaward, 'Hyde, Edward, first earl of Clarendon (1609–1674)', in *Oxford Dictionary of National Biography* (Oxford, online edn., 2008), available from www.oxforddnb.com/view/article/14328, last access 6 February 2016.

[39] For Colepeper's career, see D. L. Smith, 'Colepeper, John, first Baron Colepeper (bap. 1600, d. 1660)', in *Oxford Dictionary of National Biography* (online edn., 2005). Available from www.oxforddnb.com/view/article/5876, last access 6 February 2016.

[40] See RGADA, f. 35, op. 1, d. 176, ll. 40ff., for a list of food provided to the members of the embassy. Ibid., l. 2, mentions a group of twenty-seven people.

[41] 'The relation of the Lord Culpepers reception at the emperiall Cittie of Mosco, and his Lopps quitting thereof, Anno Domini 1650', in *Correspondence of Sir Edward Nicholas, Secreatary of State*, ed. G. F. Warner, 4 vols. (London, 1886), I, pp. 182–85, here on p. 183.

[42] RGADA, f. 35, op. 2, d. 83, for the English letter, dated 16 September 1649, and RGADA, f. 35, op. 1, d. 187, l. 82, for the quote from the Russian translation.

representative: he represented a power whose people had just ousted the king and abolished the monarchy. Therefore, the most important information conveyed in his account was that the tsar rose from his throne and doffed his hat to ask about the health of Charles II. This particular movement of the tsar, performed at the public audience, had been an essential element of recognising the *honores regii* of a foreign power, and its standing in the international hierarchy, at the Russian court.[43] This token of honour was only given to crowned heads, as Kotoshikhin also noted.[44] (Besides recounting that crucial gesture, Colepeper also detailed the daily share of one sheep, a quarter of beef, four hens, a side of bacon, wood, water, bread, beer, vodka, and honey ['though not of the best'] and the sables that he had received as gifts from the tsar.)[45]

The Commonwealth's Embassy to Russia (1655)

Asking about the English king's health and the tsar's standing up posture signalled Moscow's awareness of the competing claims to sovereignty over the English state then asserted by the parliamentarians and Charles II. The Russian court faced a dilemma. On the one hand, it could not ignore the Republican regime; on the other, it supported royalist efforts to regain power.[46] In order to communicate its recognition of the royal prince's claim to the throne while at the same time acknowledging the new English government, it deployed finely tuned gestures.

Oliver Cromwell's first embassy to Russia, sent in 1654/55 to restore the trade privileges at the behest of English merchants, was treated quite differently when compared with the envoy of Charles II.[47] At first glance, however, it may seem difficult to discern the disparity, as all the weight of the political message was captured in a punctilio.

William Prideaux was chosen as Parliament's representative to Russia. His task was to convince Aleksei about the legitimacy of the new government and to revive the trade relations with the

[43] See Iuzefovich, 'Russkii posol'skii obychai xvi veka', p. 121.

[44] Kotoshikhin, *O Rossii*, p. 76.

[45] 'Relation of the Lord Culpepers reception', pp. 183, 185. For the defrayment of the diplomat's expenses, compare the list of food and drinks detailed in the *posol'skaia kniga*, see RGADA, f. 35, op. 1, d. 186, ll. 20ff., 40ff.

[46] Lubimenko, 'Anglo-Russian relations', pp. 53f.

[47] For the new government's awareness of the importance of trade with Russia, see Ibid., p. 49. A second embassy, headed by Richard Bradshaw, was dispatched to Russia in 1657, but it was denied entry into the tsar's realm. For the two embassies, see C. I. Arkhangel'skii, 'Diplomaticheskie agenty Kromvelia v peregovorakh s Moskvoi', *Istoricheskie Zapiski*, 5 (1939), 118–40.

Commonwealth.[48] The first thing he learned from his *pristav* upon his arrival in Moscow was that he could not be received, as he wrote back to England, 'in the same manner as ministers from kings and great princes, in the quality I ame sent from his highness, lord protector, to the emperor'.[49]

In his report to the secretary of state John Thurloe, Prideaux recounted his first reception on 16 February 1655 in great detail. He described the throne that was 'sayed to be of silver gilt with gold, handsomely wrought and adorned with pretious stones', mentioned the tsar's 'vest of cloth of gold with long hanging sleeves, and lyned with sables', his 'capp of purple velvet, lyned with sables, and imbroidered with pearle'. However, his report less described the Russian court and its splendour than it actually pointed to the activities of the diplomat and his ability to gain honour and respect through the grandeur which was put on display by his host. Most importantly, Prideaux hid a crucial detail from his superiors in London, namely that the tsar did not stand up while he asked about the health of 'Oliver Utaditela (that is the sole commander or sole director)'.[50] Instead, the tsar addressed the question to the diplomat while moving his body only slightly on the throne (*nemnogo pripodyvsia*). This gesture was a clear sign that the Russian court was prepared to accept the head of the Commonwealth as the representative of a minor (if not temporary) power, but not as the legitimate authority of the English state. Prideaux was granted the right to negotiate through acknowledgement of his credentials, but the legitimacy of his master was contested through ritual degradation. The scribes in the *Posol'skii prikaz* made sure that the tsar's indication about the lack of sovereign majesty found an entry in the records.[51]

Prideaux realised the impact of this gesture. In a meeting with the head of the ambassadorial chancellery, Almaz I. Ivanov, he entered a series of complaints, or 'an advertisement to his Lordship, to be humbly represented to his imperial majesty', pressing for the appropriate honours to be granted, in particular that the tsar should stand while pronouncing the name of the Lord Protector.[52] He argued that despite the reforms of government, England 'hath not for that diminished any thinge of it's

[48] For Prideaux, see T. Venning, 'Prideaux, William (1604/5–1660)', in *Oxford Dictionary of National Biography* (Oxford, online edn., 2008). Available from www.oxforddnb.com/view/article/66273, last access 6 February 2016.

[49] Prideaux to Thurloe, 24 February 1655, printed in *A collection of the state papers of John Thurloe, volume 3: December 1654– August 1655*, p. 173. Available from www.british-history.ac.uk/report.aspx?compid=55367#s14, last access 6 February 2016.

[50] Ibid., p. 174. [51] RGADA, f. 35, op. 1, d. 183, ll. 32–33.

[52] The conversation between Ivanov and Prideaux is recorded in RGADA, f. 35, op.1, d. 183, ll. 61ff. For Ivanov, see Rogozhin, *U gosudarevykh del byt' ukazano*, pp. 139–56.

greatness and condition, but is rather augmented, if the just conquest and addition of countrys be an augmentation to a state in several wayes'.[53] European courts like that of France, Portugal, Spain, as well as the Republic of Venice had allegedly shown their respect to Cromwell as they had done to previous kings. The Swedish court, according to Prideaux, had received an English representative with full honours in 1654. Prideaux shrewdly referred to the practice of European states, hoping that the tsar, who counted himself a member of the Christian *société des princes*, would follow suit. What he did not mention was that the Commonwealth's ambassador at Stockholm, Bulstrode Whitlocke, faced serious ceremonial difficulties. The Swedish master of ceremonies told him that the representative of Denmark insisted on his right to take precedence over England because he was sent by an anointed king 'and you are only ambassador to the protector, a new name, and not sacrée'.[54] Cromwell had no place in the system of honours and norms that constituted monarchical society, and the Russian court was well aware of this fact.

Prideaux, therefore, miscalculated his tactics. The *Posol'skii prikaz* was not impressed by his examples and continued to refuse him the royal honours which were so important for the acknowledgement of the sovereignty of the state that he represented. He was told that other courts' practices were no example to the tsar. The diplomat was rebuked for having brought this up, as 'it would not become him to raise such matters'.[55] The position that 'the behaviour of diplomats from other states are no example to us' is a typical reaction to ceremonial dispute among members of the *société des princes*. There are numerous examples of this phrase in the Russian documentation of diplomatic protocol.[56] It has been suggested that this attitude exposed the characteristics of the early modern Russian court, namely an insistence on its own ceremonial forms.[57] A further interpretation construes the tsars' tenacious grip on ceremony as a failure to adapt to foreign practice, and a tendency to isolate itself through obsolete tradition. What is more, this approach is taken as proof of the Russian

The quotation is from Prideaux to Thurloe, 24 February 1655, printed in *A collection of the state papers of John Thurloe, volume 3: December 1654–August 1655*, p. 256.

53 Ibid.

54 See B. Whitlocke, *A journal of the Swedish ambassy, in the years M.DC.LIII. and M.DC. LIV. from the Commonwealth of England, Scotland, and Ireland*, 2 vols. (London, 1772), II, pp. 47ff., for an interesting conversation between the English diplomat and the Swedish master of ceremonies. Quotation on p. 48. Cf. Anderson, *Modern diplomacy*, p. 60.

55 RGADA, f. 35, op. 1, d. 183, l. 62ob.

56 The quoted example is from 1654 when Russian diplomats announced Aleksei's accession to the throne and the beginning of the war against Poland to the emperor in Vienna, see *PDS*, III, col. 198.

57 See, for example, Cf. Iuzefovich, '*Kak v posol'skikh obychaiakh vedetsia*', p. 9.

ceremonial *Sonderweg* (and its implication for Russia's place in the world more generally), its uniqueness which separated Russian diplomacy from developments in Western Europe: Europe scoffed at the 'small-minded stubbornness of Muscovite diplomats'.[58]

While it is true that some monarchs considered the ceremonies of other courts in crafting their own practices, it would be misleading to construe Russia's diplomatic practice as *sui generis*.[59] The Russian court cannot be said to have exhibited an ambition to distinguish itself from Europe with practices that befitted its national character or cultural identity. Rather than being a conscious reference to cultural heritage, the defence of familiar norms and local practice emerged from the logic of ceremony itself. If status was at stake, the court relied on the precedents it knew and the documentation it drew from its own archives. Ancient letters and ceremonial records in the archive seemed to be much more reliable witnesses to the established norms than the rumours of a diplomat advancing unjustified claims to honour and prestige. The imperial court at Vienna deployed the same argument in 1698, when Russian diplomats asked for a modification of the ceremonial procedure, emphasising that their request was common practice in all Christian states. In response, the imperial court implied that the customs of other states were no example for Leopold I, for he was the only emperor on earth, and lived by the rules of ancient establishment.[60] An argument along these lines was also made by the father of international law, Hugo Grotius. Grotius had been appointed to an ambassadorial post in Paris, in the service of Sweden's Queen Christina (r. 1632–1654). At the public entry of the Dutch ambassador into the town in 1637, Grotius sought to take a place ahead of the coaches of the two attending English ambassadors, as he was defending the pre-eminence of Sweden. In response to Grotius' attempt at placing the Swedish over the English crown, the ambassadors argued that the Swedes should, following the precedent of Norway and Denmark, yield precedence to England. In reply, Grotius made it clear that the examples of their Scandinavian neighbours did not mean anything to the Swedes.[61]

[58] For example, G. N. Peskova, '"Zamysly nashi, mozhet byt', velikie …": K 300-letiiu Velikogo posol'stva Petra I', *Mezhdunarodnaia Zhizn'*, 11–12 (1997), 140–49. Available from www.idd.mid.ru/letopis_dip_sluzhby_05.html, last access 6 February 2016. Similar already, Veselovskii, 'Tatarskoe vliianie'.

[59] An important Soviet survey of international diplomacy, for example, uses the above quotation to show that the Russian court developed a distinctly 'Russian' ceremonial to set itself apart from Byzantine and eastern traditions, and, having adopted western elements, overgrew it with Asian customs: Potemkin et al., eds., *Istoriia diplomatii*, I, p. 304. This interpretation is largely adopted by Peskova, 'Zamysly nashi'.

[60] *PDS*, VIII, col. 1380.

[61] K. Colegrove, 'Diplomatic procedure preliminary to the congress of Westphalia', *American Journal of International Law*, 13 (1919), 450–82, here on p. 461. For English

This example epitomises the common weapon of citing other courts' behaviour in ceremonial struggles. The reaction that that weapon provoked was often strong enough to mute an opponent's arguments to disapprove of foreign examples if they contradicted one's own dynastic interests.

Therefore, the Russian court's response to Prideaux' foreign examples did not exhibit a typical Russian stiffness and cultural self-centredness. It was the politically equivocal status of his master in the social hierarchy that made any attempt to press for royal honours ineffective. The Russian court knew this very well. Nevertheless, strikingly, the English diplomat recounted the episode as if he had won a ceremonial dispute.[62] He reported back to London that when he took leave of the tsar, the latter 'putt his hands on his lyps, and moved a little up from his throne, and said unto me, that I should remember him to *Vladitela* (Cromwell), to whom he wished good health'. The republican envoy also pointed out that the present boiars were standing, doffing their hats as a sign of respect. He hastened to add that this 'ceremony would not have beene done, had I not used to the chancellor the discource above mentioned touching this matter'.[63] His principle task as a diplomat was to uphold the sovereignty of his master, hence his concern for ceremony and recognition.

The tsar's body movement ('moved a little up from his throne') may seem politically insignificant. However, Aleksei's gesture signified that the Russian court denied Cromwell the royal or sovereign honours. In order for the envoy to be recognised as a representative of the English state, as had previously been done, the tsar would have had to stand and hold his body in a particular position while pronouncing the name of the Lord Protector. The *Posol'skii prikaz* had a clear understanding of the different implications of sitting (*sidia*), rising just a little (*pripodniavsia* or *pripodyvsia*), and standing (*vstav*).[64] These were gestures of legal import and not performances of diplomatic niceties. As Stieve explained in his *Europäisches Hof=Ceremoniel*, such elements of diplomatic procedure

precedence claims, see C. Kampmann, 'Die Balance of Europe und die Präzedenz der Englischen Krone: zur Rechtgertigung Englischer Gleichgewichtspolitik im 17. Jahrhundert', in *Imperium, Empire, Reich: ein Konzept politischer Herrschaft im deutsch-britischen Vergleich = An Anglo-German comparison of a concept of rule*, ed. F. Bosbach, H. Hiery, C. Kampmann (Munich, 1999), pp. 69–90.

[62] Apparently not without success; see, for example, Venning's account of the episode: Venning, 'Prideaux, William (1604/5–1660)'.

[63] Prideaux to Thurloe, 24 February 1655, printed in *A collection of the state papers of John Thurloe, volume 3: December 1654–August 1655*, p. 257.

[64] See 'Vypiska ob obriadakh, kotorye byli nabliudaemy Rossiiskimi Gosudariami na audientsiiakh, pri voproshenii Poslov, Poslannikov i gontsev Evropeiskikh i Aziiatskikh Dvorov o zdorov'e ikh Vladetelei – Pisana 1676 goda', printed in *Sobranie gosudarstvennykh gramot i dogovorov*, IV, pp. 342–43. See also Iuzefovich, *Put' posla*, p. 183.

were understood to be an expression of legal recognition.[65] Official diplomatic relations could only be successfully established if the ritual of the reception was congruent with the claims to recognition on both sides. A misalignment of expectations and rituals could derail ambassadorial missions. More often than not, ambassadors cut short their mission and returned home empty-handed if disputes over ceremonies indicated that they were going to be received with a ritual that did not match their expectations of social, and by implication political, respect.

Timothy Hampton has argued that 'to receive an embassy or have an embassy received by someone else is to be "recognized," to be acknowledged as a legitimate political agent. In fact, the two terms, "receive" and "recognize" are used interchangeably in discussions of the right of legation'.[66] Without doubt, the relationship between a public performance and its legal response was a prerequisite for physical manifestations of the abstract concept of sovereignty. Yet, Prideaux's public audiences demonstrate that 'reception' did not invariably translate into 'recognition'. Prideaux was officially received as a representative of a foreign government while recognition of this government's legitimacy was held in limbo through the denial of full ceremonial honours. International law and its symbolic manifestations accommodated such contradictions. The Commonwealth's embassy to Russia shows the subtlety and significance of early modern diplomatic ritual. Its elasticity allowed rulers to tolerate irreversible realities, while at the same time protesting against them by denying, if necessary, the legitimacy of unwarranted legal assertions.[67]

Prozorovskii's Embassy (1662/63)

Anglo-Russian relations were reset after the Restoration of the English monarchy and showed promise of recovering from the drawbacks they had suffered during the Commonwealth period. Still, the old contention about trade privileges persisted and imbued diplomatic relations with mutual distrust. The embassies exchanged between the courts of Charles II and Aleksei in the 1660s reflect this development and demonstrate to what extent ceremonies could affect the course of negotiations.

[65] Stieve, *Hoff-Ceremoniel* (1715), pp. 2ff. [66] Hampton, *Fictions of embassy*, p. 119.

[67] Barbara Stollberg-Rilinger has shown with the example of the Holy Roman Empire that this ritual-based elasticity was a basic feature of early modern politics, exhibiting a high degree of functionality in dealing with conflicting assertions of rights and entitlements. Rival legal claims coexisted and were frequently reinforced at the level of ritual: 'The result was a largely disconnected existence alongside actual practice on the one hand, and a multitude of competing counterfactual claims on the other.' See Stollberg-Rilinger, *Old clothes*, pp. 57–62, quotation on p. 62.

Protocol and politics were inseparable. While at the beginning ceremonial honours seemed to facilitate the resumption of monarchical friendship and mutual political goals, they soon became vehicles for expressing divergent interests. The English diplomats and the representatives of the tsar provoked each other, as they pitted the honour of the king against that of the tsar. Paradoxically, no side wished to raise the status of their master above that of the other. Both adhered to the principle of reciprocity and were prepared to afford as much splendour for their diplomatic guests as could be demanded. A series of miscommunications, unfortunate coincidences, and organisational inconsistencies triggered disagreements about the meaning of symbols, gestures, and titles, as well as their political consequences. This had the effect that diplomatic ceremonial entered the sphere of political negotiation and gained as much attention as trade privileges, for which the English had initially dispatched an embassy to Moscow.

The tsar learned about Charles II's accession to the throne from the Englishman John Hebdon. Hebdon had served as a translator for the English living in Moscow. In 1660, he was sent to various Western courts to represent the tsar's interests as a diplomatic resident, although he carried no official credentials with him.[68] Upon his arrival in England, the king had already returned to power. Hebdon promised that the tsar 'will send His Ambassador (according to the Custome of Nations) to Congratulate and give a further testimony of His Imperiall Majesties affection'. At the same time, he informed the monarch about Russia's state of affairs, in particular about the war against Poland-Lithuania. He then asked for permission to levy 3,000 English soldiers and officers to assist the tsar's troops, reminding Charles II of the support he had received from Russia during the Civil War.[69] The king granted the request and gave Hebdon a cordial letter to the tsar, in which he announced the restoration of the monarchy, expressed gratitude for Aleksei's support, and asked for the reestablishment of trade privileges. The tsar reciprocated with a letter proposing an exchange of ambassadors on that very issue.[70]

As Hebdon had indicated, a congratulatory embassy was soon sent to London. On 20 February 1662, the tsar gave orders to three distinguished

[68] TNA, SP 91/3 ('Translation of Russian Safe conduct for John Hebdon', 31 July 1660), fol. 80. For Hebdon's diplomatic rank, cf. Dukes, Herd, Kotilaine, *Stuarts and Romanovs*, p. 100.

[69] 'TNA, SP 91/3 ('Hebdon's remonstrance to Charles II', 15 March 1661), fols. 77–79v, quotation on fol. 77.

[70] Charles II to Aleksei, 10 May 1661, TNA, SP 91/3, fols. 85–88; Aleksei to Charles II, 28 July 1661, TNA, SP 102/49, fol. 39. See Dukes, Herd, Kotilaine, *Stuarts and Romanovs*, pp. 99ff., for Anglo-Russian relations at the beginning of the Restoration.

persons to prepare themselves for leading the ambassadorial mission.[71] Three *posly, stol'nik* Prince Petr S. Prozorovskii, *dvorianin* Ivan A. Zheliabuzhskii, and *d'iak* Ivan S. Davydov were appointed to the head of the embassy. The main goal of the mission was to re-establish the ancient friendship between the tsar and the English monarch interrupted by the Civil War.[72]

Although all three diplomats were named *posly* in the *posol'skaia kniga*, it was Prince Prozorovskii who took charge as the representational head of the mission. His responsibility was to deliver the tsar's congratulations to the king. In addition, the ambassadors had to gather information about one Frederick Albertus, an imposter who claimed to be the tsarevich of Belorussia and was supposed to reside in London at that time. In a secret instruction, the second ambassador, Zheliabuzhskii, was charged with the task of negotiating the repayment of the loan which Aleksei had advanced to Charles II in 1650. Given that the tsar had helped the English king when he was in need, he hoped that he would now receive a loan in return, on top of the repayment, and left it to Zheliabuzhskii to solicit a credit from the English court. The money would later be repaid with commodities such as hemp or potash. Furthermore, Zheliabuzhskii was instructed to take out a loan from the merchants in London.[73] Davydov fulfilled secretarial functions.[74]

The ambassadors were accompanied by a large retinue, as was customary for a Russian grand embassy (*velikoe posol'stvo*).[75] Many noblemen and servants, soldiers, translators, and a priest accompanied the ambassadors. The *stateinyi spisok* also lists a number of living animals, for example falcons, hawks, pelicans, martens, and Persian horses. The birds and mammals were given to the English king as presents, complementing gifts of sable, velvet, carpets, and 150 tonnes of hemp to facilitate trade and diplomatic relations.[76]

[71] RGADA, f. 35, op. 1, d. 8, l. 3.

[72] See *nakaz*, RGADA, f. 35, op. 1, d. 8, ll. 17ff. The Russian nineteenth-century historian A. Lodyzhenskii provided a short overview of the 1662 embassy, emphasising the congratulatory aspect of the mission that had little or no real political or economic implications: A. Lodyzhenskii, *Posol'stvo v Angliiu kniazia Prozorovskago, dvorianina Zheliabuzhkago i d'iaka Davydova v 1662 godu: istoricheskii ocherk po dokumentam Moskovskago Glavnago Arkhiva Ministerstva Inostrannykh del* (St Petersburg, 1880), p. 5. Similar on the distinction between diplomatic politeness, monarchical amity on the one side and political or economic business on the other, S. Konovalov, 'England and Russia: Three Embassies, 1662–1665', *Oxford Slavonic Papers*, 10 (1962), 60–104, pp. 60–63.

[73] Lodyzhenskii, *Posol'stvo*, pp. 5f. [74] Ibid., p. 12.

[75] RGADA, f. 35, op.1, d. 8, ll. 3ob ff., 96ob–98, 320ob–321. Lodyzhenskii, *Posol'stvo*, p. 13, counts up to hundred persons.

[76] RGADA, f. 35, op. 1, d. 8, ll. 93ob ff. The hemp was kept in Archangel to be picked up by the English, ibid., l. 96, and RGADA, f. 35, op. 1, d. 192, l. 287. See also, Lünig, *Theatrum Ceremoniale*, I, pp. 622–23; Rousset de Missy, *Cérémonial diplomatique*, II,

The embassy was set to make a magnificent entry into London. It sailed from Riga via the Baltic Sea and arrived in Gravesend on the south bank of the Thames, a few miles from London. After John Hebdon had announced the embassy to the king, the English master of ceremonies, Charles Cottrell, visited the ambassadors to discuss the ceremonial of their procession through London.[77] The Russians appeared to be demanding. For example, they requested that their suite should be permitted to ride on horseback from the Tower Wharf to their residence in London, so that the gifts could be presented to the onlooking crowds while the embassy proceeded through the town. Cottrell accepted the ambassadors' demands. But he reminded them that the exceptional alterations of the proposed ceremonial were only made because of the king's particular friendship with and love for the tsar.[78] Lavishly decorated barges collected the embassy from its temporary dwelling on the south bank of the Thames on 27 November 1662. The first ambassador, Prince Prozorovskii, had fallen ill so that he could not participate in the solemn entry and was directly brought to the ambassadors' residence. A few miles from London, Zheliabuzhskii and Davydov changed to another vessel on which they were greeted by a noble in the name of the king. The embassy continued its journey on the Thames. Cannon shots were fired from other ships to honour the ambassadors, and people watching the procession welcomed them with loud shouts.[79]

On landing at the wharf, the diplomats were welcomed by a group of distinguished persons sent to convey the king's 'love and friendship' to the tsar. The author of the *stateinyi spisok* noted that the ambassadors were told by their hosts that no diplomat of any other foreign monarch had yet received such an honourable reception.[80] The ambassadors entered the king's coaches together with Baron William Crofts, a gentleman of the bedchamber ('boiarin Wiliiam Crafts'), who was sent to accompany the ambassadors to their residence. The train then proceeded through London, from the Tower to their official residence at York House in the Strand, accompanied by the Russian suite on horseback, the king's horse

pp. 502f. For a detailed analysis of these gifts, see J. Hennings, 'The failed gift: ceremony and gift-giving in Anglo-Russian relations (1662–1664)', in *International Diplomacy. Volume I: Institutions*, ed. I. Neumann, H. Leira (London, 2013), pp. 91–110.

77 Hebdon initially refused to offer his service to the ambassadors because they failed to produce a letter from the tsar that asked for his assistance. He did, however, concede to inform the king about their arrival when the ambassadors promised Hebdon to request a reward for him from the tsar. Lodyzhenskii, *Posol'stvo*, pp. 16f.

78 RGADA, f. 35, op. 1, d. 8, ll. 168ob ff. See also Lodyzhenskii, *Posol'stvo.*, pp. 17f.

79 RGADA, f. 35, op. 1, d. 8, l. 186–86ob. For a full account of the solemn entry, see ibid., ll. 175ob ff.

80 RGADA, f. 35, op. 1, d. 8, l. 188ob.

guards, trumpeters, many citizens, and the merchants of London, blending the embassy into the symbolic fabric of crown and city.[81] York House was situated across the palace of the Queen mother. According to the *stateinyi spisok*, the king and his wife had come there to watch the ambassadors' arrival.[82] Andrei N. Lodyzhenskii, who studied the embassy, remarks that the author of the *stateinyi spisok* noted the presence of the king 'with obvious satisfaction'.[83] Although there is no evidence for such an assessment by the diplomats about their treatment, it is clear that the presence of the king was viewed as a special honour, not least because back home in Moscow Tsar Aleksei also observed the spectacle of incoming embassies from a special lookout.

Reading between the Gestures I: Aleksei Mikhailovich vs. Louis XIV

The Russian embassy of 1662/63 must have left an impression not only on the ambassadors but also on the crowds who witnessed the ceremonies. Individual observers commented on the scene and offered their interpretation of the ceremonial and its message. Their observations largely match the accounts of the *stateinyi spisok*.[84] The diarist John Evelyn, for example, noted that the king gave orders to receive the embassy 'with much state' because the tsar had supported his cause during the Civil War and banished all trade with the king's enemies. Evelyn described the event as follows:

> The City Companies & Traind bands were all in their stations, his Majesties Army & Guards in greate order: his Excellency came in a very rich Coach, with some of his chiefe attendants; many of the rest on horse back, which being clad in their Vests, after the Eastern manner, rich furrs, Caps, & carrying the present, rendred a very exotic and magnificent shew: Some carrying Haukes, furrs, Teeth, Bows &c.[85]

The naval official and future Member of Parliament Samuel Pepys also observed the scene. It is interesting to note that he, as a member of the political establishment, described the entry as a regular diplomatic event but at the same time made a mocking remark about the common people who attended the ceremonies in the streets: 'But Lord, to see the absurd nature of Englishmen, that cannot forbear laughing and

[81] See L. Manley, *Literature and culture in early modern London* (Cambridge, 1995), pp. 212–93, for London as a ceremonial space.

[82] RGADA, f. 35, op. 1, d. 8, l. 191. [83] Lodyzhenskii, *Posol'stvo*, p. 18.

[84] See Konovalov, 'England and Russia', pp. 60–63, for English accounts. Konovalov did not have access to the *stateinyi spisok*.

[85] E. S. de Beer, ed., *The diary of John Evelyn*, 6 vols. (Oxford, 1955), III, pp. 344f.

jeering at everything that looks strange.'[86] For him, the solemn entry was a necessary and common element of diplomatic procedure:

> We [. . .] went to the next house upon Tower Hill to see the coming by of the Russia Embasador – for whose reception all the City trained=bands do attend in the streets, and the King's Life-guard, and most of the wealthy citizens in their black velvet coats and gold chains (which remain of their gallantry at the King's coming in); but they stayed so long that we went down again home to dinner. And after I had dined, I heard that they were coming, and so I walked to the Conduict in the *quarrefour* at the end of gracious-street and cornhill; and there (the spouts thereof running, very near me, upon all the people that were under it) I saw them pretty well go by. I could not see the Embassador in his coach – but his attendants in their habitts and fur-caps very handsome comely men, and most of them with Hawkes upon their fists to present to the King.[87]

The observation of ambassadors and their ceremonial treatment was central to the tasks of foreign representatives. A diplomat had to be able to read between the gestures to elicit the meaning of specific ceremonies. The slightest deviation from the protocol could have serious consequences. If an irregularity was suspected, it had to be placed in a wider diplomatic context. All occurrences contrary to custom were scrutinised to determine whether they posed a threat to the honour of one's own master and potentially constituted a precedent to be followed upon by others.

Diplomats residing at the English court struggled to make sense of the solemn entry of the Russian embassy. The interpretation of the reception proved to be a difficult task, as there were some contradictions in the arrangement of the solemn entry. On the one hand, the Venetian resident reported what the English had told the Russian ambassadors, namely that their procession included extraordinary honours that no other monarch had hitherto received. On the other, he noted that the diplomats were fetched by a baron who was lower in rank than an English earl who usually attended the reception of ambassadors.[88] He made it clear, however, that the special treatment was only a reciprocal reaction to the treatment of English representatives in Moscow. This remark pre-empted further speculation about the implications which any additional, or lesser, honour granted to the tsar might have had for the status of other European rulers:

[86] R. Latham, W. Matthews, eds., *The diary of Samuel Pepys: a new and complete transcription*, 11 vols. (London, 1970–1983), III, p. 268.

[87] Ibid., III, pp. 267f.

[88] Cf. Rousham, Box 1 ('Concerning the Reception of Ambassadours, Envoyés etc. in the Court of England', ca. 1672–1674), fol. 4.

Yesterday the Muscovite ambassadors made their public entry with great pomp, their followers carrying a number of falcons to present to the king. Other animals for the same purpose have not yet been seen and will not be shown before the day of audience. Besides the royal coach they only had a baron for this function, but the streets were lined with troops from the Tower, where they landed, to the other end of the city, where they lodge, and they were preceded by a troop of the king's horse guards and his Majesty's trumpets, an honour not shown to any other foreign minister and shown because it was used by the Muscovite with the ambassadors of this nation.[89]

The *Mercurius publicus* published a short account of the public audience in January 1663, including a long list of presents brought to the king by 165 people.[90] The ambassador delivered the credentials and gave a very long speech – so long that the king, who had initially risen from his throne, decided to sit whilst Prozorovskii finished his monologue. The ambassador interrupted his speech and prompted Charles II to rise: it behoved the king to listen to the words of the tsar (in the person of his ambassador) standing, out of the brotherly love the two rulers felt for one another, recognising each other's sovereign status.[91]

Other observers perceived the audience as 'very handsome'[92] and confirmed that the procession was held with 'extraordinary State'.[93] Again, the Venetian resident had a different impression. He pointed to the fact that, although the ambassadors were received with 'great outward formalities', they 'were only introduced by Sir Cotterel, master of the ceremonies, and the earl of Loderdale, whose title is Scotch and who is only considered in England as a baron. They [the ambassadors] learned this afterwards and complained, saying that their master, one of the first monarchs in the world, has been treated worse than his peers'.[94]

[89] Giavarina to the Doge and Senate, 8 December 1662, printed in 'Venice: December 1662', in *Calendar of State Papers Relating to English Affairs in the Archives of Venice, Volume 33: 1661*–1664 (1932), pp. 216–24. Available from www.british-history.ac.uk/report.aspx?compid=90111, last access 6 February 2016.

[90] *Mercurius publicus: comprising the sum of forraign intelligence; with the affairs now in agitation in England, Scotland, and Ireland*, vol. 1, 1 January 1663, pp. 1–4. See also the descriptions in, Lünig, *Theatrum Ceremoniale*, I, p. 622; Rousset de Missy, *Cérémonial diplomatique*, II, pp. 502f.

[91] The audience had been delayed for several weeks because of Prozorovskii's illness. For the procession, see RGADA, f. 35, op.1, d. 8, ll. 224ff.

[92] Latham, Matthews, eds., *Diary of Samuel Pepys*, III, p. 297.

[93] De Beer, ed., *Diary of John Evelyn*, p. 349. See also A. Keay, *The magnificent monarch: Charles II and the ceremonies of power* (London, 2008), p. 254, fn. 52.

[94] Giavarina to the Doge and Senate, 19 January 1663, printed in 'Venice: December 1662', in *Calendar of State Papers Relating to English Affairs in the Archives of Venice, Volume 33: 1661*–1664 (1932), pp. 225–28. Available from www.british-history.ac.uk/report.aspx?compid=90112, last access 6 February 2016.

Despite this setback, the Russians had managed to wrestle additional honours from the English court to enhance the prestige of the tsar. While Prince Prozorovskii was still ill, Charles Cottrell visited the ambassadors several times to ask about the tsar's health and to negotiate the ceremonial of the imminent visit to the king.[95] The Russians demanded that the royal coach carry them all the way to the Banqueting House where the audience was to be held. That honour was not extended to any other monarch, since ambassadors usually descended from the coach and continued on foot before being admitted into Whitehall.[96]

The Russian representatives also asked for permission to remain uncovered before the king because the tsar required foreign ambassadors to doff their hat when being admitted to his chambers.[97] The headgear was a central element in the communication between rulers through their ambassadors: 'Doffing the hat and exposing the head is a sign of submission.'[98] Why did the ambassadors insist on leaving their head uncovered before the king? The latter even protested against this ceremony.[99] One answer is that the diplomats simply followed their instructions of the *Posol'skii prikaz*, without considering the implications of that gesture. Another, more probable, explanation is that the Russians feared that if they put on their hat before the king, as he demanded, then the English could lay claim to the same privilege when they visited the tsar in Moscow, which in the tsar's eyes could be perceived as a humiliation. The latter interpretation about how the Russians were received by Charles II was advanced by the French ambassador, the comte de Cominges. For Cominges, the case was not quite so clear as for the Venetian resident. The pomp of the Russian ambassadors' public audience with the king raised his suspicion. Although direct diplomatic exchanges between Moscow and Paris had been rare, there had been earlier concerns at the French court about the rank of the king vis-à-vis the Russian monarch.[100] A late fifteenth-century precedent had been

[95] RGADA, f. 35, op.1, d. 8, ll. 193ff. [96] Ibid., ll. 196ob ff., 207ob–209.

[97] Ibid., ll. 212ob ff.

[98] *Philosophia Elegantiarum & Ceremoniarum Aulicarum* (Frankfurt a. M., 1689), p. 1, as quoted in Krischer, *Reichsstädte*, p. 62. See also P. J. Corfield, 'Ehrerbietung und Dissens in der Kleidung. Zum Wandel der Bedeutung des Hutes und des Hutziehens', in *Zum Wandel von Zeremoniell und Gesellschaftsritualen in der Zeit der Aufklärung*, ed. K. Gerteis (Hamburg, 1992), pp. 5–19.

[99] *Mercurius publicus*, p. 2 (as in fn. 566): 'The Earl of Lauderdale and Sir Charles Cottrel Master of the Ceremonies conducted the Ambassadors to his Majesty in the Banqueting-house, where they delivered their Credential Letters under their Masters Seal (which all the way were exposed to the view of the people) and past the rest of their Adress all the while uncovered, though his Majesty spake to forbear that Ceremony.'

[100] Cf. Schaub, 'Diplomates russes et français', for Franco-Russian relations and the French perception of Russian diplomacy in the seventeenth century.

recorded to prove that King Charles VIII's ambassador took precedence over Grand Duke Ivan III's representatives during the marriage ceremony of King (and later Emperor) Maximilian I and Bianca Maria Sforza in the Cathedral of Milan in November 1493.[101]

Cominges, who stayed in London incognito at the time of the arrival of the Russian embassy, awaited his own solemn entry into the town. Having witnessed the procession of the Russians, as well as their public audience, he now feared that he would not be able to compete with the splendour of the tsar's representatives. He wondered if he should make the same request regarding ceremonies to stand on the same footing with his colleagues from Moscow.[102]

Cominges had good reason to worry about his presentation to the English king and its political consequences. He followed the comte d'Estrades into office, whose struggle for precedence over the Spanish ambassador, in 1661, had resulted in bloodshed and commotion in the princely world.[103] In order to avoid such disorder at his court in the future, Charles II forbade other diplomats to be present at the receptions of newly arrived ambassadors.[104]

As such, Cominges had no reason to fear jeopardising the international prestige of his master, since no diplomat from other courts was present at the reception of the Russian embassy to challenge his place in the hierarchy. Cominges nevertheless saw himself in an awkward position. After his predecessor had embarrassed himself before the Spaniard, Louis XIV now faced the competition with the Russian tsar if the splendour of

[101] AN, KK 1438, fols. 24–25v. The diplomats of Ivan III abstained from the ceremonies on the grounds that they were denied the first place in the ambassadors' seating plan in the Cathedral. Nevertheless, Beatrice d'Este, the wife of the duke of Milan, wrote to her sister in the usual formulaic style of reporting ceremonial events that 'the Ambassador of Russia, who was numbered amongst them, declared that he had never witnessed such an extraordinary display of pomp. The Nuncio of his Holiness the Pope said the same thing, as well as the Ambassador of France, who declared that, although he had been present at the Coronations of the Pope and of his own King and Queen, he had never seen anything more splendid'. See Robert de La Sizeranne, *Beatrice d'Este and Her Court*, trans. N. Fleming (London, 1924), p. 212. Ivan III was highly engaged in pursuing dynastic prestige in the 1490's. He adopted imperial insignia in diplomatic exchanges with Maximilian I and sent ambassadors to Italy for his plans of restructering the Kremlin palace. See also Alef, 'Adoption'. For the architectural pursuits of the Russian 1493 embassy to Milan, see E. Welch, 'Between Italy and Moscow: cultural crossroads and cultural exchange', in *Cultural exchange in early modern Europe, Volume IV: forging European identities 1400-1700*, ed. H. Roodenburg (Cambridge, 2007), pp. 59–99, here on pp. 88ff.

[102] J. J. Jusserand, *A French ambassador at the court of Charles the Second: le comte de Cominges* (London, 1892), pp. 66ff. See also Konovalov, 'England and Russia', p. 61.

[103] See Introduction, fn. 80.

[104] Rousham, MC Box 1 ('An act of State by his Majesty in Councell', 2 October 1661 and 6 February 1662).

Cominges' reception did not equal that of the Russians. He wrote to the secretary of state for foreign affairs in Paris:

> You will know, sir, that an entree on an unparalleled scale was arranged for him [the Russian ambassador(s)]; all the merchants were under arms; the aldermen, who are what we call échevins, went to pay him a visit and congratulate him upon his coming; the King defrays all his expenses and provides him with lodgings. After a month's stay he had today his audience, when fifteen or sixteen foot soldiers were under arms. [. . .] His coach was admitted into Whitehall, contrary to custom. He did not, it is true, cover himself when talking to the King of Great Britain; but as for me, and whatever the English may say, I do believe that it is not so much out of respect for his Majesty as out of pride; for they hope by this means to prevent the English Ambassador from covering himself when addressing the Muscovite Prince. All I think we can reasonably pretend to is admittance for our coach into Whitehall; for the additional pomp displayed in the entree into town had no cause but the interests of the London merchants who trade with Muscovy, and in consideration of which they treated him to such a fanfare.[105]

Cominges saw two reasons as to why the Russians seemed to have outperformed other ambassadors in gaining symbolic capital from the English court. First, although standing uncovered before the king initially resulted in a diminution of prestige, that gesture preserved the status of the tsar who could, in turn, demand the same from an English ambassador visiting his court. Second, he related the unexpected honours, bestowed on the Russians, to the English court's ambition of restoring the trade privileges in Russia. The king was willing to grant ceremonial prestige and send a sign of symbolic generosity in order to help the merchants. Cominges' account makes clear how ceremonies became the focus of speculation. The ritual not only revealed reciprocal honour relations between the courts (and their implications for one's own position) but also gave an impression about the state of political affairs which were wedded to the ceremonial representation of the negotiating parties.

No threat to the status of Louis XIV could thus be inferred from Cominges' comments. On the contrary, if the additional honours were a product of Russian-English business relations, or emerged from the logic of reciprocity practiced between London and Moscow, then the increased prestige of the tsar did not affect the French king's rank. Nevertheless, Cominges took this issue very seriously. He even pondered on whether he should make his solemn entry at all, given the

[105] Cominges to Lionne, 8 January 1663 (NS), as quoted in English translation in Jusserand, *French ambassador*, p. 67. See p. 194, for excerpts in French.

head start in prestige the Russian embassy had gained as they progressed through London.[106]

The matter was so important that Louis XIV took it into his own hands. The king wrote a long letter to Cominges, deliberating the hat questions and the honours that Cominges would have to grant to the Russian ambassadors during the customary visit. His comments show that there was no straightforward rule by which the ambassador could act. The king relied on the confidence he placed in his representative to take the right decision on the ground. Rather than assessing the problem from afar and giving orders, he encouraged the diplomat to follow his advice but to act on his own, carefully balanced judgement. Louis XIV's reasoning demonstrates how pressing decisions on ceremony were made by aligning a diplomat's actions with the ongoing practice in other places. The king compared various precedents and practices in Copenhagen, Moscow, Münster, Frankfurt, and London in order to help Cominges assess the situation regarding the status of the tsar. He concluded that, however favourable the treatment of the Russians was in London, to avoid a solemn entry all together would come at the expense of losing his ability to state his precedence over other rulers, in particular over the Spanish king.[107] The upshot is that diplomatic ritual was not a static system of norms. Rather, the protocol underwent a constant process of negotiation, which produced the norms to which diplomats had to mould their behaviour.

Cominges had to face the Russian competition so that Louis XIV would not lose this important instrument of power. The presence of the Russian embassy and Louis XIV's insistence on his ambassador's full participation in the merry-go-round of international prestige forced Cominges to arrange his diplomatic reception in an equally elaborate ritual. In letters to Lionne, he described his solemn entry and public audience. He duly reported that a big crowd watched his procession on his way to the king's palace, when 'I was led to Whitehall, the Guards being drawn in a line, with the drums beating, and the cavalry sounding their trumpets. I went on, still seated in the King's coach, by which doing I received the same honour as was allowed to the Muscovites'. The French proudly adopted Russian practice. Downplaying the issue, Cominges hastened to add that 'the thing, besides, is considered as of little import in this Court'.[108] However, the tsar's place in the ceremonial pecking order could not be neglected and was sufficiently important to be

[106] Ibid., p. 67.

[107] Louis XIV to Cominges, 21 January 1663 (NS), AAE, CP Angleterre, 78, fols. 16–18v. My thanks to Niels May for sending me a copy of the manuscript. An incomplete excerpt from this letter can be found in Jusserand, *French ambassador*, pp. 194–96.

[108] Cominges to Lionne, 19 April 1663 (NS), quoted in English translation in ibid., p. 74.

discussed in great detail with the king. Cominges' report was received with great satisfaction in Paris, but the French king realised 'that the people who flocked there [to the ceremonies] in such large numbers were drawn more by curiosity than by love'.[109] It appears that curiosity was a common motivation among the onlookers, who were drawn to the public site of glory to witness the assertion of royal rank.

Curiosity, then, was a common element accompanying the spectacle of a diplomatic entry, be it the 'strangeness' of the Russian embassy, which, according to Pepys, was noted by the English, or the lavish train of a French ambassador. Here, the categories of perception – strangeness, barbarism, or curiosity – are blurred and cannot readily be presented as specific to Russian diplomacy's ostentation and exoticism: they appear to be much more general. Cominges himself was amazed by the poor quality of coaches of the Spanish or Danish diplomats. He mocked a Tuscan representative who 'looks quite abashed, being entirely unused to the part he has to play. [...] Never was seen on the back of a merchant, of the Rue aux Fers, on his marriage day, a coat of such glowing and puffing-out stuff, with his ill-drawn woollen hose, a large flat collar, and huge white feathers'.[110] Cominges also felt a sort of estrangement at the English court. He was disgusted by the 'gross and barbarous incivility' of his English hosts who, after inviting him to dinner at the Lord Mayor's house, had started to dine before the appointed hour, eating from dishes made of wood, and without napkins.[111]

The French diplomat and author Jean J. Jusserand, who published extracts of Cominges' correspondence in the late nineteenth century, made an interesting remark about the ambassador's concerns regarding court etiquette: 'The stiffness of the rules, and the importance of the smallest items, seem at the present day very strange, people being no longer accustomed to such a tone of deep seriousness in matters of this sort, except in dispatches referring to imperial courts in Asia.'[112] Jusserand's marvelling at Cominges' actions is a striking example of how nineteenth-century scholarship viewed diplomatic ceremonies and influenced later attitudes about issues of precedence. Jusserand's perspective also gives a hint as to why Russian early modern diplomatic practice has often been associated with 'Asian' practices. What Jusserand's comment actually demonstrates is how foreign (or 'Asian') early modern Europe had become to him. Cominges' anxiety about his ceremonial position relative to that of the Russian ambassadors reveals the extent to which Russia had been an integral part of the diplomatic

[109] Louis XIV to Cominges, 29 April 1663 (NS), quoted in English translation, in ibid., p. 75.
[110] Cominges to Lionne, 6 October 1663 (NS), quoted in ibid., p. 76.
[111] Quoted in ibid. [112] Ibid., p. 66.

culture of the old regime precedence system, a culture which did not exhibit 'Asian' features but rather shaped the relations between Europe's dynastic courts.

Carlisle's Embassy (1663/64)

From the English perspective, the effort expended on receiving the 1662 embassy from Russia did not lead to success in negotiating the trade privileges. A written exchange ensued between the court and the embassy. The English were keen to know why their merchants were expelled from Moscow, why their houses and properties were confiscated, and whether the former trading rights could be restored. The ambassadors assured the court that the decision to ban the merchants, who sided with the rebels, was made out of the tsar's love and friendship for the king. However, they said that their *nakaz* did not vest them with the authority to negotiate trade privileges. The court informed the ambassadors that Charles II planned to send an embassy to the tsar to resume negotiations on this issue. The king returned the loan received from the tsar soon after his father's death.[113] Yet he refused to return the favour and did not advance credit to the tsar. According to the court, the sum Zheliabuzhskii requested was too high; the king's treasury did not find itself in the position to extend such a loan even to his brother, the tsar. After the prospect of returning to the old privileges failed, the English court made no further attempts to placate the ambassadors with extraordinary ceremonies. Their departure turned out to be much more modest than the promising reception they had received on their arrival.[114] The ambassadors left England in July 1663. Upon their return to Russia, Prozorovskii sent a messenger from Archangel to the *Posol'skii prikaz* to announce the imminent arrival of an English embassy of which Charles II had given notice to the Russian ambassador. Prozorovskii wrote to the tsar in the typical diminutive form – as slave Petrushka[115] – that Charles Cottrell told him that the king was making arrangements to send 'his great ambassadors, his privy council boiar Charlus Govart and with him persons of various ranks'.[116]

Charlus Govart – or, Charles Howard, the first Earl of Carlisle (1628–1685) – was selected by King Charles II as England's ambassador extraordinary to Russia. Carlisle was accompanied by a retinue, along with his wife, the countess Anna of Carlisle, and his son, Edward, viscount

[113] TNA, SP 91/3 ('Receipt of Prozorovskii', 3 July 1663), fols. 100–01.
[114] For the negotiations, see Lodyzhenskii, *Posol'stvo*, pp. 20–23.
[115] See Poe, 'What did Russians mean'. [116] RGADA, f. 35, op. 1, d. 11, l. 5ob.

Howard of Morpeth. According to the Russian records, more than eighty people travelled with the embassy,[117] including the poet Andrew Marvell who served as a secretary, a physician, several musicians, a chaplain, clerks, interpreters, and Guy Miege, who published an important account of the embassy.[118] Carlisle's main responsibilities were to reciprocate the honour that the tsar had shown to Charles II in sending his diplomats to London, as well as to build the promising momentum in their relationship by negotiating the trade privileges which the English hoped to restore.[119] It can safely be concluded that Carlisle's diplomatic mission resulted in a great failure. Ceremonial disputes and diverging economic interests precipitated a decline in Anglo-Russian relations and left the two monarchs in a state of mutual resentment. Why and how did this happen?

Carlisle has been described as unfit for the job, as 'impatient and peevish, arrogant and ignorant, over-concerned with ceremony and etiquette'.[120] A haughty nobleman, the young ambassador lacked experience and diplomatic skill. From a modern perspective, this criticism suggests an inability to focus on facts and business and to navigate the waters of protocol in a detached and deliberate manner. Carlisle's contemporaries are quoted as saying that 'he was more of use for parade than for "business"'.[121] Until now, the unquestioned assumption that one can reach conclusions about a person's motivations and political intentions based on an individual's disposition has been invoked to explain the ill-fated course of Carlisle's mission. But this line of reasoning can readily be turned on its head. Could the ambassador's concern for parade have been precisely the reason why the choice fell on him? Guy Miege, whose account was published with the authorisation of Carlisle, may have answered this question positively,

[117] The exact numbers vary. A report from Archangel names eighty-eight people (excluding the ambassador's wife and son) and a further twenty-nine who came on a different boat, see RGADA, f. 35, op. 1, d. 11, l. 17ob. Cf. the list of all the embassy's personnel, see ibid., ll. 20ob–23.

[118] G. Miege, *A relation of three embassies from His Sacred Majestie Charles II to the great Duke of Muscovie, the King of Sweden, and the King of Denmark, performed by the Earl of Carlisle in the years 1663 and 1664* (London, 1669). A vivid paraphrase of this account is given by J. Jolliffe, 'Lord Carlisle's embassy to Moscow', *Cornhill Magazine*, 176 (1968), 217–32. For Miege, see V. Larminie, 'Miege, Guy (bap. 1644, d. in or after 1718)', Oxford Dictionary of National Biography (Oxford, online edn., 2004). Available from www .oxforddnb.com/view/article/18687, last access 6 February 2016.

[119] For an overview that puts Carlisle's embassy in the context of seventeenth-century Anglo-Russian relations, see Dukes, Herd, Kotilaine, *Stuarts and Romanovs*, pp. 105–11.

[120] Konovalov, 'England and Russia', p. 65. For Carlisle, see G. Goodwin, S. Kelsey, 'Howard, Charles, first earl of Carlisle (1628–1685)', in *Oxford Dictionary of National Biography* (Oxford, online edn., 2009). Available from www.oxforddnb.com/view/article/ 13886, last access 6 February 2016.

[121] Dukes, Herd, Kotilaine, *Stuarts and Romanovs*, p. 106; Konovalov, 'England and Russia', p. 65.

boasting of his master's 'comely and advantageous stature, a *Majestick* mine'. He attributed to Carlisle a 'peculiar grace and vivacity in his discourse, and in his actions a great promptitude and diligence'.[122] Of course, Miege was writing in Carlisle's name. Still, the exaggerated praise of his master is not much less convincing than the critique brought against Carlisle. What follows deliberately avoids seeking answers in Carlisle's character. It focuses instead on the 'parade' side of the English embassy and asks about its consequences on 'business'.

At the outset, Carlisle could have expected a grand welcome in Russia. He was informed on his arrival in Archangel that Prozorovskii had given a constructive report to the tsar regarding his entertainment in London. He spoke in the highest terms about the incoming English ambassador.[123] Prozorovskii's account could be construed as a guarantee for an equally honourable treatment of the English nobleman. Indeed, the *Posol'skii prikaz* made great efforts to arrange a comfortable reception for the diplomatic dignitary. The landing stage for the ambassador's ships was to be 'filled with people and everything be put in orderly fashion according to diplomatic custom'.[124] After enquiring about the rank of the ambassador and the social composition of his entourage, the *prikaz* gave order to Archangel to supply enough food and drinks for Carlisle's entire embassy. The ambassador and his company were to be given a second helping upon request.[125] The food was plenty. The register of provisions lists barrels of German and French white wine and German beer and honey in great quantity.[126]

It would be wrong to conclude, however, that this copious supply of food and drink signalled the Russian court's exceptional hospitality. The tsar's lavish reception of Carlisle proceeded in strict accordance with the principle of diplomatic reciprocity. This was not an independent expression of hospitality or goodwill. The embassy was not accommodated in accordance with the daily needs of the English diplomats. Nor were the ambassador's requests regarding food and drink determined by his own desires; instead, those requests were proffered in accordance with the demands of the international prestige of the state he represented, and the position of his monarch in the ceremonial hierarchy.[127]

The honour that the *Posol'skii prikaz* was willing to grant to Carlisle was articulated in the quantities of food and drink. The so-called sovereign's grant (*gosudarevo zhalovan'e*) for the embassy was calculated on the basis

[122] Miege, *Relation*, p. 4.
[123] Carlisle to Clarendon, 27 August 1663, Bodl. Libr., MS Clarendon 80, fol. 165v. Letter quoted in Konovalov, 'England and Russia', p. 67.
[124] RGADA, f. 35, op. 1, d. 11, l. 10. [125] Ibid., l. 8. [126] Ibid., ll. 23–25.
[127] See Kotoshikhin, *O Rossii*, pp. 73ff.

of what the recent Russian embassy had received in England. Carlisle's first *pristav*, Andrei Bogdanov, the head of a *strel'tsy* unit who was appointed because he seemed 'adroit and not of scanty appearance', was instructed accordingly. He also watched over the embassy's rations provided by the tsar, so that they matched Prozorovskii's expenses which had been defrayed by the English king.[128] At another point, the *posol'skaia kniga*, which deals with Carlisle's reception, even quoted the registers of food and drinks from Prozorovskii's *stateinyi spisok* to make sure that the principle of equal exchange was sustained.[129] Bogdanov's report to the *Posol'skii prikaz* on the embassy's reception in Archangel stressed that Carlisle's victuals had not been reduced or increased when compared with Prozorovskii's provisions.[130]

The reception in Archangel pleased the ambassador. His lodgings were in good order, and he had no reason to complain about the food or the drinks, although he preferred to have his meat prepared and his bread baked by his own cooks. Only a little incident cast a shadow on the promising welcome in Russia. The first *pristav* assigned to Carlisle refused to yield him the more honourable right-hand side on their first encounter, which provoked the ambassador's stern protest. The *pristav* assented after he had consulted his superiors who advised him to let Carlisle take the place of honour, as he wished.[131] Despite this punctilio, Miege noted that the ambassador 'had all manner of good entertainment, which tasted very pleasant to us', but hastened to add 'that we were mistaken in it, for we experienced the contrary in several places upon a very bad account'.[132]

The *Posol'skii prikaz* instructed the local *pristavy* to arrange Carlisle's journey from Archangel to Moscow (via Ustiug, Vologda, and Iaroslavl') and to 'provide a safe conduct and to preserve the honour of the foreign dignitary in the towns'.[133] Miege's account mentions only relatively minor quarrels about accommodation, food, and protocol that punctuated the embassy's route to the Russian capital.[134] The major incident that overshadowed all the *Posol'skii prikaz*' earnest efforts to arrange an

[128] RGADA, f. 35, op. 1, d. 11, l. 11.

[129] Such lists and instructions where produced at all stages of Carlisle's embassy on its way from Archangel to Moscow, and for its stay in Moscow. See for example, ibid., ll. 143ob ff.

[130] Ibid., l. 38–38ob (This comparison did not include the second helpings which the English ambassador was offered).

[131] Carlisle to Clarendon, 27 August 1663, Bodl. Libr., MS Clarendon 80, fol. 165. Letter quoted in Konovalov, 'England and Russia', p. 68. See also the Russian documentation, RGADA, f. 35, op. 1, d. 11, l. 17–17ob.

[132] Miege, *Relation*, pp. 81f. [133] RGADA, f. 35, op. 1, d. 11, l. 53.

[134] For a vivid description of the journey, see Miege, *Relation*, pp. 88–112.

agreeable voyage for the ambassador happened near Moscow in the run-up to the ambassador's solemn entry into the city.

The embassy stayed in Sergiev Posad – 'Troitza' in Miege's account – where the ambassador saw the famous monastery, but complained that he was denied access to the churches.[135] The *pristavy, stol'nik* Afonasei I. Nesterov and *d'iak* Ivan Davydov, who had been appointed to accompany Carlisle from Vologda to Moscow, received the order on 3 February 1664 to collect the ambassador from his temporary lodgings.[136] The embassy was brought to the *podkhozhii stan poslov* (the ambassador's point of departure for his solemn entry) at Rostokino, a small village just a few kilometres outside Moscow, from where the solemn entry was to begin on the 5th.

On 4 February, the tsar sent an order to the *Koniushennyi prikaz* (equerry chancellery) that solemnly dressed sleighs, padded with white furs of polar bears, as well as thirty-three saddled horses, be provided for the ambassador and his entourage. A new and higher ranking *pristav, dumnyi dvorianin* Ivan A. Pronchishchev, was appointed together with *d'iak* Grigorii Bogdanov. They were meant to proceed towards the embassy's train in order to meet it on its way to Moscow, exactly 'one pistol shot away from the earthen rampart' of the city. At the same time, a *d'iak* of the *Razriadnyi prikaz* (military service chancellery) was advised to assemble a large group of the court nobility, townsfolk and servicemen, consisting of *dvorianye, striapchie, deti boiarskie, prikaznye liudi*, and others. That sundry group was instructed to cheer the guests when the *pristavy* welcomed the ambassador. It is worth noting that participation in diplomatic receptions was seen as an important service to the tsar. As such, the names of those who participated in the ceremonies were recorded in the military service books (*razriadnye knigi*). These records served as a source for calculating the rank of servitor families within the *mestnichestvo* system and helped to settle disputes over precedence quarrels among themselves.[137] This is an important reminder that although official diplomatic ceremonies centred around the honour of the sovereign host relative to the foreign guest, there were many instances where ranking systems overlapped with the international hierarchy.[138]

After the *d'iak* of the *Razriadnyi prikaz* had signalled that everyone stood ready for the reception, a messenger would be sent to Rostokino to tell the embassy that it might commence its journey. It should follow Tver

[135] Ibid., pp. 112f. [136] RGADA, f. 35, op. 1, d. 11, ll. 121–23ob.

[137] See *Dvortsovye razriady*, 4 vols. (St Petersburg, 1850–1855), III, cols. 553ff. For *mestnichestvo* and ritual, see Kollmann, 'Social drama'. For the *razriadnyi prikaz*, see more recently, O. V. Novokhatko, *Razriad v 185 godu* (Moscow, 2007).

[138] For more examples, see the reception of Peter I in Paris in Chapter 4.

street to Red Square, and from there proceed to their lodgings which had been prepared in the *posol'skii dvor*.[139]

Carlisle's servants began preparing the festive train for the procession. Miege never missed a chance to stress the splendour of Carlisle's retinue. Accordingly, he wrote that 'our Liveries were so rich [. . .] that the Pages[']' Liveries amongst others cost near thirty pound sterling a piece, being almost covered quite over with silver lace. Each of them had a good plume of feathers in his hat, and in short there was nothing in all this Equipage unworthy the greatness of the Master'.[140] Nesterov had duly informed the ambassador that he would be collected at nine o'clock on 5 February to make his entry. Clad in their lavish dresses, the embassy impatiently awaited its hosts to convey them to Moscow by the appointed hour. The messenger who was to give the sign for the start of the procession did not show up until the evening. Nevertheless, the embassy set forth to Moscow, still expecting a lavish reception. When the city was in sight, the embassy was told to retire to a little village nearby. Carlisle was informed that the entry must be delayed until the next day. The *d'iak* Lukian Golozov came before the ambassador to apologise for the disorder. The preparations had not been finished in time, and the messenger arrived late because he lost his way. As a consequence, the tsar cancelled the entry that day entirely, for it did not seem comely to receive the ambassador in the dark.[141]

As orders for the solemn entry's preparation were issued only on 4 February, it is reasonable to assume that difficulties in arranging the procession on such short notice caused the delay. However, Carlisle foretold damaging repercussions for his master's prestige at other European courts, fearing that 'this delay would become every where a matter of laughter and contempt'.[142] Miege concluded melodramatically that 'this day, which should have been a day of Pomp and Magnificence proved a day of fasting of trouble and discontent; this day in which his Excellence ought to have received the extraordinarie Markes of the greatest Amity that ever was betwixt two Crownes, was a day in which he received but the tokens of indignity and contempt'.[143]

Carlisle's secretary wrote a letter to the tsar, asking for a full explanation of the incident. He also announced that the ambassador refused to proceed with his entry until full reparation – through 'the blood of the

139 RGADA, f. 35, op. 1, d. 11, ll. 146ob ff., for the preparations of the solemn entry.
140 Miege, *Relation*, p. 113.
141 See ukaz to Golosov's from 5 February 1664, in the *stolbtsy*, RGADA, f. 35, op. 1, d. 200, ll. 9–11.
142 Miege, *Relation*, p. 116. 143 Ibid.

Criminals' – was paid by the Russian court.[144] The Russians promised to give immediate satisfaction to the ambassador and asked to continue with the solemn occasion. Carlisle agreed. On 6 February, the embassy finally made its solemn entry into Moscow, albeit again too late to be watched in daylight. Carlisle's further protest had caused a delay, so that a huge number of torches were mounted in the streets of Moscow to illuminate the diplomatic spectacle. The Russian court stressed that many foreigners lived in the capital. It was essential that those foreigners witnessed and reported to their masters the splendour of the reception, which was a testimony of the great friendship between the tsar and the English king, Charles II.[145]

As if the delay was not a significant enough affront to the ambassador, that incident was followed by another troubling episode. The *pristav* Pronchishchev, who had been ordered to receive Carlisle with a ceremonial speech before continuing the procession into Moscow, had been advised that, on the first encounter, he should wait until the ambassador dismounted from his sleigh.[146] When the two parties met at the designated location, Pronchishchev sent a messenger to the ambassador to request that he step down from his sleigh in order to hear the words of the tsar. Only when Carlisle stood before the *pristav* was Pronchishchev himself allowed to dismount and begin the speech. Carlisle, who again felt on the verge of compromising the status of the English king, protested. He urged Pronchishchev to come off his sleigh first, which the latter refused to do. The two men sat in the freezing cold, exchanging arguments about their ceremonial rights, until Carlisle proposed a solution to the stand-off. They should dismount from their sleighs simultaneously. The *pristav* agreed but, in Miege's words, 'tooke occasion to deceive his Excellence, and falsify his word, hanging in the aire betwixt the armes of his servants, and but touching the earth with his tiptoes, whilst the Ambassador came out freely'.[147] Clearly, this was not a cultural misunderstanding but a shrewd response to a complicated face-to-face situation in which both parties knew what was at stake.

The ambassador perhaps breathed a sigh of relief when he at last passed through the city gates of Moscow; it had been a long, tiring journey. Only after being drawn into the protracted argument over the ceremonial that was to usher the English embassy into the capital could Carlisle and his

[144] Carlisle to Aleksei, 6 February 1664, printed in ibid., pp. 118–26 (Latin and English translation). The letter stresses that Carlisle's reputation and with it that of his master would be subject to ridicule around the world.

[145] See ibid., p. 192. [146] RGADA, f. 35, op. 1, d. 11, ll. 151ob–152ob, 178ff.

[147] Miege, *Relation*, p. 132. Compare with Kotoshikhin's description of a diplomatic reception in Moscow; see Kotoshikhin, *O Rossii*, pp. 74ff.

entourage finally enjoy the splendid parade as the festive train slowly marched into the town:

All these ceremonies, and the slowness of our march took up so much time, that the night overtook us before we could enter the Town, our frequent stoppings and pawses having consum'd above three houres in going of about two miles. Therefore, because the Sun had withdrawn himself before we were ready to appear in the Town, the Citizens had made great fires in their streets, and provided great numbers of torches to render every thing visible about his Excellence; so that the night as well as the day did seem to participate in the Glory of this Entry.[148]

Immersed in the twilight magic of the passing day, the Russians put such grandeur on display with 'rich furrs, cloth of gold and silver, velvets and other rich stuffs [...] that it was reported every where in the court, that the City of *Mosco* never saw the Entry of any Ambassador so glorious as this'.[149] Despite the ceremonial defeat that Carlisle suffered during the first encounter with a Russian official near the capital (or perhaps because of it), Miege never tired of informing the reader about the magnificence of the ambassador's solemn entry. Patrick Gordon, a Scottish general in the tsar's service, noted with much less enthusiasm that Carlisle 'was received with great splendor after the usuall way'.[150] The claim that a diplomatic reception was unique in its splendour was of course itself a ceremonial trope, often deployed by diplomats to underline the unsurpassed prestige of their master. As mentioned above, Prozorovskii was told by the English that his reception was suffused with unusually high honours. Augustin Freiherr von Meyerberg, the Holy Roman Emperor's diplomat, who had visited the tsar's court in 1661/62, shortly before Carlisle's arrival, also claimed that his reception was endowed with unprecedented honours.[151]

What were the ramifications of Carlisle's ceremonial treatment? Courtly representation and political negotiation were inseparable. It is no wonder that Miege suggested that both aspects of diplomatic exchange should be discussed simultaneously: 'It follows now that we display the Ambassador['] s negotiation, and at the same time the Ceremonies which are practised in that Court.'[152] In the case of Anglo-Russian relations, the intimate connection between ceremony and politics bore disastrous consequences for Carlisle's goal of restoring the trade privileges. The disputes over ceremonies, and in particular Carlisle's complaints about his treatment during the solemn entry, threatened to set the topic of the trade

[148] Miege, *Relation*, p. 133. [149] Ibid., p. 127.
[150] D. Fedosov, ed., *Diary of General Patrick Gordon of Auchleuchries, 1635–1699. Volume II: 1659–1667* (Aberdeen, 2011), p. 189.
[151] Adelung, *Meyerberg*, p. 29. [152] Miege, *Relation*, p. 143.

privileges aside and put the issue of monarchical status squarely on the agenda.

The first public audience with Tsar Aleksei was held on 11 February 1664, shortly after the embassy had arrived in Moscow. Miege was pleased that the Russians had arranged the first meeting in the Kremlin so quickly in order to honour the ambassador, although a two-day delay followed the invitation which had originally been scheduled for 9 February.[153] This time the ceremonies were not punctuated with quarrelsome interruptions. Carlisle wished to wear his hat during the audience, despite Prozorovskii's head having been uncovered when before the English king. Whether this request was honoured by the Russian court is uncertain. But it did not seem to prompt further dispute.[154]

Carlisle offered numerous valuable gifts to the tsar, one of which stands out as a direct link to the restoration of trade privileges. Carlisle handed to Aleksei two pistols, explaining 'that pair of Pistolets his Majestie [the king] delivered me also with his own hand, commanding me to excuse their oldness, which he thought would not make them less acceptable, when you knew they where those, with which after so long adversity, He rid in His triumphant Entry into His Metropolitan City of London'.[155] This special gift signified the continuity of the English monarchy. It could be seen as an incentive to restore trade privileges because the justification for their abolition in 1649 had become obsolete with the monarchy's restoration. Following the presentation of the credentials and the presents, the ambassador was invited to a feast during which numerous lengthy toasts were raised in honour of the king and the tsar.

After Carlisle had attended a second audience in the Kremlin, the negotiations with the appointed boiars began. The ambassador submitted two papers drafted by the secretary, Andrew Marvell.[156] In the first, Carlisle, referring to the delay of his entry, complained that 'forasmuch as in the eye and discourse of the whole World, the honour of the King my Master has thereby exceedingly suffered, and will daily more without a satisfaction as publick and notorious as the miscarriage'. Carlisle feared that he could be held responsible for what he thought was a debasement of the king's honour. Accordingly, he demanded 'that his Imperial Majestie

[153] Ibid. For the audience and its preparation, see ibid., pp. 144 84. For the Russian account, see RGADA, f. 35, op. 1, d. 11, ll. 192ff., 274ff.

[154] However, the point was raised again later. It caused some serious difficulties when Peter I received Queen Anne's ambassador, Charles Whitworth, in 1710. This episode will be discussed in Chapter 5.

[155] Miege, *Relation*, p. 182.

[156] Some of the papers, which Marvell submitted to the *Posol'skii prikaz* in the course of the negotiations, have been preserved in the Russian state archive, see RGADA, f. 35, op. 1, d. 205. They match Miege's account and formed part of the basis of his book.

will be pleased to command that a perfect narrative in the most authentick manner of the reason of that disorder, of names of the persons criminal both principals and accessory, and what example of justice his Imperial Majestie [...] has shewed upon them, may be delivered to me under the hands and seales of the Lords Commissioners for my justification'.[157] The ambassador thereby created a new item of political interest: the ceremonies became an object of the negotiations, or were brought in as a bargaining chip in the arguments exchanged over trade.

The second paper produced by Marvell underscores this conclusion. It dealt with the trade privileges that Carlisle had hoped to restore by linking them to the 'happy Correspondency and great Amity betwixt the Kings of England and Emperours of Russia'.[158] According to Carlisle, those privileges formed the foundation of the special relationship between the two monarchs. Their mutual ties would strengthen even further if the tsar allowed the merchants to return to Moscow and continue their business under the old regulations. To 'raise a building of perpetual friendship' ultimately meant the restitution of trade privileges.[159] It becomes clear that the economic-political goal of Carlisle's mission was interrelated on a symbolic level with the personal relationship between the two sovereigns, that is, their brotherly love. This friendship, in turn, was dependent on the degrees of honour that both were willing to grant each other in the ceremonies. All three elements of diplomatic exchange – trade, monarchical friendship, and courtly representation – merged into an inseparable act of political communication, impacting on each other in an unfortunate way.

In a series of ensuing conferences, the boiars laid out the position of the tsar and exchanged further arguments with the ambassador. Eventually, the negotiations ended in a stalemate. The Russian court reiterated that the solemn entry was postponed because it had become dark on the appointed day and that the ambassador 'should lodge that night nearer *Mosco*, so that the next day he might be received betimes with a splendour answerable to his quality; And so, that so many strangers who lived in Mosco might see by this Reception, how great is the Amity which their Great Lord beares to his Majestie, and that they might discourse of it in their several Countries'.[160] Carlisle's worries, as well as the boiars' response, already hint at the important role that the ever-present but distant addressee – the *société des princes* – played in diplomatic ritual.[161]

[157] Miege, *Relation*, pp. 187f. [158] Ibid., p. 189. [159] Ibid., p. 190.
[160] Ibid., p. 192 (190 in the book due to a printing error).
[161] See Chapter 4 which elaborates the role of the courtly public in diplomatic ritual.

The boiars also listed the reasons for the abolition of the privileges, notably the late rebellion in England and the illegal trade that the English merchants were pursuing in Russia.[162] In particular, the boiars were irritated about the fact that Carlisle had emphasised economic relations as the basis of the relationship between his master and the tsar, which in turn surprised Miege: 'They den[ied] the foundations of Friendship between the two Crowns to be [...] the Grant of the Priviledges, but only the mutual Love of both Princes.'[163] The Russians argued that it was this love out of which Aleksei had supported Charles II during the Civil War, but without receiving anything in return (apart from repayment). After all, the Russian ambassador Prozorovskii was denied a loan in support of the tsar's war against Poland.

What is more, the boiars protested that Carlisle – in the Latin version of the speech that he delivered after submitting his credentials to the tsar – addressed the tsar as *illustris*. The Russian court considered the offence to consist in replacing the previously used term *serenissimus*. The offence was assigned especially high importance because it was committed in public. Carlisle gave a long-winded explanation in which he quoted various ancient authors, boasting his literary knowledge. *Serenus* meant nothing but 'still and calm', whereas '*Illustris* in its proper derivation and signification expresseth that which is all resplendent lightsome and glorious', which seemed more appropriate to a ruler so great as the tsar.[164] The Russians, who had no literature according to the ambassador, were not impressed by this etymological hair-splitting. What mattered was the fact that, according to them, all princes in Europe used the word *serenissimus* when referring to the tsar. The boiars produced a text from the Holy Roman Emperor to impress this point on the English ambassador. Carlisle's countered the boiars' complaint by arguing that they had omitted the phrase 'defender of the faith', when addressing the English king on their part.[165]

The written word, uttered in public in a ceremonial speech, belonged to the spectrum of diplomatic ritual. This incident demonstrates that it did not matter what the words in question actually meant. It did not matter whether the Russian monarch was serene, or should be characterised as such. The term *serenissimus* had ritual importance because of documented precedent, not meaning. One may assume that, had the tsar been addressed as *illustrissimus* in the past, the *Posol'skii prikaz* might as well have taken umbrage at *serenissimus*. The fear was that altering a word in the tsar's title might establish a new, unintended precedent and signal

[162] For the details of the negotiations, see Konovalov, 'England and Russia', p. 81.
[163] Miege, *Relation*, p. 220. [164] Ibid., p. 216. [165] Ibid., pp. 215–20.

a change in his status. In diplomatic protocol, the relation between words/gestures and their meanings was, to some degree, an arbitrary one. What counted was their correct, precedent-informed performance.

After making every attempt to reach an agreement with the boiars concerning the reparation of the ceremonial insult and trade privileges, Carlisle hoped for a private audience with the tsar. The request was honoured, but the boiars made it clear that such an audience would only serve to deepen the amity between the tsar and the king, not to do business. The ambassador decided to avail himself of a very special trick to urge the Russian ruler to make a decision in favour of English interests.

After starting the conversation with a summary of the good nature of Anglo-Russian relations, Carlisle proposed: 'I shall as I have the honour to represent his Royal majesties person, to take the liberty to represent his words upon this occasion, as if He and You could meet together, and did in presence to contemplate both Your unspeakable Majesties in that glasse of friendship the most clear eyes of one another.'[166] The wording of this address lay at the heart of the metaphoric inventory of Russian diplomatic ceremonial which placed the senses and the presence of the sovereign in the centre of diplomatic dialogue. In Russia, an audience was commonly referred to as the act of 'seeing the clear eyes' of the tsar.[167] By loosening the abstract rules of diplomatic representation, Carlisle aimed to engage Aleksei in a direct exchange with Charles II. The ambassador suspended the symbolic link to his king, which invested him with the surrogate authority of his master, and assumed the voice of the sovereign, not as his representative of but as the monarch himself. Ingeniously, Carlisle decided to represent the sovereign by ventriloquizing him, rather than simply by speaking on his behalf. He continued his speech before the tsar in the first person: 'Had I desired any new thing of Your Tzarskoy majesty my dear and loving brother [. . .] I might with less unkindness have taken your so long deliberation and perhaps have digested the refusal [of restoring the privileges].'[168] By changing the grammatical person in his speech (from 'His majesty' to 'I'), the ambassador took the role of his sovereign and created a playful inversion in the laws of diplomatic representation. Carlisle's diplomatic artifice was quite

[166] Miege, *Relation*, p. 257.

[167] This expression was used until the early eighteenth century. For a late example, see the French envoy de Baluze's reception in 1703, RGADA, f. 93, op. 1 (1703), d. 3, l. 36. See also F. P. Sergeev, *Formirovanie russkogo diplomaticheskogo iazyka* (L'vov, 1978), pp. 50–54; Iuzefovich, *Put' posla*, pp. 177f. This formula also appears in Lünig's descriptions of diplomatic ceremonies arranged at Moscow for an embassy from the Netherlands (1665), Lünig, *Theatrum Ceremoniale*, I, p. 556.

[168] Miege, *Relation*, p. 258.

a theatrical achievement. In a professional diplomatic context, it might appear somewhat strange from a modern point of view. Early modern diplomacy allowed, and even necessitated, such manoeuvres. By putting himself in the place of the king, Carlisle hoped to overcome the difficulty of having to recreate the authority and defend the interest of a sovereign who was absent. If he spoke in the voice of the king, he imagined that he could strengthen his master's personal bond to the tsar and thus agitate the latter to act in favour of the English merchants.

However, Carlisle's tactic did not yield the desired results. On the contrary, the case he made for restoring trade privileges and the complaints he entered about the affront to his honour further upset the Russian court. In particular, Carlisle's speech fuelled the anger of the tsar on account of an allegation that Prozorovskii had requested an excessive loan at the English court. Ostensibly, the Russian easily foresaw that such a large loan would be denied, and the boiars used this denial as a convenient pretext for rejecting English requests regarding trade privileges. Carlisle submitted another four papers in which he reiterated his trade-related demands and his criticism of the *pristav*'s supposed misbehaviour. The answers that he received from the *Posol'skii prikaz* defended the tsar's position and warned the ambassador that the tsar intended to write a report to the king about his unacceptable behaviour and false accusations. Here, the negotiations ended.

In June 1664, Carlisle requested a departure audience with the tsar in order to leave Moscow at the earliest opportunity. One final occasion worsened the relations between the two countries. The ambassador was presented with a gift of sables for him, his family, and other members of the embassy. However, Carlisle explained, his 'Embassy had had no success, and that in this case it was not proper for him to receive any favour from his Tsarskoy Majesty till he had first received the Justice he demanded'.[169] Patrick Gordon summarised Carlisle's stay in Moscow as follows:

> But his Excellency, takeing himself to be affronted at his first reception at the sea port, and then much more at his comeing into Mosko, which albeit done by a mistake and not of purpose, he urged the reparation thereof with too much heat. Whereupon followed some irritations on both sides, so that the ambassadour, urging reparation at diverse conferences and at a private audience, and not getting any to his satisfaction, as also being denyed the priviledges, the chieffe business for which he came, refused the presents which were sent him by the Tzaar.[170]

[169] Ibid., p. 305. [170] Fedosov, ed., *Diary of General Patrick Gordon*, p. 223.

Gift exchange was a state affair in early modern diplomacy. The rules of *do ut des* applied to international relations beyond the implications of diplomatic niceties. The transfer of objects, art and luxury goods, trade ware, precious metals, and exotic animals revealed the political, economic, social, and cultural intricacies of diplomatic practice.[171] Rejecting objects formed as much a part of giving as offering and accepting them.[172] Refusing gifts at the end of a diplomatic mission sent a clear political message.[173] For the ambassador, the rejection of the gifts was a last means of restoring the sensitive equilibrium between his ambassadorial honour and that of the tsar, as the ceremonial affronts had put this equilibrium out of balance and the court had not offered any reparation.[174] The Russians responded instantly by returning the Englishmen's gifts given to the tsar at the first public audience. The ambassador's mission in Moscow was over. But more dispute was still to come.

In 1664, shortly after the departure of Carlisle, Aleksei sent two envoys, Vasilii Ia. Dashkov and Dmitrii Shipulin, to Charles II to deliver a complaint about the ambassador's behaviour.[175] Carlisle had already warned the king about the Russians' nature: 'They are a people that neither know to manage affairs nor practise courtisy and as for truth or honour they would thinke it a disreputation to be guilty of them. Hence, it is that to give the Ly is here accounted no affront and to professe themselves slaves is their only ingenuity.'[176] The Russian court, in turn, held

[171] M. Jansson, 'Measured reciprocity: English ambassadorial gift exchange in the 17th and 18th centuries', *Journal of Early Modern History*, 9 (2005), 348–70. For a discussion of Carlisle's case, see Hennings, 'The failed gift', esp. pp. 97–103. For examples of the growing scholarship on material culture and gifting in early modern diplomacy, see H. Jacobsen, *Luxury and power: the material world of the Stuart diplomat*, 1660–1714 (Oxford, 2012); P. Burschel, 'Der Sultan und das Hündchen. Zur politischen Ökonomie des Schenkens in interkultureller Perspektive', *Historische Anthropologie*, 15 (2007), 408–21; Martin, 'Gifts For the Bride'; D. Carrió-Invernizzi, 'Gift and diplomacy in seventeenth-century Spanish Italy', *Historical Journal*, 51 (2008), 881–99; M. Häberlein, C. Jeggle, eds., *Materielle Grundlagen der Diplomatie: Schenken, Sammeln und Verhandeln in Spätmittelalter und Früher Neuzeit* (Konstanz, 2013); T. Sowerby, '"A memorial and a pledge of faith": portraiture and early modern diplomatic culture', *English Historical Review*, 129 (2014), 296–331; F. Heal, *The power of gifts: gift-exchange in early modern England* (Oxford, 2014), esp. pp. 149–79; Windler, *Diplomatie comme expérience de l'Autre*, pp. 485-548.

[172] M. Mauss, *The gift: the form and reason for exchange in archaic societies*, trans. W. D. Hall (London, 2002), pp. 52–55.

[173] H. Duchhardt, 'Das diplomatische Abschiedsgeschenk', *Archiv für Kulturgeschichte*, 57 (1975), 345–62, esp. pp. 354, 356; J. Falcke, *Studien zum diplomatischen Geschenkwesen am brandenburgisch-preussischen Hof im 17. und 18. Jahrhundert* (Berlin, 2006), pp. 306–11.

[174] Hennings, 'Failed gift', pp. 101f.

[175] For Dashkov's *stateinyi spisok*, see RGADA, f. 35, op. 1, d. 12.

[176] Carlisle to Charles II, 14 June 1664, TNA, SP 91/3, fols. 105–05v. Letter printed in C. Robbins, 'Carlisle and Marvell', *History of Ideas Newsletter*, 3 (1957), 8–17, pp. 12–13. But 'to place responsibility for the failure of the embassy [. . .] fully on the

the ambassador responsible for offending the tsar and his counsellors in the papers he submitted to the *Posol'skii prikaz*. The envoys explained that Carlisle was received with great honours. He was even permitted to step out of his carriage near the entry to the palace, a privilege which had not been granted previously to any other ambassador. (This was the response to the special honours that were shown to Prozorovskii in 1662 and which raised Louis XIV's concern about the position of the Russians in the system of precedence.) The Russians returned the favour and blamed the failure of Carlisle's embassy on his fixation on ceremony: 'Failing to address the matters of state, which exist between the two great sovereigns to the advancement of their monarchical love and amicable friendship, he provoked long quarrels about his solemn entry into Moscow, the city of the tsar.'[177] However, to distinguish, as the Russians did, between matters of state, on the one hand, and ceremony, on the other, did not imply that the ritual side of diplomacy was treated separately from the negotiations.[178] Mutual recognition on the ritual level was the precondition to any successful diplomatic negotiation. Both Carlisle and his opponents knew that the symbolic consequences of ceremony could not be ignored in favour of state business. In response to Dahskov's complaints, Miege included in his account a long report in defence of the ambassador.[179] He wrote that 'the Ambassador being still further off any reparation of the former affront [...] was not in [the position] to propound any further matter of State'.[180] This observation underscores again how important it is to devote equal attention both to ceremony and negotiation in order to fully understand the intricacies of early modern diplomacy.

Dashkov had, then, a cold reception in England. The king wrote back to the tsar, 'We find noe evidence or argument to perswade us, that hee the said Earle of Carlisle hath been wanting in his respect of your Imperiall Ma[jes]tie nor in his duty to Us according to his character wherewith Wee honoured him.'[181] The letter's further well-wishing and reconfirmations of the 'perpetuall brotherly love and close alliance' could

nature of the Russians [was], of course, disingenuous in the extreme', is a recent response to Carlisle's embassy by Dukes, Herd, Kotilaine, *Stuarts and Romanovs*, p. 110.

177 For the Russian complaint against Carlisle (July 1664), see Bodl. Libr., MS Barlow 52. Transcribed and reproduced in Konovalov, 'England and Russia', pp. 95–104 (quotation on p. 95).

178 On this topic, see also Roll, 'Zeremoniell und Politik', esp. p. 55.

179 'My Lords Apology against the *Russ* Ambassador', in Miege, *Relation*, pp. 435–61.

180 Ibid., p. 444.

181 Charles II to Aleksei, 20 March 1665, RGADA, f. 35, op. 2, d. 95, l. 2. Also quoted in Dukes, Herd, Kotilaine, *Stuarts and Romanovs*, p. 113.

not forestall the derailment of Anglo-Russian relations as a result of Carlisle's embassy and the politics of ceremony.

Reading between the Gestures II: Perception and Deception

What was the legacy of Carlisle's embassy, and how was this legacy formed by Miege's account? (see Figure 3.1). Miege constantly emphasised the great honours bestowed on his master by the Russian court. In particular, the solemn entry, which, paradoxically, served as the catalyst for all ensuing disputes, was depicted as a testament to the English king's glory. But why did Miege dwell on this praise, if the way in which the honours were granted to the king were, as he wrote, 'another ridiculous example of the pride and the rusticity of the Moscovites'[182]? Why would an Englishman value the ceremonial honours granted by a 'barbarous' despot?

Sovereignty and might were bound up with the experience of pomp and ceremony in diplomatic rituals. It is not a coincidence that Miege used the term 'majestic' to convey the core message of the solemn entry – the prestige of his sovereign – to the reader of his account: 'The pretious stones, darting about the rays of their refulgency, made the clearness of the night in some respect more majestique than the brightness of the day.' For Carlisle, it was just as important as it had been for Prozorovskii to show that the king was respected by the tsar as a powerful sovereign.[183] If a diplomat failed to uphold the honour of his master, the failure had to be concealed or excused.

For Carlisle, concealment was not an option, given the public's presence in the events. To describe the Russian court as the centre of exotic and barbarous practice was thus a necessary strategy to downplay Carlisle's ceremonial defeats. Miege cited selected themes of barbarism to shroud the ambassador's embarrassment behind a curtain of cultural otherness.[184] At the same time, he celebrated the 'unprecedented' honours the embassy was granted by the Russian tsar as proof of England's elevated international prestige. He mixed the genre of ethnographic description (which placed the tsar outside the *société des princes*) with that of a diplomatic report in which the tsar was recognised as a member of the European monarchical society, as well as an important contributor

182 Miege, *Relation*, p. 131.

183 Hence Carlisle's concerns about ceremony in a letter to the king: Carlisle to Charles II, 12 March 1664, TNA, SP 91/3, fols. 103–04v. Carlisle's letters to the king are printed in Robbins, 'Carlisle and Marvell'.

184 Miege, *Relation*, preface, pp. 56f., 61f., 124f., 131, 184f. 341.

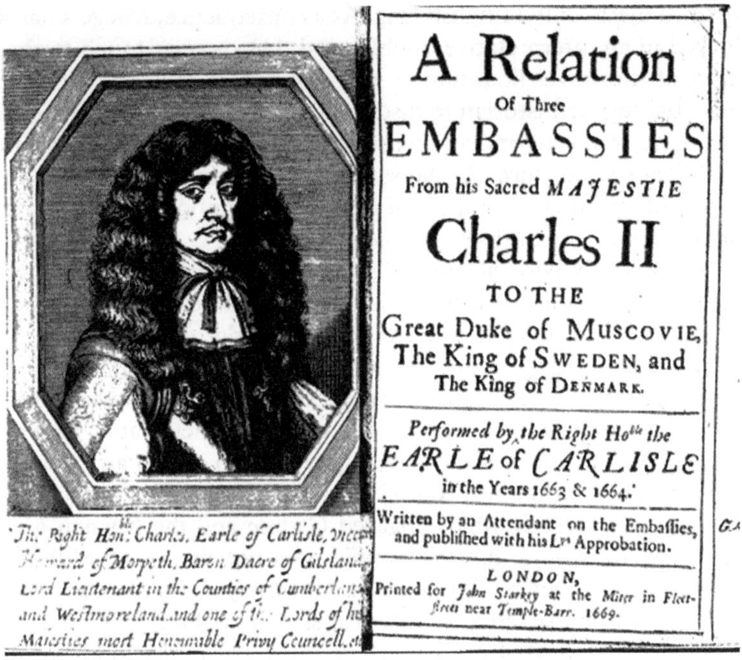

A Relation
Of Three
EMBASSIES
From his Sacred MAJESTIE
Charles II
TO THE
Great Duke of MUSCOVIE,
The King of SWEDEN, and
The King of DENMARK.

Performed by the Right Ho[ble] the
EARLE of CARLISLE
in the Years 1663 & 1664.

Written by an Attendant on the Embassies,
and published with his L[rs] Approbation.

LONDON,
Printed for John Starkey at the Miter in Fleet-
street near Temple-Barr. 1669.

The Right Hon[ble] Charles, Earle of Carlisle, Viscount Howard of Morpeth, Baron Dacre of Gilsland, Lord Lieutenant in the Counties of Cumberland and Westmoreland and one of the Lords of his Maiesties most Honourable Privy Councell, etc.

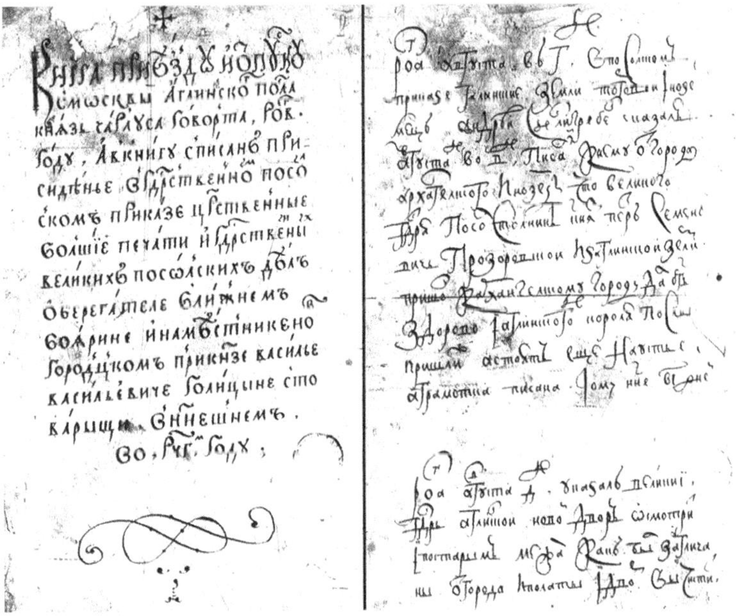

Figures 3.1 and 3.2 Two different genres: travel account juxtaposed with ceremonial documentation. Published account of Carlisle's embassy and two pages from the Russian *posol'skaia kniga* of the embassy's stay in Moscow.

to the majesty of the English king. As a consequence, Miege's narrative is locked in an interpretative double-bind that owes as much to the exoticism of the travel literature as to reporting of ordinary protocol. It is essential for the historian to discriminate between these two constitutive elements of the narrative: discourses of barbarism and descriptions of diplomatic procedure. At the same time, one must read them together when interpreting the impact of Miege's descriptions on the contemporary perception of Carlisle's embassy.

It has rightly been acknowledged that Miege wrote his account as an apology for Carlisle's actions that had failed to restore English trade privileges.[185] In order to absolve the ambassador of wrongdoing, Miege's narrative spanned the entire gamut of cultural demarcation, from the tropes of barbarism to accusations of arrogance. The Russians were blamed for their ignorant behaviour and inability to conduct negotiations in a civilised way. True, the ceremonial disputes spiralled into a clash and worsened the relations between the two courts. However, a closer look at the diplomatic norms and practices, which engaged Carlisle and the Russian *pristavy* to equal extent, shows that this conflict was not the result of the cultural boundaries erected by Miege to explain away the ambassador's failure. The English ambassador and the Russian court both defended – on the common battle field of symbols and gestures – what they thought were their inviolable sovereign rights.

The *posol'skaia kniga* (see Figure 3.2) provides a useful example. Amidst the instructions to the *pristavy* regarding Carlisle's embassy, the clerks inserted a long quote from Prozorovskii's *stateinyi spisok*, which gave a detailed account of the Russian ambassadors' reception in London.[186] The London ceremonial thus was retrieved from the archives of the *Posol'skii prikaz* to serve as a concrete model for Carlisle's ceremonial treatment. As such, the basis of Carlisle's experiences in Russia was not some obscure or 'Byzantine' practice, but the diplomatic ceremonies that the English court had arranged for Prozorovskii.[187]

Nevertheless, Miege's deliberate misrepresentations contributed to the barbarous image of seventeenth-century Russia.[188] They also encroached on the writings of contemporary scholars of precedence who had otherwise no difficulty in culling out Russia's barbarous image in order to

[185] Konovalov, 'England and Russia', pp. 66f.
[186] RGADA, f. 35, op. 1, d. 11, ll. 170–78.
[187] Cf. S. Lachs Phyllis, *The Diplomatic corps under Charles II & James II* (New Brunswick, 1965), p. 106.
[188] See Voltaire's remarks on Carlisle's embassy (fn. 293).

include the tsars in the European *theatrum praecedentiae*.[189] Numerous editions of Miege's *Relation* were published in English (London, 1669, 1705, and 1715), French (Amsterdam, 1669, 1672, 1700; Rouen, 1670 and 1700), and German (Leipzig, Frankfurt a. M., 1701).[190] Thanks to his account, the discourse of barbarism and descriptions of diplomatic procedure coalesced in works of diplomatic theory, introducing a degree of uncertainty about Russia's place in the world. Wicquefort, for instance, noted that Russians were uncivil and barbarous:

> The Muscovites are rude, barbarous and bruthish. For although Birth makes some distinction among the last, yet they are all Slaves to the Czar; and in this servile and mean Education there is nothing to be seen but what is abject, gross and rustical. The Czar or Great Duke, causes all Embassadors to be receiv'd at the entrance into his Dominions, and defrays them as long as they stay there; but then this treatment, and the Honour that is done them is accompanied with an arrogancy that is almost beastly. Whereas in other courts, the Masters of the Ceremonies and the Introductors of Embassadors, do all the Civilities imaginable [...] the *Muscovite Pristave* does all he can to take the place of Honour; makes difficulty to alight from his Horse till the Embassador has quitted his. [...] There are several relations from those parts [...] But it is not any where that their impertinence is more lively represented, than in what we have of the Journey the Earl of *Carlisle* took thither in the Year 1663.[191]

Then Wicquefort went on to paraphrase the ceremonial incidents that Miege had conveniently constructed as affronts against the ambassador and his master. Miege's account also inspired Rousset de Missy to make mocking remarks about the Russian *pristav* who seemed so serious about upholding the majesty of his ruler that he turned into a marble column. In particular, he referred to the dispute about who ought to dismount from his sleigh first. According to the author, the Russian celebrated his glorious victory attained through deception, by making the unsuspecting ambassador touch the ground first.[192]

Was this the typical approach of a stubborn and backward Russian courtier who was preoccupied with outward appearance and had no concern for diplomatic substance? Certainly not. Swedish diplomatic protocol also showed concern about the moment when ambassadors,

[189] Another prominent example is, Lünig, *Theatrum Ceremoniale*, II, pp. 1461ff., where Russia is not mentioned in the section on non-European ceremonial practice.

[190] Poe, *Foreign descriptions of Muscovy*, p. 133.

[191] Wicquefort, *Embassador*, I, p. 145.

[192] The fact that Rousset concentrates on Carlisle's embassy when describing the diplomatic ceremonial exercised at the Russian court, shows just how influential Miege's account was. Rousset de Missy, *Cérémonial diplomatique*, II, p. 649. See also Lünig, *Theatrum Ceremoniale*, I, pp. 646ff.

coming from the sea, disembarked and stepped onto Swedish soil.[193] The Russians might have borrowed the *pristav*'s trick from Herberstein who had applied the same odd technique at one point during his embassies in the first half of the sixteenth century, in order to preserve the status of the Holy Roman Emperor. Herberstein commented on his furtive ceremonial manoeuvres as follows:

> The interpreter Istoma came forward and called upon me to dismount. I excused myself as being very tired; [. . .] After spending some time over such pompous talk I wanted to make an end of it, and shook my foot out of the stirrup. Upon this the other [Russian] envoy dismounted at once, whilst I climbed slowly from the saddle. I too wished to preserve reverence for my master among these wild people.[194]

Herberstein's comment illustrates how difficult it is to distinguish between ceremonial details and cultural perception. On the one hand, he projected the image of the savage onto the Russians in their attempt to preserve or increase the international prestige of the tsar; on the other, he abided by the rules of the savage, as if they were his own, and he invented ceremonial tricks to avoid humiliating the emperor. As Wicquefort's account demonstrates, these 'German' tricks were later foisted on Russians as proof of their haughtiness and uncivilised culture. Who is the savage here?

Whether diplomats from Moscow were beastly or arrogant is not the point. The German envoy behaved in an equally underhand way, and the same 'beastliness' could be ascribed to the French and Spanish diplomats whose ceremonial quarrel in London in 1661 left several people dead, or to Carlisle whom the Russians blamed for his 'ceremonious stomack'.[195] The crux of the matter is that all the diplomats – Dokhturov, Colepeper, Prideaux, Prozorovskii, and Carlisle – shared common knowledge about symbolic rivalry. They knew perfectly well that symbols did the work of fact in a world where the sovereignty of a state was inextricably interlinked with the ritual 'fabrication' of a monarch's sovereignty or international prestige.[196] Neither cultural incompatibility between Russia and England nor personal qualities such as 'impatience, peevishness and arrogance' led

[193] RGADA, f. 156, op. 1, d. 153, l. 2. See also the reception of Swedish ambassadors on their way to Moscow as described by Kotoshikhin, *O Rossii*, p. 74.

[194] Picard, ed., *Herberstein*, p. 54.

[195] See Chapter 2, fn. 178. The term 'ceremonious stomacks' was used by an English master of ceremonies to describe the behaviour of Russian diplomats, see the quote in Anderson, *Modern diplomacy*, p. 61.

[196] The term 'fabrication' is from Burke, *The fabrication of Louis XIV*.

to the ceremonial stalemate.[197] Conflicts over diplomatic ceremonies emerged from the mounting claims to status and the logic of ritual itself, from the unpredictability and contingency of face-to-face communication.

A contrasting example can clarify this point. When Christopher Columbus set foot on an island in the Caribbean Sea in 1492, to take possession of the newly discovered land, he unfurled the royal standard in a legal ceremony and declared in a series of recorded speech acts that this land now belonged to the territory of the sovereign of Spain. Regarding the natives' reaction to the solemn performance, he reported back to Spain: 'And I was not contradicted.'[198] This transatlantic encounter – in contrast to Russian-European quarrels over ceremony – resulted in a genuine cultural misunderstanding. The indigenous people failed to recognise the ritual of taking possession and the legal basis of the ceremonial. They lacked the cultural connection to the intruders to raise any voice of protest.[199] The Russian ceremonial contradictions, however, against European attempts to assert equal or superior status in the territories which were in possession of the tsar (and vice versa), show that Europeans and Russians were conscious actors in a world of converging norms and that they participated in the same cultural practices: they were caught in the delicate web of mutually granted honours and prestige that shaped early modern diplomatic culture.

[197] Cf. Konovalov, 'England and Russia', p. 65; Anderson, *Modern diplomacy*, pp. 61f.; M. V. Unkovskaya, 'Anglo-Russian diplomatic relations, 1580–1696' (unpublished DPhil dissertation, University of Oxford, 1992), p. 292. But compare K. Boterbloem, 'Russia and Europe: The Koenraad van Klenk Embassy to Moscow (1675–76)', *Journal of Early Modern History*, 14 (2010), 187–217, who revisits the notion of Muscovy as a 'barbarous outsider'.

[198] S. Greenblatt, *Marvelous possessions: the wonder of the New World* (Oxford, 1991), p. 58.

[199] For an inspiring study of the rituals of taking possession of foreign lands in the age of European expansion, see Seed, *Ceremonies of possession*.

4 Stage and Audience

The Grand Embassy to Vienna (1698) and Peter I's Visit to Paris (1717)

Both Peter I's Grand Embassy to Vienna in 1698 and his travels to Paris in 1717 illustrate the theatricality of diplomatic dialogue in the age of baroque culture, the way in which rulers and diplomats changed the scenery in the *theatrum praecedentiae* in order to reconcile seemingly incompatible ceremonial demands and to advance negotiations with other polities. This chapter investigates the semiotic dimensions of the tsar's Grand Embassy to the court of the Holy Roman Emperor Leopold I as well as his stay at the court of Louis XV (r. 1715–1774), as an example of the role of politics in ceremony and ceremony in politics.[1] It ignores the reasons for Peter I's visits to Vienna and Paris – his wish to persuade Emperor Leopold I to prolong the war with the Ottoman Empire in 1698, and the 1717 negotiations of an alliance treaty between France, Prussia, and Russia – and does not dissect the ceremonies for evidence of the differences between Habsburg, Russian, or French traditions. Rather, it examines the role of the courtly public sphere more closely and asks how far ceremony constrained or facilitated political communication.

Vienna 1698

However rigid were the rules governing precedence, and however greatly they constrained rulers as well as their subjects, ceremonies were understood to be a system of signs, to be adjusted and manipulated short of undermining the established hierarchical system. The crucial arena for such manoeuvres was the court. The degree to which spectators, most often aristocrats and courtiers, took part determined the degree to which symbolic communication between the negotiating parties was perceived to be binding. In 1698, the relations between the tsar and the emperor

[1] For concise overviews of the Grand Embassy, see E. Schlöss, 'Über die Begegnung des Zaren Peter I mit dem Kaiser Leopold I', *Wiener Geschichtsblätter*, 49 (1994), 149–62; I. Schwarcz, 'Velikoe posol'stvo i Venskii dvor: K voprosu o prebyvanii Velikogo Posol'stva v Vene', in *Tsentral'naia Evropa v novoe i noveishee vremia: sbornik k 70-letiiu T. M. Islamova*, ed. A. S. Stykalin (Moscow, 1998), pp. 55–68.

necessitated the communication of conflicting political messages. These passed through three separate, if interconnected, channels of communication (see Figure 4.1) that followed distinct sets of semiotic rules and involved the court, as a witness, in varying degrees. First, public ceremonies expressed, and thus substantiated, the established hierarchical relationship between tsar and emperor in the political order. Second, private ceremonies facilitated a personal relationship between two royal allies, portrayed as equal brothers. Third, the negotiations about the Ottoman war were kept secret, away from public view, to prevent the disagreements over the war from challenging the symbolically established order and striking at the foundations of monarchical authority.

At the time of the Grand Embassy, neither the tsar nor the Holy Roman Emperor maintained a resident ambassador at the other's court. Instead, a series of short-term embassies had settled questions arising from their relations with their common neighbour, Poland-Lithuania, and their potential enemy, the Ottoman Empire.[2]

Two Muscovite embassies with ambassadorial rank were sent to Vienna between the end of the Thirty Years' War and Peter I's arrival in 1698, in 1679 and 1687.[3] In 1679, imperial officials responsible for the reception of the ambassadors had difficulty in deciding where to place the tsar within the hierarchy of European monarchs. After a search through the court archives failed to turn up a precedent, the emperor called a conference at which his officials recommended him to recognise the tsar to be a '*monarcha et princeps coronatus autocrator etc.* as much as the king of Spain and other absolute potentates'.[4] Thus, the embassy was received with the *honores regii* accorded to crowned heads as an unambiguous sign of the recognition of the sovereignty manifest in their dignified appearance. At Vienna in 1679, imperial officials recognised the tsar as a sovereign among Christian sovereigns, though of lesser rank than the emperor who

[2] The imperial court did not have an official resident in Moscow until 1711 (Anton Otto von Pleyer, agent 1691–1710, resident 1711–1718). The first Russian diplomatic mission at Vienna was established under the leadership of Prince Petr A. Golitsyn (the tsar's representative at Vienna from 1701 to 1705), see L. Bittner, et al., *Repertorium der diplomatischen Vertreter aller Länder seit dem Westfälischen Frieden, 1648*, 2 vols. (Oldenburg, Berlin, Zurich, 1936–1965), I, pp. 434f. See W. Leitsch, *Moskau und die Politik des Kaiserhofes im 17. Jahrhundert. Teil 1* (Graz, 1960), and Roll, 'Beobachtungen', for Austro-Russian relations.

[3] Bittner et al., *Repertorium*, I, pp. 434f.

[4] Quoted from the *Zeremonialprotokolle*, HHStA, ZA Prot, 3, fol. 204v. The *Zeremonialprotokolle* of the 1679 Russian embassy are now available in transcription in H. D. Körbl, 'Zeremonielle Aspekte des diplomatischen Verkehrs: Der Besuch der moskowitischen Großbotschaft im Wien des Jahres 1679', in *Der Wiener Hof im Spiegel der Zeremonialprotokolle (1652–1800): Eine Annäherung*, ed. I. Pangerl, M. Scheutz, T. Winkelbauer (Vienna, 2007), pp. 573–625.

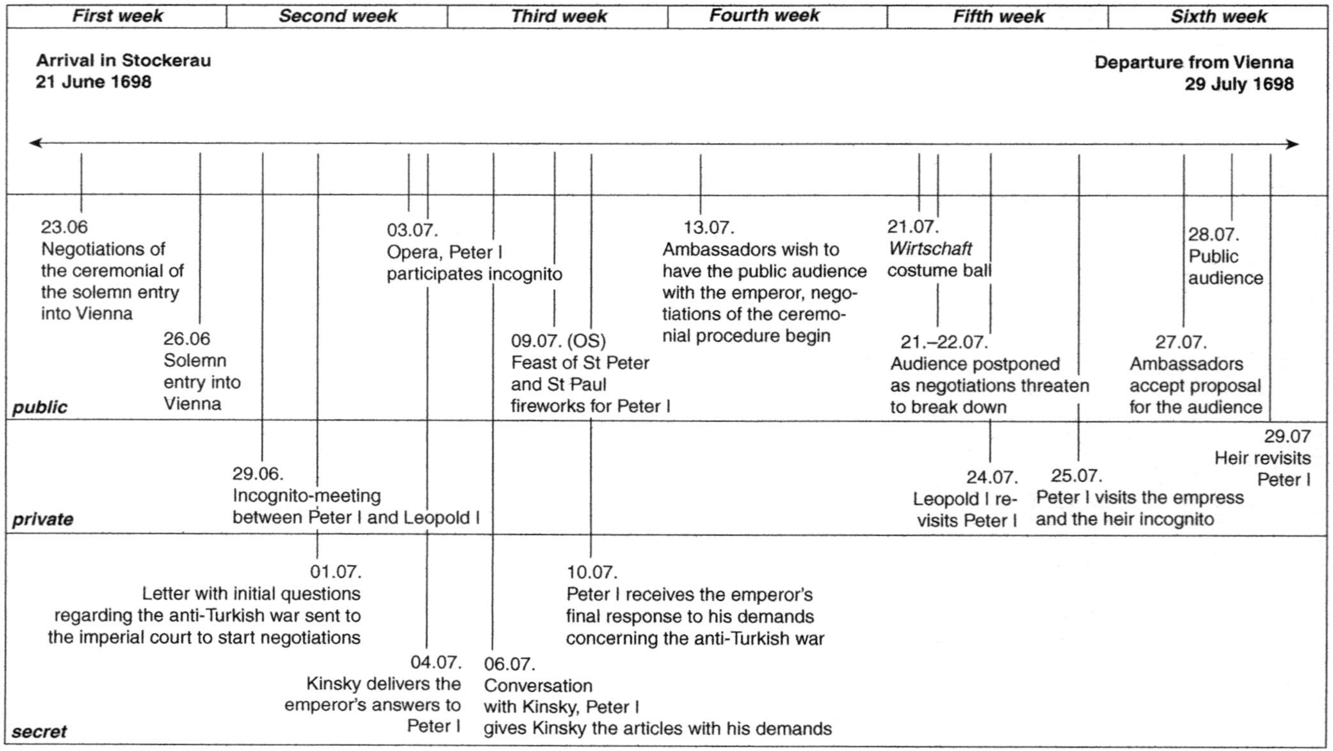

Figure 4.1 Bird's-eye view of Peter I's Grand Embassy's sojourn in Vienna (1698)

placed himself above kings. The ceremonies observed at that time also determined the honours paid to Peter I's diplomats in 1698.[5]

By an *ukaz* of December 1696,

> the Sovereign decreed ... to send grand ambassadors with full powers [*poslat' velikikh i polnomochnykh poslov*] to neighbouring countries, to the emperor, to the kings of England and Denmark, to the Roman pope, to the Netherlands, to the elector of Brandenburg, and to Venice ... for the confirmation of ancient friendship and love, for common affairs of the whole of Christendom: the weakening of the enemies of the cross of the Lord, the Turkish sultan, the Crimean khan, and all Muslim hordes.[6]

The itinerary listed in the official instructions to the ambassadors did not match the embassy's route. First, they were to travel through Swedish Livonia and Courland (avoiding Poland) to Vienna, to conduct negotiations with the Holy Roman Emperor, Peter I's ally in the struggle against the Ottomans. From there, they were to continue to Rome, Venice, the Netherlands, England, Denmark, and, finally, to visit the elector of Brandenburg, Frederick III. In the event, the route was changed, as Peter I's envoy to Vienna, Koz'ma N. Nefimonov, had renewed the anti-Ottoman alliance shortly before the embassy's departure from Moscow in March 1697. Rather than going to Vienna, it first spent two months visiting the elector of Brandenburg at Königsberg. From there it travelled to the Dutch Republic. In January 1698, Peter and a small entourage sailed for England, where he stayed until April. In both countries, he familiarised himself with the political situation in western Europe and studied navigation and shipbuilding. When he learned that, despite Nefimonov's efforts, the Holy League was likely to make peace with the Ottomans through the mediation of William III, the visit to the imperial court was revived. After Peter I had re-joined the embassy in the Dutch Republic, it travelled to Vienna by way of Bielefeld, Minden, Hildesheim, Halle, Leipzig, and Dresden.[7]

[5] For 1687, see Augustynowicz, 'Moskauer Grossgesandtschaft'.

[6] *Ukaz*, 6 December 1696 (OS), quoted in N. G. Ustrialov, *Istoriia tsarstvovaniia Petra Velikago*, 6 vols. (St Petersburg, 1858–63), III, p. 6.

[7] R. Wittram, 'Peters des Großen erste Reise in den Westen. Herrmann Aubin zum 23. Dezember 1955', *Jahrbücher für Geschichte Osteuropas*, 3 (1955), 373–403. For the practical motives of the embassy regarding shipbuilding, navigation, and general craftsmanship, see D. Iu. Guzevich, I. D. Guzevich, *Velikoe posol'stvo* (St Petersburg, 2003), ch. 3. The literature on the Grand Embassy is huge. For a comprehensive and analytical bibliography, see D. Iu. Guzevich, I. D. Guzevich, *Pervoe Evropeiskoe puteshestvie tsaria Petra: analiticheskaia bibliografiia za tri stoletiia, 1697–2006* (St Petersburg, 2008). See also D. Iu. Guzevich, I. D. Guzevich, *Velikoe posol'stvo: Rubezh epokh, ili Nachalo puti: 1697–1698* (St Petersburg, 2008), and A. G. Gus'kov, *Velikoe Posol'stvo Petra I: Istochnikovedcheskoe issledovanie* (Moscow, 2005), for a source description with rich materials from the Russian archives.

The ambassadorial chancellery in Moscow, in organising the Grand Embassy, followed long-established tradition.[8] As mentioned earlier, in Muscovy, unlike Europe, the doctrine of 'representative character' did not determine the rank of the diplomat. The three Muscovite ranks of *posol, poslannik,* and *gonets* reflected mainly the importance of the mission or the social status of the men appointed.[9] The task of fostering the alliance against the Ottomans warranted giving the Grand Embassy ambassadorial rank, and before their arrival at Vienna, the imperial court recognised them as 'grand ambassadors with full powers' (*gevollmächtigte grossgesande*), to be addressed as 'Excellenz'.[10] This form of address, which signified ambassadorial rank to listeners as well as the addressed, also signified the emperor's acceptance of the ambassadors as 'representatives' of the tsar.[11]

According to Muscovite custom, three officials were appointed jointly to head the embassy. Peter I's favourite, Franz Lefort, appointed as chief ambassador, had mainly ceremonial responsibilities.[12] The second and third ambassadors, Fedor A. Golovin and Prokopii B. Voznitsyn, were responsible for the practical organisation of the embassy and negotiations. Both were experienced diplomats; Voznitsyn, in particular, was said to be knowledgeable about the customs and manners of foreigners.[13] The embassy numbered around 250. Lefort alone was accompanied by six pages, four dwarfs, servants, musicians, trumpeters, surgeons, a pastor, and well-equipped guards.[14] Among them was Peter I, travelling incognito as a soldier, Petr Mikhailov.

The tsar's concealment as a member of the embassy's guard is often attributed to his remarkable character – in particular, his alleged dislike of ostentation. In modern scholarship, contemporary observations and historical interpretation often coalesce into a heroic image filled with deep admiration. The incognito 'reflects Peter's deeply held belief that what really mattered was a man's innate worth, a compound of knowledge, energy and public spirit, not titles, ceremonies, or outward

[8] Cf. Kotoshikhin, *O Rossii*, ch. 4, with the embassy's *nakaz* in *PDS*, VIII, cols. 661–99; M. M. Bogoslovskii, *Petr I: materialy dlia biografii*, 5 vols. (Moscow, 1940–1948), II, pp. 8f.

[9] See also Grabar, *International law*, pp. 56–59.

[10] Dietrichstein to Lefort, 23 April 1698, HHStA, ÄZA, Kart. 18 ('Diarium über den Aufenthalt des Czar Peter I. in Wien'), fol. 56–v.

[11] Rohr, *Ceremoniel-Wissenschaft der grossen Herren*, p. 377.

[12] For Lefort, see M. C. Posselt, *Der General und Admiral F. Lefort. Sein Leben und seine Zeit: ein Beitrag zur Geschichte Peter's des Grossen*, 2 vols. (Frankfurt a. M., St Petersburg 1866).

[13] *Theatri Europaei Continuati Funffzehender Theil/Das ist: Abermalige Außführliche Fortsetzung Denck- und Merckwürdigster Geschichten* (Frankfurt a. M., 1707), pp. 330ff.

[14] A. Babkin, 'Pis'ma Frantsa i Petra Leforta o "Velikom Posol'stve"', *Voprosy istorii*, 6 (1976), 120–32, here p. 123; Ustrialov, *Istoriia tsarstvovaniia*, III, pp. 572–76.

appearances',[15] wrote a respected biographer and historian of diplomatic relations to evoke the words of the Austrian diplomatic secretary, Johann Georg Korb, who described the tsar as 'a great contemner of all pomp and ostentation about his own person'.[16] It is generally accepted that he travelled under an assumed identity to enable him to study carpentry and shipbuilding in the countries he visited without being inhibited by protocol and public responsibilities. The incognito took odd forms if one is to believe contemporary accounts that the tsar, who was six feet seven inches tall, sometimes lifted up a dwarf to cover his face.[17] However curious it may appear, however deep the insights into Peter I's fabled character, it can be explained by recognising its diplomatic functions.

As the Habsburgs awaited the embassy's arrival, imperial officials planned a programme for the tsar's entertainment: visits to the imperial treasury (*Schatzkammer*), picture galleries, libraries, and gardens.[18] Nevertheless, the tsar's presence had to remain, officially, unacknowledged ('"all" incognito').[19] But how to treat him as if he were not there? And why was it important to disguise his majesty when everybody knew who he was?[20]

Rohr stated in 1729 that 'the [Holy] Roman Emperors always [...] claimed the prerogative never to have to give the *place d'honneur* at the right hand to any other crowned head [...] in their own houses or courtly camps [...] Therefore, the Muscovite Tsar Peter [...] residing in Vienna in 1698, could only see and visit the Roman Emperor [...] incognito and without ceremonies.'[21] The tsar's arrival at the imperial court reignited a long-standing ceremonial rivalry.

Leopold I's long reign had been punctuated with arguments over Russia's claim to equality. The emperor treated any claim by a Christian ruler to equality as a contradiction in terms: Christian sovereigns deferred

15 M. S. Anderson, *Peter the Great*, 2 edn. (Harlow, 1995), pp. 39f.

16 J. G. Korb, *Diary of an Austrian secretary of legation at the court of Czar Peter the Great*, trans. C. C. Macdonnell, reprint edn., 2 vols. (London, 1968), II, p. 155.

17 *Theatri Europaei*, p. 334. For Peter I's physical appearance, see Hughes, *Age of Peter the Great*, pp. 357–63.

18 HHStA, ÄZA, Kart. 18 ('Diarium über den Aufenthalt des Czar Peter I. in Wien'), fol. 72–v.

19 HHStA, ZA Prot, 5, fol. 420v. For the 1698 *Zeremonialprotokolle* in facsimile with parallel transcription, see now E. Schlöss, 'Zar Perter der Grosse in Wien: Übertragung der Blätter 411 bis 452 der Ceremonialprotocolle 1698 (ZA Prot. 5) in die Schrift unserer Zeit wort- und zeilengetreu', *Mitteilungen des Österreichischen Staatsarchivs*, 51 (2004), 375–546.

20 The tsar's presence was reported in the press; see W. Griep, F. Krahé, *Ausstellungskatalog 'Peter der Große in Westeuropa': die grosse Gesandtschaft 1697–1698 [Ausstellung 'Schätze aus dem Kreml – Peter der Große in Westeuropa']* (Bremen, 1991), pp. 43ff.

21 Rohr, *Ceremoniel-Wissenschaft der grossen Herren*, p. 343.

to the emperor as the protector of the church.[22] The imperial envoy at Moscow in 1661/62, Augustin von Meyerberg, had disputed with Muscovite officials over whether the emperor and the tsar should be addressed and address one another as 'Majesty'. Meyerberg complained that the Muscovites referred to his sovereign as 'his imperial high-mightiness' (*kayserliche grossmächtigkeit*) and not as 'his imperial majesty'. In Moscow, this inferior form of address (*vel'mozhnost'* in Russian) was employed because Leopold I, too, had refused to address Tsar Aleksei, Peter I's father, as 'Majesty' to avoid jeopardising his own claim to superior status.[23] In 1675, the head of the ambassadorial department, Artamon S. Matveev, gave the imperial envoys Hannibal F. von Bottoni and Johann C. Terlinger von Guzman a memorandum that urged the emperor, first, to present future Russian diplomats with their recredentials in person and from his own hands at an audience, and not to employ courtiers to hand them over according to Habsburg practice; and second, to address the tsar as 'Majesty' (*velichestvo*) in official correspondence. The ambassadorial department gave as the reason: 'so that His Tsarist Majesty and His Imperial Majesty were equal in honour [*v ravnoi chesti*], for these two Great Sovereigns have for one another agreeable brotherly friendship and love, and they address each other as brothers in their instruments'.[24] Sovereigns addressed one another as equal brothers.[25] If the imperial court refused to grant these privileges, as they did, the Muscovite court would reciprocate.

Given these experiences, the presence, in Vienna, of a tsar whose behaviour was known to be unpredictable was an obvious challenge to Leopold I's status. As Peter I, as the Russian tsar, embodied all of his predecessors' demands for equal status, any deviation from established ceremonial might have implied a serious challenge to the emperor's claim to the highest rank among sovereigns. Therefore, the imperial court had to ensure that the two men did not meet in public, in their capacities as emperor and tsar. The ceremonies between them were planned and executed as if the tsar were not present.

Incognito did not require the disguising of the person, and body, of the prince, or of his individual identity. It simply implied that a monarch, having put aside his majestic attributes when appearing before the court,

[22] Cf. Duchhardt, 'Imperium'.

[23] K. Meyer, '"Kayserliche grossmächtigkeit". Titularfragen bei den Verhandlungen zwischen Kaiser und Zar 1661/62', in *Rossica Externa. Studien zum 15.-17. Jahrhundert. Festgabe für Paul Johansen zum 60. Geburtstag*, ed. H. Weczerka (Marburg, 1963), pp. 115–24. For the tsars' title, see the section 'Imperator' in Chapter 5.

[24] *PSZRI*, I, no. 610 (9 October 1675, OS), p. 1011.

[25] Grabar, *International law*, p. 6; Iuzefovich, *Put' posla*, pp. 14–23.

invited everybody to pretend that he was absent.[26] Incognito was a political strategy used in the symbolic context of diplomacy, and not a game of hide-and-seek.[27]

Public Ceremonies

Several pageants (see Figure 4.1) formed the basis of diplomatic dialogue during the Grand Embassy's stay at the imperial court. Of these, the solemn entry into Vienna, on 26 June 1698, was the first step in the symbolic process by which the hierarchical relationship between tsar and emperor was reaffirmed and displayed before selected witnesses.[28] The entry gave a foretaste of the next ceremonial occasion, namely the public audience that brought the ambassadors to the seat of power, that is, before the emperor himself.

The audience with the emperor staged the presentation of the ambassadors' credentials. As a legal document, the credentials qualified an ambassador to act on behalf of his sovereign, who guaranteed his diplomat's reliability and demanded assurances of his safety.[29] Under normal circumstances, credentials were presented shortly after an embassy's arrival. The ceremony began with the collection of the foreign diplomats from their residence, continued with a parade through the city to the court, and, after the diplomats had presented their credentials to the monarch, ended with a feast. The public audience for Peter I's ambassadors took place more than a month after its solemn entry and only one day before the Grand Embassy departed.[30] The negotiations over the audience almost broke down as the Russian ambassadors argued with imperial officials over ceremonies designed to affirm – in the ambassadors' eyes, to decrease – the tsar's prestige relative to the emperor's. The protracted argument led Peter I to postpone his departure, even after he had received alarming news of the uprising in June of the musketeers (*strel'tsy*) in Moscow. As Peter I wished Lefort and Golovin to return with him to Moscow (Voznitsyn stayed in

[26] See also F. C. v. Moser, *Teutsches Hof-Recht*, 4 vols. (Frankfurt a. M., Leipzig, 1761), II, p. 266: 'A travelling master reveals his innate character [status] sometimes but appears incognito if he says that he wishes to appear incognito'.

[27] For the political significance of Peter I's love for mockery, inversions of social structures, and play, see Hughes, *Age of Peter the Great*, pp. 248–97; Zitser, *Transfigured kingdom*, pp. 12ff. For a *longue durée* study of incognito, see V. Barth, *Inkognito: Geschichte eines Zeremoniells* (Munich, 2013).

[28] For a detailed account, see *PDS*, VIII, cols. 1319ff. Cf. Wicquefort, *Embassador*, pp. 127–64.

[29] Stieve, *Hoff-Ceremoniel* (1723), pp. 235f. For the credentials, see *PDS*, VIII, cols. 1399ff.

[30] The account derives from HHStA, ZA Prot, 5, fols. 428–39, 440v–41v, 443v–51 and *PDS*, VIII, cols. 1368ff.

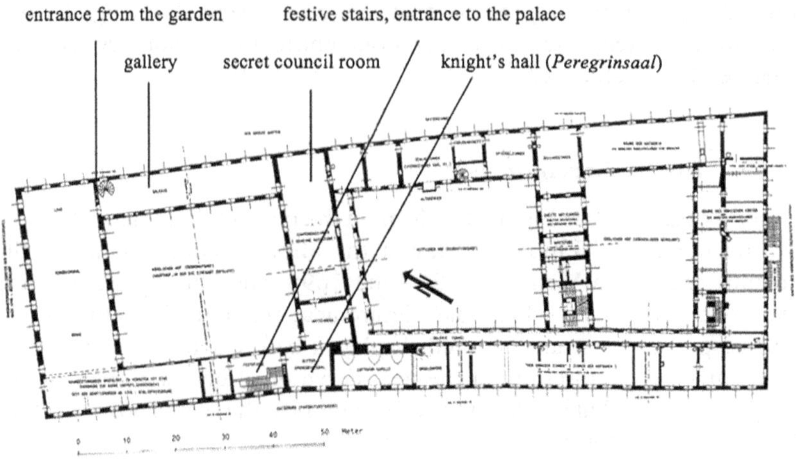

Figure 4.2 Reconstruction of the floor plan of the Favorita (first floor)

Vienna), he was obliged to wait until they had had their public audience with the emperor.

On 13 July, when the Muscovite ambassadors were certain that the customary gifts for the emperor would arrive from Moscow in time, they asked for their public audience. The emperor's cup-bearer, Baron Königsacker, who had led the solemn entry into Vienna, proposed a ceremony modelled on the precedent of 1679. The imperial court would convey the ambassadors and their entourage from their lodgings in carriages reserved for such solemn occasions. The mayor would supply forty Viennese townsmen to carry the tsar's gifts for the emperor. The procession through the streets of Vienna, to be headed by a Muscovite diplomatic secretary, on horseback, holding the credentials aloft, would accompany the ambassadors as far as the inner courtyard of the emperor's residence, the Favorita (Figure 4.2). From here, they would ascend the grand staircase leading to the knights' hall (*Ritterstuben*), in which foreign diplomats were usually welcomed and in which they would remove their hats. The knights' hall was also called the *Peregrinsaal* (derived from the Latin word *peregrinus*, meaning foreigner) because foreign diplomats had to pass through it before entering the emperor's chambers.[31] From there, the chief steward, also with his head uncovered, would lead them towards the antechamber, past the imperial guards and townsmen who would stand on both sides of the room with the gifts in their hands. The chamberlain

[31] E. Schlöss, *Baugeschichte des Theresianums in Wien* (Wien, 1998), p. 48.

would accompany them through the first antechamber to the entrance to the secret council room in which the audience would be held. There, the ambassadors and the Muscovite nobles would wait for the invitation to approach the emperor, who would be standing on a pedestal beneath a canopy. He would ask about the tsar's health while gently touching his hat, though not removing it. From his elevated position, he would legitimise the ambassadors' diplomatic mission through the acceptance of their credentials. Muscovite nobles would then be invited to kiss the emperor's hand, and to lay the tsar's gifts at his feet.

The relationship between the tsar and the emperor implied by these arrangements did not satisfy Muscovite expectations. For example, first, the ambassadors demanded more carriages and twice the number of townsmen in attendance as signs of the emperor's esteem for the tsar. Second, they objected to removing their hats when passing through the knights' hall; this honour should be paid to the emperor in person, not to his subjects. Third, the ambassadors interpreted the delay while they waited outside the secret council room until the audience was granted as a humiliation: they wished to be presented to the emperor immediately by announcing the tsar's title in his presence. And fourth, they argued that the way they gave their gifts – placing them at Leopold I's feet – would be perceived as the payment of tribute.

In almost every respect, the ambassadors' pretensions broke with the precedent from 1679. The imperial court noted in a record, dated July 1698, the reasons for its refusal to agree.[32] First, an ambassador might not pass through the antechambers wearing a hat; the emperor would not grant such a privilege to a crowned head. Nor, second, might an ambassador enter the audience chamber while being announced by reading his master's title in the presence of the emperor; it would imply that the emperor was obliged to wait for the ambassador, instead of the Muscovite ambassador's being obliged to wait for the highest ruler on earth. Third, the imperial court denied that the established way of giving the gifts could be viewed as the payment of tribute. As the emperor gave gifts in return, an act of mutual courtesy did not imply further obligation. And fourth, the number of men assigned to carry the gifts could not be increased because, the imperial court claimed, it did not want to place an additional burden on the inhabitants of Vienna.

Imperial officials had offered a few alterations to established usage, to accommodate the Russian requests. One was the enquiry about the tsar's

[32] With an explicit disdain for court ceremony Ustrialov considers the draft to be an expression of imperial court's arrogance and hauteur, but discusses every single point of the ceremonial quarrel, see Ustrialov, *Istoriia tsarstvovaniia*, III, pp. 124, 137ff.

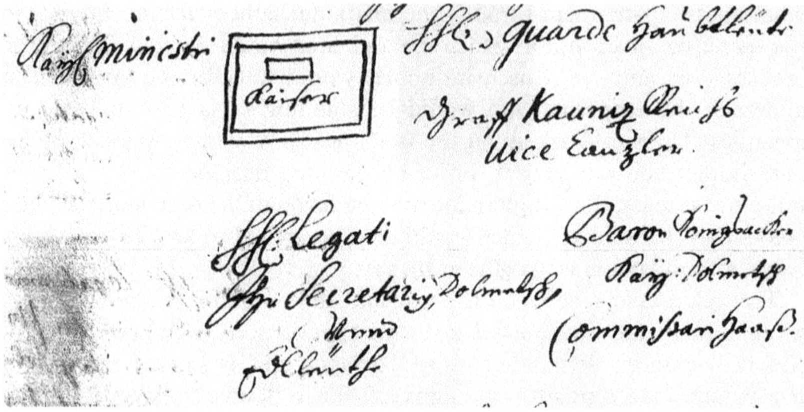

Figure 4.3 Viennese ceremonial records: Sketch of the assembly at the audience. Left to right: imperial ministers, Emperor Leopold I, imperial guards, the imperial vice-chancellor Count Kaunitz, the Russian ambassadors, their secretary, interpreter, Russian ambassadors, Baron Königsacker, imperial interpreter, commissary Haaß.

health at the reception of the ambassadors halfway up the grand staircase. But as the imperial officials objected to changes that denied the emperor his precedence, they threatened to cancel the public audience if the ambassadors continued to make difficulties. On 27 July, after a long and vexatious argument, the Muscovites gave way, to avoid the embarrassment of not having had their presence publicly acknowledged prior to their departure. The next day, the day before Peter I, Lefort, and Golovin left Vienna, the Grand Embassy was received in public audience by the emperor before the imperial court and finally submitted its credentials (see Figures 4.3 and 4.4). The issue of recredentials did not arise as Vosnitsyn stayed on in Vienna.

The imperial officials grounded their refusal to accept the ambassadors' demands on the practice at other courts. Concessions to the tsar carried the risk that other European monarchs, treating the concessions as a precedent, would try to increase their status in relation to the emperor by their own ceremonial innovations at the imperial court or during the reception of an imperial ambassador. In more abstract terms, the presentation of credentials was a ritual that confirmed the place of an ambassador's sovereign within the hierarchy acknowledged by the manner of his solemn entry into the city. Without the performance of the ceremonies, the credentials themselves and the monarch's address to his guests had no meaning. The symbolic language of the audience gave legal status to the script embodied

Figure 4.4 Russian ceremonial records: The Russian sketch of the meeting.

in the ceremonies by communicating its meaning to a witness, that is, the wider public.[33] The ritual of the public audience with the emperor, by translating a diplomatic document into the language of honour, gave every diplomatic relationship its place in the established political order. The prerequisite for such a relationship was the ceremonial acknowledgement by the Muscovite ambassadors of the emperor's primacy.

Public ceremonies constrained all the participants. Only a strictly choreographed ritual could express the hierarchical relationship of the parties by anticipating the ever-likely disputes. Until the ceremony of presentation had reaffirmed the relative status of the two states, personal meetings between their rulers in view of the court were prohibited, lest they jeopardise an agreement over the issue of status. For this reason, Peter I, despite being incognito, did not attend the audience but only the banquet afterwards in the Grand Embassy's residence.

Divertissements

One way to enable Leopold I to meet Peter I without prejudicing the outcome of the negotiations over the ambassadors' public audience was a *divertissement.* The imperial court invited the Grand Embassy to

[33] See also P. Bourdieu, *Language and symbolic power*, trans. G. Raymond, M. Adamson (Cambridge, MA, 1991), ch. 2; Stollberg-Rilinger, 'Symbolische Kommunikation', p. 516.

a costume ball, a *Wirtschaft*, on 21 July.[34] The event was staged on two floors of the Favorita which was turned into the mock-up of a tavern in which the innkeeper entertained travellers from different countries played by eighty imperial courtiers aided by forty of their servants (Figure 4.5).[35]

Leopold I chose the programme, the identities for the travellers, and the costumes. He himself took the role of the innkeeper, then sent Peter I the list from which he asked him to choose. After Peter I had chosen the role of Frisian peasant, the other costumes/roles were assigned by lot (Figure 4.6).[36]

The seating at dinner (Figure 4.7) made witty allusions to political and social antagonisms – impersonators of Spaniards placed opposite impersonators of Frenchmen, Muscovites opposite Poles, a shepherd near a soldier, and a hunter near a gardener, and so on – in a stereotypical view of the world. The emperor's conspicuous position as the host – sitting with only his wife, Empress Eleonore Magdalena, at the head of the table in a position of unchallenged superiority – implied that the rules of precedence were not entirely suspended.[37] Elsewhere, however, the order of precedence of both the guests and their assumed personae were ignored. Pierre Lefort, the nephew of the Muscovite ambassador, explained to his father that 'all people attending the feast were equal to each other', and that 'there was not the least hierarchy'.[38]

The political implications of the ball were different from those of the solemn entry and the public audience with the emperor. Free from the constraints of ceremony, the ball allowed political relationships between Russia and the Habsburgs to be expressed more freely.

During the ball, the innkeeper (Leopold I) approached the Frisian peasant (Peter I), to propose a toast to the friendship between the tsar and the emperor, both of them supposedly 'absent':

> He [the innkeeper] assumed that he [the Frisian peasant] knew the Grand Tsar of Moscow, to whom he wished well. Whereupon the ostensible Frisian peasant thanked him politely, raising the cup and giving his answer: he had to admit that he indeed knew the Grand Tsar of Moscow inside out. He was a friend of His Imperial Majesty and an enemy of his enemies. For the sake of the emperor's love

[34] For a description, see HHStA, ZA Prot, 5, fols. 439ff.

[35] For Wirtschaften, see C. Schnitzer, *Höfische Maskeraden: Funktion und Ausstattung von Verkleidungsdivertissements an deutschen Höfen der Frühen Neuzeit* (Tübingen, 1999), pp. 220–43. For court festivities see also the classic R. Alewyn, *Das grosse Welttheater. Die Epoche der höfischen Feste in Dokument und Deutung* (Hamburg, 1959).

[36] The list was printed in Lünig, *Theatrum Ceremoniale*, I, pp. 157f.

[37] Schnitzer, *Höfische Maskeraden*, pp. 231–43. The seating plan was printed in *Theatri Europaei*, p. 474, and Lünig, *Theatrum Ceremoniale*, I, p. 159.

[38] Quoted in Posselt, *Lefort*, II, p. 495.

Figure 4.5 A depiction of the *Wirtschaft* in the Favorita.

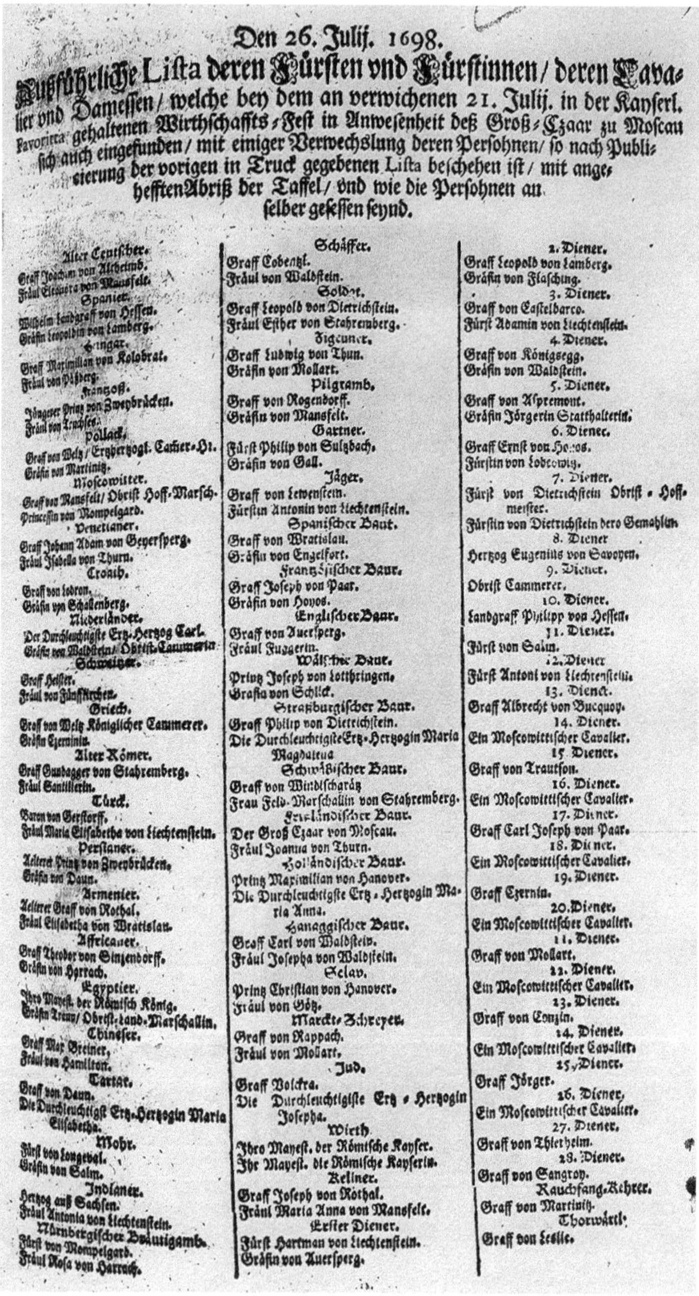

Den 26. Julij. 1698.

Außführliche Lista deren Fürsten und Fürstinnen / deren Cavalier und Damessen / welche bey dem an verwichenen 21. Julij. in der Kayserl. Favoritta gehaltenen Wirthschaffts-Fest in Anwesenheit deß Groß-Czaar zu Moscau sich auch eingefunden / mit einiger Verwechslung deren Persohnen / so nach Publicierung der vorigen in Truck gegebenen Lista beschehen ist / mit angehefften Abriß der Taffel / und wie die Persohnen an selber gesessen seynd.

Alter Teutscher.
Graff Joachim von Altheimb.
Fräul Eleonora von Mansfelt.
Spanier.
Wilhelm Landgraff von Hessen.
Gräfin Leopoldin von Lamberg.
Hungar.
Graff Maximilian von Kolobrat.
Fräul von Pötting.
Frantzoß.
Jüngerer Printz von Zweybrücken.
Fräul von Truchses.
Pollack.
Graff von Weltz / Ertzhertzogl. Cammer-Hr.
Gräfin von Martinitz.
Moscowitter.
Graff von Mansfelt / Obrist Hoff-Marsch.
Princessin von Mompelgard.
Venetianer.
Graff Johann Adam von Geyersperg.
Fräul Isabella von Thurn.
Croath.
Graff von Lodron.
Gräfin von Schallenberg.
Niederländer.
Der Durchleuchtigste Ertz-Hertzog Carl.
Gräfin von Waldstein / Obrist-Cammerin.
Schweitzer.
Graff Heister.
Fräul von Fünffkirchen.
Griech.
Graff von Weltz Königlicher Cammerer.
Gräfin Czernin.
Alter Römer.
Graff Gundagger von Stahremberg.
Fräul Santillerin.
Türck.
Baron von Gerstorff.
Fräul Maria Elisabetha von Liechtenstein.
Persianer.
Aelterer Printz von Zweybrücken.
Gräfin von Daun.
Armenier.
Aelterer Graff von Rothal.
Fräul Elisabetha von Wratislau.
Africaner.
Graff Theodor von Sinzendorff.
Gräfin von Harrach.
Egyptier.
Ihro Mayest. der Römisch König.
Gräfin Traun / Obrist-Land-Marschallin.
Chineser.
Graff Max Breiner.
Fräul von Hamilton.
Tartar.
Graff von Daun.
Die Durchleuchtigst Ertz-Hertzogin Maria Elisabetha.
Mohr.
Fürst von Longeval.
Gräfin von Salm.
Indianer.
Hertzog auß Sachsen.
Fräul Antonia von Liechtenstein.
Nürnbergischer Bräutigamb.
Fürst von Mompelgard.
Fräul Rosa von Harrach.

Schäffer.
Graff Cobentzl.
Fräul von Waldstein.
Soldat.
Graff Leopold von Dietrichstein.
Fräul Esther von Stahremberg.
Zigeuner.
Graff Ludwig von Thun.
Gräfin von Mollart.
Pilgramb.
Graff von Rogendorff.
Gräfin von Mansfelt.
Gartner.
Fürst Philip von Sultzbach.
Gräfin von Gall.
Jäger.
Graff von Lewenstein.
Fürstin Antonin von Liechtenstein.
Spanischer Baur.
Graff von Wratislau.
Gräfin von Engelfort.
Frantzösischer Baur.
Graff Joseph von Paar.
Gräfin von Hoyos.
Englischer Baur.
Graff von Auersperg.
Fräul Fuggerin.
Wälscher Baur.
Printz Joseph von Lotthringen.
Gräfin von Schlick.
Straßburgischer Baur.
Graff Philip von Dietrichstein.
Die Durchleuchtigste Ertz-Hertzogin Maria Magdalena
Schwäbischer Baur.
Graff von Windischgrätz
Frau Feld-Marschallin von Stahremberg.
Friesländischer Baur.
Der Groß Czaar von Moscau.
Fräul Joanna von Thurn.
Holländischer Baur.
Printz Maximilian von Hanover.
Die Durchleuchtigste Ertz-Hertzogin Maria Anna.
Hanaggischer Baur.
Graff Carl von Waldstein.
Fräul Josepha von Waldstein.
Sclav.
Printz Christian von Hanover.
Fräul von Götz.
Marckt-Schreyer.
Graff von Rappach.
Fräul von Mollart.
Jud.
Graff Volckra.
Die Durchleuchtigiste Ertz-Hertzogin Josepha.
Wirth.
Ihro Mayest. der Römische Kayser.
Ihr Mayest. die Römische Kayserin.
Kellner.
Graff Joseph von Rothal.
Fräul Maria Anna von Mansfelt.
Erster Diener.
Fürst Hartman von Liechtenstein.
Gräfin von Auersperg.

2. Diener.
Graff Leopold von Lamberg.
Gräfin von Flasching.
3. Diener.
Graff von Castelbarco.
Fürst Adamin von Liechtenstein.
4. Diener.
Graff von Königsegg.
Gräfin von Waldstein.
5. Diener.
Graff von Aspremont.
Gräfin Jörgerin Statthalterin.
6. Diener.
Graff Ernst von Hoyos.
Fürstin von Lobcowitz.
7. Diener.
Fürst von Dietrichstein Obrist-Hoffmeister.
Fürstin von Dietrichstein dero Gemahlin.
8. Diener
Hertzog Eugenius von Savoyen.
9. Diener.
Obrist Cammerer.
10. Diener.
Landgraff Philipp von Hessen.
11. Diener.
Fürst von Salm.
12. Diener
Fürst Antoni von Liechtenstein.
13. Diener.
Graff Albrecht von Bucquoy.
14. Diener.
Ein Moscowittischer Cavalier.
15. Diener.
Graff von Trautson.
16. Diener.
Ein Moscowittischer Cavalier.
17. Diener.
Graff Carl Joseph von Paar.
18. Diener.
Ein Moscowittischer Cavalier.
19. Diener.
Graff Czernin.
20. Diener.
Ein Moscowittischer Cavalier.
21. Diener.
Graff von Mollart.
22. Diener.
Ein Moscowittischer Cavalier.
23. Diener.
Graff von Conzin.
24. Diener.
Ein Moscowittischer Cavalier.
25. Diener.
Graff Jörger.
26. Diener.
Ein Moscowittischer Cavalier.
27. Diener.
Graff von Thierheim.
28. Diener.
Graff von Sangroy.
Rauchfang-Kehrer.
Graff von Martinitz.
Thorwärtl.
Graff von Leslie.

Figure 4.6 The list of the *Wirtschaft*'s participants and their costumes went into print and was enclosed with the ceremonial records.

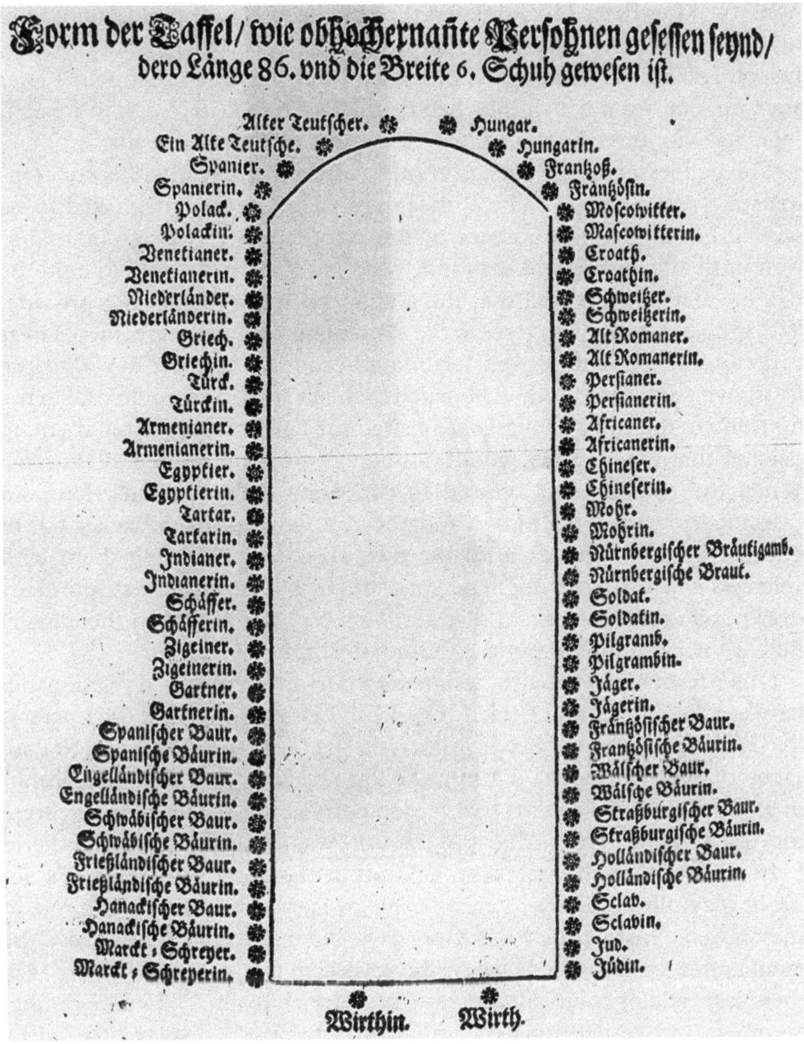

Figure 4.7 The seating plan at dinner at the *Wirtschaft*.

and interest, he would drink down this cup and return it empty, even if it was filled with poison.[39]

In this way, the roles played by the princes allowed them to make light-hearted allusions to their political relationship before Europe's high

[39] Lünig, *Theatrum Ceremoniale*, I, 159.

nobility. After Peter I had drained the cup, he again assured Leopold I of his goodwill before passing the cup to the heir to the Habsburg throne, Joseph I, king of the Romans, disguised as an Egyptian. Leopold I later gave the cup from which they had drunk, a *Cristallo di Rocca*, to Peter I, together with three Spanish horses as a personal, exclusive gift.[40]

The ball lessened the tension resulting from the negotiations concerning state ceremonies.[41] The Russian ambassadors had first asked to be received in the public audience by the emperor on 13 July, to be told to wait until after the 21st: Leopold I, who had already decided to hold the ball on that day, insisted that the audience should follow, not precede, it.[42] If his intention was to ease the settlement of the disagreements over ceremonies, the date proved fortunate because it was the day after the Muscovite ambassadors had objected to the proposed ceremonies. On the morning of the 21st, Königsacker visited the ambassadors to tell them, in person, that the emperor would not agree to their proposed alterations. When the ambassadors refused to withdraw their demands, Leopold I decided to cancel the public audience but advised Königsacker not to inform the ambassadors until the next day.[43] Conciliating them with splendid *divertissements* might persuade them to give way in the arguments over public ceremonies and distract Peter I's attention from the equally difficult negotiations about the Ottoman Empire.

Other festivities were also designed to portray an idealised relationship between Leopold I and Peter I. On 3 July, Peter I attended the opera at the court's invitation.[44] Six days later, on the Feast of St Peter and St Paul (according to Muscovite dating), the ambassadors returned the compliment by inviting 500 guests to a garden party at the residence to celebrate the tsar's name day.[45] The programme was designed to flatter Peter I. In a speech on the occasion, a Jesuit at the Habsburg court, Father Wolf, playfully compared Peter I's role as tsar with Saint Peter's role in the church: 'Just as the Lord God gave Peter the Apostle the keys, he would offer them to His Majesty, the sovereign tsar, to enable him to take these keys and open up and possess the Turkish realm.'[46] In the evening, trumpets and kettledrums accompanied a fireworks display ordered by Leopold I, in which the letters '*VZPA [sic] – Vivat Czar Petrus Alexiowiz*' lit up the night sky.[47]

[40] *Theatri Europaei*, p. 474. HHStA, ZA Prot, 5, fol. 441v. For horses as diplomatic gifts, see M. Bayreuther, 'Pferde in der Diplomatie der frühen Neuzeit, in *Materielle Grundlagen*, ed. Häberlein, Jeggle, pp. 227–56.

[41] See also Bauer, *Typologie*, p. 58.

[42] HHStA, ZA Prot, 5, fol. 428–28v.

[43] Ibid., fol. 437.

[44] Ibid., fol. 423–23v.

[45] *Pokhodnyi zhurnal: 1698*, 2nd edn. (St. Petersburg, 1911), p. 27.

[46] *PDS*, VIII, col. 1363.

[47] HHStA, ZA Prot, 5, fol. 427v.

The acknowledgement of Peter I at such imperial festivities carried no legal or politically binding implications. The Habsburgs, by their behaviour, conveyed the impression that they supported him against the Ottomans, even if political circumstances prevented the emperor from taking any action. The role of the festivities was to disguise and, ideally, to reconcile the differences that had arisen between Russia and the Holy Roman Empire over status as well as peace or war with the Ottomans.

Private Meetings

The use of costumes facilitated personal contact between Peter I and Leopold I, but not their meeting as allies. A relationship that implied loyalty to an alliance required a different vehicle: a private space in which the two men could meet as tsar and emperor, and not as pretend innkeeper and peasant, but unburdened with the sign language of public ceremonies that would have reopened the argument about status.

Shortly after the Grand Embassy's arrival, the vice-chancellor of Bohemia, Count Tschernin, visited the embassy to discuss Peter I's stated wish to meet the emperor incognito. Tschernin explained that 'grandees usually have preliminary negotiations about the subjects to be discussed, so that one can give more adequate answers, and, no less important, know how they ought to behave to one another in the ceremonial'.[48] On such occasions, explicit reference to state affairs was taboo. The tsar replied 'that he would not assert any pretensions and that his treatment should instead rest with His Majesty [the emperor]. He would also not mention the negotiations [about the Ottoman war] which he would leave to his ambassadors.'[49]

On 29 June, Tschernin collected Peter I and a small entourage, and brought them, in his own carriage, to the garden behind the Favorita. They crossed the garden to the back door of the palace and ascended the winding staircase to the gallery. As they crossed the threshold, Leopold I and his ministers entered the gallery from the opposite side, approaching Peter I to meet him beside the window in the middle of the room. Peter I, however, increased his pace as soon as he caught sight of Leopold I, and advanced one window too far. Leopold I, who was wearing a hat, asked Peter I, who had removed his, to put it back on. Peter I did so, with a reluctant gesture, to take it off again and to show his preference for meeting the emperor bare-headed. Then Leopold I, too, took off his hat.

The two men conversed out of earshot of their entourages. Only Lefort, who acted as interpreter, could later recall the words of Peter I's greeting

[48] HHStA, ZA Prot, 5, fol. 421. [49] Ibid., fol. 421–21v.

to Leopold I: 'My brother! [...] I expressly came here to meet you and to affirm the alliance which already exists between us.'[50] The meeting seemed to please both men, according to the Habsburg account: 'For the rest, as one could glimpse his [Peter I's] face, he was in good spirits, and it seemed as if he departed from His Majesty with good cheer.'[51] Lefort was even more enthusiastic: 'Never have I witnessed such a great brotherhood between these two monarchs. Until now, everything has met the wishes of both monarchs.'[52]

As mentioned earlier the tsar addressed the emperor as 'brother' to indicate their equal status. This rule did not apply at the Habsburg court. In the quarrel over forms of address in 1675, Matveev had claimed that the emperor should acknowledge the tsar's equality by referring to him as 'Majesty' in official correspondence because they already addressed one another as brothers. Bottoni and Guzman had replied that the recognition of 'Majesty' could not be inferred from the alleged brotherhood between monarchs: the emperor's biological brother (his brothers had already died) would not be addressed thus; nor, they supposed, would the brother of the tsar.[53] During the Grand Embassy's public audience on 18 July, the emperor inquired after the health of his 'beloved brother' the tsar without, in his own opinion, acknowledging their equality.[54]

In private, the Habsburgs did not challenge the notion of brotherly equality.[55] Such a compliment would help to establish a personal relationship between the two sovereigns and strengthen the alliance between the states they embodied as absolute monarchs. The gallery of the Favorita seemed better suited than the secret council room for the ceremonial representation of equality, with its implication of friendship and alliance.

Its two entrances were placed diagonally in the opposite corners (Figure 4.8, nos. 1 and 2). One led to the secret council room, the other to the garden; a design that enabled the two rulers to enter the room simultaneously, approach each other at the same pace, and meet in the middle (as marked by the windows) on an equal footing. When Peter I entered from the garden, outside, while Leopold I entered from inside, from the seat of imperial authority, the meeting created the perfect symmetry between guest and host. Their embrace of one another as equal brothers and allies signalled the two monarchs' friendship. Leopold I neither made his guest wait nor stood on

[50] Quoted in Posselt, *Lefort*, II, p. 486. [51] HHStA, ZA Prot, 5, fol. 422v.
[52] Quoted in Posselt, *Lefort*, II, p. 487.
[53] Wickhart, *Moscowittische Reiss-Beschreibung*, p. 113.
[54] HHStA, ZA Prot, 5, fol. 431, 448.
[55] Cf. Rousset de Missy, *Cérémonial diplomatique*, I, p. 512, who contradicts the notion of brotherhood.

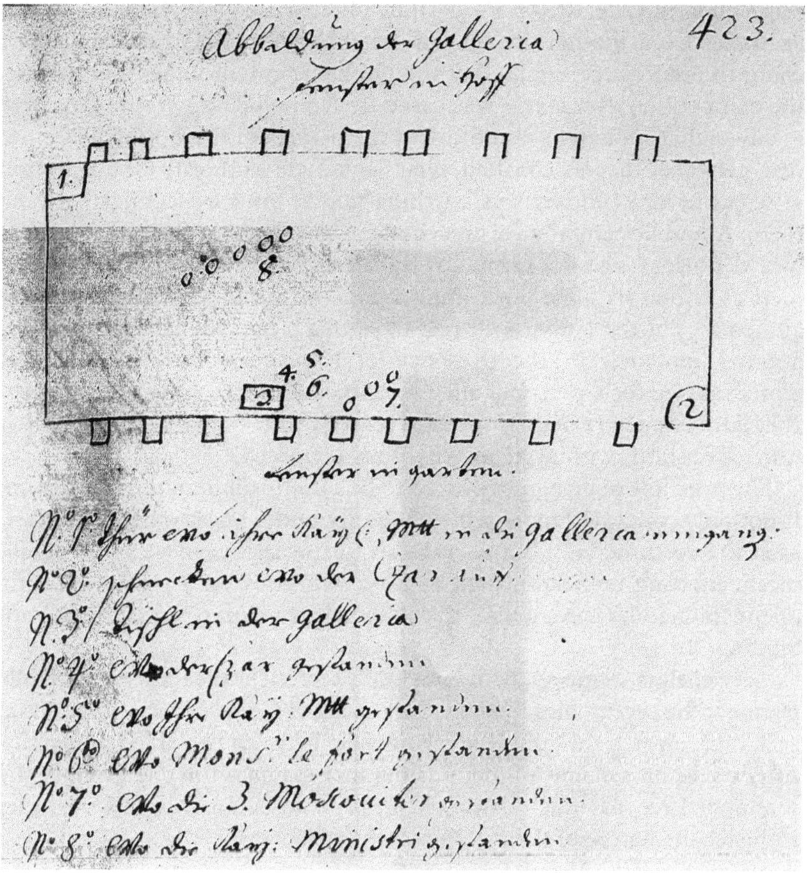

Figure 4.8 Viennese ceremonial records: Sketch of the gallery in the Favorita, depicting the positions taken by the participants during the private meeting between Peter I and Leopold I. (1) entrance from which the emperor entered the room, (2) winding staircase from which the tsar entered the palace coming from the garden, (3) small table, (4) tsar, (5) emperor, (6) Lefort, (7) three Muscovites nobles, and (8) imperial ministers.

a pedestal to receive him, as he would at the ambassadors' public audience. He met Peter I on the same level, after both had moved forwards at the same time.

The most obvious symbolic expression of equality was the outcome of Peter I's insistence on taking off his hat. Both men were supposed to wear hats to signify that neither need acknowledge the other's superior status.

As a consequence, Peter I's gesture obliged Leopold I to follow his example. Even though the sign of equality contradicted the emperor's claim to precedence signified at the public ceremonies, here, in private, the competition over status was eased by symbolic parity.

Given that monarchs could divest themselves of their public ceremonial personas that established their legitimate authority, the question arises as to how binding was anything said at private meetings between them. At public ceremonies, precedence – as a signal of claims to status as well as power – was confirmed by the attendance of the court or townsmen as witnesses. The legal implications of the proceedings at public audiences put the emperor at risk of setting a precedent when meeting another monarch in the presence of the court. Its exclusion was a prerequisite for a personal encounter meant to strengthen the Austro-Russian alliance to a degree not represented by the public symbols of their respective status within the international hierarchy.

The principle of incognito proved to be a useful diplomatic mechanism. It not only concealed monarchical identity under an assumed character, as at the costume ball, but also, as on this occasion, meeting incognito meant meeting 'unbeknownst', without witnesses. At a private meeting unconstrained by ceremonial, the acknowledgement of equality was not binding.[56]

Nevertheless, as incognito did not imply secret, the meeting was carefully planned; the ceremonies – the records speak of *Caeremoniali* – symbolised and, thus, created the amicable relationship between two allied monarchs. Afterwards, an account of the meeting that matches the one given in the ceremonial records was distributed in print to communicate to a wider audience the nature of the two monarchs' alliance:

> As they were approaching one another, the tsar made a deep bow to which the emperor responded likewise, and they embraced each other. The emperor urged the tsar to cover his head, which he did, but he doffed his hat shortly afterwards, whereupon the emperor did the same in return. The conversation lasted for about twenty minutes, and nobody was allowed to join . . . They addressed each other as brothers [. . .] and, in the salutation, the emperor attested his delight to meet the tsar as a glorious monarch and his ally [. . .] The tsar replied in the same manner [. . .] and he mentioned that everything in his country stood ready for the emperor's order.[57]

[56] On the role of the public as a witness to legally binding rituals, cf. G. Althoff, 'The variability of rituals in the Middle Ages', in *Medieval concepts of the past: ritual, memory, historiography*, ed. G. Althoff, J. Fried, G. Patrick (Cambridge, 2002), pp. 71–87, esp. p. 74.

[57] *Die Entreveüe zwischen dem Kayser/ und dem Czaar/ den 29. Junii 1698* (n.p., 1698).

The court (and later, historians) received word of a ceremony that symbolically acknowledged the equal status of the two sovereigns for the sake of representing a strong personal bond.[58] The public's physical distance to a face-to-face encounter, and the lack of direct witness, ensured that the ceremony did not undermine the hierarchical order as represented in its public counterpart.

A few weeks later, on 24 July, Leopold I visited Peter I at his lodgings. This meeting followed the same pattern. The emperor, accompanied by a small group of courtiers, was brought to the garden of the palace in which the Grand Embassy was accommodated. Peter I received the group in the garden and entered a room in the palace alongside the emperor. Neither wore a hat and they exchanged mostly compliments for a quarter of an hour. The next day, the tsar took leave of the emperor, the empress, and the king of the Romans, Leopold I's designated successor as emperor.[59] The meeting made the two rulers 'even more allied through the [...] granted honour', as the historian Matthias Fuhrmann understood in 1739.[60]

It may appear paradoxical that Leopold I repaid Peter I's compliment at the moment that Königsacker's negotiations about ceremonies with the Russian ambassadors had been suspended on the 21st, owing to the dispute about the tsar's status. Yet, there was no contradiction between the emperor's willingness to acknowledge the tsar as an equal brother while simultaneously ordering imperial officials to reject the claim when made by the Muscovite ambassadors. The private ceremonies served a different purpose – to buttress the alliance – and they implied a lesser degree of political obligation.

The role of the private meeting also makes clear why the emperor refused to discuss affairs of state, however urgent. As a device to place the relations between two states in an established hierarchy, the public ceremonies buttressed a ruler's authority, not only his status in the hierarchy but also his political power. The lack, at the private meeting, of such symbolism of power projection inhibited the resolution of affairs of state. The meeting lacked both a legal and a representative foundation

[58] See also T. V. Civ'jan, 'Etiquette as a semiotic system', in *Soviet semiotics: an anthology*, ed. D. P. Lucid (Baltimore, London, 1977), pp. 103–05, here on p. 104: 'Behaviour in etiquette is usually intended for at least two addressees, the immediate addressee and the distant addressee or "public"; in this sense it can be compared to an actor's stage performance, which is oriented toward both his co-actor and the audience. It is assumed that the distant addressee is always present, and the first commandment of etiquette is to behave "as if in public" even when alone in private'.

[59] HHStA, ZA Prot, 5, fols. 441v–443v.

[60] M. Fuhrmann, *Alt- und neues Wien, oder dieser [...] Stadt chronologisch- und historische Beschreibung [...]*, 2 vols. (Vienna, Lintz, 1738/39), II, p. 1193.

from which to proceed; it was, itself, the buttress to a political relationship. Moreover, as nobody other than Lefort was supposed to participate in the conversation, Leopold I could not turn to his officials for expert advice, reason enough not to discuss the affairs of the Ottoman Empire.

From a modern perspective, a meeting between heads of state implies that pressing political issues are being discussed. Naturally, one might expect that the emperor and the tsar, when they met, were bound to have talked about political issues of importance to both of them.[61] However, the prevailing diplomatic practice at the imperial court did not allow for such discussion. Personal encounters between monarchs were rare, not least because of the difficulties that arose over the staging of ceremonies.[62] The fact that Leopold I and Peter I met at least four times was itself extraordinary. Peter I's presence in the Grand Embassy and his interest in meeting other rulers in person were novel and complicated late seventeenth-century international relations.[63] The two rulers' avoidance of serious topics is attributable less to the disenchantment with politics usually attributed to Leopold I,[64] than to the constraints imposed by symbol and ceremony on the monarch's political activities in early modern diplomacy.

Secret Negotiations

Peter I's goal – to persuade the Holy League of Austria, Poland, Venice, and Muscovy to prolong the war against the Ottoman Empire – seemed likely from the outset to prove unattainable.[65] The coalition was disintegrating because Leopold I had shown an interest in allowing William III of England to mediate peace with Sultan Mustafa II. Without Leopold I's support, however, Peter I doubted whether he could expel the Ottomans from the northern shore of the Black Sea. Having evicted them from Azov

[61] As do Posselt, *Lefort*, II, p. 487; Schwarcz, 'Velikoe posol'stvo', pp. 58f.; Ustrialov, *Istoriia tsarstvovaniia*, III, p. 127.

[62] See Paulmann, *Monarchenbegegnungen*, pp. 30–37.

[63] For Peter I's meeting with William III of England at Utrecht in September 1697, see G. Barany, *The Anglo-Russian entente cordiale of 1697–1698: Peter I and William III at Utrecht* (Boulder, 1986), esp. p. 67.

[64] See, for example, Bogoslovskii, *Petr I*, II, p. 471; Schwarcz, 'Velikoe posol'stvo', p. 59. See also J. P. Spielman, *Leopold I of Austria* (London, 1977), p. 9.

[65] Russia had joined the Holy League in 1686, through the bilateral Eternal Peace with Poland. See R. P. Bartlett, *A history of Russia* (Basingstoke, 2005), p. 74. For Russia's membership in the Holy League, see B. L. Davies, *Warfare, state and society on the Black Sea steppe: 1500–1700* (London, 2007), pp. 175ff. For Russia's military involvement as a member of the Holy League, see C. B. Stevens, *Russia's wars of emergence, 1460–1730* (Harlow, 2007), pp. 189–211.

in 1696, he aimed at evicting them from the Crimea by capturing Kerch.[66]

The emperor, in his turn, needed friendly relations with Russia to form a bulwark against the Ottomans to dissuade them from renewing the war; the private meeting represented the need of each for the other's alliance.[67] Nevertheless, the Habsburgs' decisive victory over the Ottomans at Zenta in September 1697 had enabled Leopold I to propose peace on the basis of *uti possidetis*: the negotiations led in 1699 to the Treaty of Karlowitz.[68] Leopold I sought peace owing to the cost and the possibility of a new struggle in western Europe: the Treaty of Ryswick had ended the Nine Years' War with France in 1697 without resolving the conflict between France and the Habsburgs, at a time when the deteriorating health of Charles II of Spain (r. 1665–1700) was likely to provoke a new war with France over the succession to the Spanish throne.[69] Thus, although the Austrian Habsburgs wished Peter I to succeed against the Ottoman Empire, Leopold I could not allow the ceremonies at the private meetings to represent more than a degree of general political goodwill that did not jeopardise his own dynastic interests. Nor could he fulfil the implications of the remarks made to Peter I during the festivities.

No attempt was made to represent, in a ceremony, the two rulers' stances towards the Ottoman war. Imperial officials and Peter I exchanged information during the negotiations without concerning themselves with status and prestige. Naturally, the negotiations, being verbal exchanges, are distinguishable from contacts that relied for communication on a nonverbal language of symbol. Nonetheless, the negotiations may not be separated from the other two forms of diplomatic encounter, nor did they occupy the political arena while the others were confined to courtly pageantry. Both ceremony and secrecy formed part of the raison d'état in early modern foreign relations.[70] In this particular case, the negotiations were constrained by the forms of diplomatic dialogue. Although the prerequisite for official negotiations was the public audience with the emperor, the Grand Embassy only requested an audience three days after the negotiations had come to an end. Therefore, the negotiations had to remain secret.

What is more, the negotiations had to be secret because they were conducted in a way that contradicted the political messages the ceremonies conveyed. This point is exemplified in a conversation on 6 July between Peter I and Count Kinsky, who led the imperial

[66] Hughes, *Age of Peter the Great*, p. 22. [67] Schwarcz, 'Velikoe posol'stvo', pp. 65f.
[68] See V. Matveyev, *The Karlowitz congress and the debut of Russia's multilateral diplomacy (1698–99)* (Leicester, 2000).
[69] See Mckay, Scott, *Rise*, ch. 3. [70] Bély, *Espions*, pp. 741f. and passim, for secrecy.

delegation.[71] The tsar wished to discuss the war in person once an exchange of letters between the court and the embassy had revealed that peace between the Austrian Habsburgs and the Ottomans was inevitable.[72] As negotiating with the emperor in person was inconceivable, the Grand Embassy sought to make personal contact between the tsar and a senior Habsburg official who, unlike the Russian ambassadors, were not assigned 'representative character'. As Kinsky, supposedly, merely conveyed information to the Grand Embassy on the emperor's behalf, conversations with him need not be constrained by the issue of monarchical precedence nor need the tsar appear incognito.

Evgenii F. Shmurlo argued that Peter I stripped off his disguise and replaced it whenever it suited him, that the incognito was under his sole control: he 'declined meetings with rulers nowhere [...] he gave visits to them and received them in return [...] he conducted negotiations, visited banquets, gave and received gifts – and all this was performed in his privileged position as tsar'.[73] It is true that Peter I conducted the negotiations at Vienna in his capacity as ruler of Russia. But this does not imply that he slipped out of his incognito when attending balls or meeting with officials and courtiers. The symbolic forms of communication used at the imperial court prohibited such behaviour. As the tsar of Russia, he could meet the emperor's officials to discuss state affairs *in camera*. On all other occasions, he was bound by the rules of diplomatic practice. To have appeared before the imperial court in his majestic persona without prearrangement would have openly challenged the emperor's authority.

In conversation with Kinsky, the tsar criticised the emperor on the grounds 'that the conditions of the peace are determined according to the will of his Imperial Majesty, although it should have been agreed by consent of all [his] allies'.[74] He managed to make Kinsky admit that the peace was attributable to the emperor's debts. Such a statement mismatched the ceremonial symbols that represented the Holy Roman Emperor as the pre-eminent ruler on earth whose prestige should have been an indicator of his wealth and power. Such criticism from Peter I's diplomats, in their official role as his representatives, or more rigorous demands for changes to the ceremonies, would have been perceived as an

[71] For Kinsky, see S. Sienell, *Die geheime Konferenz unter Kaiser Leopold I.: personelle Strukturen und Methoden zur politischen Entscheidungsfindung am Wiener Hof* (Frankfurt a. M., 2001), pp. 190f.

[72] *PDS*, VIII, cols. 1334.

[73] E. Shmurlo, 'Kriticheskie zametki po istorii Petra Velikago', *Zhurnal Ministerstva Narodnogo Prosveshcheniia*, 329 (1900), 54–95, here p. 73, followed by Bogoslovskii, *Petr I*, II, p. 15; Hughes, *Age of Peter the Great*, p. 23; R. Wittram, *Peter I. Czar und Kaiser: zur Geschichte Peters des Großen in seiner Zeit*, 2 vols. (Göttingen, 1964), I, p. 133.

[74] *PDS*, VIII, col. 1355. For the negotiations, see Bogoslovskii, *Petr I*, II, pp. 474–81.

insult from a lesser to a greater power. The forthright discussion required by divergent political interests was inconceivable, in public, given the established hierarchy. The negotiations had to be secret lest they contradict the public ceremonial messages witnessed by the court or released to the press. It is no wonder that, in the press, pomp and ceremony formed the political focus on the Grand Embassy; the information about the Ottoman war remained scarce and vague.[75]

The ceremonies at the private meetings also, by implication, belied the substance of the negotiations. Kinsky told Peter I that the emperor did not want to be called to account before God for the Christian blood being shed, when he had the opportunity to end the fighting. Peter I, openly questioning Leopold I's loyalty, replied that the Ottomans were weak. He added, accurately, that 'the Emperor hurries to make peace because of the succession to the Spanish throne and the war with the French, and thus leaves his allies in great displeasure';[76] he accused him of being willing to abandon his allies and renege on his agreements.

Peter I's language contradicted the symbolic language used at both the private meetings and the public ceremonies and explains why negotiations with other states were walled off, in secret, from the sphere that represented claims to status. Secrecy – that is, the absence of ritual-imposing witnesses – permitted mutual criticism without the risk of destabilising relationships between courts.[77]

Whereas the Russian ambassadors feared the lowering of their sovereign's status, the emperor saw his position at the top of the hierarchy confirmed by the reassertion of his prestige. The emperor won the zero-sum game in that the ambassadors failed to extract a single token of higher status for the tsar. The ambassadors saw the empire's answer to Russia's claim to equal status as a humiliation:[78] one that fitted Russia into the hierarchy as a power ruled by a monarch equal to any other sovereign, including the emperor. Only by refusing the tsar further honours could the emperor buttress his claim to pre-eminence.

The treatment of the Grand Embassy may suggest that, at the end of the seventeenth century, the tsar was still not seen to be an ally but, at best, as an associate. The setback over ceremonies, the failure to persuade

[75] A. Blome, *Das deutsche Russlandbild im frühen 18. Jahrhundert: Untersuchungen zur zeitgenössischen Presseberichterstattung über Russland unter Peter I* (Wiesbaden, 2000), p. 84.

[76] *PDS*, VIII, col. 1357.

[77] This relation between honour and the antagonism between public and secret knowledge was not only present in diplomacy but pervaded all levels of early modern society. For a parallel observation on seventeenth-century English local government see, Braddick, 'Administrative performance'. For a discussion of secrecy in early modern politics in Gestrich, *Absolutismus und Öffentlichkeit*, ch. 2.

[78] *PDS*, VIII, cols. 1385–87.

the emperor to continue the war against the Ottomans, and the disregard of Muscovy's interests during the peace negotiations at Karlowitz – when the tsar was confronted with a fait accompli that belied the promises the emperor had made – show that Muscovy was a weak power in the eyes of its European contemporaries: had the emperor perceived the tsar to be a powerful ruler and potent ally against the sultan, he might have buttressed the alliance by granting Peter I more public ceremonial recognition. If, however, ceremonial signals represented and thereby created power relationships, the emperor had no choice other than to refuse the demands made by the Russian ambassadors, even if he had valued the tsar as an important ally. Imperial officials understood that both emperor and tsar operated in a hierarchical world in which concessions to allies over ceremonies could amount to the loss of power in the face of enemies. Austria, after containing the Ottoman Empire at Zenta and halting the expansion of France by the Treaty of Ryswick, was one of the strongest of the European powers. But the emperor predicted a new struggle to maintain his power and status relative to France in the struggle over the Spanish succession. Thus, the emperor could not imperil his own status by paying greater honours to the tsar than were usually paid to kings such as the king of France whom he conveniently ranked below the Russian court. Peter I, who asked for the emperor's assistance, lacked what Lünig called the 'preponderant might' of levering the imperial court into recognising his ceremonial claims to higher authority.[79]

The constraints of public ceremony and the needs of secret negotiations did not preclude the representation of strong personal bonds. In an age when international politics were more a personal affair between rulers than a business between nation states, an alliance was an interpersonal relationship. The alliance between Peter I and Leopold I and the emperor's personal esteem for the tsar are not disproved by their failure to influence the public ceremonies; they were communicated privately. The political messages exchanged between the Grand Embassy, the emperor, and the court as witness conflicted with one another. The language of hierarchy represented in the public ceremonies contradicted the language of brotherhood represented at the private meetings, and both conflicted with the language of practical politics represented in the negotiations about the Ottoman war. Political symbolism and ritual (today sometimes referred to as the power of soft) and tangible political power did not constitute separate spheres of action: ceremonial representation and political practice were contingent upon each other. All the parties involved – emperor, tsar, Muscovite

[79] See Introduction, fn. 62.

ambassadors, imperial ministers, and Habsburg courtiers – proved to be versatile actors when balancing the pomp of monarchy with the circumstance of foreign affairs.

Paris 1717

A gold medal commemorates Peter I's journey to France in 1717. Struck in his presence during a visit to the mint of medals in Paris, the front shows his bust surrounded by an inscription: '*Petrus Alexiewitz, Tzar Mag[nus] Russ[orum] Imp[erator]*'. The reverse accommodates a winged allegory of fame blowing a trumpet in front of a wide, sun-flooded valley framed by the motto '*vires acquirit eundo*'.[80] A contemporary observer noticed that these words, 'he grows as he goes', were an allusion to the Russian ruler's travels of the past twenty years.[81] Indeed, the political landscape of the continent had changed since Peter I had set out on his first travels to Europe at the end of the seventeenth century: Russia had grown into a formidable military power.

The first two decades of the eighteenth century saw Russia rise and eclipse Sweden as a great power in the north. Europeans feared that the tsar 'will be as though a Turk of the north', as Leibniz famously put it in a comment on the Battle of Poltava (1709).[82] In 1714, Peter I registered an important victory over the Swedish fleet in the Baltic, allowing him to explore the possibility of peace and to look for suitable partners in support of Russia against her northern rival. This move was timely. The tsar had to take an active role in the European alliance system lest western powers interfere in northern affairs in favour of Sweden after a series of peace treaties signed at Utrecht, Rastatt and Baden (1713/14) had put an end to the War of the Spanish Succession.[83] In February 1716, he once again

80 For the representation of fame, or *renommée*, in seventeenth century iconology, see C. Ripa, *Iconologie où les principales choses qui peuvent tomber dans la pensée touchant les Vices et les Vertus*, trans. Jean Baudoin (Paris, 1643), part II, pp. 80f. I am indebted to Till Hennings for drawing my attention to this reference.

81 *Le Nouveau Mercure May–Juin 1717* (Paris, 1717), pp. 189f.

82 Quoted in V. I. *Guerrier, Leibniz in seinen Beziehungen zu Russland und Peter dem Grossen: eine geschichtliche Darstellung dieses Verhältnisses nebst den darauf bezüglichen Briefen und Denkschriften* (St. Petersburg, Leipzig, 1873), p. 81. For European responses to Russia's military successes in the first quarter of the eighteenth century, see Schnakenbourg, *La France*, pp. 471–75. For Leibniz' views on Russia, see C. Roll, 'Barbaren? tabula rasa? Wie Leibniz sein neues Wissen über Russland auf den Begriff brachte. Eine Studie über die Bedeutung der Vernetzung gelehrter Korrespondenzen für die Ermöglichung aufgeklärter Diskurse', in: *Umwelt und Weltgestaltung: Leibniz' politisches Denken in seiner Zeit*, ed. F. Beiderbeck, I. Dingel, W. Li (Göttingen, 2015), pp. 307–58.

83 Hughes, *Age of Peter the Great*, pp. 52–54.

embarked on a journey through Europe in order to strengthen his newly gained position of power and to foster relations with foreign courts.[84]

The diplomatic situation grew complex. Relations with Great Britain had deteriorated. The presence of Russian troops in northern Germany (a result of the marriage contract between Peter I's niece, Ekaterina Ivanovna, and Karl Leopold of Mecklenburg-Schwerin) posed a threat to British naval power in the Baltic and alienated King George I. The flight of the Russian heir to the throne, Aleksei Petrovich, to his brother-in-law, Emperor Charles VI in Vienna, had worsened relations with the Habsburgs. Meanwhile, Britain and France had signed a defence treaty, promising each other support against Stuart pretenders and Spanish claims to the French throne. In January 1717, the two countries formed a triple alliance together with the Dutch Republic.[85]

While Peter I, who was staying in Amsterdam at the time, feared that this new coalition could turn against Russian interests in the Great Northern War, France signalled rapprochement with Russia.[86] Franco-Russian relations had been recovering slowly since a diplomatic huff over protocol in Paris in 1687,[87] and Louis XIV had been showing little interest in meeting the tsar throughout his long reign. Peter I's plan of visiting France during the Grand Embassy was met with a circumspect response by the king. The memoirist Saint-Simon noted that Louis XIV continued to be indifferent towards a visit of Peter I when the latter was contemplating a sojourn in Paris in the last year of the Sunking's reign.[88]

The situation changed when the then five-year-old Louis XV acceded to the throne in 1715. The regent, Philippe d'Orléans was prepared to reconsider the king's traditional ties with Sweden in order to look for stronger partners in the long-standing rivalry with the Habsburgs.[89] In October 1716, Prussia proposed to involve Russia in a closer relationship together with France. The plans gained momentum in a meeting

[84] For a brief overview of Franco-Russian relations, see *Recueil des instructions données aux ambassadeurs et ministres de France: depuis les traités de Westphalie jusqu'à la Révolution française, vols. VIII–IX: Russie, tome premiere, des origines jusqu'a 1748* (Paris, 1890), pp. 137f., and chs. 8–11, for selected documents relating to Peter I's stay in France. For the broader context of the second tour to western Europe, see Wittram, *Peter I.*, II, pp. 305–23.

[85] Hughes, *Age of Peter the Great*, pp. 52–54.

[86] S.M. Solov'ev, *Istoriia Rossii s drevneishikh vremen*, 15 vols.(Moscow, 1959–1966, originally published 1851–1879), IX, pp. 63f.

[87] For an account of the 1687 embassy, see *SIRIO*, XXXIV, pp. 15–19. See also Grönebaum, *Frankreich in Ost- und Nordeuropa*, pp. 101–11.

[88] S. A. Mezin, *Vzgliad iz Evropy: frantsuzskie avtory XVIII veka o Petre I* (Saratov, 2003), pp. 19f.

[89] This was met with strong opposition from Dubois who feared that an all too friendly relationship with Russia could alienate the British with whom France and the Dutch Republic had just negotiated a triple alliance. See Schnakenbourg, *La France*, pp. 508f.

between Peter I and Frederick William I (r. 1713–1740) at Havelberg in November. In the following month, Peter I received word that France was prepared to enter friendly relationships with both Prussia and Russia as guarantors of the treaties of Utrecht and Baden and to engage the two countries in a defence agreement.[90] The marquis de Châteauneuf, Louis XV's ambassador in The Hague, was instructed to assure the tsar of the king's highest esteem for his person and for the glory that he had acquired. The French court looked very favourably upon entering 'direct and reciprocal correspondence'.[91] Petr P. Shafirov drafted a five-point proposal for the king. After a revision of the proposal, facilitated by the Prussian representative to the Hague, Peter I gave the French ambassador a new version, stipulating four conditions: (1) that the tsar guarantee the Peace of Utrecht and the Peace of Baden, (2) that the French king abstain from any subsidies to Sweden during the war between the tsar and the Swedish king, (3) that the French king make all effort to achieve a peace in the north short of any partiality for the Swedish king, and (4) that the French king provide support to Russia in the region of 25.000 Ecus per month during the course of the Great Northern War.[92] The tsar might have been aware that his demands were unwarranted and that a personal visit was in order to facilitate the alliance.[93]

The sway of personal presence seems conducive to alliance building in a society in which sovereigns expressed loyalty in the language of family relationships and addressed each other as brothers.[94] But, as mentioned earlier, such visits remained the exception and complicated early modern international relations for want of standard procedure. Unlike modern diplomatic protocol, that discriminates between state visits, official visits, working visits, and private visits, with clearly defined organisational rules and distinctions,[95] the presence of a foreign monarch confronted a court with a novel situation and many problems, particularly during the reception of Peter I. As was the case in Vienna, the French had to reconcile the pomp of monarchy with the circumstance of foreign affairs. As a result, Peter I's visit to Paris exhibited inter-related forms of political communication very

[90] Solov'ev, *Istoriia Rossii*, IX, pp. 65f.

[91] Louis XV to Châteauneuf, 5 January 1717, in *Recueil des instructions*, pp. 138–45, here on p. 140.

[92] *SIRIO*, XXXIV, pp. XXIV-XXV; Wittram, *Peter I*, II, pp. 308ff.

[93] *SIRIO*, XXXIV, p. XXV.

[94] R. Lesaffer, '*Amicitia* in Renaissance peace and alliance treaties (1450–1530)', *Journal of the History of International Law*, 4 (2002), 77–99, p. 93.

[95] *Le service du Protocole*, homepage of the French Ministry of Foreign Affairs and International Development, available from www.diplomatie.gouv.fr/fr/le-ministere-et-son-reseau/organigramme-de-l-administration/article/le-service-du-protocole, last access 6 February 2016.

similar to those at the Habsburg court: entertainments, private meetings, and secret negotiations.

In April 1717, Peter I, and a selected delegation of his ministers, departed from the Netherlands and set out to the French capital in order to expedite the alliance. Negotiations were to be kept secret while both the tsar's passion for travel and educational interests served to give the impression that a 'simple curiosity' and the 'natural inquietude' of his personality were the motives behind the journey, as was noted by M. de Liboy in his report about the reception of the Russian delegation at the French border.[96]

Peter I's 1717 visit to Paris resembled his 1698 journey to Vienna in that the tsar travelled incognito and insisted that his presence remain unbeknownst.[97] This did not prevent the contemporary media, and individual observers, from producing ample evidence about his itinerary in and around the capital and about various private meetings with the members of French court society.[98] The tsar took every opportunity to immerse himself in the world of arts, architecture, and science. His travel agenda included visits to the Louvre, the Arsenal, the Hôtel des Invalides, the observatory, the Jardin de Plantes, the Basilica of Saint Denis, and Versailles, with its rich decorations, elaborate canal systems, fountains, statues, and terraces, which provided a model for the Peterhof palace and gardens near St Petersburg. He cruised the Seine in a gondola, was taken out to balls and operas by his host. He also peeked into French academic and legal culture at the Sorbonne and the Parlement. Peter I studied maps and books, assisted in chemical experiments, attended a cataract surgery, and marvelled at objects in the famous cabinet of curiosities of

[96] Wittram, *Peter I.*, II, p. 314. Liboy's report quoted from *SIRIO*, XXXIV, p. 145. See also ibid., p. 171.

[97] BM, ms 2747, fol. 242; See also AAE, MD Russie, 3 ('Sur les Honneurs faits de la part du Roy au Czar de Moscovie Pierre 1.er'), fols. 139–40.

[98] P. F. Buchet, *Abrégé de l'histoire du Czar Peter Alexiewitz avec une relation de l'etat présent de la Moscovie, & de ce qui s'est passé de plus considerable, depuis son arrivée en France jusqu'a ce jour* (Paris, 1717), esp. pp. 176–210; J. Buvat, *Journal de la régence: 1715–1723* (Paris, 1865), pp. 261–77; Le Père Furcy, 'Venu en France du Czar ou grand duc de Moscovie, son arrivée a Paris', in *Bulletin de la Société de l'histoire de Paris et de l'Ile-de-France*, 18 (1891), 15–18; *Journal du marquis de Dangeau, avec les additions inédites du duc de Saint-Simon*, ed. E. Soulié, L. Dussieux, 19 vols. (Paris, 1854–1860), XVII, pp. 74–114; *Historical memoirs of the duc de Saint-Simon: a shortened version*, ed. and trans. L. Norton, 3 vols. (London, 1967–1972), III, pp. 120–31. Despite extensive contemporary interest in Peter I's travels, his journey to France has received far less attention from historians than the Grand Embassy. For a full account, and a detailed discussion of the published primary sources, see Mezin, *Vzgliad iz Evropy*, pp. 12–39, and Schnakenbourg, *La France*, pp. 475–91. A useful chronology of Peter I's stay in France, based on brief excerpts from published materials, is B. Lossky, 'Le séjour de Pierre le Grand en France', *Le Monde Slave*, 9 (1932), 278–303.

Louis Léon Pajot d'Ons-en-Bray. He went to see the art galleries of Paris, followed an invitation to the Academy of Sciences and conversed with notable scholars, scientists, and engineers. He visited artisans and manufacturers in their workshops as well as factories such as the glassworks and the Gobbelins Manufactory, gathering an array of objects, books, and instruments for his own collections.[99] The tsar also recruited specialists and craftsmen to work in St Petersburg.[100] In short, the presence of the Russian monarch was impossible to mask.

Yet, Peter I's stay in France differed significantly from his European travels some twenty years earlier. In 1717, he did not dispatch a diplomatic mission as such, or camouflage himself as a simple soldier travelling among the suite of publicly accredited diplomats, as he did at the court of the Holy Roman Emperor. Neither was there a fully authorised ambassador at court when Peter I arrived in France, although Russia had begun to include Paris in its growing network of permanent diplomatic representations.[101] The tsar's entourage consisted of sixty-one persons, among them some of the most prominent figures of Russian foreign policy at the time, accompanied by guards, a physician, several chefs, singers, servants, and a priest. The list of Peter I's suite includes Prince Boris I. Kurakin (the then-ambassador at The Hague), Vice-Chancellor Petr P. Shafirov, Prince Vasilii V. Dolgorukov, Heinrich J. Ostermann, General Ivan I. Buturlin, Petr A. Tolstoi, and others.[102] Apart from the general diplomatic imperative of keeping alliance negotiations undisclosed, the fact that the Russian delegation did not act in any officially recognised role was another formal reason to keep negotiations secret. As it soon became clear that the tsar's curiosity could not have

[99] See C. Henry, 'Le séjour de Pierre le Grand à Paris: contribution à l'histoire de la formation du cabinet de Saint-Pétersbourg', *Publications du Groupe Histoire Architecture Mentalités Urbaines*. Available from www.ghamu.org/IMG/pdf/Pierre1er txt-def-20-04-2011.pdf, last access 6 February 2016. For a list of Peter I's activities, see *Le Nouveau Mercure May-Juin 1717*, pp. 182–206.

[100] Wittram, *Peter I.*, II, p. 317 mentions the list that registered the names and professions of more than sixty artisans that were willing to work in Russia's new capital: AAE, CP Russie, 8 ('Liste des personnes qui desirent aller travailler à St. Pétersbourg pendant l'espace de cinq années, 6 July 1717'), fols. 216f. Already in 1716, before Peter I's arrival, the French court had drafted registers of names for the same purpose; see AN, K 1352, no. 69–71: 'L'Estat des Ouvriers qui desirent se rendre á St. Petersbourg pour travailler aux Ouvrages de sa Majestcé Czarienne' (17 November 1716); 'L'Estat des personnes qui desirent aller à St. Petersbourg pour travailler au service de Sa Majesté Czarienne' (15 April 1716). See Henry, 'Séjour de Pierre le Grand', p. 22.

[101] Ageeva, *Diplomaticheskii tseremonial*, p. 34f. A number of diplomatic representatives had resided at the French court intermittently in various capacities, albeit for relatively short periods of time: P. V. Postnikov (1702, continued to live in Paris until 1710 without diplomatic accreditation), A. A. Matveev (1705–1706), G. Volkov (1711), A. Lefort and Zotov (1715/16), see Bantyzh-Kamenskii, *Obzor*, IV, pp. 85–88.

[102] *SIRIO*, XXXIV, pp. 168–70; Buchet, *Abrégé*, p. 208.

been the only motive to come to France, the regent ordered the Marshal de Tessé, to 'confer with the ministers of the tsar secretly' under the direction of the marquis d'Uxelles, president of the Council of Foreign Affairs.[103] Peter I left all negotiations to Shafirov, and Kurakin, rather than treating with the duke of Orléans himself.[104]

From the point of view of protocol, the child-king Louis XV did not receive an official embassy from Russia but a monarch who wanted to remain unrecognised and delegated all diplomatic business to his ministers. However, diplomacy without ceremonial complication proved impossible. The incognito, informal visits, the reduction of symbolic forms, the pretend absence of ceremony was an inverted form of ritual recognition. The suspension of public ceremonial became as intricate as finding an agreement that would accommodate conflicting claims to honour. The stakes were higher because of both the unpredictability of the tsar's behaviour and an image of Russia that was still framed in the discourse of barbarism and thus likely to cause resentment. The archivist Nicolas-Louis Le Dran, who completed a survey of Russian-French relations in 1726, gave a telling impression by filling the margins of his text with a quote by the marshal de Villeroy who, as the owner of Peter I's accommodation in Paris, had met the tsar and written to Madame de Maintenon: 'I cannot relay to you the honours, favours, and kindness, with which the king arranged the visit of the tsar, but I have to tell you at the same time that this prince, who is known to be barbarian, is not that at all; he conveyed a sense of grandeur, generosity, and politeness that we had not anticipated.'[105] Saint-Simon had expected that 'the expense [of Peter I's visit] would be prodigious, and the trouble scarcely less so with a prince so powerful, so capricious, so inquisitive, and still tinged with some remnants of barbarism', and he feared that 'the behaviour of his staff would greatly differ from the conduct agreeable to western countries. They were certain to be full of strange whims and outlandish customs, as prone to take offence as their master, and very positive about their rights

[103] See the instructions to Tessé in *Mémoires et lettres du maréchal de Tessé, contenant des anecdotes et des faits historiques inconnus, sur partie des règnes de Louis XIV et de Louis XV*, ed. P.-H. de Grimoard, 2 vols. (Paris, 1806), II, p. 321.

[104] Wittram, *Peter I.*, II, p. 317.

[105] AAE, MD Russie, 4 ('Negociations entre la France et le tsar de la Grande Russie, Pierre Ier, par Le Dran', 1726), fol. 19v. Le Dran's notes were included in *SIRIO*, XXXIV, pp. IVff., the quote is on p. XXV, fn. 1. Similar *Journal du marquis de Dangeau*, XVII, pp. 80f. On Peter I's image in western Europe, see Schnakenbourg, *La France*, pp. 475f. See also Schnakenbourg's insightful discussion of contemporary French reactions to Peter I's personality and manners which were often reminiscent of the widespread barbarism discourse. The author rightly concludes that alterity patterns continued to inform the perception of Russia in France despite the positive image of Peter I., ibid., pp. 482–90.

and dues.'[106] Peter I was aware of the image that preceded him and his court. Before their arrival, Kurakin had already warned Liboy that the tsar and his entire entourage took offense at being called 'Muscovite'.[107]

No wonder, then, that from the arrival at the French border in April 1717 to the signing of the alliance treaty in Amsterdam in August the same year, the Russian diplomats insisted on correct procedure in order to balance Russia's ceremonial status against the tsar's rejection of public ceremonies. Kurakin requested written assurance that the French court confirmed it granted all honours according to the tsar's demands. Liboy was asked to pre-date the letter to the day before the tsar's arrival so as to lead people to believe that all ceremonies, whatever form they might take, had been pre-arranged with the consent of the Russian ruler.[108] The Russians had to hedge their bets against the immense prestige of the French court while suspending ceremonial rules through the incognito. Such a written agreement would provide enough leverage to prove that Peter I was placed in control of his own status management and that the French court did not gain any prestige at the expense of the Russians by reducing the ceremonies.

Such concerns were not unfounded. Peter I may have slipped out of his role as the Russian ruler in public, moving swiftly from sight to sight. But dynastic competition continued to keep the diplomats busy behind the scenes, especially where the results of secret negotiations and the written fixation of tangible political interests were entangled with claims to honour and status. The alliance resulting from the negotiations in Paris was of rather low practical significance according to most historians.[109] The treaty makes an interesting showcase for Franco-Russian relations at another level. The friendship alliance with both France and Prussia indicated a new departure in the political order of the power system in which Russia's reach now extended to central and western Europe.[110] Already during the secret negotiations, Peter I's chief negotiators had shown a clear awareness of the tsar's newly acquired position, reminding Tessé that 'the system of Europe [had] changed' and Russia had replaced

[106] *Historical memoirs of the duc de Saint-Simon*, III, p. 91. According to Dangeau, the French court spent around 500 to 600 écus per day on the tsar's visit, *Journal du marquis de Dangeau*, XVII, p. 98. Lünig, *Theatrum Ceremoniale*, I, p. 215, gives a similar figure: the total amounted to 4,000 Livres a day. 1,500 livres per day were allocated to provide for the tsar's and his suite's table, see Buvat, *Journal de la régence*, pp. 263f.

[107] AAE, MD Russie, 3 ('Sur les Honneurs faits de la part du Roy au Czar de Moscovie Pierre 1.er'), fol. 148.

[108] *SIRIO*, XXXIV, pp. 155f.

[109] Mezin, *Vzgliad iz Evropy*, p. 36. For a more positive assessment, see Wittram, *Peter I*, II, pp. 322f., and Schnakenbourg, *La France*, pp. 506–25, esp. pp. 518f. For the terms of the treaty, see *Recueil des instructions*, pp. 189f.

[110] Wittram, *Peter I*, II, p. 323.

Sweden as a great power.[111] The Russians swiftly converted their gains in power into claims to status. In the treaty, they suggested to style the title of their ruler as 'Maj[esté] Czarée'. After all, the French court willingly had pleased the tsar by acknowledging him as *Petrus Alexiewitz, Tzar Magnus Russorum Imperator*, at least on the medal struck in his honour. In the arena of official status exchange, and its documentation, this suggestion raised the suspicion of the French who insinuated that the Russians were trying to arrogate to their crown the title 'Caesarea Majestas', a claim that, according to them, would not pass with other monarchs. Insisting on equality as they did, the French were not shy, either, of trying to place themselves above both the Prussian and the Russian signatories. According to Le Dran, Châteauneuf put his signature on the treaty higher than that of the Russian minister so that the French king took precedence over both the tsar and the Prussian king in all copies. The French court played the oriental card and informed the 'Muscovite ministers' that 'the oriental powers made no difficulties in conceding the place of honour in this or that copy [of the treaty] to the crown of France'.[112] After much deliberation, the diplomats agreed to hand out six original copies of the treaty, two for each delegation. Châteauneuf placed his signature in the first column on the two copies for the French court while the signatures of the other two parties were relegated to the second column. The Prussians received a similar version. However, on the copy for the tsar, the Russian plenipotentiaries were allowed to sign the treaty in the first column, while the French had to content themselves with the second, lesser column.[113] The signatures on the treaty inscribed the performance of rank into the document itself.

Throughout the entire stay, long before the signing of the official document, court officers had been kept in thrall by ceremonial incertitude. Peter I's status expectations vacillated between the complete suspension of monarchical honours and an uncompromising assertion of Russia's ceremonial dignity. The tsar's presence resulted in a paradox between holding his monarchical identity in limbo, on the one hand, and

[111] *Mémoires et lettres du maréchal de Tessé*, II, p. 315. The Russians argued that France had lost her traditional ally in the German lands and should therefore resort to Russia. They urged Tessé to break Sweden out of the French alliance system and let the tsar take its place. During the Great Northern War, Sweden had been expelled militarily from northern Germany by 1716, although it would retain Bremen, Verden, and a small part of western Pomerania in the final peace settlement of Nystad in 1721.

[112] AAE, MD Russie, 4 ('Negociations entre la France et le tsar de la Grande Russie, Pierre Ier, par Le Dran', 1726), fol. 41v; *SIRIO*, XXXIV, p. XLII.

[113] AAE, MD Russie, 4 ('Negociations entre la France et le tsar de la Grande Russie, Pierre Ier, par Le Dran', 1726), fol. 41v–43. *SIRIO*, XXXIV, pp. XLII-XLIV. See also the king's instructions on this matter: Louis XV to Châteauneuf, 28 July 1717, in *Recueil des instructions*, pp. 190–95, here on p. 191.

the French's court responsibility to acknowledge his status according to international norms, on the other. The incognito was taken quite literally. Instructions to Peter I's hosts at the French border in Dunkirk mentioned the tsar but referred to him as 'a gentleman from abroad' (*un seigneur étranger*) and 'the person of distinction who is to be received' (*la personne de distinction qu'il s'agiroit de recevoir*).[114] The local officer received an order from the regent to show all marks of consideration to the tsar without breaching the rules of the incognito. He was instructed to leave the tsar in no doubt that the regent was prepared to receive his distinguished guest with all due honours but he withdrew from any public celebrations because Peter I desired to pass through France unacknowledged.[115] The tsar had a clear idea of how he wanted to pass through French towns, demanding that three salutes be fired by the artillery upon both his entry and departure. He refused to accept a public, solemn entry, but he took the compliments and the customary wine offerings from the town officials on his way to Paris, passing through Calais, Boulogne, Montreuil, Abbeville, Amiens, Beauvais, and Beaumont.[116]

Meanwhile, in the capital, the regent made enquiries to Charles Trudaine, the provost of the merchants of Paris, as to whether representatives of the township might greet the tsar upon his entry into the city. Desgranges, the master of ceremonies, reported that such honours were only given to kings, queens, and princes who proceeded through the city in open splendour, in coaches provided by the French monarch, but not incognito. He produced a list of precedents, including the visits of the Polish and Swedish royal consorts in 1645–1665 and 1664, the duchess of Savoy (1679), the queen consort of Spain (1673), the duchess of York, and Philip V of Spain in 1700.[117] Desgranges also alluded to Philip V's journey through Provence and Languedoc on his return from Italy in 1702. The Spanish king travelled incognito. The provincial governors furnished the coaches and provided guards to accompany him while Louis XIV offered the king to send the towns' mayors and aldermen as an expression of the highest honours in the form of a 'simple reverence without compliments (*sans compliment*)' and with 'much respect and politeness [...] but without ceremonies (*sans cérémonies*)'.[118] These

114 AAE, MD Russie, 3 ('Sur les Honneurs faits de la part du Roy au Czar de Moscovie Pierre 1.er'), fols. 139–40v.

115 Ibid. fols. 139v–40v; For the instructions, see *SIRIO*, XXXIV, pp. 123–27.

116 BM, ms 2747, fols. 242v–43.

117 AAE, MD Russie, 3 ('Sur les Honneurs faits de la part du Roy au Czar de Moscovie Pierre 1.er'), fols. 148–49.

118 Ibid., fol. 149v.

informal formalities conveniently absorbed the ambiguity that emerged with the fiction of incognito suspending status and the presence of a prince requiring due status recognition. The French court adopted the same ritual formula for Peter I's stay in Paris: respect, politeness, and deference without ceremonies.

While the master of ceremonies was studying the list of precedents, organising the arrival of the Russian tsar in the capital, Liboy awaited Peter I at the French border, making sure that this ceremonial formula did not result in a major diplomatic affront. There was a fine line between informal politeness and the failure to acknowledge the rank of the foreign monarch. After the first meeting with Peter I and Kurakin, Liboy reported back to Paris that despite the incognito the tsar had no reason to assume that he was not treated as a majesty. But he worried that the poor state of the coaches he managed to obtain for the Russian delegation would damage the relationship with the tsar: 'the augmentation of the court of the tsar' would make the French effort of staging an appropriate reception look very feeble'.[119] Liboy, who had been appointed to this task because of his 'wisdom' and 'zealousness', was endowed with full powers to decide ceremonial issues on the ground. His instructions permitted enough flexibility in making ad hoc concession in ceremonial questions to the tsar's full satisfaction. Liboy was also instructed to make it clear to the Russians that the French would have been prepared to receive the tsar with all public honours due to his rank and that the relinquishment of public ceremonies only accommodated Peter I's own demands.[120] The balancing act between the absence of public ritual and informal status recognition proved difficult, especially since Peter I refused to be part of a scenario in which his honours could be put on display. And yet, some commentators ignored ceremonial intricacies on the ground. Contemporary reports registered in a rather standard language that on 21 April 'the tsar arrived in Dunkirk where he was received as he had demanded, with all the honours due to crowned heads'.[121] It seems as though the court cared more about the public perception of the events than some of their observers.

Complications continued when Peter I arrived in Paris. The marquis de Nesle delivered the king's greetings to the tsar in Calais and escorted the delegation through the Picardie region. On 5 May, the regent sent Tessé to accompany the tsar and his retinue from Beaumont to Paris and

[119] *SIRIO*, XXXIV, pp. 139–41.
[120] For Liboy's instructions, see *SIRIO*, XXXIV, pp. 127–31; *Recueil des instructions*, pp. 158–65. See also AAE, MD Russie, 3 ('Sur les Honneurs faits de la part du Roy au Czar de Moscovie Pierre 1.er'), fols. 142–42v.
[121] Buchet, *Abrégé*, p. 377. Similar Furcy, 'Venu en France du Czar', p. 16.

throughout his stay in the capital. The *maître d'hotel du roi* and further officers were in charge of organising the tsar's arrival in Paris. Thomas de Dreux, the grand master of ceremonies, took over the role of the grand marshal of lodgings.[122] With so many court officials involved, status issues concerning the Russian monarch percolated through the ranking system of the French court to the competition between the master of ceremonies and the *introducteur des ambassadeurs*. To participate in the reception of a prince was a source of status with which individual office holders hoped to bolster their own prestige.[123]

The Russian delegation arrived in Paris on 7 May at 9 o'clock at night.[124] Many members of French court society attended the occasion. Peter I passed through the crowd in a six-horse carriage but, according to Lünig, remained unrecognised, as the court had forbidden to illuminate the scene with torches.[125] The tsar and his entourage walked into the Old Louvre where a lavish dinner awaited them and eight chambers had been furnished for the most distinguished members of the delegation. Peter I inspected the rooms, rejected the invitation to dine and hurriedly retired to a more humble abode away from the pomp of the Louvre, to the Hotel Lesdiguières near the Arsenal where he downed two glasses of beer and went to sleep.[126] The St Petersburg published gazette *Vedomosti* gave the grandeur (*velikost*) of the old royal palace as the reason for the tsar's discomfort.[127]

However, courtly splendour, the rules of hospitality and diplomatic protocol could not be avoided so easily and continued to restrict Peter I's stay in Paris. In a letter to his wife, Ekaterina Alekseevna, he complained that he had not been able to see anything for three days following his arrival, as he was obliged to stay in his lodgings until he had completed a series of visits, particularly the first meeting with the king of France.[128] Meanwhile, the Regency Council convened to discuss the organisation of the first encounter of the two heads of state shortly after the regent's first ceremonial visit in the tsar's residence.[129]

The situation was equally difficult as in 1698 when the Viennese court arranged a rendezvous between the German emperor and the Russian tsar. The symbolism of the meeting between Peter I and Louis XV marked a key moment in the relations between the two courts, as it put the question of precedence on the agenda of both organisers and

[122] BM, ms 2747, fol. 243. [123] Ibid., fols. 243v–244. [124] Ibid., fol. 244v.
[125] Lünig, *Theatrum Ceremoniale*, I, p. 213. [126] Ibid.; BM, ms 2747, fol. 244v.
[127] *Vedomosti vremeni Petra Velikogo. Vypusk vtoroi: 1708–1709 gg.* (Moscow, 1906), p. 246.
[128] *Pis'ma russkikh gosudarei i drugikh osob tsarskago semeistva. Vol. I: Perepiska Petra I s Ekaterinoiu Alekseevnoiu* (Moscow, 1861), p. 66
[129] BM, ms 2747, fols. 245ff; *Vedomosti*, pp. 245f.

observers. Similar to the private encounter between Leopold I and Peter I in Vienna, the unofficial character of the meeting permitted more flexibility than a public audience. Nevertheless, a less formal ceremonial required a carefully arranged ritual. The Council decided that Louis XV should visit Peter I in his lodgings and that the two should treat each other as equals (d'*égal à égal*).[130] The asymmetry between the seven-year-old child king and the experienced tsar – 'a huge man', as Saint-Simon noted – belied all claims to equality.[131] But in diplomatic ceremonial, the physical appearance of the two monarchs was secondary to the ritual choreography that framed their encounter.

On 10 May, Louis XV paid Peter I the first visit. The king came in an eight horse-drawn carriage accompanied by distinguished office holders of his court and representatives of the town. The citizens of Paris had been ordered to present gifts to the tsar in honour of his stay in the capital: wine and marmalade. Peter I, who according to the records had grown impatient to meet the French monarch, received Louis XV in the courtyard of his residence at 5 o'clock in the afternoon.[132] He approached the king, as the latter descended from his coach. The child embraced the tsar, expressing his joy about the honour of hosting such a distinguished guest in his realm.[133] Such tributes were duly recorded and conveyed to the public at courts throughout Europe, including St Petersburg.[134] Peter I, known for his impulsive character, reciprocated the compliment but added a personal note to the ritual: 'All were astounded to see the Czar pick the little King up under his arms, and swing him up to his own level in order to embrace him. The king, young as he was, was quite unafraid.'[135] Saint-Simon, who made this observation, was adept at precedence disputes and gave a finely tuned political interpretation of Peter I's personal behaviour: 'It was very moving to see the Czar's gentleness with [the king]; he appeared to grow fond of him, showing innate courtesy, mingled with royal dignity, equality of rank, and some slight superiority because of his age.'[136] And as if pressed by circumstances he endowed his words with the authority of a witness, adding: 'All this was clearly visible.'[137]

The notes of the master of ceremonies, like most published accounts, emphasise that the king was in possession of the right hand throughout their meeting, a privilege usually granted to ambassadors during their visits of other diplomats in their house. But Desgranges' records make no

[130] BM, ms 2747, fol. 245.
[131] *Historical memoirs of the duc de Saint-Simon*, III, p. 123. [132] BM, ms 2747, fol. 245v.
[133] Ibid., fol. 246.
[134] Buchet, *Abrégé*, p. 188; Buvat, *Journal de la régence*, pp. 265f.; *Journal du marquis de Dangeau*, XVII, pp. 83f.; Lünig, *Theatrum Ceremoniale*, I, p. 214; *Vedomosti*, p. 246.
[135] *Historical memoirs of the duc de Saint-Simon*, III, p. 124. [136] Ibid. [137] Ibid.

mention of Peter I's breach of protocol. Instead a brief description of the spatial arrangement of the encounter (not dissimilar to the meeting with Leopold I) created the perfect symmetry between the two princes who sat, with their heads uncovered, on two chairs placed opposite each other on the same line.[138] The tsar returned the visit, calling on the king in the Tuileries Palace around the same time the next day. He received the same honours as he had given Louis XV the previous day. The ramification is that the sheer presence of the prince translated arbitrary behaviour, or carefully calculated gestures, into a message of political import that could either be counter-balanced or facilitated by the language of ritual. Precedence issues were unavoidable. Even the mise-en-scène of equality was a strategy of dealing with the problem of rank. The slightest deviation from the choreography, often unintended, caught the attention of the onlookers who construed the resulting symbolism in the light of dynastic supremacy.

So prestigious was the meeting of the two heads of state that a quarrel arose between the *introducteur des ambassadeur*, the marquis de Magny, and Tessé. Magny hoped to escort Peter I in his coach in order to derive symbolic profit from the honours that the king put on display before the French court. His hopes were dashed when he was told that he was the *introducteur des ambassadeurs* and not an *introducteur des princes*, a function that, on this occasion, Tessé fulfilled in his role as the *introducteur du tsar*.[139] Again, while the hierarchical world of diplomacy developed its own codes of honour – emerging from the culture of court society – it often overlapped with domestic ladders of prestige.[140]

The meetings with the king released the tsar from this 'house arrest'. Once the relationship between king and tsar had been established through ritual, he was free to explore the city while his ministers were negotiating the terms of the alliance treaty. Ceremonial duties continued to occupy the tsar, the court and the diplomatic corps in the French capital. Peter I departed from Paris on 20 June. His one and a half months' stay in Paris was punctuated with various encounters, demonstrating the ongoing tensions between personality and protocol.[141] Peter I's approach to ceremony extended from loathing ceremonial duties to very unceremonious behaviour. When the tsar arrived at the Palais-Royal to visit Françoise Marie de Bourbon, the duchess of Orléans, the entire palace remained closed because the tsar wished not to be recognised. He was seen to lower his head and hide his face under his hat when he walked out of the

[138] BM, ms 2747, fol. 246. [139] Ibid., fol. 247. [140] See also Chapter 3, p. 143.

[141] There were further visits of both the king, the regent and members of the French court. Peter I received the papal nuncio and other foreign diplomats. Cf. Schnakenbourg, *La France*, p. 484, on Peter I's personal take on protocol.

apartments.[142] On another occasion Peter I caused eyebrows to raise when he visited Madame de Maintenon, the second wife and 'informal *premier ministre*',[143] of the deceased Louis XIV. Expecting the tsar on 10 June at Saint-Cyr, the eighty-two-year-old woman retired to bed, pretending to be ill in order to dispense with the ceremonial. On the next day she wrote to her niece, Madame de Caylus: 'He sat down by my Bed's-Side, and asked me by an Interpreter whether I was sick? I said that I was; he asked what my Ailment might be; and I answered, great Age and a pretty weak Constitution. He knew not what to reply, and his Interpreter seemed not to understand me. His Visit was very short; he caused the Curtain to be open'd at the Bed's-Feet, in order to have a Peep at me: You may well judge that it must have given him a great deal of Satisfaction.'[144] Saint-Simon recounted the episode in slightly more dramatic terms: 'The Czar entered, flung wide first the window-curtains, then all the bed-curtains, took a long, leisurely look at her, uttered not a word, nor she to him, and then went his way, without the smallest suspicion of a bow'.[145]

Even when the tsar consciously side-stepped etiquette, or unintentionally breached the ceremonial order, precedence and the associated expectations were inevitable. Diplomatic protocol did not lose its significance because of Peter I's personal penchants for pretence and play. The ritual persona of the prince and both his character and physical appearance – the king's two bodies – were inseparable in the monarch's presence.[146] This was a structural condition of early modern statehood and diplomacy that neither individual power holders, nor their representatives, could escape. However, the tsar's stay in Paris demonstrates the flexibility with which the court handled the presence of a monarch whose aura still carried notions of barbarism and who was at the same time establishing himself firmly on the political map of Europe. Similar to his stay in Vienna, Peter I's incognito and encounters *sans cérémonie* resolved status questions but they did not de-ritualise diplomatic practice. On the contrary, strategies of reduced formality increased the complications of ritual procedure. The French court officials were very insecure in hosting the

142 Buvat, *Journal de la régence*, p. 269. 143 Duindam, *Vienna and Versailles*, p. 230.

144 Madame de Maintenon to Madame la comtesse de Caylus, 11 June 1717, in *Lettres de Madame de Maintenon, vol. VI: 1714–1719*, ed. J. Schillings (Paris, 2011), pp. 609f. English translation from *The letters of madam de Maintenon; and other eminent persons in the Age of Lewis XIV. To which are added, some characters* (London, 1753), pp. 295f.

145 *Historical memoirs of the duc de Saint-Simon*, III, p. 128. Similar, Buvat, *Journal de la régence*, p. 271; *Journal du marquis de Dangeau*, XVII, p. 104. See also, Mezin, *Vzgliad iz Evropy*, p. 29.

146 E. H. Kantorowicz, *The king's two bodies: a study in mediaeval political theology* (Princeton, 1997).

foreign guest while, at the same time, the bureaucratic ranks tried to gain symbolic capital from the occasion. Informality permitted contemporaries to balance inherited claims to rank with coexisting concepts of state equality. The rituals negotiated the ambiguities that resulted from the contradictions between surviving notions of dynastic precedence and the idea of equality in post-Westphalian diplomatic practice.

Questions of rank, and its symbolic manifestations, continued in the official diplomatic channels. Shortly after his departure from Paris, Peter I dispatched Johann C. von Schleinitz as Russia's first publicly accredited permanent resident to the French court in order to continue friendly relations with the king.[147] The second item on his list of instructions ordered the diplomat to demand the honours that the French granted to the first crowned heads, in particular the Holy Roman Emperor and the king of Great Britain.[148] In his report from 20 December 1717, Schleinitz duly informed his sovereign that he received 'the usual honours' upon his arrival in France, submitting a full report of the ceremonies shortly afterwards.[149]

In contrast, when the Grand Embassy arrived in Vienna in 1698, the Russian ambassadors still followed the old protocol as instructed by the *Posol'skii prikaz* in Moscow. These codes allowed little deviation from the precedent collections in the archives of the ambassadorial chancellery in which other courts' practices provided no model for preserving the honour of the tsar. The instructions to Schleinitz, and the routine language of his reply, suggest that significant changes were underway during the period between the Grand Embassy and Peter I's visit to France in 1717. Within less than twenty years, Russia had not only grown into a major military power that was gradually melding into the European alliance system, gaining the tsar the fame of a powerful and enterprising ruler. Russian diplomatic practice, the approach to ritual and its organisation also witnessed a period of reform. The following chapter will trace the continuities and changes in this process.

[147] *Recueil des instructions*, pp. 197ff. [148] RGADA, f. 93, op. 1 (1710), d. 10, ll. 1–7.
[149] Ibid., ll. 27ff. For a full account of the ceremonies, see RGADA, f. 156, op. 1, d. 171.

5 From Insult to Imperator

Changes and Continuities in the Reign of Peter I

Anti-ceremonial Peter?

The film *Peter I*, by the Soviet film director Vladimir M. Petrov, gives imaginative insights into the diplomatic culture at the court of Tsar Peter I.[1] An ambassador of the Holy Roman Emperor arrives in the Neva Bay near the fortress of Kronstadt. The Russian officer, who is asked to pilot the ship into the harbour, is hopelessly drunk. Embarrassed about his fellow countryman, Peter I takes the matter into his own hands and boards the diplomat's sailing-ship. There he eavesdrops the ambassador's conversation. The diplomat and his attendants discuss how western powers needed to evict the Russian barbarians from the Baltic Sea and prevent them from invading the rest of Europe. Taken aback by these words, but with increased confidence, Peter I steers the ship towards the newly erected Peter and Paul Fortress and exclaims: '*Peterburg*!' On their arrival, at the landing stage, the haughty Austrian nobleman drops five guilders of gratuity into the hands of the pilot-tsar and says: '*na vodku*!' (for Vodka!). A change of scene places the ambassador in the interior of a palace where he is told that he will be received by the tsar without grand ceremonies (*malyi priem*). 'Excellent', he replies and adds: 'They say that Tsar Peter is a man of very simple spirits.' A courtier, attending the ambassador, comments ambiguously: 'In his demeanour, the sovereign is simple!' The diplomat is surprised to behold the pilot among the illustrious society in the palace, but sees his expectation fulfilled that, at the Russian court, one is surrounded by commoners. Peter I, with a victorious twinkle in his eye, discloses himself to the ambassador by seizing the hand of Tsaritsa Ekaterina Alekseevna. The monarch's suddenly revealed presence ridicules the European diplomat and forces him to perform an automated series of bows in a submissive but, at the same time, vainglorious manner.

In real life, too, Peter I expressed dismissive views about diplomatic protocol in terms 'reminiscent of those in which foreigners once spoke

[1] V. M. Petrov, *Petr Pervyi* (Lenfil'm, 1937–1938).

of Muscovite diplomacy'.[2] In February 1713, he wrote to his favourite Menshikov, who had been appointed to serve as his ambassador at the peace congress in Brunswick: 'Act with as much flattery and obligingness (*nizost'*) to the Danish court as possible, for even if you speak the truth, unless you are compliant they will take it ill; you know what they are like, they have more regard for the protocol than the actual business.'[3] While these episodes endorse the prevailing image of Peter I as an unassuming man with both a practical sense and a love for pretence and play, it is hard to maintain that, in reality, the Petrine administration ever ignored the rules of diplomatic ceremonial as Peter I does in the film.[4]

It has rightly been suggested that in order to assemble trustworthy people around him and bind their loyalty to his charismatic appearance, Peter I created an anti-ceremonial mock court.[5] Foreign ministers witnessed the games and wild ceremonies of the 'All-Mad, All-Jesting, All-Drunken Assembly' and often unwillingly participated in the bacchanalian debaucheries which took place during lavish festivities arranged for the tsar and his illustrious entourage.[6] Diplomatic dignitaries were invited to dress up in 'very extraordinary and inconvenient' Muscovite costumes to celebrate a mock wedding according to old customs.[7] Diplomats were also at risk of experiencing Peter I's humour at their expense. In 1715, the English representative at St Petersburg, George Mackenzie, became the object of laughter. Much to his embarrassment, the Englishman had presented the tsar with credentials signed by Queen Anne (r. 1702–1714), who had passed away before he could deliver the letter to the tsar. Peter I threatened Mackenzie and, in the presence of other foreign ministers, told the diplomat that he would issue the recredentials in the name of his dead mother, Natalia Naryshkina. He also suggested that

[2] Hughes, *Age of Peter the Great*, p. 51. [3] Quoted in ibid.

[4] For Peter I's 'plainness', an image that already became commonplace during his lifetime, see Hughes, 'Courts', pp. 312f. For the tsar's image(s) which evolved after his death, see N. V. Riasanovsky, *The image of Peter the Great in Russian history and thought* (Oxford, 1985). See also I. Kondakov, '"Poriadok" vs. "khaos": Petr I v intellektual'noi istorii Rossii', in *Petr Velikii*, ed. E. V. Anisimov (Moscow, 2007), pp. 9–33.

[5] Zitser, *Transfigured kingdom*, esp. p. 12.

[6] The theme of alcohol is also picked up by Petrov's film. For contemporary accounts, see, for example, the descriptions by the Prussian envoy Gustav von Mardefeld: Mardefeld to Frederick Wilhelm I, letters of 1 and 11 August 1721, *SIRIO*, XV, pp. 191, 195. For drinking culture and the All-Drunken Assembly, see L. A. J. Hughes, *Playing games: the alternative history of Peter the Great* (London, 2000); Hughes, *Age of Peter the Great*, pp. 249–57, Keenan, *St Petersburg*, pp. 42–48, and Zitser, *Transfigured kingdom*, with further references on the subject.

[7] Whitworth to St John, 8 June 1712, *SIRIO*, LXI, p. 215.

henceforth any further compliments from the queen should be addressed to the deceased tsaritsa.[8]

However, it would be misleading to assume, on the basis of the carnival nature of the mock court, that Petrine diplomacy was completely devoid of the strict ceremonial rules that determined rank and status, even in court entertainments and festivities. On the contrary, the descriptions by foreign ministers show how important they regarded the seating order at a dinner table or how perceptive they were about their position in a solemn parade.[9] Such baroque representations complemented diplomatic protocol. Ol'ga G. Ageeva wrote that courtly divertissements 'became an organic element of Petrine reforms [...]. The creation of a system of new kinds of secular festivities may itself be considered as one of the cultural transformations in the first quarter of the eighteenth century'.[10]

As such, the idea of exploiting festivities as a political medium was not Peter I's invention. The court of Aleksei had already involved foreign diplomats in solemn events that followed a carefully prescribed ceremonial. The Epiphany ceremony, for example, served to address foreign diplomats with special honours.[11] Furthermore, in 1675, the tsar used his pilgrimage to the Trinity Lavra of St Sergius as an occasion to stage a parade, demonstrating the power of the tsar's troops to the attending diplomats. The message of the solemnities were primarily directed towards the envoys of the Holy Roman Emperor, Hannibal F. von Bottoni and Johann C. Terlinger von Guzman, who, of all foreign representatives, had been given the best observation point. The scenario presented a comprehensive section of Muscovite society. Watching the boiars, the *okol'nichie*, the *blizhnie i dumnye liudi*, the *stol'niki*, the *striapchie* passing by, the imperial diplomats asked who all these people were and what ranks they carried. They also wondered if this order would have been the same under Emperor Augustus. If the tsar had an army as rich as this, he would not only beat the Ottomans but everything else would be secure in his hands.[12] Admittedly, this is the impression that is conveyed by the Russian sources. But the diplomats confessed that what they saw 'was a very glorious and, to

[8] Mackenzie to Townshend, 11 April 1715, *SIRIO*, LXI, pp. 372–79. For another, more subtle, example of Peter I's humour, see Zitser, *Transfigured kingdom*, pp. 101f.

[9] See, for example, La Vie's account from 4 February 1715, *SIRIO*, XXXIV, p. 101.

[10] O. G. Ageeva, 'Prazdniki v chest' poltavskoi pobedy v XVII v.', in *Poltava: k 300-letiiu poltavskogo srazheniia: sbornik statei*, ed. O. G. Ageeva (Moscow, 2009), pp. 257–73, here on p. 258. For court festivities in St Petersburg, see also Keenan, *St Petersburg*, ch. 3.

[11] See the description by Wickhart, *Moscowittische Reiss-Beschreibung*, pp. 76–82. For the Epiphany ritual and its origins, see Bushkovitch, 'Epiphany'.

[12] *PDS*, V, col. 229.

say the truth, majestic procession'.[13] Bottoni and Guzman promised to inform the emperor in writing about all the magnificence which they witnessed.[14] The then three-year-old tsarevich and future tsar, Peter I, was complimented by the imperial diplomats who removed their hats as Aleksei and his two sons Ivan and Peter passed by.[15]

And yet, the way in which Tsar Peter I used court festivities to communicate his political ambitions was quite distinct from the seventeenth-century practice as exercised by his father, as Richard Wortman has shown.[16] While solemn celebrations and domestic court ceremonies remained an asset of Russian diplomacy, they now departed from Orthodox ritual and were remodelled on Western imagery, primarily addressing the wider European public both at the Russian court and in the newly established residencies abroad. Important military victories and peace treaties – Azov (1696), Poltava (1709), and Nystad (1721) – were marked by lavish celebrations. These celebrations were intended to let other monarchs know about the achievements of their potential ally or terrifying enemy, Tsar Peter I.[17] Gavriil I. Golovkin, Russia's head of foreign affairs since 1706, distributed pamphlets about the victory of Poltava among foreign diplomats in order to diffuse this courtly knowledge to other fellow monarchs more effectively.[18] Descriptions of the triumphal arch set up in Moscow to celebrate the peace with Sweden went into print.[19] After the conclusion of the Treaty of Nystad (1721), Peter instructed his diplomats in Paris, The Hague, Berlin, Gdańsk, Vienna, Copenhagen, Hamburg, Dresden, and Constantinople to stage a festivity at their local residencies. The diplomats were instructed to light fireworks and arrange a huge feast on the day on which the peace

[13] Wickhart, *Moscowittische Reiss-Beschreibung*, p. 102. The Russian court produced very detailed descriptions of the ceremonies (including the Epiphany ceremony) and the dialogues that informed the diplomats about the constitution of the Russian army during the procession. For an example, see RGADA, f. 375, op. 1 (1675), d. 15. Reproduced in *PDS*, V, cols. 302–13.

[14] *PDS*, V, col. 231. See their description, translated from Latin into Russian, *PDS*, V, cols. 339ff.

[15] *PDS*, V, col. 229. [16] Wortman, *Scenarios*, I, ch. 2.

[17] For the imagery of the events celebrating Azov, Poltava, and Nystad, see ibid., I, pp. 42f., 48–50, 60f. For Poltava in particular, see Ageeva, ed., *Poltava: k 300-letiiu poltavskogo srazheniia*. Music played an important role in these festivities; for the Poltava celebrations, see G. J. Buelow, *A history of baroque music* (Bloomington, IN, 2004), pp. 455f. For an interpretation of the entertainments at the Petrine court, see Hughes, *Age of Peter the Great*, pp. 264–70. A good example of the many contemporary descriptions is Whitworth to Boyle, 22 December 1709 and 5 January 1710, *SIRIO*, L, pp. 291ff., 299.

[18] Whitworth to Boyle, 13 July 1709, *SIRIO*, L, pp. 200ff. See D. O. Serov, *Administratsiia Petra I* (Moscow, 2007), pp. 35f., for Golovkin.

[19] RGADA, f. 17, op. 1, d. 149. For triumphal arches, see E. A. Tiukhmeneva, *Iskusstvo triumfal'nykh vrat v Rossii pervoi poloviny XVIII veka* (Moscow, 2005).

celebrations took place in St Petersburg. The tsar may have envisaged the festivities to take place simultaneously, so that the spark of his empire, sent out from the newly founded capital, would illuminate the night sky of all major cities across Europe, including the Ottoman Empire – in the name of peace (see Figure 5.1).[20]

At the other end of such baroque representations were the restraints of war, which led to what might at first sight appear as a 'de-ceremonialisation' of Russian diplomatic practice. Russia was in a semi-permanent state of military struggle during Peter I's reign.[21] The tsar was constantly on the move, which made it difficult to gain access to him, let alone to arrange proper public receptions. Charles Whitworth, Queen Anne's representative to Russia (1704–1712),[22] wrote to the secretary of state in 1706: 'You will please to observe [. . .] how unsettled the court is and is like to be during the present war. They travel so fast by the help of relays, and their stays are so short, that it is impossible for the envoys to keep pace with them.'[23] The French envoy, Jean C. de Baluze learnt on his arrival in Moscow in 1703 that he was going to be received by the tsar without any ceremonies.[24] Peter I's equipage had been prepared for war, and the tsar was just about to leave his court to join the troops.[25]

But here, too, the constraints dictated by war and the austerity regime of military camp life did not remove the rules of protocol from the agenda of diplomatic encounter. On the contrary, diplomats insisted on the correct procedure to protect their status despite, or because of, the circumstances owing to the ongoing wars. Surprised about his modest reception in Moscow, the French diplomat Baluze enquired if it were possible to be brought to a meeting with Peter I in the tsar's personal carriage so as to simulate the impression of a public reception. The *pristav* declined the diplomat's request but offered the coach of Fedor A. Golovin, who had accompanied Peter I to western Europe and was now directing foreign affairs. Baluze pressed the *pristav* for two hours to send a coach appropriate to the occasion. As a result of the diplomat's perseverance, the *pristav* fetched him in a 'large golden sleigh, lined with

[20] RGADA, f. 156, op. 1, d. 181. The Russian embassy in Paris produced a draft (probably for publication) with descriptions of the festivity, AVPRI, f. 93, op. 93/1 (1721), d. 7, ll. 399–403. Similar festivities took place after the battle of Poltava in 1709; see Andrei A. Matveev's descriptions of the celebrations in the Netherlands: *PiB*, IX, pp. 1098ff. For further contemporary published descriptions, see Steppan, *Akteure*, p. 187.

[21] See Hughes, *Age of Peter the Great*, pp. 21–59.

[22] For Whitworth's career and his stay in Russia, see J. M. Hartley, *Charles Whitworth: diplomat in the age of Peter the Great* (Aldershot, 2002).

[23] Whitworth to Harley, 16 January 1706, *SIRIO*, XXXIX, pp. 211f.

[24] RGADA, f. 93, op. 1 (1703), d. 3, ll. 65ob–66.

[25] See Baluze's account of his reception, *SIRIO*, XXXIV, p. 23.

Figure 5.1 Depiction of the peace celebrations at the Russian ambassador's residence in Paris.

velvet, drawn by grey dappled horses and covered with a crimson velvet blanket, trimmed with golden fringes and double marten furs'.[26] This must have pleased the Sun King in France. For Baluze, the symbolism of the carriage was a legal instrument which showed that he was properly confirmed in his public office and thus endowed with all diplomatic privileges. During the audience, Peter I assured Baluze that his reception *sans cérémonies* would not result in a disadvantage vis-à-vis other envoys. Golovin, in the presence of the tsar, promised that he would provide Baluze with a writing that guaranteed the equal treatment relative to the status of the diplomats from Vienna.[27] Baluze, in turn, promised to report to the king how well he was received at the Russian court.[28] The issue of daily provisions of food and drinks also remained an element of ceremonial procedure, as Baluze constantly demanded to be treated on the same terms as the envoys of the Holy Roman Emperor. He would not accept any food if it amounted to less than what the imperial envoys were given.[29]

These examples show that neither Peter I's personal dislike of protocol, which found expression in his love for social inversion and play, nor the constraints of war completely eradicated the principles that determined and communicated status and rank in diplomatic culture. The tsar may not have been very fond of diplomatic ceremonial, but he and his diplomats had to take it as seriously as their Muscovite predecessors.[30] The question arises as to what extent diplomatic ceremonial was reformed during the reign of Peter I.

Ceremony and Reform

If a state saw such extensive reforms as did Russia under Peter I, one may assume that the diplomatic institutions and their constitutive rituals also underwent radical transformation.[31] Any response to this supposition

[26] Ibid., p. 24.
[27] Ibid., p. 25. A copy of this letter can be found in RGADA, f. 93, op. 1 (1703), d. 3, ll. 96f.
[28] Ibid., l. 67. [29] Ibid., ll.185ob–188ob, 246ob–258.
[30] Simon Dixon, in his survey of the Russian court, reaches a similar conclusion: Dixon, *Modernisation*, pp. 118–26. See also Grabar, *International law*, p. 66, and Sakharov, ed., *Istoriia*, III, pp. 14f.
[31] The institutional changes of Petrine diplomacy are emphasised by D. Altbauer, 'The diplomats of Peter the Great', *Jahrbücher für Geschichte Osteuropas*, 28 (1980), 1–16; Bohlen, 'Changes in Russian diplomacy'; and Matveyev, *The Karlowitz congress*. The literature on the reforms of Peter I is too vast to be fully cited here. For an overview, see Wittram, *Peter I.*, II, ch. 3. For a summary of the classics, see Bushkovitch, *Peter the Great*, pp. 1–11, and E. A. Zitser, 'Post-Soviet Peter: new histories of the late Muscovite and early imperial Russian court', *Kritika: Explorations in Russian and Eurasian History*, 6 (2005), 375–92, for a review of the more recent literature. For a balanced assessment of Peter I's reforms, see Hughes, *Age of Peter the Great*, pp. 462–70. For diplomatic practice, see also Steppan, *Akteure*, pp. 155ff., passim.

must lead to contradictory conclusions, if it takes heed of the 'historiographic commonplace' about Peter I's reign as a turning point in Russian history but at the same time seeks to acknowledge indisputable continuities.[32]

On the one hand, change in ceremonial procedure did undoubtedly happen. An observer of the Petrine court wrote in 1702 that the tsar intended to 'reform the chancelleries and regulate the court ceremonies for ambassadors, princes, counts, knights of orders, and gentlemen [...] after the example of other crowned heads'.[33] A few years later, Friedrich C. Weber, a Hanoverian who represented English interests at the Russian court between 1714 and 1719, confirmed that diplomatic ceremonies were now arranged on the European model.[34] On the other hand, as will become clear in the following case studies, a closer look at the sources of diplomatic protocol reveals that Peter I's diplomacy inherited a pool of precedents from previous centuries and continued to use them as his predecessors had done before him, which renders the distinction between 'Petrine' and 'Muscovite' obsolete.

A transformation of diplomatic ceremonial occurred, but not under the label of a 'cultural revolution' in the sense that Peter I jettisoned Muscovite diplomatic procedure in order to replace it with a new political culture which was exclusively modelled on a foreign, essentially 'Western' archetype.[35] Rather, the change of diplomatic culture happened at the level of adaptation of pre-existing norms. This is not surprising if one accepts that diplomatic practice before Peter I had evolved from an exchange with other powers, which, in the process, enabled Petrine diplomats to align their behaviour with other courts' ceremonial conventions. Diplomatic ceremonial was an organic part of court drama and display, but as such it had always belonged to the arena of foreign relations, to a wider spectrum of converging diplomatic cultures. It remained distinct from and outlasted domestic court ceremonies which, by contrast, had been inspired by Orthodox ritual and did undoubtedly see

[32] On the concept of 'turning point', see Hughes, *Age of Peter the Great*, p. 462. The contributions in H.-J. Torke, ed., *Von Moskau nach St. Petersburg: das russische Reich im 17.* Jahrhundert (Wiesbaden, 2000), attempt to challenge this notion and trace the origins of both reform and change in the seventeenth century.

[33] See Huyssen de Wigland's letter about the reforms of the tsar (1702), *SIRIO*, XXXIV, p. 21.

[34] F. C. Weber, *Des veränderten Rußlandes zweyther Theil, worinnen die Folge derjenigen wichtigen Veränderungen, welche der Rußische Kayser Petrus der Erste zur Aufnahme seines Reichs in allen Ständen vorgenommen* (Hanover, 1739), p. 184. Similar Lünig, *Theatrum Ceremoniale*, I, p. 492.

[35] On the notion of 'cultural revolution', see the works by James Cracraft, in particular his *The revolution of Peter the Great* (Cambridge, MA, London, 2003). See also Wortman, *Scenarios*, I, ch. 1.

a substantial transformation in image, function, and meaning under Peter I.[36]

What, then, was the nature of change in diplomatic procedure in the Petrine era? Seventeenth-century Russian diplomats shared with their Western peers a common understanding of the norms of symbolic competition. When diplomats from London, Vienna, or Paris deplored Russian ceremonial practice, they did this out of the fear that a new precedent might challenge their master's honour, as the Russians might use a common ceremonial element differently (the *pristav*'s claim to the place of honour on a diplomat's arrival, for example). Muscovite diplomacy based protocol on the information that the clerks of the *Posol'skii prikaz* drew from their own archives. This knowledge, in turn, stemmed from direct encounters with dynastic courts. Muscovy did not observe the practice of other courts through the mediums of *Zeremonialwissenschaft*, international law or diplomatic theory. Recognition of sovereignty depended much more on the participation in shared practices, and their uninterrupted documentation in the *posol'skie knigi*, rather than on the involvement in discourse. In order to avoid disputes about specific gestures, attempts were made to fix the procedure in bilateral contracts, notably with Sweden (1674), Austria (1675), Denmark (1684), and Brandenburg (1687).[37] Each decision regarding protocol in Russia emerged from the paperwork that Russian embassies produced abroad or that the chancellery collected in relation to diplomatic receptions in Moscow. In other words, Muscovite diplomatic ceremonial was *self-referential* in that it relied almost exclusively on the documented experiences of Russia's own diplomats and administrators.

It was this uroboric nature of Muscovite diplomacy which was modified by Peter I. From his reign onwards, diplomatic ceremony ceased to be exclusively determined by the precedents as sanctioned by the *starina* and written down in the *posol'lskie knigi*. Other courts' practices were now accepted as examples to solve ceremonial conflicts.[38] Petrine diplomatic culture continued the traditions of the ambassadorial chancellery, but at

[36] For domestic court ceremony, its focus on the church and the changes under Peter I, see Bushkovitch, *Peter the Great*, pp. 21–26; Hughes, *Age of Peter the Great*, pp. 248ff.

[37] For Sweden, see, *PSZRI*, I, no. 574 (24 March 1674), pp. 977–78. For Austria, see, *PSZRI*, I, no. 610 (9 October 1675), pp. 1009–14. For Denmark, see *PSZRI*, II, no. 1088 (10 August 1684), pp. 636–38. For Brandenburg, see *PSZRI*, II, no. 1250 (16 June 1687), pp. 860–62. Cf. Iuzefovich, *Put' posla*, p. 13.

[38] A good example is Prince Vasilii L. Dolgorukov's dispute with France's head of foreign affairs, Guillaume Dubois, over the place of honour during a visit to Dubois' house in 1721. Dolgorukov closely observed other diplomats' reactions and finally accepted Dubois' claim, following the examples of others. See the introduction to this book (fn. 1).

the same time it became *relational* to the customs of other courts. Existing forms of old concepts were filled with a new sense of pragmatism.[39]

Adaptation to other courts' ceremonial conventions happened at the spur of the moment. There was no direct *ukaz* that wrought a 180-degree change upon diplomatic protocol. It seems natural that this process started with the return of the Grand Embassy to Moscow in 1698. When the envoy Charles Whitworth arrived in Moscow in 1705, the Russian court consulted a number of precedents from the seventeenth century to arrange the reception of the diplomat. Examples include the ceremonies granted to the *poslannik*, Vasilii T. Postnikov, at the English court in 1687 (which was punctuated with ceremonial disputes) and the receptions of John Hebdon and John Hebdon Junior in Moscow in 1667/68 and 1677/78 respectively.[40] These 'Muscovite' examples provided the setting for Whitworth's reception, but the Russian court now adjusted established practice to avoid foreseeable ceremonial conflicts. For example, the *pristav* received the instruction to alight his sleigh before delivering a speech to the envoy at their initial encounter. He was also ordered to yield the 'right hand' to the diplomat at all occasions.[41] This was a clear response to the disputes that had once protracted the solemn entry of the Earl of Carlisle, triggering a series of further insults and complaints. Whitworth noted this change and informed the secretary of state in London about his reception in Smolensk as follows:

> I took leave to be so particular [in the description of the ceremonies] that you might better observe the Changes now made in the customes of the moscovites, whose pristaffs formerly disputed the right hand with all forreign Ministers, as happened in my lord Carlisles Embassy; also to acquaint you with an unusual mark of respect, which has been shown to Her Majesty on this occasion, the woywode [of Smolensk] having never used to give the first visit to any forreign ministers. In 1698 after a dispute of 2 days, the Emperor's envoy extraordinary monsieur Guarient was oblidged to pay him that civility, the woywode having at last pretended an indisposition, though there appeared no signs thereof in m-r Guarient's reception.[42]

The imperial envoy Ignaz C. von Guarient und Rall, whom Whitworth mentioned, had arrived in Moscow before Peter I's return from his

[39] Cf. H. Doerries, *Russlands Eindringen in Europa in der Epoche Peters des Grossen: Studien zur zeitgenössischen Publizistik und Staatenkunde* (Königsberg, Berlin, 1939), pp. 22ff., 97ff., who concludes that Peter I did away with the 'exotic' Muscovite ceremonial to introduce 'modern concepts of monarchical honour'.

[40] RGADA, f. 35, op. 1, d. 294, ll. 22–39, 46–55ob, passim. For a description of Postnikov's stay in London, see Vinogradoff, 'Russian missions', here on pp. 64–72; See also L. A. J. Hughes, 'V. T. Postnikov's 1687 mission to London: Anglo-Russian relations in the 1680s in British Sources', *Slavonic and East European Review*, 68 (1990), 447–60.

[41] RGADA, f. 35, op.1, d. 294, l. 80ob.

[42] Whitworth to Harley, 18 February 1705, *SIRIO*, XXXIX, pp. 29f.

journey to western Europe, which suggests that the incentive to alter the ceremonies must have come about sometime between the end of the Grand Embassy and Whitworth's reception.[43]

It is clear why the Russian court avoided ceremonial difficulties in its relations with England. In his struggle to strengthen his international position against Sweden, Peter I was convinced that England's interests were in line with his own and should result in an alliance with Queen Anne.[44] Whitworth's reception was arranged accordingly. The public audience with the tsar was held in private. But the honours given at his solemn entry were far above what an envoy might have expected (as opposed to an ambassador). They were used 'to let[ting] the world see the particular esteem he [Peter I] had for Her Majesty [Queen Anne]'.[45] The honours were intended to gratify the English diplomat and thereby tempt his master to support Russia in the ongoing war against Charles XII of Sweden. Whitworth understood the message of the diplomatic ceremonial: 'I perceive this court was in the hopes, that I was sent on purpose to offer Her Majesty's mediation in the war with Sweden [...] and perhaps this expectation was the chief motive of the unusual honours, that were shown at my reception.'[46]

Another example demonstrates how Muscovite precedents were adjusted. It had been more than twenty years since, in 1680, an accredited diplomat from France, François G. de Béthune, had come to the Russian court.[47] The ceremonial quarrels between Prince Iakov F. Dolgorukov's embassy and the French court in 1687 had led to a break in Franco-Russian relations.[48] The French envoy Baluze thus was moving in dangerous terrain when he was dispatched to Russia in 1703. As mentioned earlier, Baluze requested that he be received on an equal footing with other diplomats of his rank, notably those of the Holy Roman Emperor.[49] He said that, although all powers conceded the highest honours to the

[43] For Guarient's reception, see RGADA, f. 32, op. 1, d. 20. There is a Russian translation of a printed description of Guarient's embassy in Latin, which I was not able to locate. For the translation, see ibid., d. 21. Guarient's own reports have been used as a major source for Petrine court politics by Bushkovitch, *Peter the Great*, pp. 198ff.

[44] For a very informative account of Anglo-Russian political relations, see D. A. Collyer, 'Notes on the diplomatic correspondence between England and Russia in the first half of the eighteenth century', *Transactions of the Royal Historical Society*, New Series, 14 (1900), 143–74.

[45] Whitworth to Harley, 21 February 1705, *SIRIO*, XXXIX, p. 32. [46] Ibid., p. 34.

[47] For Béthune's description of his reception in Moscow, see *Receuil des instructions*, pp. 67ff.

[48] See the French account of the Russian 1687 embassy to France, *SIRIO*, XXXIV, pp. 15–19; *Receuil des instructions*, pp. 85ff. See also Grönebaum, *Frankreich in Ost- und Nordeuropa*, pp. 101–11.

[49] Baluze had been advised that he should under no condition yield precedence to the representatives of the Holy Roman Empire; see his instructions in *SIRIO*, XXXIV,

ambassadors of the Holy Roman Emperor, envoys were entitled to demand an equal treatment among each other.[50] The Russian court compiled a list of precedents to align Baluze's reception with previous ceremonies. In particular, it consulted the ceremonies arranged for Bottoni and Guzman in 1675, apart from the ones for Petr I. Potemkin in Paris (1681) and the ceremonies given to envoys from Brandenburg.[51] These examples were altered through small but significant gestures. Unlike Béthune before him, Baluze was allowed to dismount from his sleigh after the *pristav* had done so, and he was also given the place of honour.[52] As Baluze was going to see the tsar privately, he enquired if his audience would be any different from that organised for other envoys. The court's answer is a good example of how other European courts' practice became an additional point of reference for diplomatic ceremonies next to previous precedents: The tsar ordered to arrange an audience for Baluze 'in the ordinary former manner according to which other European great sovereigns deign to receive envoys privately'.[53]

The adaptations of ceremonial were an important element of the general reforms of foreign policy through which Peter I hoped to buttress Russia's place in the European *société des princes*.[54] The most salient feature of Petrine diplomacy was the establishment of permanent residencies at foreign courts.[55] Aleksei had made a similar attempt, albeit on a much smaller scale.[56] Peter I implemented permanent representations at all major European courts as well as in other parts of the world. By 1725 he could resort to diplomatic residents in the Dutch Republic, France, Spain, Poland, Austria, Prussia, Denmark, Sweden, Hamburg, Lithuania, the Ottoman Empire, China, Bukhara, Gilan, and at the

pp. 408–14. For a comparison, see Christian Steppan's analysis of the reception of an Austrian diplomat at the Petrine court: Steppan, *Akteure*, pp. 174ff.

50 RGADA, f. 93, op. 1 (1703), d. 3, l., 34ob.

51 RGADA, f. 93, op. 1 (1703), d. 3, ll. 1–23. For the diplomatic ceremonial used in diplomatic contacts between Brandenburg and Russia, see Prudovskii, 'K voprosu'.

52 RGADA, f. 93, op. 1 (1703), d. 3, l. 52.

53 RGADA, f. 93, op. 1 (1703), d. 3, l. 64.

54 For a comparative study that attempts to evaluate Petrine innovations in foreign policy against seventeenth-century diplomacy (including an appraisal of Peter I's reforms), see G. A. Sanin, 'Novatsii Petra I v upravlenii vneshnepoliticheskimi delami po sravneniiu s vtoroi polovinoi xvii veka', in *Rossiiskaia diplomatiia*, ed. Ivanov et al., pp. 148–52.

55 Aleksandrenko, *Agenty*, I, pp. 1–17.

56 Artamon S. Matveev, the head of the *Posol'skii prikaz*, proposed to the imperial envoys in 1675 that the tsar and the emperor should establish permanent residencies at their courts for the sake of 'good correspondence'. However, the project failed because the imperial envoys had no authority of negotiating such a proposal, see Wickhart, *Moscowittische Reiss-Beschreibung*, p. 113. For the Polish residence in Moscow, see Kaminski, *Republic vs. autocracy*. Thomas Eekman identified Johan van Keller as the official representative and 'permanent agent' of the Netherlands in Moscow (1676–1698): T. Eekman, 'Muscovy's international relations in the late seventeenth century: Johan van Keller's observations', *California Slavic Studies*, 14 (1992), 44–67.

Kalmyk Khanate.[57] In most cases, diplomats were sent to other courts incognito or as ministers without ambassadorial rank in order to save the cost of furnishing an ambassador's equipage and to avoid quarrels over precedence.[58]

The establishment of resident diplomacy abroad (and in St Petersburg) went hand in hand with institutional changes at home. The relatively late introduction of the table of ranks (1722) had left a blank space in the court hierarchy for Russian diplomats' whose social rank was an important factor in their appointment to a diplomatic mission. In 1722 Peter I issued an *ukaz* which determined that diplomats without a specific rank should be made *kamer-iunker* before they embarked on their mission, or *legatsions-rat* if they were sent to important (*znatnye*) courts.[59]

The restructuring of foreign policy institutions began with the Great Northern War.[60] From around 1700, a 'field ambassadorial chancellery' (*Pokhodnaia posol'skaia kantseliariia*) oversaw Russia's diplomatic activities. Renamed *Posol'skaia kantseliariia*, this new organization became a permanent institution in St Petersburg in 1710 and soon outgrew the Moscow-based *Posol'skii prikaz* in importance, especially after Count Golovkin, who had been presiding over foreign affairs since 1706, was appointed to the rank of chancellor in 1709. Petr P. Shafirov became vice-chancellor. Around the same time, foreign diplomats started to move from Moscow to the new capital in the north, a process that found a conclusion around 1718.[61] With the introduction of the collegiate system into Russian

[57] AVPRI, f. 2, op. 2/6, d. 57 ('Reestr ministrov russkikh pri inostrannykh dvorakh i konsulov', 1725). For Peter I's diplomats, see Altbauer, 'Diplomats'; E. Amburger, 'Das diplomatische Personal des russischen auswärtigen Dienstes unter Peter I.', in *Das Vergangene und die Geschichte. Festschrift für Reinhard Wittram zum 70. Geburtstag*, ed. R. v. Thadden, G. v. Pistohlkors, H. Weiss (Göttingen, 1973), pp. 298–311. For brief biographical sketches of the most important diplomats who served under Peter I, see Grabar, *International law*, pp. 46ff.

[58] T. K. Krylova, 'Stateinye spiski petrovskikh diplomatov (1700–1714 gg.)', *Problemy Istochnikovedeniia*, 9 (1961), 163–81, here on pp. 163f. This practice continued through the eighteenth century. Anderson, *Modern diplomacy*, p. 83, states that Russia had no full ambassador at other European courts (except for Warsaw) as late as the third quarter of the eighteenth century. There were, however, exceptions. For example, in 1720, Prince Vasilii L. Dolgorukov was sent to Paris as an ambassador (*posol'*), see AVPRI, f. 93, op. 93/1 (1720), d. 10, l. 1.

[59] *PSZRI*, VI, no. 3969 (17 April 1722), p. 656.

[60] An informative survey of the remodelling of Russian foreign policy institutions is Grabar, *International law*, pp. 51–53.

[61] For the beginnings, see Weisbrod to Rowe, 14 September 1710, *SIRIO*, L, p. 362: 'And the Czar, having been informed that the Prussian envoy, m-r Kayserling, was buying a house here [Moscow], asked him what he would do with a house in Moscow, His Majesty intending to make Petersburgh his residence and to order most people of quality down to build there; and some have writ hither, that they do not believe the court will come up next winter to this place'. For the court's move from Moscow to St Petersburg,

government in 1718, the chancellery became a 'college'. It was renamed *Kollegiia inostrannykh del* and received its final structure by an *ukaz* in 1720.[62] Heinrich J. Ostermann, a German born clerk, who started out as a translator in the *Posol'skaia kantseliariia,* worked his way up through the ranks to vice-chancellor and led the peace negotiations with Sweden, summarised the activities of the *Kollegiia* as follows: The foreign affairs college was a 'perpetual state archive and a permanent [source of] information about everything old and which has transpired in state affairs, behaviour, conduct, and the measures taken'.[63]

Ceremonial Knowledge

Ostermann's remark makes clear that the new institution continued the *Posol'skii prikaz'* mission as a collector and keeper of vital political information. Ceremonial knowledge and diplomatic theory was particularly important if the desired adaptations to other courts' practices would be successful. The *starina,* written into the *posol'skie knigi,* delivered the precedents, but seventeenth-century Russia had not participated in the legal discourse on ceremony, precedence, social hierarchy, and diplomatic practice apart from Kotoshikhin's descriptive account of ceremonial written in Swedish exile.[64] The first Russian treatise on international law appeared as late as 1717, as a justification of the war against Sweden.[65] Although it is 'regarded as a landmark in Russian international legal history', it remained an 'isolated and lonely document, not emulated by another Russian work of comparable scope [...] for many decades'.[66]

Petrine diplomats sensed an urgent need to gather further systematic information on diplomatic practice. In the early eighteenth century the Russian court began to collect foreign language materials on 'law and

see O. E. Kosheleva, *Liudi Sankt-Peterburgskogo ostrova Petrovskogo vremeni* (Moscow, 2004), ch. 4; Keenan, *St Petersburg,* pp. 17f. For an inspired interpretation of the symbolism of St Petersburg in the context of diplomacy and ceremonial, see D. Geyer, 'Peter und Petersburg', *Jahrbücher für Geschichte Osteuropas,* 10 (1962), 181–200, esp. pp. 191ff.

62 On the institutional history of the *Kollegiia innostrannykh del,* see *Ocherk istorii Ministerstva inostrannykh del, 1802–1902* (St Petersburg, 1902, reprint 2002), pp. 35–70. For an updated account on the early history of the college of foreign affairs including a discussion of the *ukaz* that gave the college its final form, see S. L. Turilova, *Istoriia vneshnepoliticheskogo vedomstva Rossii (1720–1832)* (Moscow, 2000), pp. 4–21.

63 Quoted in Grabar, *International law,* p. 52.

64 For a compararison between European and Muscovite theories and practices of honour, see Kollmann, *By honor bound,* pp. 58–63.

65 Shafirov, *Discourse.* For a Russian perspective on the 'just war', see P. Robinson, 'The justification of war in Russian history and philosophy', in *Just war in comparative perspective,* ed. P. Robinson (Aldershot, 2003), pp. 62–75.

66 Butler, 'On the Origins of International Legal Science in Russia', p. 41.

legislation of neighbouring states'.[67] In 1710, for example, Chancellor Golovkin requested that all books which Petr V. Postnikov, a western European-educated Russian scholar and diplomat, had bought and collected in France be sent back to Russia, including, for example, works on French law.[68] The instructor of the tsarevich, Heinrich von Huyssen, was ordered to tutor Aleksei Petrovich on aspects of international affairs.[69] Two important treatises of international law were translated on order of the tsar: Hugo Grotius' *De jure belli ac pacis* (1625) and Pufendorf's *Juris naturae et gentium* (1672). Postnikov translated Wicquefort's *L'ambassadeur et ses fonctions.*[70] However, none of these translations appeared in print.[71]

The first Russian newspaper *Sankt-Peterburgskie Vedomosti*, founded in 1702, established itself as a source of information about foreign relations, its reports stemming directly from military officers or Russian diplomats abroad (for example, Prince Boris I. Kurakin or Prince Vasilii L. Dolgorukov) or from copies of European periodicals.[72] The *Vedomosti* regularly reported on ceremonial occasions in Europe, including coronations, royal weddings, funerals, etc., as well as diplomatic receptions.[73] Andrei A. Matveev (1666–1728), son of the former head of the *Posol'skii prikaz* and one of Peter I's chief diplomats (serving in London and The Hague), acquired an extensive library over his lifetime. The catalogue of his books lists such important works as Godefroy's *Le ceremonial françois* (1649), Leibniz's *Codex juris gentium diplomaticus* (1693) as well as his *De jure suprematus ac legationis* (1678), Lünig's *Staats-Titularbuch* (1709), Vera y Figueroa's *Le parfait ambassadeur* (an edition of 1709), Zwantzig's *Theatrum praecedentiae* (1706), Wicquefort's

[67] Grabar, *International law*, pp. 36f.

[68] I. F. Tokmakov, 'Delo 1710 g. 21 marta po pis'mu kantslera grafa Golovkina o prisylke v S.-Peterburg, kuplennykh vo Frantsii i Gollandii doktorom Petrom Postnikovym knig', *Bibliograf*, 4 (1885), 75–81.

[69] On Huyssen's syllabus for the tsarevich, see Korzun, *Heinrich von Huyssen*, pp. 33–36.

[70] The Russian translation manuscript is preserved in RGADA, d. 93, op. 1 (1713), d. 3.

[71] Grabar, *International law*, pp. 38–43. For translation activities under Peter I, see G. Marker, *Publishing, printing, and the origins of intellectual life in Russia, 1700–1800* (Princeton, NJ, 1985), ch. 1; P. P. Pekarskii, *Nauka i literatura v Rossii pri Petre Velikom*, 2 vols. (St Petersburg, 1862), I, pp. 214–20, 323–32.

[72] S. R. Dolgova, 'Pervaia russkaia gazeta "Vedomosti" o diplomaticheskikh sviaziakh i tseremoniale v Rossiiskom gosudarstve', in *Representatsiia vlasti v posol'skom tseremoniale i diplomaticheskii dialog v XV – pervoi treti XVIII veka. Tret'ia mezhdunarodnaia nauchnaia konferentsiia tsikla "Inozemtsy v Moskovskom gosudarstve", posviashchennaia 200-letiiu Muzeev Moskovskogo Kremlia. Tezisy dokladov*, ed. A. K. Levykin, V. D. Nazarov (Moscow, 2006), pp. 41–44.

[73] S. M. Tomsinskii, *Pervaia pechatnaia gazeta Rossii (1702–1727)* (Perm, 1959), pp. 70–75. See also Marker, *Publishing*, pp. 27ff.

L'ambassadeur et ses fonctions (1690), and an extensive collection of Grotius' works.[74]

The import and translation of Western literature formed only one basis of the ceremonial knowledge that the *Posol'skaia kantseliariia* and its successor, the college of foreign affairs, sought to expand. A range of unpublished materials, mostly descriptions of the ceremonies practiced at individual courts, were collated to complement the new libraries. The first account, a description of Swedish ceremonies, was obtained around 1694.[75] A new wave of descriptions flowed into the Russian archives with the Grand Embassy. A handwritten German extract of the *Ceremoniale Brandenburgicum* was acquired around 1697, most likely during Peter I's stay at the court of the elector.[76] A Russian description of English diplomatic ceremonial found its way into the Russian archives around 1700.[77] The journal of the English diplomat Hans W. Bentinck, earl of Portland (1649–1709), which is a detailed description of French ceremonial produced during his mission to Paris, was obtained and translated into Russian in 1698.[78]

In 1706, Matveev, who apparently used the books from his library to compile his diplomatic reports,[79] sent to Moscow an exhaustive hand-written account of the manner in which diplomats were received in France, Great Britain, and the Dutch Republic.[80] Kurakin also gave

[74] N. S. Kartashov, I. M. Polonskaia, *Biblioteka A. A. Matveeva (1666–1728): katalog* (Moscow, 1985), pp. 100, 102f., 30f., 39, 85, 89f., 92.

[75] RGADA, f. 156, op. 1, d. 153.

[76] RGADA, f. 156, op. 1, d. 156. The *Ceremoniale Brandenburgicum* elaborates on the ceremonial that Russian diplomats received in Berlin and the elector's representatives in Moscow (ibid., l. 33–33ob). It acknowledged that the tsar demanded to be treated like the Holy Roman Emperor but reserved the royal honours for the Russian ruler. The *Ceremoniale Brandenburgicum* was one of the more unfortunate acquisitions. The work appeared in 1699 but was banned in the same year. Its sale was put under punishment by the Prussian authorities because, as they argued, it disclosed the mystery of the ceremonies at the elector's (and future king's) court, something that should not be left in the hands of private authors (or scholars). See Vec, *Zeremonialwissenschaft*, pp. 236ff.

[77] RGADA, f. 156, op. 1, d. 158.

[78] The original French copy is in RGADA, f. 93, op. 1 (1698), d. 1. For the Russian translation, see RGADA, f. 35, op. 1, d. 268. For a description of Portland's embassy to France, see also Rousham, MC 15, pp. 52–69. The systematic acquisition of such accounts continued through the first half of the eighteenth century, in particular during the years 1738/39 and 1747, see: RGADA, f. 156, op. 1, d., 209, 211, 213, 214 and 228–232, for descriptions of ceremonies in England, Austria, France, Prussia and Sweden. See also D. J. Taylor, 'Russian foreign policy 1725–1739: the Politics of stability and opportunity' (unpublished PhD thesis, University of East Anglia, 1983), esp. p. 316.

[79] N. A. Kopanev, 'Knigi A. A. Matveeva iz biblioteki Mikhalkovykh', in *Knizhnye sokrovishcha. K 275-letiiu Biblioteki AN SSSR*, ed. L. I. Kiseleva, N. P. Kopaneva (Leningrad, 1990), pp. 130–37, here on p. 136.

[80] RGADA, f. 93, op. 1 (1706), d. 5. Matveev was one of the last Russian diplomats who compiled a *stateinyi spisok* (see below). In addition, he wrote a private diary in which he

a comprehensive report about the ceremonies he observed in Hanover, England, France, and Venice.[81] The descriptions of individual audiences arranged for Russian diplomats were also collected,[82] and the Petrine court closely observed the reception of foreign ambassadors at other courts, for example that of an Ottoman ambassador in Vienna.[83]

All these collections are a testament to the increased demand for information on diplomatic ritual. Peter I's diplomats as well as his court were in great need to study what David Cannadine called the 'vocabulary of pageantry', the 'syntax of spectacle', and the 'ritualistic idioms' of foreign courts.[84] The Muscovite court had done the same through the *stateinye spiski*, which continued to serve as an ancient library of diplomatic protocol under Peter I. But Petrine diplomacy needed to continue 'collecting' rituals, as ceremonial procedures were in continuous flux, with old precedents becoming obsolete while new ones were being added in 'an unending pursuit'.[85]

The institutional changes also entailed a change in correspondence and administration. Diplomats ceased to produce the *stateinyi spisok* which had kept their predecessors busy for two centuries. Rather than filling long scrolls with their daily observations, which had to be submitted at the end of a diplomatic mission, they now embarked on an entirely new system of correspondence, sending their diplomatic reports (*reliatsii*) with the regular post back to Russia. These dispatches did not follow the strict code of the *stateinyi spisok* and its contrived congruence with the diplomat's *nakaz*. The *reliatsii* enabled envoys and ambassadors to react on the spot and respond to important issues as the given situation demanded. Content and style varied from diplomat to diplomat. However, the *Posol'skaia kantseliariia* was not so quick in adopting this new form of communication, especially as far as matters of protocol were concerned. Diplomatic ceremonial relied on a precedent-based system that underwent constant changes and variations. Generic descriptions

noted many observations on the states to which he was sent, including many notes of diplomatic ceremonies: Sharkova, ed., *Russkii diplomat*, esp. pp. 141–48.

81 Semevskii, ed., *Arkhiv kniazia F. A. Kurakina*, II, pp. 201–05, III, pp. 78–81, 194–200, 262–75, 301–14.

82 See, for example, the reception of Johann C. von Schleinitz in Paris in 1717, RGADA, f. 156, op. 1, d. 171. A Russian translation of a description of diplomatic ceremonies at the court of Louis XIV, authored by a Habsburg representative at Versailles, dates from 1776, but the original German manuscript may have reached Russia around 1704; see RGADA, f. 93, op. 1 (1704), d. 5.

83 RGADA, f. 156, op. 1, d. 180; RGADA, f. 15, op. 1, d. 15. For a comparison, see the reception of an Ottoman representative at the court of Peter I, RGADA, f. 159, op. 2 (1721–1725), d. 474.

84 D. Cannadine, 'The context, performance and meaning of ritual: the British monarchy and the "invention of tradition", c. 1820–1977', in *The invention of tradition*, ed. E. J. Hobsbawm, T. O. Ranger (Cambridge, 1983, reprint, 1984), pp. 101–64.

85 Duindam, *Vienna and Versailles*, p. 181.

like those gathered since 1694 did not suffice to provide a picture of the most recent developments in ceremonial practice. Ceremonial information had to be constantly updated. But the diplomats often failed to provide enough details about their ceremonial receptions at foreign courts, as they were changing to the new system. The *stateinyi spisok*, in contrast, had proven a reliable form of information transmission. Thus, in 1712, when Peter I decided to send Prince Boris I. Kurakin to The Hague to take the place of Matveev, both diplomats were ordered to submit a *stateinyi spisok* to the *Posol'skaia kantseliariia*. As odd as this may seem, the diplomats were requested to report on their previous as well as future diplomatic missions in the old style inherited from Muscovite times.[86] The same directive was reissued in 1719. As most diplomats failed to honour the earlier order from the *kantseliariia*, the *Kollegiia inostrannykh del* re-summoned all diplomats to revert to the old style and compile reports in the form of a *stateinyi spisok* to complement the lengthy *memorialy* and *reliatsii* they had already sent.

Such an instruction was a typical product of a period of transition, an example of how the combination of old and new revealed itself in concrete administrative measures. This may, on the face of it, demonstrate the inner conflict between the old bureaucracy, that had difficulties to digest the changes from *prikaz* via *kantseliariia* to *Kollegiia* on the one hand, and the diplomats whose lives thrived in the centres of diplomacy, at places like The Hague, London, Vienna, Berlin, or Paris, on the other. But the reason for this attempted return to the old system might have been of a much more practical nature. Chancellor Golovkin needed to update his ceremonial accounts to be able to instruct his diplomats properly and to arrange the ceremonies at the Russian court according to current practice. He ordered virtually all active diplomats to compile *stateinye spiski* regarding 'the ceremonies with which they were received at foreign courts as well as all things on which they have not informed the court of the [tsar] in their reports'.[87]

The diplomats' reactions were mixed. While Matveev's and Petr A. Tolstoi's (former accredited ambassador to the Ottoman Empire) *stateinye spiski* arrived safely, others were trying to excuse themselves for various reasons.[88] Tolstoi's notes were interrupted in 1710, when he was thrown into prison after Charles XII, who had escaped to the Porte, had

86 RGADA, f. 50, op. 1 (1712), d. 3, l. 22, d. 4, ll. 22, 70. The same order was sent to Prince Vasilii L. Dolgorukov in Denmark: RGADA, f. 53, op. 1 (1712), d. 3, l. 80. See also Krylova, 'Stateinye spiski petrovskikh diplomatov', p. 164, and 164ff., 174ff., for the description of other diplomats' *stateinye spiski*.

87 RGADA, f. 158, op. 1 (1719), d. 117, l. 1.

88 Matveev's *stateinyi spisok* on his stays in The Netherlands, Great Britain and France: RGADA, f. 50, op. 1 (1700), d. 2. For an analysis of Tolstoi's *stateinyi spisok*, see Krylova, 'Stateinye spiski petrovskikh diplomatov'. For an account that is much different in its

convinced the sultan to declare war on Russia.[89] Shafirov, who as a result of the Treaty of the Pruth (1711) was kept as the sultan's hostage, claimed that to draft a *stateinyi spisok* was impossible because of the 'dangerous situation and deadly terror in which I and my whole suite found ourselves'.[90] Prince Vasilii L. Dolgorukov sent a message from Paris, explaining that his relocation from Copenhagen to Paris had caused him to leave all his notes in Hamburg. Further cordial reminders dispatched to him and other diplomats fell on deaf ears. Prince Petr A. Golitsyn, who served as the governor of Kiev at the time, wrote that he had already submitted a *stateinyi spisok* regarding his mission to Vienna on his return to Moscow in 1706, and that the rest of his papers probably fell victim to a fire in his house in Moscow in 1711. A clerk of the *Kollegiia inostrannykh del* was sent to the archive of the former *Posol'skii prikaz* to check if the requested report ever arrived, as Golitsyn alleged. But the clerk concluded that such a document had never been written.[91]

It becomes clear that the old forms of correspondence were incompatible with the new diplomacy under Peter I. However, this episode also supports the case that the Petrine court could not dispense with ceremonial and its record-keeping once it had restructured diplomatic administration and the forms of correspondence. The demand for ceremonial knowledge increased with the introduction of resident diplomacy; an adaptation to 'European' diplomacy did not make Russian foreign policy less ritualistic than it had been before. On the contrary, Russia used diplomatic ritual in a way that shrewdly blended old and new, as the following case studies show.

Peter I's Honour and the British Constitution

In 1708, in response to an ill-received arrest of the indebted Russian ambassador, Andrei A. Matveev, at the English court, Parliament passed '[a]n act for preserving the privileges of ambassadors and other public ministers of foreign princes and states'.[92] To criminalise breaches of international law, which had hitherto relied on the comity of nations, and to declare by parliamentary statute that a diplomat enjoyed protection against arrest or prosecution, was undoubtedly a landmark achievement in the history of diplomatic practice. As is well known, Catherine II of Russia (r. 1762–1796) pursued a similar law in the 1770s. Fascinated by William Blackstone's *Commentaries on the laws of England* – which

nature, see Tolstoi's diary on his travels to Italy, M. J. Okenfuss, ed., *The travel diary of Peter Tolstoi: a Muscovite in early modern Europe* (DeKalb, 1987).

[89] RGADA, f. 158, op. 1 (1719), d. 117, l. 32–32ob. [90] Ibid., l. 38–38ob.

[91] Ibid., ll. 23–25, 47–48. [92] 7 Anne, ch. 12.

celebrated the progressiveness of English legal culture in distinction to the customs of barbarous states – Catherine II sought to implement international law in the national legal system in her failed attempt to create a progressive new criminal code (*ugolovnoe ulozhenie*).[93]

What is less known is that Peter I had already introduced such legal sanction in a direct response to the arrest of his diplomat in London, shortly after the publication of the Act of Parliament.[94] In Russia, the word of the sovereign was the law.[95] As such, a letter by Peter I, which instructed the tsarevich on how to proceed with indebted diplomats from other courts, was treated as a legal enactment.[96] Peter I wrote to his son that foreign diplomats, who committed a legal offence in Russia, must neither be held in detention nor be punished, as any such action was against international law and resulted in conflicts between states.[97] If diplomats incurred debts and refused to settle them, then no other authority than the *Posol'skaia kantseliariia* should attend to the matter and propose an agreeable solution. On the same day as he devised the letter to his son, Peter I also issued a secret order in which he instructed the chancellery to keep an eye on the English envoy, Whitworth, if necessary with the help of soldiers, so that he would not leave the town until the queen had given due satisfaction to the tsar in response to Matveev's arrest.[98]

William Butler has pointed out that 'it is extremely difficult to say when a particular rule of conduct has been accepted by the international community of states as a legally binding norm for all'. The Matveev affair is one of the few cases whose direct contribution to the 'development of international law down to the present' can be pinned down.[99] The Act of Parliament and Peter I's letter to the tsarevich mark the awareness of

93 W. Blackstone, *Commentaries on the laws of England*, 4 vols. (Oxford, 1765–1769), I, pp. 245–48. See G. O. Babkova, 'Mezhdunarodnoe pravo v ugolovno-pravovoi doktrine Ekatariny II', *Novyi Istoricheskii Vestnik*, 14 (2006), 90–98.

94 Grabar, *International law*, pp. 59–61.

95 Hughes, *Age of Peter the Great*, p. 132.

96 The letter was copied from the original held by the *Blizhniaia kantseliariia* and forwarded as an *ukaz* to the *Posol'skii, Malorossiiskii, Novgorodskii and Smolenskii prikaz*: RGADA, f. 158, op. 3, d. 8. The same edict was reconfirmed in 1719 and distributed to all colleges and police officers, RGADA, f. 158, op. 2 (1719), d. 66.

97 *PSZRI*, IV, no. 2206 (14 September 1708), p. 419. See also *PiB*, VIII, p. 131.

98 Peter I to Gagarin, 14 September 1708, *PiB*, VIII, no. 2626, p. 132; See also Peter I's letter to Gagarin sent on 15 September 1708, in *PiB*, VIII (primechaniia k no. 2626), pp. 676–78.

99 W. E. Butler, 'Anglo-Russian diplomacy and the law of nations', in *Great Britain and Russia in the eighteenth century: contacts and comparisons: proceedings of an international conference held at the University of East Anglia, Norwich, England, 11–15 July 1977*, ed. A. G. Cross (Newtonville, 1979), pp. 296–305, here on p. 301. Diplomatic immunity continued to rely on the tacit agreement between states. Its codification as an international law custom was agreed at the Vienna Convention on Diplomatic Relations of 1961.

contemporaries of the need to make tacit conventions in foreign relations part of the national legal system in order to effectively protect diplomatic privileges. Yet, is it right to interpret the Act and the letter as their authors' enlightened effort to standardise and thus rationalise the relations between states through legal sanction, or, as in the case of Catherine II, to free her country of the barbarous image by introducing Western law? An examination of the legal context of these documents will neither reach to the core of their contemporary significance nor provide an adequate historical assessment.[100] In order to understand the 'meaning' of these legal texts and their place in diplomatic history, one has to turn once again to the issues of ceremony and diplomatic representation. The following analysis of the Matveev case emphasises what most examinations of it do not, namely that international law and the legal protection of diplomats was closely tied to the cause of monarchical honour and its ritual manifestation.[101]

The 1708 Act of Parliament was the result of 'one of the most embarrassing diplomatic incidents of the eighteenth century'.[102] In May 1707, Matveev was dispatched to London as ambassador extraordinary. Russia sought the mediation of Queen Anne to expedite a peace with Sweden that would allow the tsar to keep Ingria and Livonia. Peter I intended to join the Grand Alliance and was willing to send troops and naval forces if the queen were willing to take the role as mediator. Matveev soon realised that the English secretaries of state Robert Harley (1704–1708) and Henry Boyle (1708–1710) showed no real intention of accepting the tsar's offer. He decided to return to The Hague, where he had served as the Russian representative since 1699.[103]

On 21 July 1708, between 8 and 9 in the evening, shortly after his valedictory audience with Queen Anne, Peter I's ambassador was attacked on an open street by English bailiffs. At first Matveev thought he was going to be robbed. 'Facing the coming of his death', his secretary

[100] The Matveev case has been analysed from the perspective of legal history by E. R. Adair, *The extraterritoriality of ambassadors in the sixteenth and seventeenth centuries* (London, New York, 1929), pp. 87ff., 239ff. See also Anderson, *Modern diplomacy*, p. 54; E. M. Satow, *A Guide to Diplomatic Practice*, 4th edn. (London, 1957), pp. 177, 183.

[101] An exception is L. Frey, M. Frey, *The history of diplomatic immunity*, pp. 226–30.

[102] The Matveev case was reconstructed on the basis of the published and unpublished Whitworth papers held by the Bodleian Library, in Hartley, *Whitworth*, pp. 69–77, quotation on p. 77. For an account (albeit biased) that sets the case in the context of Anglo-Russian relations and praises the correct behaviour of the Russian diplomat, see L. N. Nikiforow, *Russisch-englische Beziehungen unter Peter I.*, trans. W. Müller (Weimar, 1954), pp. 82–93.

[103] For Matveev's negotiations, see Hartley, *Whitworth*, p. 70, based on A. Rothstein, *Peter the Great and Marlborough: politics and diplomacy in converging wars* (Basingstoke, 1986), ch. 6.

wrote in the *stateinyi spisok*, he screamed at the attackers who violently removed him from his coach, tore his clothes to pieces and divested him of his weapons. He was then brought to a tavern where the bailiffs held him in custody for several hours. There Matveev heard the reason for his arrest: he was accused of owing £50 to two merchants.[104] In reality, the arrest was arranged by order of a number of suspicious creditors who feared that Matveev would not voluntarily pay the debts which he had incurred prior to his departure from the English court. According to a list of creditors, his debts amounted to more than £400 owed to a fishmonger, a locksmith, a silkman, a confectioner, a gardener, and other tradesmen.[105]

The detention of an ambassadorial dignitary was a clear breach of the law of nations that protected his privileges at a foreign court and constituted the prerequisite for successful negotiations in the relations with other states.[106] The incident came as a shock to the diplomatic corps in London. Many residents visited Matveev in his prison to express their sympathy and declare that they perceived this arrest as an affront against the whole diplomatic community. After Henry Boyle had been informed of the incident by the Portuguese envoy, he immediately arranged Matveev's release from custody.[107] The English court realised that this affair was 'a crying Insolence, and likely to make a great noise in the world', as Boyle warned Whitworth, the Queen's envoy in Moscow, in a letter written two days after the event.[108] The news spread like wild fire, and soon the Matveev affair caused furore at all European courts. This was also noted by Dietrich H. Kemmerich, professor of law at the *Ritterakademie* in Erlangen, in the preface to a book that he exclusively devoted to the case in 1710.[109]

The incident did not only attract the attention of diplomats and legal experts. In 1723, Daniel Defoe, whose dismissive attitude towards Russia had caused resentment between the two courts – in particular his comparison of Peter I with a raging bear – anonymously published an 'impartial' history of the reign of Peter I, including a compilation of documents

[104] RGADA, f. 50, op. 1 (1700), d. 2, ll. 161ob–162ob.

[105] Matveev owed another £422 14s to people who were not involved in his arrest. The list of Matveev's creditors is published in S. Dixon, ed., *Britain and Russia in the age of Peter the Great: historical documents* (London, 1998), pp. 77f.

[106] See also J. J. Murray, 'The Görtz-Gyllenborg arrest – a problem in diplomatic immunity', *Journal of Modern History*, 28 (1956), 325–37.

[107] RGADA, f. 50, op. 1 (1700), d. 2, ll. 162ob–163. See also Boyle to Goodfellow, 30 July 1708, in Dixon, ed., *Britain and Russia*, pp. 71f.

[108] Boyle to Whitworth, 23 July 1708, *SIRIO*, L, pp. 32f.

[109] D. H. Kemmerich, *Grund=Sätze des Völker=Rechts von der Unverletzlichkeit der Gesandten. Samt einer Relation von dem Affront, welcher dem Moscowitischen Abgesandten in Engelland Anno 1708 erwiesen* (n.p., 1710).

referring to the Matveev incident which brought England into 'a little Demellez, or Broil, with his Czarish Majesty'.[110] John Mottley published the letters exchanged between Matveev and Boyle as well as the correspondence between the tsar and the queen sixteen years later to show the affair 'in a Clear light'.[111]

The case did not concern the physical integrity of the diplomat alone. The inviolability of an ambassador rested on two legal fictions: first, 'extraterritoriality', meaning that a foreign representative was exempt from the law of the state he visited; second, 'representative character', which implied that a diplomat directly represented his sovereign.[112] The fact that in the early modern period the ambassador (as opposed to envoys or residents) embodied his master's persona and all ceremonial dignity attached to it has already been discussed in Chapter 2. Matveev enjoyed this particular rank or 'character', and as such his arrest addressed questions of international law, and, by implication, the ceremonial integrity of the tsar. Consequently, any offence against an ambassador was perceived as a direct affront against his master's dignity. It is no surprise, then, that Golovkin was quick in pointing out that the incident in London was 'an affront offer'd his Czarish Majesty himself in the person of his ambassador at London'.[113]

Matveev himself regarded the affront a violation of the law of nations, a 'high insult committed to his majesty the tsar in my person'.[114] This circumstance brought about a new political dimension to the incident: it precipitated a crisis in Anglo-Russian relations. The status of the tsar before the queen was in danger, his international prestige dented by some 'brutal sort of people' who were, after all, subjects of the English Crown.[115] The queen assured the tsar that she was 'deeply pained by the sense of the grave insult' and promised to 'arrest the perpetrators of this vile and inhumane deed and to condemn them and subject them to the cruellest punishment which can be inflicted under the laws and statutes of our imperial realms for their offence in daring to violate the

[110] [D. Defoe], *An impartial history of the life and actions of Peter Alexowitz, the present Czar of Muscovy. Written by a British officer in the service of the Czar* (London, 1723), pp. 259–301, quotation on p. 259. For Defoe's views on Russia, see A. G. Cross, *Peter the Great through British eyes: perceptions and representations of the tsar since 1698* (Cambridge, 2000), pp. 52ff.

[111] J. Mottley, *The history of the life of Peter I.*, 3 vols. (London, 1739), I, pp. 312–26, II, pp. 49–75, quotation in I, p, 12. See also Cross, *Through British eyes*, pp. 68f.

[112] B. Sen, *A diplomat's handbook of international law and practice*, 3rd edn. (Dordrecht, 1988), pp. 95f.

[113] Golovkin to Whitworth, 16 September 1708, in Dixon, ed., *Britain and Russia*, p. 73.

[114] Matveev to Boyle, 16 November 1708, TNA, SP 104/120, fol. 125v.

[115] Boyle to Goodfellow, 30 July 1708, in Dixon, ed., *Britain and Russia*, p. 72.

sacred laws and privileges of diplomacy in such a foul manner'.[116] The tsar demanded a punishment 'proportionate to the affront', namely that 'the sheriff[,] the occasion of all this mischief[,] may at least be condemned to death, afterwards diverted of all his employments, and declared infamous; that his servants who attacked the ambassador [...] may actually be put to death'. All others involved in this affront, 'should be punish'd according to the severity of the law, that Her Majesty may thereby convince the world of her love to justice and her sincere friendship for His Czarish Majesty as well as wash off the scandal of violating the Law of Nations from her people'.[117] The desired punishment of the assailants correlated with the honour of the Russian monarch, which explains the extreme legal consequences with which the Russian court wished to settle the matter. However, considering the death penalty in a case where the sovereign dignity of a monarch was damaged was not so unusual. The Earl of Carlisle, visiting Moscow in 1663/64, had equally asked for 'the blood of the Criminals', who in his opinion had violated his ceremonial rights during his reception in Russia.[118]

The English court promised that no means should be neglected to make ample reparation for the assault. Henry Boyle assured the Russians that everything in the queen's power would be pursued to offer the tsar all possible satisfaction, and to convince him of the queen's esteem and friendship for his person. The queen had expressed her willingness to take legal action against the bailiffs in very careful terms. Punishment could only 'be inflicted under the laws and statutes of our imperial realms',[119] she had written in her letter to the tsar. Notwithstanding her sovereign authority, the power of the queen did not extend to punishing the bailiffs in the way that the tsar would have liked it. Boyle informed Charles Whitworth in Moscow, that the assailants and other persons involved in the incident had been arrested but that no more could be done as 'the laws of our constitution' forbade harsher punishments at this point.[120] In the course of events he later wrote to the envoy that English justice could not be stretched to a death penalty: 'It is certain that the laws of this kingdom will never go near that length, and it cannot be expected that we should break in upon our constitution, and overturn the foundations of our government to come at the satisfaction demanded'.[121]

116 Anne to Peter I, 19 September 1708, in ibid., p. 75.

117 Golovkin to Whitworth, 16 September 1708, in ibid., p. 73. See also Golovkin to Whitworth, 12 November 1708, TNA, SP 91/5, fol. 343, in which Golovkin claims that the convicts 'by all laws of the world cannot deserve less than death'.

118 See Chapter 3, fn. 144. 119 See fn. 116.

120 Boyle to Whitworth, 30 July 1708, *SIRIO*, L, p. 36.

121 Boyle to Whitworth, 28 January 1709, *SIRIO*, L, p. 136.

Whitworth presented Golovkin and Shafirov with the English view. He expressed his hope that a reparation, which the queen was in the position to offer, would not lead to a break in Anglo-Russian relations. He could not imagine that a merciful prince like the tsar would take satisfaction in the death of 'one or two mean persons'.[122] The queen's hands were 'bound by the fundamental Constitutions of Great Britain', a breach of which would 'put the wholle Nation into Confusion'.[123] According to Whitworth, a pro forma condemnation of the offenders was not compatible with the law. Golovkin accepted that the queen's actions were limited by the rulings of the court of justice and Parliament. He also stressed that these institutions should be prepared to contribute, on their side, to the reputation of the queen and the English nation by duly considering the tsar's position and preserving the law of nations. Only then could the tsar show his mercy. Golovkin let the English court know that Peter I started to wonder why it took them so long to settle this case, asking why the English so vigorously defended the rights of their own diplomats if they were not able to prosecute the convicts in their own country.[124]

In fact, the court hearings of this case were protracted. They lasted more than a year and never led to a legal sentence.[125] The immunity of an ambassador was guaranteed by royal protection. The ambassador was personally accredited to the monarch and not to Parliament. Diplomatic privileges were subject to the prerogative of the queen. The English Common Law, however, could not accommodate civil suits brought against crimes of international law. While the attorney general acknowledged the guilt of the assailants, who had committed a breach against the immunity of ambassadors, the question of whether they had committed a crime by suing Matveev for his debts remained unresolved. It was concluded that the persons investigated could not be sentenced since no offence known to English law had been perpetrated.[126] Legal historian Edward R. Adair wrote:

[122] Whitworth to Golovkin, 17 January 1709, TNA, SP 91/6, fol. 6v.

[123] Whitworth to Shafirov, 28 February 1709, TNA, SP 91/6, fol. 62.

[124] Golovkin to Whitworth, 18 February 1709, TNA, SP 91/6, fols. 56–57v. There were cases when the English envoy complained about the treatment of foreigners whose houses were searched and their Russian servants taken away: Whitworth to Shafirov, 4 March 1708, *SIRIO*, XXXIX, pp. 467–70. After the Matveev affair had come to an end (and after Peter I' had issued the *ukaz* regarding the prosecution of foreign diplomats at his court), Ludwig Christian Weisbrod, who replaced Whitworth as a diplomatic agent, complained that his own servants were attacked and thrown into prison. He asked for public satisfaction to restore his privileges as a diplomatic representative: Weisbrod to Rowe, 28 September 1710, *SIRIO*, L, pp. 367–69.

[125] Hartley, *Whitworth*, pp. 71–72.

[126] Adair, *Extraterritoriality*, pp. 87, 230, 241. Cf. the review of Adair's work by K. Berriedale, 'The extraterritoriality of ambassadors', *Journal of Comparative Legislation and International Law*, 12 (1930), 126–28.

The English government did not for one moment deny the immunity of an ambassador from civil jurisdiction, but it found that, with the decay of prerogative action, it was no longer convenient to punish men by imprisonment if they were guilty of no crime at common or statute law; for it must be remembered that though the men who had sued the Russian ambassador were found guilty of the facts alleged, it was never decided that these facts were criminal and they were therefore never legally punished by sentence of the court.[127]

In short, international law was incompatible with English law. Settling the dispute was thereafter left to the queen (and her council), whose undisputed prerogatives included war and peace as well as the treatment of foreign ministers. Anne was under pressure to meet the expectations of her fellow monarch, the Russian tsar, but realised the impossibility of punishing through prerogative action men who were not found guilty of any crime. This was the internationalisation of an internal problem.[128] The conflict between the prerogative of the queen (that had been in decline since 1688) and Common Law inhibited a legal decision by which the bailiffs could have been sentenced to whatever punishment in order to save the face of the tsar. In other words, the Matveev affair resulted in a clash between the social norms of early modern court society, based on the reciprocal balance of status relations on the one hand; and the fundamental principles of the British constitution, hammered out in civil war and revolution in the seventeenth century, on the other.[129] How then, if not by direct jurisdictional action, did the queen manage to appease the tsar without breaching the constitution of the country she ruled?

Shortly after Matveev's arrest, Anne considered the possibility of sending 'some person of quality and distinction' to Moscow as a sign of her respect for the tsar and the seriousness with which she perceived the incident.[130] Whitworth informed the Russian court about the plan to present the queen's apologies through a formal embassy. Defending the English legal system, he suggested that the dispatch of a representative of the queen reinforced the good personal relations between the two monarchs and compensated the unfulfilled expectations of the tsar, who was still waiting for a definite legal response to the affront.[131]

127 Adair, *Extraterritoriality*, p. 239. For the relationship between Parliament and international law, see D. Armitage, *Foundations of modern international thought* (Cambridge, 2013), ch. 8, esp. pp. 143f. for the significance of the Matveev case.

128 I wish to thank László Kontler who pointed this out to me.

129 The Queen's dilemma of having both to appease the tsar and at the same time protect the laws of the state she ruled, was pointedly summarised by Kemmerich. See his description of the public audience and the conclusion he makes about the Matveev affair, Kemmerich, *Grund=Sätze des Völker=Rechts*, pp. 40ff.

130 Boyle to Whitworth, 30 July 1708, *SIRIO*, L, p. 36.

131 Whitworth to Golovkin, 21 September 1708, TNA, SP 91/5, fols. 96–99; Whitworth to Golovkin, 28 February 1709, TNA, SP 91/6, fols. 60–61v.

In addition, Parliament passed the Diplomatic Privileges Act, indicating that an apology delivered by an ambassador was insufficient and that the British government undertook all measures to act against crimes against international law if not retrospectively, then at least for the future. Breaches against the civil immunity of ambassadors and their suite were no longer part of the queen's prerogative; they were to be prosecuted and the convicts punished on the basis of this new law. This Act of Parliament described the legal position of diplomats at the English court. Therefore, it was undoubtedly a valuable contribution to the development of international law. However, the outward gloss of judicial procedure cannot obscure the fact that the real intention of this Act was the conciliation of the unpremeditated friction between the tsar and the queen. A clear judgement of the Matveev affair must point to the nature of the personal relations between sovereigns which were rooted in the world view of court society rather than in exclusive principles of positive law. The Act does not prove the overriding significance of law in early modern diplomatic relations. Neither can it be taken as indicative of the queen's respect of the independence of international law, nor of Parliament's serious effort to regulate through legal means the relations between states. Rather, the Act must be understood as a goodwill gesture, used to symbolise Queen Anne's esteem for the tsar. The law itself was a ritual act. This is not to say that this Act of Parliament was of merely 'ornamental character'.[132] While its judicial purpose – however significant – was certainly secondary,[133] the Act served as an effective vehicle of honour in the process of repairing the tsar's sovereign status and Russia's international prestige.

In a letter to Whitworth, sent in April 1709, Boyle stressed that the Act 'expresse[d] the sense of Her Majesty and the whole nation upon the affront offered to the moscovite ambassador'. Parliament's public commitment to the case was meant to show how Britain detested the violence committed against Matveev. Boyle instructed the English envoy 'to make the [Russian] court highly sensible of this extraordinary instance of Her Majesty's endeavours to use all practicable methods towards due satisfaction'. He realised that this message needed to be conveyed in a special way and suggested to Whitworth that 'if you think that an exemplification of this act under the great seal and finely embellished would be acceptable at your court and make a greater impression, I shall take care to have such an one prepared, and sent to you'.[134]

132 Berriedale, 'The extraterritoriality of ambassadors', p. 128.

133 No prosecution for a breach of the Diplomatic Privileges Act has been reported after it had been issued, see Adair, *Extraterritoriality*, p. 238. See also Berriedale, 'The extraterritoriality of ambassadors', p. 128.

134 Boyle to Whitworth, 26 April 1709, *SIRIO*, L, p. 172.

The queen's apology and the Act of Parliament had to be communicated through an effective medium in order to increase the credibility of Anne's intentions. As legal procedures proved insufficient in the Matveev affair, it was monarchical honour that served to mediate and settle the conflict between the queen and the tsar through a solemn ritual act. A public audience in which an English ambassador presented the apologies of the queen to the tsar as if she were present herself lent itself well to this purpose.

The plan of sending a 'person of quality' to Moscow had already been conceived, as mentioned before. In order to save time and further costs, the then-representative at the Russian court, Whitworth, was vested with the corresponding 'character', his rank being elevated from that of envoy to fully accredited ambassador extraordinary.[135] At the public audience, Whitworth asked the tsar to accept the queen's request for forgiveness, beseeching him not to impute some wrongdoers' crime to the whole 'nation'. He alluded to the circumstance that these persons had already been 'stigmatised by the solemn voice of the nation in Parliament, by an act' and declared further that

> to make these Testimonies of Her Majestys Justice and friendship more signal and authentic I am also honour'd [...], with full power to represent Her Majestys Person, as if she was here present, and declare Her just Concern and abhorrence for this rash attempt on a publick minister she so highly esteemed, to excuse the Defect of our former Constitutions, which would not come up to your Imperial Majestys desires, and the severe punishments due for so enormous a Breach of the Law of nations; and to assure your Imperial Majesty of Her sincere Inclinations, to maintain that ancient friendship and good Correspondence, which has so long and happily florish'd between both Imperial Crowns; as you may please to see more at large by this [Queen Anne's] letter, which will remain a lasting monument of Her Majestys tender regard and Esteem for your Imperial Person.[136]

The Act of Parliament, then, became an important ritual element of the attempt to exculpate the queen from the guilt of having failed to restore

[135] Anne to Peter I, 15 August 1709, in Dixon, ed., *Britain and Russia*, pp. 83–85. See also the records of a conference (11 January 1710) attended by Whitworth, Golovkin, and Shafirov during which the then-envoy is asked why he had been 're-sent' as ambassador extraordinary, RGADA, f. 35, op. 1, d. 334, ll. 35–36ob, 138–44ob.

[136] Whitworth' speech presented to the tsar during the public audience (draft), RGADA, f. 35, op. 1, d. 334, ll. 50–52 (quotation on l. 50ob). TNA, SP 91/6, fols. 126–27. The text was printed in a contemporary collection of important political speeches: J. C. Lünig, *Grosser Herren, vornehmer Ministren und anderer berühmten Männer gehaltene Reden.*, 6 vols. (Hamburg, Leipzig, 1722–1734), III, pp. 892ff. See also 'From an announcement concerning the formal audience at which Peter I accepted Queen Anne's public apology about the Matveev incident, as communicated by her ambassador extraordinary, Charles Whitworth, February 1710', in Dixon, ed., *Britain and Russia*, pp. 91–93.

the tsar's honour through punishing the convicts. The Act was much more than just the result of pure law-making. The criminalisation of legal actions against a diplomat was part of a performance of reconciliation, based on the concept of monarchical prestige, requiring that the honour of the diplomatic partner be preserved in every instance. When presented to the Russians, this text of seemingly purely legislative quality was thus imbued with additional meaning, communicating the queen's intact friendship with the tsar to the Russian court. It is important to note that the speech was read out in English, German, and Russian, so that everyone present at the public audience, including foreign ministers in Moscow, would witness the ceremonial and hear the voice of the queen in a language that they would understand.[137] Accounts of the audience and the ambassador's speech were published in French, German, and Russian and distributed to foreign diplomats.[138] In this way, foreign courts received word of the ceremonial treatment of the ambassador and the respect shown to the tsar. In response to Whitworth's plea, Peter I kindly accepted the queen's apologies, as Great Britain had shown great concern through the Act of Parliament and because Whitworth's embassy had delivered much honour to him.[139]

The public audience was held on 5 February 1710 and coincided with Russia's rising status in Europe during the course of the Great Northern War. It is commonly known that Peter I gained supremacy in eastern Europe, as Russia eclipsed Sweden as a European great power.[140]

[137] Ibid., p. 92: 'And when he [Whitworth] had given His Czarish Majesty three ordinary bows, stepping then onto the dais, the envoy gave the following speech in the English language. So that it should be understood by all foreign and other actual potentates, it was read in German by the secretary of the embassy and then on behalf of the Russian people by the Czar's secretary in Russian'.

[138] *Relation von der öffentlichen Audientz, welche Ihro Majestät der Königinn von Großbritanien ambassadeur Herr Charles Whitworth bey Ihro grossczarischen Majestät in Moskau den 5 Februar gehabt* (n.p., 1710). A copy of the German version is preserved in RGADA, f. 35, op. 1, d. 334, ll. 1–4ob. The title of the French translation is *Relation de ce qui s'est passé à Moscou de 5/16 fevrier 1710, le jour que sa majesté czar Pierre I, empereur de la Grande Russie, admit à l'audience publique son excellence monsier Charles Whitworth etc.* (n.p., 1710). In May 1710, Peter I ordered to translate and publish the text in Russia. The original Russian translations, including a translation of the Privileges Act, can be found in RGADA, f. 35, op. 1, d. 334, ll. 5–23. A printed version was included in Semevskii, ed., *Arkhiv kniazia F. A. Kurakina*, II, pp. 235–38. See also Pekarskii, *Nauka*, I, 211.

[139] See Peter I's answer to Whitworth's speech, *PiB*, X, no. 3589 (5 February 1710), p. 34. A final meeting between Whitworth and Golovkin took place on 9 February. Whitworth and Golovkin met again on 9 February to confirm the settlement of the affair; see RGADA, f. 35, op. 1, d. 334, l. 18.

[140] Cf. Aleksandrenko, *Agenty*, I, pp. 16f. Aleksandrenko cites S. M. Solov'ev, who expressed this view. At the same time Aleksandrenko critically remarks that Russia remained a 'second rank power' in the circle of European states until the reign of Catherine II. His statement does not of course refer to ceremonial honours, prestige and monarchical status, but to Russia's perceived rank as a military great power.

As could be expected, the tsar took every opportunity to demand treatment as a victor after he had defeated Charles XII at Poltava.[141] The timing of the audience proved fortunate for the Russian court. Increased power status and the strengthening of Peter I's membership in the European *société des princes* materialised in the ritual acknowledgement of Russia's new position.

If it is accepted that diplomatic ritual in the age of court society not only reflected power relations, but also constituted the political order, then the significance of the ceremonies performed by the British ambassador is striking. The triumph over another major European power had to be communicated to other courts in order to exploit the victory for glory and prestige and to pursue elevation within the pecking order of princes.

Knowledge alone of Peter I's success over Sweden was not enough to secure the symbolic profit he wished to gain from the victory. Therefore, the Russians planning the audience were pressing to let it take place after the triumphal entry into Moscow following the battle of Poltava. Before Poltava (June 1709), Whitworth had already sensed a connection between a triumph over Charles XII and the affront against the ambassador in London: 'Chiefly their late success against the swede have prevailed with them to insist on high terms of reparation, and to prefer his [Matveev's] revenge and reputation before their solid interest.' And as if to blame the consequences of the incident on cultural difference, Whitworth explained that 'the methods of this government, and especially their administration of justice differ more from those of Great Britain than the severity of their climate from the gentleness of english air, and therefore it is no wonder they are so little understood'.[142] Whether, in reality, there was a lack of understanding on the Russian side is uncertain. The tsar knew, however, that the Matveev affair provided a convenient platform on which to back up ceremonial claims to increased international prestige. After the battle of Poltava, Whitworth's worst expectations became true. The sending of an ambassador was now

141 See Hartley, *Whitworth*, pp. 74f. See also J. M. Hartley, 'Poltavskaia bitva i anglo-rossiiskie otnosheniia', *Voprosy istorii i kul'tury severnykh stran i territorii*, 3 (2009), available from www.hcpncr.com/journ709/journ709hartley.html, last access 6 February 2016.

142 Whitworth to Boyle, 9 March 1709, *SIRIO*, L, p. 153. Cf. J. M. Hartley, 'A clash of cultures? An Anglo-Russian encounter in the early eighteenth century', in *Russian society and culture and the long eighteenth century: essays in honour of Anthony G. Cross*, ed. R. P. Bartlett, L. A. J. Hughes (Münster, 2004), pp. 48–61, here on p. 58, who states that 'Whitworth was aware that the fundamental problem was cultural'. It seems, however, that this was not a specifically Anglo-Russian problem, for Whitworth complained about other countries' customs (especially ceremonial procedures) in a similar manner. His contempt for the Dutch Republic even surpassed that which he had expressed about Russia (ibid., pp. 59–60).

inevitable, 'for since their vast success they will almost be untractable'.[143] The apologies of a powerful western monarch – made to pay deference to the Russian tsar – were going to be framed in an elaborate ceremonial that granted Peter I highest honours and thereby conveyed Russia's new standing in the world: the public audience being the perfect scenario in which to communicate and thus make Russia's rise in status a reality.

Given the significance of the impending ceremonies, the negotiations of the ceremonial procedure were long and problematic. Whitworth's public audience is particularly important for understanding Petrine diplomatic protocol, for Whitworth was the first diplomat to be received as an ambassador, with all the ceremonial implications attached to this rank.[144] For the Englishman, the ceremonial became the subject of great concern. The ritual that had hitherto been employed when the English ambassador, the Earl of Carlisle, saw the 'clear eyes' of the tsar

> was suited to the constitutions and temper of all the eastern nations, but would be very disadvantagious to Her Majesty in the present juncture. Now the Czar altered the ancient maxims of his government to the method of other european courts; and I, being the first person likely to appear with the honour of ambassador since this reformation, shall be obliged to proceed with greater caution and exactness.[145]

One of Whitworth's fears was whether he could use the title 'emperor' to address the tsar, as Carlisle had done before him. Isabel de Madariaga argued that Whitworth's worries emerged from the fact that Russia had just made its debut for the *theatrum praecedentiae* through the reforms and military victories of Peter I. She noted that the ambassador's anxiety about his presentation to the tsar in these novel circumstances confirmed that 'in the seventeenth century [...] Russia was considered on a par with the empires of the East which did not form part of the Christian commonwealth of nations'.[146] True, Whitworth found himself in novel circumstances, and the wider discourse of barbarism, which was often interwoven with diplomatic practice, supports this argument. However, as the previous chapters have shown, both seventeenth- and early eighteenth-century *Zeremonialwissenschaft* and ceremonial practice had made Russia

[143] Whitworth to Boyle, 8 September, *SIRIO*, L, p. 248. See also Hartley, *Whitworth*, p. 75.

[144] The imperial resident at Moscow, Otto Pleyer, noted that Whitworth's public audience was the first notable official ceremony since the capture of Azov, see Bushkovitch, *Peter the Great*, p. 293, fn. 1

[145] Whitworth to Boyle, 20 October 1709, *SIRIO*, L, pp. 261f.

[146] I. de Madariaga, 'Tsar into emperor: the title of Peter the Great', in *Politics and culture in eighteenth-century Russia. Collected essays by Isabel de Madariaga* (London, New York, 1998), pp. 15–39, 31. Similar K.-H. Ruffmann, 'England und der russische Zaren- und Kaisertitel', *Jahrbücher für Geschichte Osteuropas*, 3 (1955), 217–24. Schaub, 'Diplomates russes et français', p. 336, draws a similar conclusion concerning Franco-Russian relations before Peter I.

a part of what Isabel de Madariaga called the 'magic circle of European states' long before Peter I.[147] In particular, Russian Orthodoxy distinguished the tsar from the 'eastern empires' that contemporary scholars of precedence painted as the barbarous contrast of Europe. Of course, in terms of geography, culture, and perceived civilisedness, Russia ranked far away from the habits and mentality of Carlisle. But this distance gave way to face-to-face proximity when the ambassador defended the honour of Charles II vis-à-vis Aleksei. Carlisle took ceremonial issues very seriously – knowing that the tsar participated in the system of symbolic competition – to the effect that his embassy resulted in a failure. Carlisle and Whitworth, then, were effectively confronted with the same problem. Whitworth's concern for 'caution and exactness' was the continuation of Carlisle's struggle to ward off ceremonial humiliation. Nevertheless, while Whitworth's observation falsely implies that Russia made its first appearance as a competitor for prestige under Peter I, it does demonstrate the contemporaries' awareness that the new tsar had to be met with even more caution, as he began to lay claim to augmented power status within the *société des princes*.[148]

Thus, the embarrassing incident involving the Russian ambassador in London was raised to yet another level of political significance. In the first instance, it brought up the issue of an ambassador's civil immunity at a foreign court. In the second, it threatened to bring about a crisis in Anglo-Russian relations. In the third, the act of satisfaction raised questions about the rank of the tsar relative to that of the queen. Now that Russia had re-asserted its place in the European monarchical world, the risk for setting a precedent to the disadvantage of the English monarch was enormous. Whitworth had the difficult task of balancing the high honours claimed by the tsar with the royal status of the queen, so that the tsar's demand for the reparation of his sovereign dignity could be fulfilled without challenging the prestige of the English crown.[149]

[147] Madariaga, 'Tsar into emperor', p. 35.

[148] This was also noted by the *Zeremonialwissenschafter*, see, for example, Rousset de Missy, *Mémoires sur le rang*, p. 48; Stieve, *Hoff-Ceremoniel* (1715), p. 131; Zschackwitz, *Einleitung*, III, pp. 350f.; Zwantzig, *Theatrum Praecedentiae*, pp. 55f.

[149] Ceremonial conflicts revolving around titles (and the higher status of an emperor than a king) caused embarrassment and resentment through the late nineteenth century. For example, Francis II took care to have himself declared emperor of Austria before agreeing to Napoleon's demand to dissolve the Holy Roman Empire: P. H. Wilson, 'Bolstering the prestige of the Habsburg: the end of the Holy Roman Empire in 1806', *International History Review*, 28 (2006), 709–36. And Queen Victoria took delight after 1876 in being able to sign herself Queen-Empress in letters to the self-proclaimed German emperor, after Benjamin Disraeli had arranged for her to be proclaimed empress of India: Cannadine, 'British monarchy', p. 126. For the decreasing significance of ceremonial, cf. L. Frey, M. Frey, 'Charlatans'.

The British diplomat asked for instructions from London: 'Though I have some little knowledge of what is practiced in other courts, yet I would not venture the least step in a matter of this consequence without full orders.'[150] London's answer remained unspecific but gave as much flexibility as the diplomat deemed necessary. The queen left the arrangement of the ceremonies in the hands of the tsar but insisted that the tsar guaranteed the same treatment for ambassadors of other courts. 'Authentic reversals' were demanded of the Russian court in order to fix the ceremonial in a contractual form, which would in turn serve as the basis for the reception of Russian ambassadors at London.[151] With these instructions in hand, Whitworth entered the negotiations.[152]

Predictably, his request for a private audience, through which he hoped to avoid the cost and effort of a public one, was declined.[153] The tsar did not wish to divest himself of the political advantages that the medium of a public audience provided. On 26 January 1710, after Whitworth had submitted a draft of his speech for Golovkin's approval, he was sent a proposal of the ceremonial of the audience. Several points of the draft seemed 'very improper' to the diplomat.[154] To discuss these issues, a conference with Golovkin and Shafirov was scheduled for the next day. In particular, Whitworth enquired about the social status of the person that was going to bring him from his residence to the palace. The second point that raised his suspicion was that he was asked to leave his head uncovered before Peter I, despite the fact that the tsar was not going to wear a hat either. Third, Whitworth refused to kiss the tsar's hand (as the Danish envoy had done before him), as this was against 'the customs of all the courts in Europe'.[155] True, kissing the tsar's hand had formed part of the Muscovite tradition. However, this was not a specifically Russian custom that stood in contrast to 'all the courts in Europe'. The imperial court in Vienna demanded the same gesture from foreign ambassadors.[156] Whitworth warned Golovkin about the 'disadvantage the Czar's ambassadors would find in their turn', referring to the question of not wearing a hat.[157] It seems unlikely that the hat issue merely reflected one of Peter I's moods. This ceremonial element invoked an older Russian convention by which the

[150] Whitworth to Boyle, 20 October 1709, *SIRIO*, L, p. 262.
[151] Boyle to Whitworth, 13 December 1709, *SIRIO*, L, p. 287.
[152] The information on the negotiations of the ceremonial and the preparation (including lists of all participants) are from, RGADA, f. 35, op. 1, d. 334, ll. 34ff., 56ff., passim.
[153] Hartley, *Whitworth*, p. 76.
[154] Whitworth to Boyle, 2 February 1710, *SIRIO*, L, p. 312. [155] Ibid., p. 313.
[156] Rousset de Missy, *Cérémonial diplomatique*, I, p. 479.
[157] Whitworth to Boyle, 2 February 1710, *SIRIO*, L, p. 312.

tsar removed his headgear at various points during the reception of an ambassador who was sent by a crowned monarch, requiring the diplomat to remain bareheaded.[158] So grave was the matter that a definite decision was postponed to a meeting of the tsar, Golovkin, and Shafirov, in consultation with Johann C. von Urbich, Peter I's former diplomatic representative at Vienna (1707–1712). During the debate, which took place on the evening of the same day, the councillors advised the tsar to model the ceremonial 'on the modern footing', as Whitworth recounted, 'but His Czarish Majesty took time to consider, being very unwilling to comply with my being covered'.[159]

Four days later, Shafirov presented to the English diplomat Peter I's decision including a written guarantee that other ambassadors would be granted the same honours. Whitworth was no longer required to kiss the hand of the tsar, but Peter I could not be moved to allow the diplomat to cover his head. Whitworth welcomed the changes but needed time to reflect on the hat issue, as he lacked clear instructions from London on this issue and found it 'difficult [. . .] to venture of myself in a point of this importance'.[160] After careful consideration, the diplomat finally agreed to accept the ceremonial. Thus, on 4 February, one day prior to the public audience, the disputes

> were all settled according to the articles which, though not so regular as in other courts, are at least much more honourable than ever were given to any ambassador here, and no better will be allowed hereafter, as you may please to see by the reverse, which I hope will prove fully to Her Majesty's satisfaction, especially since the Czar seems very well pleased with my giving up the point of the hat. I join also the countreact which I signed, and the clause at the bottom is what theses ministers would fain have added but I constantly refused as overthrowing the whole treaty, though at the same time I told them Her Majesty would doubtless have a particular consideration for their ambassadors, since, if I was not received by the several charges proportionable to those of other courts, I was very sensible it was not a mark of their neglect, but the want of a due establishment of such offices, and therefore these points must be entirely left to your disposition.[161]

[158] Kotoshikhin, *O Rossii*, pp. 75–76. The Russian court began to require foreign representatives to doff their hats in the audience chamber in the second half of the seventeenth century, see Iuzefovich, *Put' posla*, p. 179. For a discussion of the hat issue, see G. Scheidegger, 'Von alten Hüten und internationalen Staatsaffären', in *450 Jahre Sigismund von Herbersteins Rerum Moscoviticarum Commentarii 1549–1999*, ed. R. Frötschner, F. Kämpfer (Wiesbaden, 2002), pp. 263–83, esp. pp. 276ff.

[159] Whitworth to Boyle, 2 February 1710, *SIRIO*, L, p. 313. [160] Ibid., p. 314.

[161] Whitworth to Boyle, 9 February 1710, *SIRIO*, L, p. 317. A copy of the 'countreact' is included in a description of Russian diplomatic ceremonies, authored by the English master of ceremonies; see Rousham, MC 15, fols. 140–55. Whitworth report was copied upon receipt and forwarded to Charles Cottrell, see TNA, SP 104/121, fols. 10v–15r.

This episode shows how a precedent was created, determining future Russian diplomatic protocol. In 1744, Elizabeth of Russia (r. 1741–1762) issued a court regulation in the attempt to standardise ceremonial procedure.[162] The regulation included the hat gesture which required diplomats to doff their hats during the audience. The document celebrated this ceremonial element as one of Peter I's innovations, unaware or ignoring, of course, that this was established practice preceding his reign.[163] A manuscript draft of the regulation reveals the various influences that contributed to the formation of eighteenth-century Russian diplomatic protocol. Each point of the regulation has a comment in the margins to contrast Russian procedure with existing conventions of other courts in Europe.[164] However, these juxtapositions did not set 'Russian' practice apart from 'European' custom. Rather, they revealed the variations among dynastic courts that in a common political space competed for the symbolic resources of rank and status. The arrangement of Whitworth's ceremonies again demonstrates that the adaptation of Russian practice to the ceremonial used at other courts was not a process of mere imitation. The Russian court did not ape some kind of coherent western model, that painted a new European image over the old 'barbarous' customs previously practised by the tsars of Muscovy.[165] Russia was part of a wider process in which ceremonial norms were negotiated on the ground, being appropriated to the given political situation and lasting until new precedents brought about alteration of old procedures. Diversity of ceremonial forms was a hallmark of early modern diplomatic culture. These forms gradually converged in common convention through participation in shared practices and the standardisation of their rules across the Russia–Europe divide, both geographic-culturally and chronologically.

The foreign diplomats at the Petrine court realised the significance of Whitworth's public audience. The imperial resident, Otto Pleyer, interpreted the solemnities and remarked that Peter I 'began to lay his high ambitions [*Hochheitsgedanken*] before the eyes of the whole world through ceremonial'.[166] The Danish envoy, Just Juel, who attended the ceremonies, devoted several pages of his memoires to the public audience on the

[162] *PSZRI*, XII, no. 8908 (3 April 1744), pp. 58–71. [163] Ibid., p. 68.

[164] RGADA, f. 15, op. 1 (1744), d. 78.

[165] For an insightful discussion of the imitation of European court culture by the Russian tsars, see Dixon, *Modernisation*, pp. 118–26.

[166] 'Otto Pleyer's allerunterthänigste Relation von dem jetzigen moscowitischen Regierungswesen 1710', in *Zeitgenössische Berichte zur Geschichte Russlands*, ed. E. Herrmann, 2 vols. (Leipzig, 1872–1880), I, pp. 121–33 (quotation on p. 129). For Pleyer, see A. T. Hasselblat, 'Otto Pleyer, der erste förmlich accreditierte östereichische Diplomat am russischen Hofe, 1692–1719', *Russische Revue. Monatsschrift für die Kunde Rußlands*, 7 (1875), 281–435.

basis of the published German account.[167] Thus, the mise-en-scène of Queen Anne's apologies and Parliament's Diplomatic Privileges Act proved to be a great ritual success for the tsar.

One could, of course, look at the Matveev incident as a mere legalistic quarrel, first reconstructing the history of diplomatic immunity since ancient times, then retelling the affront that happened to the ambassador, and, in the end, acknowledging the progressiveness of queen and Parliament which created a new offence to meet a novel situation, passing a law in order to prosecute future crimes. However, by doing so one would fail to realise that the arguments exchanged between London and Moscow did not concentrate so much on the question whether international law was breached and how to protect diplomatic privileges. Rather, they focused on the damaged honour of the tsar and the question of how to restore it. The protagonist of the Matveev incident was not ambassador extraordinary Sergei Artamonovich but the honour of his sovereign, Tsar Peter I.

Imperator

Whitworth's public audience foreshadowed another ceremonial coup that Peter I struck against other courts in the aftermath of an important military victory. Not long after the Peace of Nystad, in October 1721, the tsar, previously known as *velikii gosudar', tsar' i velikii kniaz'* (great sovereign, tsar, and grand prince) adopted the title of '*imperator vserossiiskii*' (all Russian emperor). The Russian court had started to experiment with similar versions of the new title long before Peter I officially accepted it in 1721. Therefore, it is worth returning to the negotiation of the ceremonies, which framed the presentation of Queen Anne's public apologies to Peter I.

When Whitworth was received by the tsar to apologise for the Matveev incident, Golovkin and Shafirov engineered a ceremonial through which the ambassador was going to address Peter I as emperor, rather than tsar.[168] At a court conference, on 3 February 1710, Shafirov and Golovkin asked Whitworth that the queen should address the tsar as *imperator velikorossiiskii* in all future correspondence. The Russian ministers justified this request on the grounds that the Act of Parliament had named Peter I 'Emperor of Great Russia', and that the queen had called

[167] Iu. N. Shcherbachev, ed., *Zapiski Iusta Iulia datskago poslannika pri Petre Velikom* (1709–1710) (Moscow, 1900), pp. 149–58.

[168] After Whitworth's reception in Moscow, in 1711, Peter I's representative at the court of Vienna, Christoph Freiherr von Urbich, launched an unsuccessful attempt to elicit from the Habsburg court the acknowledgement of Peter I's imperial title, see Madariaga, 'Tsar into emperor', pp. 31f.; Wittram, *Peter I.*, II, p. 469.

him *kesarskoe velichestvo* (imperial majesty) in the text of a letter that she had sent to apologise for the Matveev incident.[169] The speech that Whitworth delivered at the public meeting with the tsar was carefully crafted to establish Peter I's imperial dignity. Whitworth was told by the Russian court to use the words 'in my full power of making this declaration as if the queen was present'.[170] This expression had the effect that anything that was said at the audience was endowed with royal recognition by Queen Anne.[171] The ceremonial of the audience could be deployed as a precedent for the acknowledgement of Peter I's imperial title, as the ambassador began his speech with the words 'most radiant, all-powerful emperor'.[172] The translator who prepared a Russian version of Whitworth's speech for publication, routinely translated this form of address as *presvetleishii derzhavneishii tsar.* But someone realised the inaccuracy, crossed out the word *tsar* and inserted *tsesar' velikorossiiskii.*[173] In the German version of the speech, the tsar is styled as *Allerdurchlauchtigster, Allergroßmächtigster Kayser.*[174]

Just Juel, the Danish envoy, wrote in his diary that Golovkin had requested his attendance at Whitworth's public audience. While Juel, together with other foreigners, awaited the ambassador's arrival in the audience chamber, Shafirov pulled out a copy of Whitworth's speech. The vice-chancellor showed the document around and drew Juel's attention to the fact that the queen's ambassador was going to address Peter I with the title 'imperial (*keizerlige*) majesty'. Juel commented, 'although I [. . .] realised this instantly, he more or less continuously repeated this fact, with the aim, of course, to indicate that other crowned monarchs should also grant the tsar this title'.[175]

[169] RGADA, f. 35, op. 1, d. 334, ll. 17, 151; Queen Anne's letter of 15 August 1709 was superscribed with the old title '*velikii tsar' i velikii kniaz"*' but addressed the tsar as '*kesarskoe velichestvo*' in the text of the letter. See the Russian translation of a German version in ibid., ll. 5–9ob, 112.

[170] Whitworth to Boyle, 18 February 1710, *SIRIO*, L, p. 312.

[171] RGADA, f. 35, op. 1, d. 334, l. 215.

[172] Dixon, ed., *Britain and Russia*, p. 92. The English court continued to call the Russian rulers 'emperor' or 'empress' in places to which they ascribed lesser ceremonial significance, for example, the text of a royal letter. However, the English avoided directly addressing the tsar as 'emperor' in the form of address that stood at the head of a letter, as this officially confirmed the title that the court was willing to recognise. For instance, George I, wrote to Catherine I of Russia after the death of Peter I as 'to the most high, most potent and most Illustrious Princess, our most dear Sister the Great Lady Czarina and Great Duchess Catharina of all the Great, Little and White Russias [. . .]'. But in the same letter he congratulated her on her 'happy accession to the Throne as Empress of all the Russias'. See George I to Catherine I, 18 March 1725, AVPRI, f. 35, op. 35/2, d. 57, l. 1–1ob.

[173] RGADA, f. 35, op. 1, d. 334, l. 107, see also ibid., l. 20ob. [174] Ibid., l. 2ob.

[175] Shcherbachev, ed., *Zapiski*, p. 155.

Eleven years later, in 1721 – Charles XII was defeated and the major reform projects had been brought on the way – the Russian Senate and the Holy Synod appealed to the tsar to accept a new title that reflected his achievements. Peter I famously refused the generous offer at first, but did not take too long to revise his decision in favour of the Senate's and Synod's proposal.[176] On 22 October 1721, in a thanksgiving service for the recent peace with Sweden, Prokopovich celebrated the tsar's achievements and justified the new title. After the sermon, Golovkin noted in a speech, scripted by Shafirov, that Peter I had 'brought his faithful subjects from the darkness of ignorance to the theatre of glory of the whole world, from not-being to being'.[177] The address ended with a triple vivat to '*Petr Velikii, Otets Otechestviia, Imperator Vserossiiskii*': Peter the Great, Father of the Fatherland, all Russian Emperor.[178]

Empire

For scholars regarding Peter I the founding father of the modern Russian state, the adoption of the new title commonly serves as explicit evidence that within the first two decades of the eighteenth-century Russia had become an empire.[179] What did the word 'emperor' mean in the context of Peter I's new appellation? The answer to this question risks conflating medieval and early modern notions of imperial dignity, precedence, and hierarchy with a distinctly modern reading of empire, put in a nutshell by Michael Doyle as 'a relationship, formal or informal, in which one state controls the effective political sovereignty of another political society', and linked by the author to imperialism which is 'simply the process or policy of establishing or maintaining an empire'.[180] The study of Russia

[176] Wittram, *Peter I.*, II, pp. 462ff.

[177] *PSZRI*, VI, no. 3840 (22 October 1721), p. 445. The English translation is from Madariaga, 'Tsar into emperor', p. 16.

[178] *PSZRI*, VI, no. 3840 (22 October 1721), p. 446. For a detailed interpretation of the speech, as well as a discussion of its authorship and the process of drafting, editing, and publication, see E. Pogosian, *Petr I – arkhitektor rossiiskoi istorii* (St Petersburg, 2001), pp. 222ff.

[179] For example, A. B. Kamenskii, *Rossiiskaia imperiia v XVIII veke: traditsii i modernizatsiia* (Moscow, 1999), p. 123; Perdue, *China marches West*, p. 84; Osterhammel, *Entzauberung Asiens*, pp. 44f.; L. Greenfeld, *Nationalism: five roads to modernity* (Cambridge, MA, London, 1992), pp. 192–99. On the question of origins of empire, national identity, and the implications of Peter I's new title, providing a useful and balanced summary of the literature and adding an important pre-Petrine angle to the discussion, see S. Plokhy, *The origins of the Slavic nations: premodern identities in Russia, Ukraine, and Belarus* (Cambridge, 2006), ch. 7, esp. pp. 250f., 283ff.

[180] M. W. Doyle, *Empires* (Ithaca, NY, London, 1986), p. 45. Among many others, see Dominic Lieven's definition: 'Empire is, first and foremost, a very great power that has left its mark on the international relations of an era. I also mean a polity that rules over

as a multi-ethnic empire, in which conquest and coherence relied on complex entanglements of official policy and ad hoc imperial momentum, has framed a new paradigm, occupying much of modern Russian historiography since the 'imperial turn'.[181] The same elements of empire can be discerned in early modern versions of Russian territorial expansion, and they have indeed been discussed at great depth.[182] Can Peter I's new title be construed to this purpose as a conscious act of proclaiming this very empire: a modern, poly-ethnic expansionist state? It is suggestive to imagine, in this regard, the adoption of the title *imperator* as a ceremonial expression of rank and try to avoid a modern state perspective of empire or, indeed, treating it as a launch pad of Russian imperial history. The fact that Peter I styled himself as 'emperor' did not mark the symbolic point of departure of a new

wide territories and many peoples, since the management of space and multiethnicity is one of the great perennial dilemmas of empire', in his *Empire: the Russian empire and its rivals* (New Haven, CT, London, 2000), p. xi. See also Jürgen Osterhammel's definition of empire as 'a large, hierarchical structure of domination of poliyethnic and multi-religious character, the coherence of which is secured by threats of violence, administration, indigenous collaboration, and the universalist programs and symbols of an imperial elite (mostly under monarchical rule), but not by social and political homogenisation and the idea of universal citizenship rights', quoted as part of a wider discussion of empire in the introduction to S. Berger, A. Miller, eds., *Nationalizing empires* (Budapest, 2015), p. 12.

181 For the imperial turn, see M. David-Fox, P. Holquist, A. M. Martin, 'The imperial turn', *Kritika: explorations in Russian and Eurasian history*, 7 (2006), 705–712; R. Vulpius, 'Das Imperium als Thema der Russischen Geschichte: Tendenzen und Perspektiven der jüngeren Forschung', *Zeitenblicke*, 6 (2007). Available from www .zeitenblicke.de/2007/2/vulpius/index_html, last access 6 February 2016, for a survey of the recent literature on the emergence and nature of the modern Russian empire.

182 See, for example, W. Sunderland, *Taming the wild field: colonization and empire on the Russian steppe* (Ithaca, NY, London, 2004), esp. pp. 3ff. and chs. 1 and 2; Boeck, *Imperial boundaries*, esp. pp. 2–5, for a nuanced discussion of 'Russian empire-building' and a critical revision of notions of conquest and anti-colonial resistance. A related but much older debate concentrates on the question of whether Muscovite foreign policy was imperialistic in its design. For an affirmative view, which applies modern concepts of empire (presupposing the existence of nations and their ultimate aim of imposing their will upon other nations) to early modern Russian history, see O. Halecki, 'Imperialism in Slavic and east European history', *American Slavic and East European Review*, 11 (1952), 1–26. Cf. Oswald Backus' response, in which he debunks the myth of Muscovite imperialism as a mere projection of nineteenth-century ideas of imperialistic politics onto sixteenth-century Russia: O. P. Backus, 'Was Muscovite Russia imperialistic?', *American Slavic and East European Review*, 13 (1954), 522–34. See also J. Pelenski, *Russia and Kazan: conquest and imperial ideology, 1438–1560s* (The Hague, 1974). Cf. G. Stökl, 'Imperium und imperiale Ideologie: Erfahrungen am Beispiel des vorpetrinischen Russland', in *Vom Staat des ancien Regime zum modernen Parteienstaat: Festschrift für Theodor Schieder zu seinem 70. Geburtstag*, ed. H. Berding et al. (Munich, Vienna, 1978), pp. 27–39. For a more recent response to the debate, which rejects the notion of pre-Petrine imperialism, see A. I. Filiushkin, 'Problema genezisa Rossiiskoi imperii', in *Novaia imperskaia istoriia postsovetskogo prostranstva: Sbornik statei*, ed. I. V. Gerasimov et al. (Kazan, 2004), pp. 375–408. See also Plokhy, *Origins*, pp. 140–45.

imperial policy, or the beginning of an empire state that was going to last until 1917.[183] To be sure, the Latin title, through its evocation of the *Imperium Romanum*, proffered a definition of the state as a territorial empire that ruled over different peoples.[184] As such it remains doubtful as to whether the new style served as an expression of imperial policy with its attendant ideological manifestations. Rather, Peter I's assertion of imperial glory spoke to foreign powers to cement Russia's place in the *société des princes*.[185] As Isabel de Madariaga rightly pointed out, the new title formed part of the 'prestige policy' that Peter I pursued in his diplomatic relations with other courts.[186] To take seriously Golovkin's and Shafirov's notion of a nation having emerged from barbarism and obscurity in order to take its place among civilisation means to ignore that such rhetoric was the import of a European discourse used to address a European audience in a long-standing competition over glory and honour. In reality, Peter I's prestige policy was the continuation of previous tsars' ceremonial strategies of challenging European rulers through adjusting symbolic and ritual practice, which, in the long run, gave rise to debates over new political identities and reorganizing the stage in the political theatre.[187]

It is worth drawing a parallel to Ivan III's adoption of the two-headed eagle on the Russian state seal in the late fifteenth century, a result of aligning Russian diplomatic procedure with the protocol of Emperor Frederick III. Gustave Alef pointed out that 'the Muscovite grand prince, discovering that the Holy Roman Emperor utilized the two-headed eagle [...], while his son and designated successor could only display a single-headed one, replied by adopting a similar device for his own'. Alef continued, 'Implicitly this intimates that Ivan III accepted the Byzantine inheritance, though he did not do much else to push the claim in theory or in deed.'[188] Adding an additional head to the Muscovite eagle

183 Ibid., p. 289, reaches a similar conclusion.

184 For the debate on whether Peter I intended to become an 'eastern emperor', as the legitimate heir to the Byzantine Empire, or whether he drew the basis for the new title from ancient Rome, see Madariaga, 'Tsar into emperor', pp. 35ff., who argues in favour of the Byzantine model. Cf. Wittram, *Peter I.*, II, pp. 462f.; Wortman, *Scenarios*, I, pp. 63f., who support the Rome-thesis. For Rome, see also S. L. Baehr, 'From history to national myth: translatio imperii in eighteenth-century Russia', *Russian Review*, 37 (1978), 1–13.

185 Already in 1718, Friedrich Christian Weber informed King George I in an unpublished diplomatic report that there were rumours at the Russian court according to which Peter I 'intended to die [as a monarch who was] declared emperor by Europe'. Quoted in, Wittram, *Peter I.*, II, p. 469.

186 Madariaga, 'Tsar into emperor', p. 35.

187 Compare Wortman, *Scenarios*, I, p. 63, who sees at the core of this policy an ideological revolution designed to instil a Western identity into the tsar's subjects.

188 Alef, 'Adoption', p. 3. See also Croskey, *Diplomatic practice*, ch. 6.

did not result from a plan of developing the Byzantine heritage into a pronounced ideology.[189] The parallel is imperfect for numerous reasons, but one might argue, in comparison, that Peter I did not invoke the ancient empires, Roman or Byzantine, as an imperial ideology that defined the future course of Russian politics. His claim to imperial dignity followed the same pattern that compelled Ivan III to adopt the two-headed eagle. If a ceremonial element signified superiority (and by implication parity with those who consider themselves superior), then it could as well be adopted into one's own protocol or title to exploit its symbolism for international prestige, provided that other powers were willing to negotiate and accept such a change. There can be no doubt that Peter I's *imperator* introduced new meanings and associations that radically departed from the semantic world of the tsars' old titles.[190] But the meaning of the title was secondary to its original purpose. Claiming that the new style was a radical break with the past would have earned Peter I little recognition among those whom he hoped to impress. Building an empire on foreign models without a Muscovite pre-history of imperial dignity was not a convincing case according to ceremonial logic. Prestige required precedent. The new title pointed to the past, not to the future. Peter I had to project himself as a monarch whose standing in the hierarchy was the natural continuation of his predecessors' recognised claims to honour. The inheritance of an ancient empire, Peter I's military success, and his grand-reform designs certainly helped to further the argument for

[189] A similar case could be made for the much discussed doctrine of Moscow as the 'Third Rome'. The idea of Moscow being the 'Third Rome' – the heir to the Roman and Byzantine empires – would have been a superb argument in quarrels over titles and ceremonial procedure. However, the doctrine seems conspicuously absent in the *posol'skie knigi*. Foreign diplomats at the Russian court didn't seem to take notice of any such ideological appropriation either. See M. Poe, 'Moscow, the Third Rome: the origins and transformations of a "pivotal moment"', *Jahrbücher für Geschichte Osteuropas*, 49 (2001), 412–29, esp. pp. 419, 421f. See also Halperin, 'Methodological Excursus', esp. pp. 109f.; D. B. Rowland, 'Moscow – the Third Rome or the New Israel?', *Russian Review*, 55 (1996), 591–614; Cf. Iu. M. Lotman, B. A. Uspenskii, 'Echoes of the notion "Moscow as the Third Rome" in Peter the Great's Ideology', in *The semiotics of Russian culture*, ed. A. Shukman (Ann Arbor, 1984), pp. 53–67. For examinations of ceremony emphasising ideology, compare Kaminski, *Republic vs. autocracy*, p. 3, and R. Wortman, 'Ceremony and empire in the evolution of Russian monarchy', in *Visual texts, ceremonial texts, texts of exploration: collected articles on the representation of Russian monarchy* (Boston, 2014), pp. 27–46.

[190] The history of the tsars' titles has been sufficiently examined. For the evolution, meaning, and usage of the Russian rulers' titles, see A. I. Filiushkin, *Tituly russkikh gosudarei* (Moscow, St Petersburg, 2006). For a semiotic study that compares the semantics of 'tsar' and 'imperator', see B. A. Uspenskii, *Tsar' i imperator: pomazanie na tsarstvo i semantika monarshikh titulov* (Moscow, 2000). A concise overview of the history of the old Russian title is M. Szeftel, 'The title of the Muscovite monarch up to the end of the seventeenth century', *Canadian American Slavic Studies*, 13 (1979), 59–81.

imperial dignity, but examples of ritual practice from Muscovite times were needed to justify increased prestige in line with the rules of the precedence system.

Therefore, Golovkin, in his speech for the thanksgiving service, emphasised that the titles 'emperor' and 'majesty' had already been granted by Holy Roman Emperor Maximilian I to Peter I's 'praiseworthy antecessors [*dostokhval'nym Antetsessoram*]', and that many other monarchs had given these titles to previous tsars.[191] The Russian court could rely on a vast collection of archival documents in support of this claim.[192] The most important piece of evidence was Maximilian I's letter of August 1514 to Vasilii III (r. 1505–1533), in which the emperor officially addressed the grand prince of Moscow as *Kayser und Herrscher aller Reußlandt.*[193] The letter was published in St Petersburg in 1718. The original was dug up from the archives in Moscow and presented to the Habsburg envoy, Count Kinsky, whose court was questioning the authenticity of the writing. The imperial court, of course, could not accept the Russian claim to imperial dignity because 'since ancient times there has only been one Christian emperor in Europe', the Holy Roman Emperor.[194]

Peter I also demonstrated continuity when he thanked Landgrave Charles of Hesse-Kassel for the recognition of the new title, stressing that 'the title imperator vserossiiskii had been granted to [him] and [his] predecessors by many potentates since ancient times'.[195] In November 1762, when Catherine II reasserted the imperial dignity of the Russian court at the beginning of her reign, the chancellor and the vice-chancellor connected her glory to that of Peter I, stating that the latter had taken – 'or better, renewed' – the imperial title for him and his successors.[196] These

191 *PSZRI*, VI, no. 3840 (22 October 1721), p. 445. For a discussion of Muscovite continuities in the new title, see Plokhy, *Origins*, pp. 285ff.

192 See, for example, a list of occasions when the English monarch addressed Tsar Aleksei as 'imperator' (1665–1678), RGADA, f. 35, op. 1, d. 213. The collections of royal letters include contemporary inventories of the titles that foreign monarchs used in each letter to the tsar. See, for example, RGADA, f. 35, op. 2 (for England) and f. 93, op. 2–4 (for France). Compare TNA, SP 91/3 ('Russian Emperor's titles', 1661), fol. 87, for England, and AAE, MD, Russie, 3 ('Sur les titres donnés au Czar de la grande Russie dans les Traités et autres actes', 1728), fols. 253–74 (for France). See also Ruffmann, 'Zaren- und Kaisertitel'.

193 Wittram, *Peter I.*, II, pp. 469f. A printed version can be found in TNA, SP 124/1.

194 HHStA, Russland I, Kart. 3 ('Gehorsambstes Reichs Hoff-Cantzlcy guthachten den Russischen Kaysers Titul [...] betr., 13 August 1725, NS), esp. fol. 45. The Austrian view, including an investigation of the letter, is summarised in this report written by the imperial court chancellery. I am grateful to Christian Steppan for making this document available to me. For a detailed account of the imperial court's reaction to Peter I's new title, see Steppan, *Akteure*, chs. 2 and 3.

195 Peter I to Charles, 4 August 1724, quoted in Wittram, *Peter I.*, II, p. 609, fn. 34.

196 AVPRI, f. 18, op. 18/1 (1722–1763), d. 3 ('Declaration faite par l'ordre exprés de sa Majesté Imperiale', 21 November 1762, by M. I. Vorontsov and A. M. Golitsyn), l. 53.

examples show that Peter I's break with the former title continued old practice. Peter I put himself in direct continuity with Muscovite tsars to project his claim to imperial honour as the Russian rulers' long-standing right. A proven precedent such as the letter by Maximilian I to Vasilii III was a much stronger argument for bolstering the court's ceremonial prestige than the introduction of a new state ideology or the contrived descent from an ancient emperor, which, in turn, only served this argument very well.

Some of the Protestant states showed no hesitation in acknowledging the tsar as emperor. In particular, Prussia accepted the title, in 1721, in return for Russia's immediate recognition of Frederick I's royal dignity as 'King in Prussia', in 1701. The court in Berlin saw no problem in this act, as Peter I's predecessor had been granted the title. The Dutch Republic and the Free and Imperial City of Hamburg followed Prussia's example in order to keep good economic relations with the Russians. Kurakin reported from The Hague in 1722 that the United Provinces accepted the title because the Russian ruler was entitled to it 'from of old' (*izdrevle*).[197] Sweden, overpowered by Russia in the Great Northern War, followed suit in 1723.[198] However, Austria, as well as France, Spain, Great Britain, and Poland, opposed Peter I's claim to imperial dignity. A pamphlet, published in Vienna in 1723, publicly condemned the arrogation of the imperial title by Peter I, denying the Russian ruler any claim to imperial continuity which the latter so emphasised.[199] The pamphlet was received and translated in Russia.[200] A counter-response was launched by the Prussian Jacob P. von Gundling, court historiographer to King Frederick I, who supported Peter I's new title. Gundling's *Bestand des Rußischen Kayser=Titels*, published in Riga in 1724, celebrated the glory of the new Russian emperor to show that he deservedly carried the imperial title which had already been granted long ago.[201] Despite such support, Russia's struggle for the acknowledgement

[197] Kurakin to Peter I, 20. April 1722, AVPRI, f. 18, op. 18/1 (1722–1763), d. 3, ll. 55ob–56ob.

[198] For the reaction of various courts, see Wittram, *Peter I.*, II, pp. 467f.

[199] B. G. Struve, *Grundmässige Untersuchung von dem kaiserlichen Titel und Würde, wobei von der Czarischen Titulatur gehandelt und Kaiser Maximilians I. angegebenes Schreiben an den Czar Iwan Wasiliewitsch beigefüget wird* (Cologne, 1723). See also F. L. v. Berger, *Bedenken über die Frage, ob der Kayserliche Titel und Nahme ohnbeschadet Kayserlicher Majestät und des römischen Staats allerhöchster Würde, nicht weniger der christlichen Könige und freien Staaten Vorrecht und Interesse, dem Czaaren von Russland communiciret werden könne* (n.p., 1722).

[200] Struve's work was translated as 'Osnovatel'noe razsuzhdenie o Imperatorskom titule' (1723), AVPRI, f. 18, op. 18/1 (1723), d. 1.

[201] J. P. v. Gundling, *Bestand des Rußischen Kayser=Titels, worbey der von Kayser Maximilian dem Ersten anno 1514. den 4. Augusti zu Brundenach geschlossene Alliantz=Tractat gegen*

of the imperial title continued into the second half of the eighteenth century.[202]

Another factor limited the success of Peter I's prestige policy. Although all courts eventually accepted Peter I's new appellation, most refused to release the corresponding honours through ceremony. Imperial dignity indicated superiority. Recognising the imperial title meant acknowledging the supremacy of the Russian court. Needless to say, no monarch was willing to hazard the consequences of decreasing their own status relative to that of the Russian ruler. The king of Denmark and Norway, Christian VI (r. 1730–1746), in 1732, therefore, stipulated that Empress Anna Ivanovna (r. 1730–1740) must not alter the ceremonial in Danish–Russian diplomatic relations if he acknowledged her imperial title. In order to guarantee the equality between the imperial Russian and the royal Danish courts, Kasimir C. von Brakel (Anna's envoy to Denmark) declared that the Russian court would preserve the two monarchs' equality in the ceremonial and make no changes to previous practice. Brakel presented the declaration to King Christian VI in August 1732. In September, the Danish representative at the Russian court, Hans G. von Westphalen, declared in a public audience with Anna that the Danish court now fully recognised the imperial title of the Russian ruler.[203] The imperial title had to be reconfirmed repeatedly during successions to the throne. At the beginning of Empress Elizabeth's reign, the Holy Roman Emperor, Charles VII (r. 1742–1745), signalled willingness to acknowledge her imperial title in certain, limited circumstances so that the empress officially recognised his diplomat. But Charles VII's representative in St Petersburg, Baron von Neuhaus, made it clear that 'the recognition of the imperial title was nothing but a pure act of courtesy which was neither harmful to the

alle bissher gemachte nichtige Einwürffe vertheidiget wird (Riga, 1724). A copy, including a handwritten Russian translation, can be found in AVPRI, f. 18, op. 18/1 (1724), d. 4. For Gundling, see Clark, *Iron kingdom*, pp. 80ff.

202 The other courts recognised the new title in the following order: Turkey, 1741; Great Britain and Austria, 1742; France and Spain, 1745; Poland, 1772. See E. A. Ageeva, 'Imperskii status Rossii: k istorii politicheskogo mentaliteta russkogo obshchestva nachala XVIII veka', in *Tsar' i tsarstvo v russkom obshchestvennom soznanii*, ed. A. A. Gorskii (Moscow, 1999), pp. 112–40, here on p. 140, fn. 54. The years vary, cf. G. A. Nekrasov, 'Mezhdunarodnoe priznanie rossiiskogo velikoderzhaviia v XVII v.', in *Feodal'naia Rossiia vo vsemirno-istoricheskom protsesse: sbornik statei, posviashchennyi L. V. Cherepninu*, ed. V. T. Pashuto (Moscow, 1972), pp. 381–88. See also A. G. Brikner, *Istoriia Petra Velikogo* (Moscow, 2007, first published 1882), p. 613. The struggle continued even after the recognition of the new title. France continued to oppose the title until the 1770s. Similarly, Emperor Joseph II denied Catherine II the title 'empress'. This was the main reason why a treaty between him and Catherine II was not signed despite his expressed desire for an alliance; see Luard, *The balance of power*, p. 139.

203 AVPRI, f. 18, op. 18/1 (1722–1763), d. 3 ('Perevod s rechi datskogo chrezvychainogo poslannika fon Vestfalena'), l. 59.

dignity of the empire, nor to that of the Emperor'.[204] When Catherine II succeeded to the throne in 1762, her court confirmed that, based on a declaration by Peter I, the imperial title of the Russian ruler did not imply any changes to established ceremonial practice.[205]

Peter I and his successors were granted the imperial title, but at the same time they were denied the ceremonies that manifested claims to imperial superiority with the political force of face-to-face. Dynastic courts discriminated sharply between ceremonial dignity and the meaning of the new title to prevent the tsar from asserting his superiority in direct diplomatic encounters. Strictly speaking, despite the acknowledgement of the title, Russia was not recognised as an empire by other European courts, as its ambassadors were not allowed to perform the honours that the title of its ruler implied. The contemporary scholar of precedence and diplomatic ceremonial, Zschackwitz, expressed it in the following terms: The acknowledgement of Peter I's title was 'an *adgnitio personalis*, but not *realis*, that is, that one concedes the title emperor to a Russian monarch but does not recognise the Russian empire as such a state'.[206] According to this interpretation, the Russian ruler was allowed to boast the new title, but the actual ceremonial counterbalanced the honours that the word 'emperor' expressed. Other courts sustained the contradiction between titulature and ritual reality in order to curb Russia's imperial ambitions, preserving their own place in the hierarchy or maintaining the fiction of equality that was gradually taking root in the early modern period. If diplomatic ritual enrobed a ruler with status, the tsar had become an emperor without clothes.

[204] AVPRI, f. 18, op. 18/1 (1722–1763), d. 3 ('Exposé de ce qui s'est passé relativement à la reconnoissance du titre Impérial depuis l'avenement au thrône de l'Impératrice Eliabeth'), l. 7ob.

[205] AVPRI, f. 18, op. 18/1 (1722–1763), d. 3 ('Declaration faite par l'ordre exprés de sa Majesté Imperiale', 21 November 1762, by M. I. Vorontsov and A. M. Golitsyn), l. 53. This declaration was sent, on the day of its issuing, to the diplomatic representatives of Austria, France, Prussia, Spain, Denmark, Great Britain, Sweden, and Saxony.

[206] Zschackwitz, *Einleitung*, III, p. 351.

Conclusion

This book traces Russia's place in early modern international relations not by modern standards of statecraft and great power concepts but in terms of the language that contemporaries used to describe the sovereignty and power of dynastic rulers: the language – verbal and non-verbal – of honour and prestige. In contrast to widespread assumptions about the irreconcilable differences between the political cultures of Russia and Western Europe, diplomatic practice drew the tsars into an arena in which rulers competed for the symbolic resources of sovereignty and power. The aim is not to decide or even to raise the question of whether Russia rested within or without Europe. The objective is to show that in the context of diplomatic ritual, the question of who belonged to the circle of sovereigns extended beyond modern ideas of Europe as a geographically defined and unified cultural sphere. The answer to this question is not determined by the variety of normative struggles over different values or civilisational belonging which suffuses post-Petrine, nineteenth- and twentieth-century notions of 'Russia and the West'. Diplomatic practice evolved within a transcultural political space of a shared pool of ceremonial norms, a space that integrated the Russian tsar who appeared a distant and foreign ruler through gradually standardised codes of behaviour and communication. Russia played a part in this evolution earlier than historians have suggested: the tsars' commitment to ritual display and the rigid institutional administration of sovereignty symbols were reflections of their acknowledged place in the early modern system of precedence, rather than remnants of the exotic 'barbarism' mocked and dismissed by many contemporary travellers.

Did Russia occupy a special place in the political sphere of ritual and ceremony? It did, not because of the cultural otherness that travel literature imputes to Russian rulers and diplomats, but because Russia joined the process of gradual standardisation of diplomatic contact at a pace which was different to that of other states. While it had always fully participated in the rivalry, and consciously sought its place among the *société des princes*, Russia was not exposed, to the same degree, to the increased flow in communication which other European courts were, especially after 1648. This book gives reasons as to why this was the case, but rather than pursuing an archaeology of ceremonial which reduces Russian diplomatic practice to its specific cultural substratum, it focuses on the flexibility of basic communication patterns that emerge in hierarchical relationships. The book thus proposes a shift in focus, away from the preoccupation with the origins of ceremonial vocabulary coupled with early modern and contemporary notions of alterity to the actual practice in which ritual was negotiated. It traces diplomatic culture in continually evolving interactions between dynastic courts, rather than in the confrontation of different political cultures rooted in rival national traditions.

As such, it is tempting to fit diplomatic culture into the broad frame of what Peter Davidson calls the 'universal baroque', a worldwide system of artistic expression exhibiting a universal symbolic language that did not have a geographical centre and was not oriented towards confessional allegiance, national borders, or cultural belonging. He sees this form of early modern art as 'an international system of communication in all the arts' that extended the boundaries of the Catholic South and the New World territories, as much as it covered the Protestant North and the Orthodox East. The baroque age was conducive to internationalism because of its ability to blend the vernacular with the universal. This hybrid nature of the baroque mode enabled people of distinct and distinctive cultural backgrounds to communicate across borders and to express themselves in two idioms at once: the indigenous and the international.[1]

Diplomacy in the heyday of court culture seemed to epitomise Davidson's vision of the period in many ways. Few aspects of early modern statecraft left more traces in written and visual sources of diplomatic encounters than the accounts of solemn parades, lavish receptions, fabulous gifts, and their assimilation into a contemporary concern with the political order. The manifestations of sovereignty and power appealed to the senses as expressions of a supranational lingua franca that drew its symbols from a pool of common gestures.[2] International norms, which were essentially the norms of court society, made communication between foreign cultures possible. This book opens by showing that ceremonial honours provided a common code of communication that served three basic functions: asserting sovereignty and substantiating claims to authority, ascribing to a sovereign a rank within the hierarchical *société des princes*, and mediating favours between befriended courts or

[1] P. Davidson, *The universal Baroque* (Manchester, 2007), esp. pp. 12–21, 182f.
[2] Garnier, 'Symbolische Kommunikationsformen'.

communicating hostilities to enemies. Despite the 'enlightened' criticism it endured, diplomatic ceremonial, which had lost its medieval notion of universal hierarchy, remained in place through the second half of the eighteenth century to 'strictly regulate forms of correspondence between states precisely because it serv[ed] as a measure of the mutual respect for each other's strength', as Catherine II's foreign policy advisor, Nikita I. Panin, observed.[3]

Diplomats were expected to acquire a high proficiency in the symbolic languages spoken and performed throughout Europe. Local accents inevitably merged into the universal idiom of ceremonial, with a French *accent* sounding more familiar, perhaps, than a heavy German or Russian inflection. Contemporary works on ceremonial and precedence often served as 'dictionaries' or guides to the rituals in which diplomats expressed their sovereigns' ambitions and exchanged political information. Despite Russia's prevailing image as an exotic and barbarous country, promoted above all in travel accounts, the tsars enjoyed wide-ranging discursive integration in the ranking system. In the eyes of most scholars of precedence, the tsars belonged to and actively participated in the ceremonial sphere. The upshot is, it would appear, that diplomatic encounters underscore the integrative force of ceremonies, their power to reconcile the cultures of such outwardly different courts like those of Versailles, Vienna, St James, Moscow, or St Petersburg. Ceremonial disputes demonstrated the widespread understanding of norms shared by all diplomats, Russian and European: as surrogates of their sovereigns, they were fighting the same battle for honour and prestige within a hierarchical international community. Conflict and failure were signs of participation in a common cultural practice.

A caveat must be introduced, however. Anthropologists have raised doubts as to whether the same verbal or symbolic expression necessarily conveys identical meaning in different cultural contexts. Clifford Geertz, in particular, has offered a valuable note of caution when discussing the universalism of diplomatic procedure. He curbed optimism concerning the similarity of words or body language. The building blocks of diplomatic relations – protocol, international law, customs, etiquette, etc. – do not exist in a cultural vacuum in which states search for a lowest common denominator of universal rules of conduct. On the contrary, according to Geertz, these principles are laden with cultural determination: they 'are projections of aspects of our own onto the

[3] Quoted in H. M. Scott, 'Russia as a European great power', in *Russia in the age of enlightenment: essays in honour of Isabel de Madariaga*, ed. R. P. Bartlett, J. M. Hartley (Basinstoke, 1990), pp. 7–39, here on p. 28. See also Dixon, *Modernisation*, p. 121. On Panin's comment, see also Scott, *Emergence*, p. 8.

world stage'.[4] In other words, the ritual surface of congruent social behaviour masks the underlying cultural difference and ultimately leads the historian astray. To believe in the universalism of ceremonial norms is 'to mistake convergence of vocabularies for convergence of views'.[5]

The analogies and discrepancies in the practical organisation of diplomatic procedure in Western Europe and Russia are a case in point: Russia and Europe were part of the same ceremonial 'semiosphere', but differences emerged in the diplomatic apparatuses of the various courts.[6] This state of affairs could yield divergent interpretations of strikingly similar administrative terminology. In a comparative survey, Chapter 2 shows that although Russian and European courts had an equally well-developed administration of ceremony, the ways in which they organised ritual procedures and kept track of ceremonial norms could and did differ. The *Posol'skii prikaz* administered a strict scheme of ritual in accordance with the precedents that Russian diplomats recorded in their *stateinyi spisok* (or which were written down in the course of a foreign embassy's stay in Russia). The pre-Petrine court based all of its knowledge of the international order on documents submitted by their own representatives at the end of every mission. Here, Russian and European practices were subtly different. European diplomats wrote lengthy reports, including ceremonial details, and sent them back home by way of the regular post. They were in direct contact with each other and with their sovereigns. Moreover, they sourced information on precedence from a growing corpus of texts compiled and published by the masters of ceremonies, diplomatic manuals, and the treatises of both *ius praecedentiae* and *Zeremonialwissenschaft*. Although the tsars were included in the discourse on the practice of precedence, pre-Petrine diplomats did not actively use or contribute to this discourse themselves, relying instead on the archives of the *Posol'skii prikaz*. As a result, the convergence of vocabulary could cause confusion about the correct meaning of words. For example, the European tripartite division of diplomatic ranks found an equivalent expression in the Russian terms *posol*, *poslannik*, and *gonets*. These ranks, however, conveyed different levels of representation, as well as divergent legal connotations, in the European and Russian contexts. These differences resulted in many misunderstandings about the nature of representation, a diplomat's rights to specific honours, and his duties as

[4] C. Geertz, 'Local knowledge: fact and law in comparative perspective', in *Local knowledge: further essays in interpretive anthropology by Clifford Geertz* (New York, 1983), pp. 167–234, here on p. 221. The cultural difference of customs and laws in diplomatic relations is emphasised by L. Frey, M. Frey, *The history of diplomatic immunity*, pp. 4f.

[5] Geertz, 'Local knowledge', p. 221. [6] Lotman, 'Semiosphäre'.

an agent of his court. The similarity of words and gestures does not support the case of the universalism of diplomatic ceremony, court ritual, and its underlying norms.

Thus, universalism and cultural specificity both seem to be applicable to diplomatic practice at the same time, which is also demonstrated by the following examples. On the one hand, the cross-cultural similarities are too obvious to be ignored or dismissed as a superficial manifestation of agreement masking deeply discordant norms. The course of ceremonial events from the first meeting at the border to the audience with the monarch before departure showed striking resemblance. The principle of reciprocity, which, for example, the English and Russian courts observed in their diplomatic exchanges, ensured that ceremonial elements were arranged in an agreed and mutually agreeable fashion. The disputes that engaged the earl of Carlisle, and the complaints about the barbarous customs of the Russians, could not disguise the fact that the honours he received in Moscow were partly based on an earlier reception of a Russian ambassador in London. In some cases, the same metaphorical vocabulary was used to describe a solemn procession, which does suggest a higher degree of commonality than the mere use of the same words. The ceremonial for Peter I's Grand Embassy in Vienna pinpointed the distance between the centre of power and the meeting point of the ambassadors by *ein Pistolenschuss* (one pistol-shot) from the city.[7] The longer the path that the court officials had to traverse to meet the ambassadors, the more honour was bestowed by the host. The distance that a bullet could travel between the gun barrel and its target also marked the meeting point of embassies according to Russian custom. The meeting point was not counted out in versts but gauged by a gunshot, so as to receive high-ranking ambassadors 'a gunshot away from the suburbs'.[8]

On the other hand, single ceremonial gestures could be misinterpreted in Russian–European diplomatic encounters due to Russia's cultural and political contacts and experiences with Eastern powers, such as the successor khanates to the Golden Horde. In 1682, for example, the tsar's emissary to the Crimea, Nikita Tarakanov, was taken under arrest and tortured because he refused to give more than the agreed number of gifts

[7] HHStA, ZA Prot 5, fol. 413.

[8] Quoted in Iuzefovich, *Obychaia*, p. 70. See also Iuzefovich, 'Russkii posol'skii obychai', p. 116. This universal metaphorical expression for the distance between the meeting point of potentially hostile parties and the court is quite telling in view of the capital's lack of defence. The first significant event of an official character took place in the passage between the pre-ceremonial, anarchical state of relations. The meeting point was placed within the reach of a bullet, where the city might still defend itself in the event that something unexpected happened before ceremonies constituted peaceful relations. See E. Muir, *Ritual in early modern Europe* (Cambridge, 1997), p. 239.

to the khan. This happened at a time when the Muscovite ruler attempted to free himself from the humiliating relationship with the Crimea.[9] In 1699–1700, during the peace negotiations with the Porte in Constantinople, the tsar's diplomats demanded that 'the tribute which formerly was paid to the Crimean khan and his officers be stopped on account of their many wrongs and not be paid in future'.[10] Any ritual that gave the impression of a submissive gesture was clearly an encumbrance to the sovereignty of the Russian ruler, and as such his diplomats feared to see it 'projected onto the world's stage', as Geertz would say. As a consequence, the Russian ambassadors in Vienna, in 1698, warned that the placing of their gifts to the feet of the Holy Roman Emperor (rather than on a table or into his hands) could be seen as a token of tribute, although the emperor had no intention of forcing the diplomats to present themselves as tributaries.[11]

These examples demonstrate that it is difficult to maintain that diplomatic ceremonial was either universal or culturally specific. Such either–or terminology is obstructive to a better understanding of what was at play in early modern diplomatic ritual. As a result, this book does not commit itself to one approach or another. It steers a middle path between the two poles of universalism and cultural determinism. It argues that ceremonial conflicts between Russian and western European diplomats did not result exclusively from a cultural clash of divergent norms. Nor did the ceremonies, however similar they may appear on the surface, represent a convenient lingua franca for cross-border communication that overrode all differences and required no further interpretation. Ceremonies were contingent upon precedent and its documentation machine. This is not to say that such symbolic representation was bereft of political ideology; they were of course as much a result as an expression of it. Cultural values did underpin these conflict-ridden diplomatic procedures, but, this book maintains, these were the values that intercourtly contacts produced, and not cultural self-representations.[12]

Three main types of conflict dominated the ceremonial battle field (more could be added to the list): First, misunderstandings owing to random

[9] S. M. Soloviev, *History of Russia, vol. 25: rebellion and reform. Fedor and Sophia, 1682–1689*, trans. L. A. J. Hughes (Gulf Breeze, FL, 1989), p. 179. Ceremonial humiliation before the Tatars was an age-old Russian fear; see Croskey, *Diplomatic practice*, pp. 122–27.

[10] S. M. Soloviev, *History of Russia, vol. 26: Peter the Great. A reign begins, 1689–1703*, trans. L. A. J. Hughes (Gulf Breeze, FL, 1994), p. 228. The Tatar khan raised the question of 'gifts' (tribute) again during negotiation of a treaty with the Turks in 1711–1713. However, discussion of the continuation of tribute to the Tatars was postponed and it remained the last. I wish to thank the late Lindsey Hughes to draw my attention to this fact.

[11] HHStA, ZA Prot 5, fol. 434.

[12] See also the notion of cultural commensurability developed in Subrahmanyam, *Courtly encounters*.

accidents and mistakes that were inadvertent (such as the adjournment of Carlisle's solemn entry into Moscow in 1663); second, conflicts owing to genuinely differing construal of relevant practice, without either side realising that they were interpreting the same gestures differently (such as the absence of the concept of 'representative character' in Muscovite diplomacy); and third, and most prominently, purposeful manipulation of shared rules and gestures for political advantage (such as Whitworth's public apology presented in 1710 to Peter I). The conflicts over ceremonies and the semiotic discomfort of diplomats over how to deal with each other underscore the fact that the norms of their conduct were still in the making (rather than culturally incompatible). Ritual gestures, which marked relations between dynastic courts, were constantly challenged and had to be battled out between negotiating parties. Competing for ceremonial claims demonstrated the difficulty of agreeing on mutually binding procedures and formalities from which negotiations could proceed without jeopardising status in face-to-face contact. This was as much a problem in the West as in Russia. True, the seventeenth century may have been the cradle of modern diplomacy. Yet the modernity of seventeenth-century diplomacy itself has been overrated.[13] Far from being standardised supranational rules, the norms that gave order to the relations between dynastic courts were still, and continued to be, in flux. These norms were less static than the notion of a modern European states-system might suggest.[14] Emerging from the principle of reciprocal exchange, their slow standardisation was itself the result of continuous cultural contact. Therefore, it would be misleading to compartmentalise diplomatic cultures and interpret Russian practices in the light of Russian–European differences in political ideology or the otherness of Russian culture, as much as it is wrong to ascribe early modern European diplomats with a specific predilection to ritualism and empty façade. Diplomatic ceremonial was driven by converging notions of honour, the symbolic language of court society, and not by incompatible national, ideological representations or by cultural incommensurability. Ceremonial quarrels were the logical consequence of face-to-face encounters that through the assumed presence of the sovereign

[13] L. Frey, M. Frey, *The history of diplomatic immunity*, p. 207, make this point. Jeremy Black, in most of his many works on diplomacy, also rejects the teleological view that points to modernity and progress in the development of Western diplomacy. See, for example, J. Black, *British diplomats and diplomacy 1688–1800* (Exeter, 2001), pp. 2ff. This view is also developed in Black, *History of diplomacy*. For a summary of the debate, see B. Teschke, 'Theorizing the Westphalian system of states: international relations from absolutism to capitalism', *European Journal of International Relations*, 8 (2002), 5–48.

[14] B. Stollberg-Rilinger, 'Herrschaftszeremoniell', in *Enzyklopädie der Neuzeit*, vol. 5, ed. F. Jaeger (Stuttgart, Weimar, 2007), pp. 416–24, esp. cols. 420f. For the states-system, see Scott, *Great power system*, p. 140.

precipitated dynastic rivalries as well as symbolic wars over conflicting legal claims. In the future, it would be worth exploring how this logic developed in Russia's diplomatic entanglements further in the East and in the borderlands, in particular in its relations with the Ottoman Empire, imperial China, and the nomadic peoples of the steppe. The Russian empire's political contacts at all extremes of its vast Eurasian territory make Moscow an ideal vantage point from which to study early modern diplomacy at a more global scale, not only to discern Russia's diplomatic place in the hierarchy of non-Christian courts but also to mediate between 'European' and 'non-European' practices and attendant historiographical traditions.[15]

This book starts by quoting Cardinal-minister Guillaume Dubois who claimed that 'there are not two courts where the ceremonial would be the same in all circumstances'.[16] True, the conventions of Russian diplomatic practice were different from those of Europeans. But within Europe such conventions differed greatly, too. The strict ritual regime of Russian diplomacy did not set the tsars apart from other monarchs. On the contrary, their insistence on their own notions of the correct treatment of diplomats is a testament to Russia's contribution to a transcultural process. This fact made it less difficult for Peter I to align Russian diplomatic practice with the conventions of other courts. Peter I did not introduce a fundamental shift which uprooted Muscovite diplomatic culture, modelling diplomacy after a new and completely different example. He adjusted (neither started nor completed) an ever-evolving paradigm by virtue of reform when within Europe's princely world itself changes were in progress over norms of diplomatic practice, the composition of diplomatic corps, the development of resident diplomacy, and the gradual emergence of a states-system. Diplomatic practice shows what the Petrine empire owed to its Muscovite past and how the diplomacy of Peter I's predecessors tied in with wider developments of early modern court culture.

[15] Useful points of departure are Perdue, *China marches West*, ch. 4, for Sino-Russian relations; A. Fisher, *A precarious balance: conflict, trade, and diplomacy on the Russian-Ottoman frontier* (Istanbul, 1999), for Russian–Ottoman relations, and Khodarkovsky, *The Russian state and the Kalmyk nomads*, pp. 58–63; Khodarkovsky, *Russia's steppe frontier*, for Russian diplomacy on the steppe frontier. For a comparative overview with an emphasis on imperial ideology, see A. J. Rieber, *The struggle for the Eurasian borderlands: from the rise of early modern empires to the end of the First World War* (Cambridge, 2014), ch. 2. See also Jeroen Duindam's recent *Dynasties: a global history of power, 1300–1800* (Cambridge, 2016).

[16] See Introduction, fn. 3.

Bibliography

Archival Materials

Haus- Hof und Staatsarchiv Wien (HHStA), Vienna

Ältere Zeremonialacten (ÄZA)
    Karton 18
Russland I
    Karton 30
Zeremonialprotokolle (ZA Prot)
    Bände 3, 5

Arkhiv vneshnei politiki Rossiiskoi imperii (AVPRI), Moscow

Fond 2 Vnutrennie kollezhskie dela
    Opis' 2/6, dela 57, 5552
Fond 23 Snosheniia Rossii s Frantsiei
    Opis' 93/1, dela 7 (1721), 10 (1720)
Fond 35 Snosheniia Rossii s Angliei
    Opis' 35/2, delo 57
Fond 18 Dela i sochineniia o titulakh
    Opis' 18/1, dela 1 (1723), 3 (1722–1763), 4 (1724)

Rossiiskii gosudarstvennyi arkhiv drevnikh aktov (RGADA), Moscow

Fond 15 Diplomaticheskii otdel
    Opis' 1, dela 15, 78
Fond 17 Nauka, literatura, iskusstvo
    Opis' 1, delo 149
Fond 32 Snosheniia Rossii s Avstriei i Germanskoi Imperiei
    Opis' 1, delo 20
Fond 35 Snosheniia Rossii s Angliei
    Opis' 1, dela 8, 11, 12, 176, 183, 186, 187, 200, 205, 213, 268, 294, 334
    Opis' 2

Fond 50 Snosheniia Rossii s Gollandiei
Opis' 1, dela 2 (1700), 3 (1712), 4 (1712)
Fond 53 Snosheniia Rossii s Daniei
Opis' 1, delo 3 (1712)
Fond 93 Snosheniia Rossii s Frantsiei
Opis' 1, dela 7 (1680–1682), 1 (1698), 3 (1703), 5 (1704), 5 (1706), 10 (1717)
Opis' 2–4
Fond 156 Istoricheskie i tseremonial'nye dela
Opis' 1, dela 153, 156, 158, 171, 173, 180, 181, 209, 211, 213, 214, 228–232
Fond 158 Prikaznye dela novykh let
Opis' 1, delo 117 (1719)
Opis' 2, delo 66 (1719)
Opis' 3, delo 8
Fond 159 Prikaznye dela novoi razborki
Opis' 2, delo 474 (1721–1725)
Fond 375 Istoricheskie sochineniia
Opis' 1, delo 15 (1675)

Bodleian Library (Bodl. Libr.), Oxford

MS Barlow 52
MS Clarendon 80

The National Archives (TNA), Kew, London

State papers foreign
Russia, SP 91/3, 5, 6
Entry books, SP 104/120
Royal letters, SP 102/49
State papers: gazettes and pamphlets
Russia, SP 124/1
Records of the Lord Chamberlain and other officers of the Royal Household
Lord Chamberlain's Department: miscellaneous Records, LC 5/2–3

Rousham Park (Rousham), Steeple Aston

MC 6, 7, 9, 10, 15
MC box 1, 4

Archives du Ministère des Affaires Etrangères (AAE), Paris

Correspondance politique (CP)
 Angleterre, 78
 Russie, 8
Mémoires et documents (MD)
 Russie, 3–4

Archives Nationales (AN), Paris

Série KK
 KK 1426
 KK 1431
 KK 1438
Série K
 K 1712
 K 1352

Bibliothèque de l'Arsenal (BA), Paris

MS 3859, 4232

Bibliothèque Mazarine (BM), Paris

MS 2737–2751

Bibliothèque nationale de France (BnF), Paris

Estampes et Photographie
 Reserve QB-201(59)-Fol-Hennin, 5223
Manuscrits français (MS f)
 10280, 10654, 14117–14120
Nouvelles acquisitions françaises (MS naf)
 3123–3133

Printed Primary Sources

A declaration, of His Imperiall Majestie, The most High and Mighty Potentate Alexea, Emperor of Russia, and great Duke of Muscovia, & c. Wherein is conteined his Detestation of the Murther of Charles the First, King of Great Britain and Ireland (n. p., 1650).

A declaration of the most Christian King, Lovis the XIIIth. [sic!] King of France and Navarre. Declaring the reasons wherefore his Majesty hath prohibited all trade with England (London, 1649).

Adelung, F. v., *Augustin Freiherr von Meyerberg und seine Reise nach Russland. Nebst einer von ihm auf dieser Reise veranstalteten Sammlung von Ansichten, Gebräuchen, Bildnissen u.s.w* (St Petersburg, 1827).

ed., *Sammlung von Ansichten, Gebräuchen, Bildnissen, Trachten usw. welche der Röm. Kaiserl. Gesandte Augustin Fryherr von Meyerberg auf seiner Reise und während seines Afenthalts in Russland in den Jahren 1661 und 1662 hat entwerfen lassen* (St Petersburg, 1827).

An act for preserving the privileges of ambassadors and other public ministers of foreign princes and states, 1708 (7 Anne, ch. 12).

Babkin, A., 'Pis'ma Frantsa i Petra Leforta o "Velikom Posol'stve"', *Voprosy istorii*, 6 (1976), 120–32.

Berger, F. L. v., *Bedenken über die Frage, ob der Kayserliche Titel und Nahme ohnbeschadet Kayserlicher Majestät und des römischen Staats allerhöchster Würde, nicht weniger der christlichen Könige und freien Staaten Vorrecht und Interesse, dem Czaaren von Russland communiciret werden könne* (n.p., 1722).

Bielfeld, J. v., *Institutions politiques*, 2 vols. (The Hague, 1760).

Blackstone, W., *Commentaries on the laws of England*, 4 vols. (Oxford, 1765–1769).

Bodin, J., *On sovereignty: four chapters from the six books of the commonwealth*, trans. and ed. J. H. Franklin (Cambridge, 1992).

Buchet, P. F., *Abrégé de l'histoire du Czar Peter Alexiewitz avec une relation de l'etat présent de la Moscovie, & de ce qui s'est passé de plus considerable, depuis son arrivée en France jusqu'a ce jour* (Paris, 1717).

Buvat, J., *Journal de la régence: 1715–1723* (Paris, 1865).

Callières, F. de, *Art of diplomacy*, trans. F. T. French (London, 1716, reprint, Leicester).

Collins, S., *The present state of Russia in a letter to a friend at London / written by an eminent person residing at the great czars court at Mosco for the space of nine years* (London, 1671).

Courtois, A. de, ed., *Lettres de Madame de Villars à Madame de Coulanges (1679–1681)*, new edn. (Paris, 1868).

De Beer, E. S., ed., *The diary of John Evelyn*, 6 vols. (Oxford, 1955).

[Defoe, D.], *An impartial history of the life and actions of Peter Alexowitz, the present Czar of Muscovy. Written by a British officer in the service of the Czar* (London, 1723).

Die Entreveüe zwischen dem Kayser / und dem Czaar / den 29. Junii 1698 (n.p., 1698).

Dixon, S., ed., *Britain and Russia in the age of Peter the Great: historical documents* (London, 1998).

Dvortsovye razriady, 4 vols. (St Petersburg, 1850–1855).

Fedosov, F., ed., *Diary of General Patrick Gordon of Auchleuchries, 1635–1699. Volume II: 1659–1667* (Aberdeen, 2011).

Finet, J., *Finetti philoxenis* (London, 1656).

Fuhrmann, M., *Alt- und neues Wien, oder dieser [. . .] Stadt chronologisch- und historische Beschreibung [. . .]*, 2 vols. (Vienna, Lintz, 1738–1739).

Galitzin, E., *La Russie du XVIIe siècle dans ses rapports avec l'Europe occidentale récit du voyage de Pierre Potemkin envoyé en ambassade par le tsar Alexis Mikhailovilch à Philippe IV d'Espagne et à Louis XIV en 1668* (Paris, 1855).

Gazette de France, no. 105 (1668); no. 17 (12 April 1687); no. 18 (19 April 1687); no. 25 (16 August 1687).

Glafey, A. F., ed., *Christoph Hermann Schweders Theatrum historicum praetensionum et controversiarum illustrium, oder Historischer Schauplatz der Ansprüche und Streitigkeiten hoher Potentaten und anderer regierenden Herrschafften in Europa* (Leipzig, 1727).

Guagnini, A., *Sarmatiae Europeae descriptio, quae regnum Poloniae, Lituaniam, Samogitiam, Russiam, Massouiam, Prussiam, Pomeraniam, Liuoniam, et Moschouiae, Tartariaeque partem complectitur* (Spirae, 1581).

Gundling, J. P. v., *Bestand des Rußischen Kayser=Titels, worbey der von Kayser Maximilian dem Ersten anno 1514. den 4. Augusti zu Brundenach geschlossene Alliantz=Tractat gegen alle bissher gemachte nichtige Einwürffe vertheidiget wird* (Riga, 1724).

Hahn, P.-M., Kiesant, K., eds., *Johann von Besser (1654–1729): Schriften*, 3 vols. (Heidelberg, 2009).

Heidenfeld, A., *Asiatischer Schauplatz / Das ist / Ausfuehrliche Beschreibung Der tuerkischen / Persianischen/ Moskowitischen und Chinischen Beherrscheren sampt Deren Inwohnern Sitten* (Frankfurt a. M., 1678).

Hennings, J. C., 'Betrachtungen über die Etiquette mit Anwendung auf die Präcedenz der Gesandten und Monarchen durch Beyspiele aus der Geschichte', in J. C. Hennings, *Verjährte Vorurtheile in verschiedenen Abhandlungen bestritten*, (Riga, 1778), pp. 1–144.

Historical memoirs of the duc de Saint-Simon: a shortened version, ed. and trans. L. Norton, 3 vols. (London, 1967–1972).

Hoevelen, C. v., *Candorins Vollkommener Teutsche Gesandte/ [...]* (Frankfurt a. M., 1679).

Hoffmann, C. G., *Entwurff einer Einleitung zu dem Erkäntniß des gegenwärtigen Zustandes von Europa. Worinnen hierzu nöthigen Wissenschaften überhaupt geurtheilet, Insonderheit aber der Ursprung von denen wichtigsten Krieges= und Friedens=Angelegenheiten dieser Zeit vorgestellet und zu dem Grunde eines Collegii Privati geleget wird* (Leipzig, 1720).

Hotman, J., *The Ambassador* (London, 1603).

Howell, J., *Proedria vasilike a discourse concerning the precedency of kings* (London, 1664).

Jansson, M., Rogozhin, N. M., eds., *England and the North: the Russian embassy of 1613–1614*, trans. P. Bushkovitch (Philadelphia, 1994).

Journal du marquis de Dangeau, avec les additions inédites du duc de Saint-Simon, ed. E. Soulié, L. Dussieux, 19 vols. (Paris, 1854–1860).

Jugler, J. F., *Beyträge zur juristischen Biographie. Oder, genauere litterarische und critische Nachrichten von dem Leben und den Schriften verstorbener Rechtsgelehrten auch Staatsmänner, welche sich in Europa berühmt gemacht haben*, 6 vols. (Leipzig, 1773–1780).

Kämpfer, F. et al., eds., *Sigismund von Herberstein: Rerum Moscoviticarum Commentarii. Synoptische Edition der lateinischen und der deutschen Fassung letzter Hand. Basel 1556 und Wien 1557* (Munich, 2007).

Kartashov, N. S., Polonskaia, I. M., *Biblioteka A. A. Matveeva (1666–1728): katalog* (Moscow, 1985).

Kemmerich, D. H., *Grund=Sätze des Völker=Rechts von der Unverletzlichkeit der Gesandten. Samt einer Relation von dem Affront, welcher dem Moscowitischen Abgesandten in Engelland Anno 1708 erwiesen* (n.p., 1710).

Korb, J. G., *Diary of an Austrian secretary of legation at the court of Czar Peter the Great*, trans. C. C. Macdonnell, reprint edn., 2 vols. (London, 1968).

Kotkov, S. I. ed., *Vesti-Kuranty: 1600–1639 gg.* (Moscow, 1972).

ed., *Vesti-Kuranty: 1642–1644 gg.* (Moscow, 1976).

ed., *Vesti-Kuranty: 1645–1646, 1648 gg.* (Moscow, 1980).

ed., *Vesti-Kuranty: 1648–1650 gg.* (Moscow, 1983).

Kotoshikhin, G. K., *O Rossii v tsarstvovanie Alekseia Mikhailovicha: text and commentary*, ed. A. E. Pennington (Oxford, 1980).

Russia in the reign of Aleksei Mikhailovich, trans. B. P. Uroff, ed. M. Poe (Berlin, Warsaw, 2014).

La Sarraz du Franquesnay, J. de, *Le ministre public dans les cours étrangères: ses fonctions et ses prérogatives* (Amsterdam, 1731).

Latham, R., Matthews, W., eds., *The diary of Samuel Pepys: a new and complete transcription*, 11 vols. (London, 1970–1983).

Le Nouveau Mercure May-Juin 1717 (Paris, 1717).

Leibniz, G. W., 'Anhang, betreffend dasjenige, was nach heutigen Völker-Recht zu einem König erfordert wird', in *Leibnitz's deutsche Schriften*, ed. G. E. Guhrauer, 2 vols. (1838–1840), II, 303–12.

Le Père Furcy, 'Venu en France du Czar ou grand duc de Moscovie, son arrivée a Paris', *Bulletin de la Société de l'histoire de Paris et de l'Ile-de-France*, 18 (1891), 15–18.

Leti, G., *Il ceremoniale historico e politico*, 6 vols. (Amsterdam, 1685).

Letiche, J. M., Dmytryshyn, B., eds., *Russian statecraft: the Politika of Iurii Krizhanich* (Oxford, 1985).

Lever, E., *Baron de Breteuil: mémoires* (Paris, 1992).

Likhachev, D. S., ed., *Puteshestviia russkikh poslov XVI–XVII vv: stateinye spiski* (Moscow, 1954).

Loomie, A. J., *Ceremonies of Charles I: the notebooks of John Finet 1628–1641* (London, New York, 1987).

Lünig, J. C., *Grosser Herren, vornehmer Ministren und anderer berühmten Männer gehaltene Reden*, 6 vols. (Hamburg, Leipzig, 1722–1734).

Theatrum Ceremoniale Historico-Politicum, oder Historisch- und politischer Schau-Platz aller Ceremonien, 2 vols. (Leipzig, 1719–1720).

Madame de Maintenon [Françoise d'Aubigné, marquise de], *The letters of madam de Maintenon; and other eminent persons in the Age of Lewis XIV. To which are added, some characters* (London, 1753).

Lettres de Madame de Maintenon, vol. VI: 1714–1719, ed. J. Schillings (Paris, 2011).

Maier, I., ed., *Vesti-Kuranty: 1656 g., 1660–1662 gg., 1664–1670 gg: Chast' 2: Inostrannye originaly k russkim tekstam* (Moscow, 2008).

Maier, I., Moldovana, A. M., eds., *Vesti-Kuranty: 1656 g., 1660–1662 gg., 1664–1670 gg: Chast' 1: Russkie teksty* (Moscow, 2009).

Mercure Historique et Politique, vol. 2 (May 1687).

Mercurius publicus: comprising the sum of forraign intelligence; with the affairs now in agitation in England, Scotland, and Ireland, vol. 1 (1 January 1663).

Mémoires et lettres du maréchal de Tessé, contenant des anecdotes et des faits historiques inconnus, sur partie des règnes de Louis XIV et de Louis XV, ed. P.-H. de Grimoard, 2 vols. (Paris, 1806).

Miege, G., *A relation of three embassies from His Sacred Majestie Charles II to the great Duke of Muscovie, the King of Sweden, and the King of Denmark, performed by the Earl of Carlisle in the years 1663 and 1664* (London, 1669).

Milton, J., *A Brief History of Moscovia and other less-known countries lying eastward of Russia as far as Cathay. Gather'd from the writings of several eye witnesses* (London, 1682).

Moser, F. C. v., *Teutsches Hof-Recht*, 4 vols. (Frankfurt a. M., Leipzig, 1761).

Mottley, J., *The History of the Life of Peter I.*, 3 vols. (London, 1739).

Okenfuss, M. J., ed., *The travel diary of Peter Tolstoi: a Muscovite in early modern Europe* (DeKalb, 1987).

Olearius, A., *The voyages and travells of the ambassadors sent by Frederick, Duke of Holstein, to the Great Duke of Muscovy and the King of Persia begun in the year M.DC.XXXIII. and finish'd in M.DC.XXXIX*, trans. J. Davies (London, 1669).

'Otto Pleyer's allerunterthänigste Relation von dem jetzigen moscowitischen Regierungswesen 1710', in *Zeitgenössische Berichte zur Geschichte Russlands*, ed. E. Herrmann, 2 vols. (Leipzig, 1872–1880), I, 121–33.

Pamiatniki diplomaticheskikh snoshenii drevnei Rossii s derzhavami inostrannymi, 10 vols. (St Petersburg, 1851–1871).

Pecquet, A., *Discourse on the art of negotiation*, trans. A. Gruzinska, M. D. Sirkis (New York, NY 2005, first published in 1737 in French).

Philosophia Elegantiarum & Ceremoniarum Aulicarum (Frankfurt a. M., 1689).

Picard, B., ed., *Herberstein, Sigmund: description of Moscow and Muscovy, 1557* (London, 1969).

Pis'ma i bumagi imperatora Petra velikago, 13 vols. (St Peterburg, 1887–), VIII-X.

Pis'ma russkikh gosudarei i drugikh osob tsarskago semeistva. Vol. I: Perepiska Petra I s Ekaterinoiu Alekseevnoiu (Moscow, 1861).

Poe, M., *Early exploration of Russia*, 12 vols. (London, New York, 2003).

Pokhodnyi zhurnal: 1698, 2nd edn. (St Petersburg, 1911).

Polnoe sobranie zakonov rossiiskoi imperii, 45 vols. (St Petersburg, 1830), vols. I–VII, XI.

Prudovskii, P. I. *Rossiia i Prussiia v seredine XVII veka. Tom 1: Posol'skaia kniga po sviaziam Rossii s Brandenburgsko-Prusskim gosudarstvom 1649–1671 gg.* (Moscow, 2013).

Pufendorf, S. v., *An introduction to the history of the principal kingdoms and states of Europe by Samuel Puffendorf. Made English from the Original* (London, 1695).

The history of the kingdoms and states of Asia, Africa and America. Both ancient and modern, 6th edn. (London, 1736).

Recueil des instructions données aux ambassadeurs et ministres de France depuis les traités de Westphalie jusqu'à la Révolution française, vols. VIII–IX: *Russie, tome premiere, des origines jusqu'a 1748* (Paris, 1890).

Relation de ce qui s'est passé à Moscou de 5/16 fevrier 1710, le jour que sa majesté czar Pierre I, empereur de la Grande Russie, admit à l'audience publique son excellence monsier Charles Whitworth etc. (n.p., 1710).

Relation von der öffentlichen Audientz, welche Ihro Majestät der Königinn von Großbritanien ambassadeur Herr Charles Whitworth bey Ihro grossczarischen Majestät in Moskau den 5 Februar gehabt (n.p., 1710).

Ripa, C., *Iconologie où les principales choses qui peuvent tomber dans la pensée touchant les Vices et les Vertus*, trans. Jean Baudoin (Paris, 1643).

Rohr, J. B. v., *Einleitung zur Ceremoniel-Wissenschaft der Privat-Personen*, ed. G. Frühsorge (Weinheim, 1990, reprint of the 1728 edn.).

Einleitung zur Ceremoniel-Wissenschaft der Grossen Herren, ed. M. Schlechte (Leipzig, 1990, reprint of the 1733 edn.).

Roginskii, Z. I., *London 1645–1646 godov: novye istochniki o poezdke gontsa Gerasima Semenovicha Dokhturova v Angliiu* (Iaroslavl', 1960).

Poezdka gontsa Gerasima Semenovicha Dokhturova v Angliiu v 1645–1646 gg.: iz istorii anglo-russkikh otnoshenii v period angliiskoi revoliutsii XVII veka (Iaroslavl', 1959).

Rousset de Missy, J., *Le cérémonial diplomatique des cours de l'Europe (= Corps universel diplomatique du droit des gens, suppl. vols. 4–5)*, 2 vols. (Amsterdam, The Hague, 1739).

Mémoires sur le rang et la préséance entre les Souverains de l'Europe et entre leurs ministres représentans (Amsterdam, 1746).

Saint-Pierre, [C.-I. Castel, abbé de], *A project for settling an everlasting peace in Europe. First proposed by Henry IV. of France, and approved of by Queen Elizabeth, ... and now discussed at large, and made practicable by the Abbot St. Pierre* (London, 1714).

Projet de traité pour rendre la paix perpétuelle entre les souverains chrétiens (Utrecht, 1717).

Sbornik Imperatorskogo Russkogo istoricheskogo obshchestva, 148 vols. (St Petersburg, 1867–1916), vols. V, VI, XI, XX, XXV, XXXIV, XXXIX, XL, XLIX, L, LII, LVIII, LXI.

Sobranie gosudarstvennykh gramot i dogovorov, khraniashchikhsia v Gosudarstvennoi kollegii inostrannykh del, 5 vols. (Moscow, 1813–1894), vol. IV.

Schweder, C. H., *Theatrum historicum paetensionum et controversiarum illustrium in Europa, oder Historischer Schauplatz der Ansprüche und Streitigkeiten hoher Potentaten und anderer regierenden Herrschafften in Europa* (Leipzig, 1712).

Selden, J., *Titles of honor* (London, 1614).

Semevskii, M. I., ed., *Arkhiv kniazia F. A. Kurakina*, 10 vols. (St Petersburg, 1891–1902).

Shafirov, P. P., *A discourse concerning the just causes of the war between Sweden and Russia: 1700–1721* (Dobbs Ferry, NY, 1973).

Sharkova, I. S., ed., *Russkii diplomat vo Frantsii (zapiski Andreia Matveeva)* (Leningrad, 1972).

Shcherbachev, I. N., ed., *Zapiski Iusta Iulia datskago poslannika pri Petre Velikom (1709–1710)* (Moscow, 1900).

Stieve, G., *Europäisches Hoff-Ceremoniel, worinnen Nachricht gegeben wird, was für eine Beschaffenheit es habe mit der Prärogativ, und dem daraus fliessenden Ceremoniel* (Leipzig, 1715).

Europäisches Hof-Ceremoniel. Andere vermehrte Auflage (Leipzig, 1723).

Stosch, B. S. v., *Von dem Praecedentz= Oder Vorder=Recht aller Potentaten und Respubliquen in Europa: Samt einer sonderbaren Zugabe von der Hoheit des Ertz-Hertzoglichen Hauses Oesterreich* (Breßlau, 1677).

Sully, [M. de Béthune, duc de], *Sully's grand design of Henry IV. From the Memoirs as translated by Charlotte Lennox. With an introduction by David Ogg* (London, 1921).

'The relation of the Lord Culpepers reception at the emperiall Cittie of Mosco, and his Lopps quitting thereof, Anno Domini 1650', in *Correspondence of Sir Edward Nicholas, Secreatary of State*, ed. G. F. Warner, 4 vols. (London, 1886), I, pp. 182–85.

Theatri Europaei Continuati Funffzehender Theil / Das ist: Abermalige Außführliche Fortsetzung Denck- und Merckwürdigster Geschichten (Frankfurt a. M., 1707).

Thynne, F., *The perfect ambassadour treating of the antiquitie, priveledges, and behaviour of men belonging to that function* (London, 1652).

Tokmakov, I. F., 'Delo 1710 g. 21 marta po pis'mu kantslera grafa Golovkina o prisylke v S.-Peterburg, kuplennykh vo Frantsii i Gollandii doktorom Petrom Postnikovym knig', *Bibliograf*, 4 (1885), 75–81.

Tsarskii tituliarnik, ed. I. M. Eskina, 2 vols. (Moscow, 2007).

Vedomosti vremeni Petra Velikogo. Vypusk vtoroi: 1708–1709 gg. (Moscow, 1906).

Vattel, E. de, *Le droit des gens, ou Principes de la loi naturelle, appliqués à la conduite et aux affaires des nations et des souverains*, 3 vols. (Paris, 1820, first published 1758).

Vera y Figueroa, J. A. de, *Le parfait ambassadeur*, trans. N. Lancelot (Paris, 1642).

Vinogradoff, I., 'Russian missions to London, 1569–1687: seven accounts by the masters of the ceremonies', *Oxford Slavonic Papers, New Series*, 14 (1981), 36–72.

Voltaire, *The works of Voltaire: a contemporary version*, trans. W. F. Fleming, 22 vols. (New York, 1901), XII (*Age of Louis XIV*), XVIII (*History of the Russian empire under Peter the Great*).

Vomperskii, V. P., ed., *Vesti-Kuranty: 1651–1652 gg., 1654–1656 gg., 1658–1660 gg.* (Moscow, 1996).

VVee have brought our hogges to a faire market; with some remembrances of the estates and conditions of the Church, King, kingdome, Parliament, Armie, and citie of London. And the one, and onely way to cure all our miseries described (London, 1648).

Weber, F. C., *Des veränderten Rußlandes zweyther Theil, worinnen die Folge derfenigen wichtigen Veränderungen, welche der Rußische Kayser Petrus der Erste zur Aufnahme seines Reichs in allen Ständen vorgenommen* (Hanover, 1739).

Whitlocke, B., *A journal of the Swedish ambassy, in the years M.DC.LIII. and M. DC.LIV. from the Commonwealth of England, Scotland, and Ireland*, 2 vols. (London, 1772).

Wicquefort, A. de, *L' ambassadeur et ses fonctions* (The Hague, 1681).

The embassador and his functions, trans. M. Digby (London, 1716, reprint, Leicester 1997).

Winterfeld, F. W. v., *Teutsche und Ceremonial-Politica*, 3 vols. (Frankfurt a. M., Leipzig, 1700).

Wickhart, C. V., *Moscowittische Reiss-Beschreibung* (Vienna, c. 1675–76).

Zedler, J. H., *Grosses vollständiges Universal Lexicon aller Wissenschafften und Künste, welche bisshero durch menschlichen Verstand und Witz erfunden und verbessert worden*, 64 + 4 suppl. vols. (Halle, Leipzig, 1732–1754).

Zschackwitz, J. E., *Einleitung zu denen vornehmsten Rechts-Ansprüchen derer gecrönten hohen Häupter und anderer Souverainen in Europa*, 3 vols. (Frankfurt a. M., Leipzig, 1733–1735).

Zwantzig, Z., *Theatrum Praecedentiae oder Eines Theils Illustrer Rang-Streit* (Berlin, 1706).

Secondary Literature

Adair, E. R., *The extraterritoriality of ambassadors in the sixteenth and seventeenth centuries* (London, New York, 1929).

Adams, R., Cox, R., eds. *Diplomacy and early modern culture* (Basingstoke, 2011).

Ageeva, O. G., *Diplomaticheskii tseremonial imperatorskoi Rossii. XVIII vek.* (Moscow, 2012).

Evropeizatsiia russkogo dvora 1700–1796 gg. (Moscow, 2006).

'Imperskii status Rossii: k istorii politicheskogo mentaliteta russkogo obshchestva nachala XVIII veka', in *Tsar' i tsarstvo v russkom obshchestvennom soznanii*, ed. A. A. Gorskii (Moscow, 1999), pp. 112–40.

'Prazdniki v chest' poltavskoi pobedy v XVII v.', in *Poltava: k 300-letiiu poltavskogo srazheniia: sbornik statei*, ed. O. G. Ageeva (Moscow, 2009), pp. 257–73.

Alef, G., 'The adoption of the Muscovite two-headed eagle: a discordant view', *Speculum*, 41 (1966), 1–21.

Aleksandrenko, V. N., *Russkie diplomaticheskie agenty v Londone v XVIII v.*, 2 vols. (Warsaw, 1897).

Alewyn, R., *Das grosse Welttheater. Die Epoche der höfischen Feste in Dokument und Deutung* (Hamburg, 1959).

Alpatov, M. A., 'Chto znal Posol'skii prikaz o Zapadnoi Evrope vo vtoroi polovine XVII v.', in *Istoriia i istoriki. Istoriografiia vseobshchei istorii*, ed. M. A. Alpatov (Moscow, 1966), pp. 89–129.

Altbauer, D., 'The diplomats of Peter the Great', *Jahrbücher für Geschichte Osteuropas*, 28 (1980), 1–16.

Althoff, G., 'The variability of rituals in the Middle Ages', in *Medieval concepts of the past: ritual, memory, historiography*, ed. G. Althoff, J. Fried, G. Patrick (Cambridge, 2002), pp. 71–87.

Amburger, E., 'Das diplomatische Personal des russischen auswärtigen Dienstes unter Peter I.', in *Das Vergangene und die Geschichte. Festschrift für Reinhard Wittram zum 70. Geburtstag*, ed. R. v. Thadden, G. v. Pistohlkors, H. Weiss (Göttingen, 1973), pp. 298–311.

Geschichte der Behördenorganisation Russlands von Peter dem Grossen bis 1917 (Leiden, 1966).

Anderson, M. S., *Britain's discovery of Russia, 1553–1815* (London, 1958).

'English views of Russia in the Age of Peter the Great', *American Slavic and East European Review*, 13 (1954), 200–14.

'English views of Russia in the 17th century', *Slavonic and East European Review*, 33 (1954), 140–60.

The origins of the modern European state system, 1494–1618 (London, 1998).

Peter the Great, 2nd edn. (Harlow, 1995).

The rise of modern diplomacy, 1450–1919 (London, 1993).

Anisimov, E. V., 'The imperial heritage of Peter the Great in the foreign policy of his early successors', in *Imperial Russian foreign policy*, ed. H. Ragsdale, V. N. Ponomarev (Cambridge, New York, 1993), pp. 21–35.

Arel, M. S., 'Masters in their own house: the Russian merchant elite and complaints against the English in the first half of the seventeenth century', *Slavonic and East European Review*, 77 (1999), 401–47.

Arkhangel'skii, C. I., 'Diplomaticheskie agenty Kromvelia v peregovorakh s Moskvoi', *Istoricheskie Zapiski*, 5 (1939), 118–40.

Armitage, D., *Foundations of modern international thought* (Cambridge, 2013).

Augustynowicz, C., '"Ablegations-negocien von keiner erhöblichkeit?": Wirken und Wirkung der Moskauer Grossgesandtschaft in Wien 1687', *Mitteilungen des Österreichischen Staatsarchivs*, 50 (2003), 43–63.

Babkova, G. O., 'Mezhdunarodnoe pravo v ugolovno-pravovoi doktrine Ekatariny II', *Novyi Istoricheskii Vestnik*, 14 (2006), 90–98.

Backus, O. P., 'Was Muscovite Russia imperialistic?', *American Slavic and East European Review*, 13 (1954), 522–34.

Baehr, S. L., 'From history to national myth: translatio imperii in eighteenth-century Russia', *Russian Review*, 37 (1978), 1–13.

Bantysh-Kamenskii, N. N., *Obzor vneshnikh snoshenii Rossii (po 1800 god)*, 4 vols. (Moscow, 1894–1902).

Barany, G., *The Anglo-Russian entente cordiale of 1697–1698: Peter I and William III at Utrecht* (Boulder, 1986).

Barker, J. C., *The abuse of diplomatic privileges and immunities: a necessary evil?* (Aldershot, 1996).

Barth, V., *Inkognito: Geschichte eines Zeremoniells* (Munich, 2013).

Baron, S. H., 'Die Ursprünge der Nemeckaja Sloboda', in *Deutsche und Deutschland aus russischer Sicht. 11–17. Jahrhundert (1)*, ed. D. Herrmann (Munich, 1989), pp. 217–37.

'Herberstein's image of Russia and its transmission through later writings', in *Siegmund von Herberstein: Kaiserlicher Gesandter und Begründer der Russlandkunde und die europäische Diplomatie*, ed. G. Pferschy (Graz, 1989), 245–79.

Bartlett, R. P., *A history of Russia* (Basingstoke, 2005).

Bauer, V., *Die höfische Gesellschaft in Deutschland von der Mitte des 17. bis zum Ausgang des 18. Jahrhunderts: Versuch einer Typologie* (Tübingen, 1993).

Hofökonomie: der Diskurs über den Fürstenhof in Zeremonialwissenschaft, Hausväterliteratur und Kameralismus (Vienna, Cologne, Weimar, 1997).

Bayreuther, M., 'Pferde in der Diplomatie der frühen Neuzeit', in *Materielle Grundlagen der Diplomatie: Schenken, Sammeln und Verhandeln in Spätmittelalter und Früher Neuzeit*, ed. M. Häberlein, C. Jeggle (Konstanz, 2012), pp. 227–56.

Behringer, W., *Im Zeichen des Merkur: Reichspost und Kommunikationsrevolution in der Frühen Neuzeit* (Göttingen, 2003).

Bell, C. M., *Ritual theory, ritual practice*, 2nd edn. (Oxford, 2009).

Belokurov, S. A., *O Posol'skom prikaze* (Moscow, 1906).

Bély, L., *Espions et ambassadeurs au temps de Louis XIV* (Paris, 1990).

Les relations internationales en Europe: (XVIIe – XVIIIe siècles) (Paris, 1992).

'Souveraineté et souverain: La question du cérémonial dans les relations internationales à l'époque moderne', *Annuaire-Bulletin de la Société de l'Histoire de France* (1993), 27–43.

La société des princes: XVIe–XVIIIe siècle (Paris, 1999).

'La négociation comme idéal et comme art: un modèle westphalian?', in *L'Europe des traités de Westphalie: esprit de la diplomatie et diplomatie de l'esprit*, ed. L. Bély, I. Richefort (Paris, 2000), pp. 604–12.

L'art de la paix en Europe: naissance de la diplomatie moderne, XVIe–XVIIIe siècle (Paris, 2007).

Benzoni, G., 'Ranke's favourite source: the relazioni of the Venetian ambassadors', *The Courier*, 22 (1987), 11–26.

Berger, S., Miller, A., eds. *Nationalizing empires* (Budapest, 2015).

Berelowitch, A., *La hiérarchie des égaux: la noblesse russe d'Ancien Régime (XVIe–XVIIe siècles)* (Paris, 2001).

Berkowitz, D. S., *John Selden's formative years: politics and society in early seventeenth-century England* (Washington, DC, 1988).

Berriedale, K., 'The extraterritoriality of ambassadors', *Journal of Comparative Legislation and International Law*, 12 (1930), 126–28.

Berry, L. E., Crummey, R. O., eds., *Rude & barbarous kingdom: Russia in the accounts of sixteenth-century English voyagers* (Madison, 1968).

Binello, E., *Muscovite politics and culture in the sixteenth and seventeenth centuries through the eyes of foreign travellers* (London, 1996).

Billington, J. H., 'The projection of power', in *Gifts to the Tsars, 1500–1700: Treasures from the Kremlin*, ed. B. Shifman, G. Walton (New York, 2001), pp. 11–19.

Bittner, L. et al., *Repertorium der diplomatischen Vertreter aller Länder seit dem Westfälischen Frieden, 1648*, 2 vols. (Oldenburg, Berlin, Zurich, 1936/1965).

Black, J., 'Russia's rise as a European power, 1650–1750', in *Russia and Europe*, ed. P. Dukes (London, 1991), pp. 69–83.

British diplomats and diplomacy 1688–1800 (Exeter, 2001).

European international relations, 1648–1815 (Basingstoke, 2002).

Great powers and the quest for hegemony: the world order since 1500 (London, 2008).

A history of diplomacy (London, 2010).

Blanning, T. C. W., *The culture of power and the power of culture: old regime Europe 1660–1789* (Oxford, 2003).

The pursuit of glory: Europe, 1648–1815 (London, 2008).

Blome, A., *Das deutsche Russlandbild im frühen 18. Jahrhundert: Untersuchungen zur zeitgenössischen Presseberichterstattung über Russland unter Peter I* (Wiesbaden, 2000).

'"Die Zeitungen sind der Grund, die Anweisungen und Richtschnur aller Klugheit . . .": Zu den Grundlagen der Rußlandhistoriographie im 17. und 18. Jahrhundert', in *Die Kenntnis Rußlands im deutschsprachigen Raum im 18. Jahrhundert: Wissenschaft und Publizistik über das Russische Reich*, ed. D. Dahlmann (Bonn, 2006), pp. 25–41.

Bogatyrev, S., *The sovereign and his counsellors: ritualised consultations in Muscovite political culture, 1350s-1570s* (Helsinki, 2000).

Boeck, B. J., *Imperial boundaries: Cossack communities and empire building in the age of Peter the Great* (Cambridge, 2009).

Bogoslovskii, M. M., *Petr I: materialy dlia biografii*, 5 vols. (Moscow, 1940–1948).

Bohlen, A., 'Changes in Russian diplomacy under Peter the Great', *Cahiers du Monde Russe et Soviétique*, 7 (1966), 341–58.

Bonney, R., *The European dynastic states, 1494–1660* (Oxford, 1991).

'The European Reaction to the Trial and Execution of Charles I', in *The Regicides and the Execution of the Charles I*, ed. J. Peacey (Basingstoke, 2001), 247–79.

Boppe, A., *Les Introducteurs des ambassadeurs. 1585–1900* (Paris, 1901).

Boterbloem, K., 'Russia and Europe: The Koenraad van Klenk Embassy to Moscow (1675–76)', *Journal of Early Modern History*, 14 (2010), 187–217.

Moderniser of Russia: Andrei Vinius, 1641–1716 (Basingstoke, (2013).

Bourdieu, P., *Language and symbolic power*, trans. G. Raymond, M. Adamson, (Cambridge, MA, 1991).

The logic of practice, trans. R. Nice, (Cambridge, 1992, reprint, 1999).

Braddick, M. J., 'Administrative performance: the representation of political authority in early modern England', in *Negotiating power in early modern society: order, hierarchy and subordination in Britain and Ireland*, ed. M. J. Braddick, J. Walter (Cambridge, 2001), pp. 166–87.

God's fury, England's fire: a new history of the English Civil Wars (London, 2008).

Brauner, C., 'Ein Schlüssel für zwei Truhen: Diplomatie als interkulturelle Praxis am Beispiel einer westafrikanischen Gesandtschaft nach Frankreich (1670–71)', *Historische Anthropologie*, 21 (2013), 199–226.

Kompanien, Könige und caboceers. Interkulturelle Diplomatie an Gold- und Sklavenküste, 17.-18. Jahrhundert (Cologne, 2015).

Brikner, A. G., *Istoriia Petra Velikogo* (Moscow, 2007, first published 1882).

Brown, P. B., 'How Muscovy governed: seventeenth-century Russian central administration', *Russian History*, 36 (2009), 459–529.

Brückner, J., *Staatswissenschaften, Kameralismus und Naturrecht: ein Beitrag zur Geschichte der politischen Wissenschaft in Deutschland des späten 17. und frühen 18. Jahrhunderts* (Munich, 1977).

Buelow, G. J., *A history of baroque music* (Bloomington, IN, 2004).

Burke, P., *The fabrication of Louis XIV* (New Haven, London, 1992).

Burschel, P., 'Der Sultan und das Hündchen. Zur politischen Ökonomie des Schenkens in interkultureller Perspektive', *Historische Anthropologie*, 15 (2007), 408–21.

Burschel, P., Vogel, C., eds., *Die Audienz: ritualisierter Kulturkontakt in der Frühen Neuzeit* (Cologne, 2014).

Bushkovitch, P., *The merchants of Moscow, 1580–1650* (Cambridge, 1980).

'The epiphany ceremony of the Russian court in the sixteenth and seventeenth centuries', *Russian Review*, 49 (1990), 1–17.

'Power and the historian: The case of Tsarevich Aleksei 1716–1718 and N. G. Ustrialov 1845–1859', *Proceedings of the American Philosophical Society*, 141 (1997), 177–212.

Peter the Great: the struggle for power, 1671–1725 (Cambridge, 2001).

'Change and culture in early modern Russia', *Kritika: explorations in Russian and Eurasian history*, 16 (2015), 291–316.

Butler, W. E., 'Anglo-Russian diplomacy and the law of nations', in *Great Britain and Russia in the eighteenth century: contacts and comparisons: proceedings of an international conference held at the University of East Anglia, Norwich, England, 11–15 July 1977*, ed. A. G. Cross (Newtonville, 1979), pp. 296–305.

'On the Origins of International Legal Science in Russia', *Journal of the History of International Law/Revue d'Histoire du droit international*, 4 (2002), 1–41.

Butterfield, H., 'Diplomacy', in *Studies in diplomatic history: essays in memory of David Bayne Horn*, ed. R. Hatton, M. S. Anderson (London, 1970), pp. 357–72.

Cannadine, D., 'The context, performance and meaning of ritual: the British monarchy and the "invention of tradition", c. 1820–1977', in *The invention of tradition*, ed. E. J. Hobsbawm, T. O. Ranger (Cambridge, 1983, reprint, 1984), pp. 101–64.

'Introduction: divine rites of kings', in *Rituals of royalty: power and ceremonial in traditional societies*, ed. D. Cannadine, S. R. F. Price (Cambridge, 1987), pp. 1–19.

Caporaso, J. A., 'Changes in the Westphalian order: territory, public authority, and sovereignty', *International Studies Review*, 2 (2000), 1–28.

Carrió-Invernizzi, D., 'Gift and diplomacy in seventeenth-century Spanish Italy', *Historical Journal*, 51 (2008), 881–99.

Chakrabarty, D., *Provincializing Europe: postcolonial thought and historical difference* (Princeton, NJ, Oxford, 2000).

Chistiakova, E. V., Rogozhin, N. M., *'Oko vsei velikoi Rossii': ob istorii russkoi diplomaticheskoi sluzhby 'XVI-XVII' vekov* (Moscow, 1989).

Civ'jan, T. V., 'Etiquette as a semiotic system', in *Soviet semiotics: an anthology*, ed. D. P. Lucid (Baltimore, London, 1977), pp. 103–05.

Clark, C., *Iron kingdom: the rise and downfall of Prussia, 1600–1947* (London, 2006).

'When culture meets power: the Prussian coronation of 1701', in *Cultures of power in Europe during the long eighteenth century: essays in honour of T. C. W. Blanning*, ed. H. M. Scott, B. Simms (Cambridge, 2007), pp. 14–35.

Colegrove, K., 'Diplomatic procedure preliminary to the congress of Westphalia', *American Journal of International Law*, 13 (1919), 450–82.

Collyer, D. A., 'Notes on the diplomatic correspondence between England and Russia in the first half of the eighteenth century', *Transactions of the Royal Historical Society*, New Series, 14 (1900), 143–74.

Conrad-Lütt, B., 'Hochachtung und Mißtrauen: Aus den Berichten der Diplomaten des Moskauer Staates', in *Deutsche und Deutschland aus russischer Sicht, 11.-17. Jahrhundert* (1), ed. D. Herrmann (Munich, 1989), pp. 149–78.

Corfield, P. J., 'Ehrerbietung und Dissens in der Kleidung. Zum Wandel der Bedeutung des Hutes und des Hutziehens', in *Zum Wandel von Zeremoniell und Gesellschaftsritualen in der Zeit der Aufklärung*, ed. K. Gerteis (Hamburg, 1992), pp. 5–19.

Cracraft, J., *The revolution of Peter the Great* (Cambridge, MA, London, 2003).

Croskey, R. M., *Muscovite diplomatic practice in the reign of Ivan III* (New York, London, 1987).

Cross, A. G., *Peter the Great through British eyes: perceptions and representations of the tsar since 1698* (Cambridge, 2000).

Croxton, D., 'The Peace of Westphalia of 1648 and the origins of sovereignty', *International History Review*, 21 (1999), 569–91.

Crummey, R. O., *Aristocrats and servitors: the boyar elite in Russia, 1613–1689* (Princeton, NJ, 1983).

'Court spectacles in seventeenth-century Russia: illusion and reality', in *Essays in Honor of A. A. Zimin*, ed. D. C. Waugh (Columbus, 1985), pp. 130–58.

Cvetkovski, R., *Modernisierung durch Beschleunigung: Raum und Mobilität im Zarenreich* (Frankfurt a. M., 2006).

Daniel, U., 'Überlegungen zum höfischen Fest der Barockzeit', *Niedersächsisches Jahrbuch für Landesgeschichte*, 72 (2000), 45–66.

Darwin, J., *After Tamerlane: the global history of empire since 1405* (London, 2008).

Davidson, P., *The universal Baroque* (Manchester, 2007).

Davies, B. L., *Warfare, state and society on the Black Sea steppe: 1500–1700* (London, 2007).

Davies, N., *Europe: a history* (Oxford, 1996).

Delanty, G., *Formations of European modernity: a historical and political sociology of Europe* (Basingstoke, 2013).

Dickmann, F., *Der Westfälische Frieden* (Münster, 1959).

Dixon, S., *The modernisation of Russia 1676–1825* (Cambridge, 1999).

Doerries, H., *Russlands Eindringen in Europa in der Epoche Peters des Grossen: Studien zur zeitgenössischen Publizistik und Staatenkunde* (Königsberg, Berlin, 1939).

Dolgova, S. R., 'Pervaia russkaia gazeta "Vedomosti" o diplomaticheskikh sviaziakh i tseremoniale v Rossiiskom gosudarstve', in *Representatsiia vlasti v posol'skom tseremoniale i diplomaticheskii dialog v XV – pervoi treti XVIII veka. Tret'ia mezhdunarodnaia nauchnaia konferentsiia tsikla 'Inozemtsy v Moskovskom gosudarstve', posviashchennaia 200-letiiu Muzeev Moskovskogo Kremlia. Tezisy dokladov*, ed. A. K. Levykin, V. D. Nazarov (Moscow, 2006), pp. 41–44.

Draper, J. W., 'Shakespeare and Muscovy', *The Slavonic and East European Review*, 33 (1954), 217–21.

Duchhardt, H., 'Das diplomatische Abschiedsgeschenk', *Archiv für Kulturgeschichte*, 57 (1975), 345–62.

'Imperium und Regna im Zeitalter Ludwigs XIV.', *Historische Zeitschrift*, 232 (1981), 555–81.

Balance of Power und Pentarchie: internationale Beziehungen 1700–1785 (Paderborn, 1997).

'"Westphalian System". Zur Problematik einer Denkfigur', *Historische Zeitschrift*, 269 (1999), 305–15.

'Die Formationsphase der Wissenschaft von den internationalen Beziehungen: Christian Gottfried Hofmanns Entwurff einer Einleitung zu dem Erkänntniß des gegenwärtigen Zustandes von Europa von 1720', in *Formen internationaler Beziehungen in der Frühen Neuzeit: Frankreich und das Alte Reich im europäischen Staatensystem: Festschrift für Klaus Malettke zum 65. Geburtstag*, ed. S. Externbrink, J. Ulbert (Berlin, 2001), pp. 37–42.

'Peace treaties from Westphalia to the revolutionary era', in *Peace treaties and international law in European history: from the late Middle Ages to World War One*, ed. R. Lesaffer (Cambridge, 2004), pp. 45–58.

Duindam, J. *Myths of power: Norbert Elias and the early modern European court* (Amsterdam, 1994).

'Ceremonial staffs and paperwork at two courts: France and the Habsburg monarchy ca. 1550–1720', in *Hofgesellschaft und Höflinge an europäischen Fürstenhöfen in der* Frühen *Neuzeit (15.–18. Jh.)*, ed. K. Malettke, C. Grell (Münster, 2001), pp. 369–88.

Vienna and Versailles: the courts of Europe's dynastic rivals, 1550–1780 (Cambridge, 2003).

'Early modern court studies: an overview and a proposal', in *Historiographie an europäischen Höfen (16. – 18. Jahrhundert): Studien zum Hof als Produktionsort von Geschichtsschreibung und historischer Repräsentation*, ed. M. Völkel, A. Strohmeyer (Berlin, 2009), pp. 37–60.

Dynasties: a global history of power, 1300–1800 (Cambridge, 2016).

Dukes, P., *The making of Russian absolutism 1613–1801* (London, New York, 1982).

'Paul Menzies and his mission from Muscovy to Rome, 1672–1674', *The Innes Review*, 35 (1984), 88–95.

'The Thirty Years' War, the Smolensk War and the modernization of international relations in Europe', in *Modernizing Muscovy: reform and social change in seventeenth-century Russia*, ed. J. Kotilaine, M. Poe (London, New York, 2004), pp. 203–22.

Dukes, P. Herd, G. P., Kotilaine, J., *Stuarts and Romanovs: the rise and fall of a special relationship* (Dundee, 2009).

Eekman, T., 'Muscovy's international relations in the late seventeenth century: Johan van Keller's observations', *California Slavic Studies*, 14 (1992), 44–67.

Ehalt, H. C., *Ausdrucksformen absolutistischer Herrschaft: der Wiener Hof im 17. und 18. Jahrhundert* (Munich, 1980).

Elias, N., *Die höfische Gesellschaft: Untersuchungen zur Soziologie des Königtums und der Aristokratie mit einer Einleitung: Soziologie und Geschichtswissenschaft* (Neuwied, Berlin, 1969).

Evans, R. J., *Cosmopolitan islanders: British historians and the European continent* (Cambridge, 2009).

Evreinov, V. A., *Grazhdanskoe chinoproizvodstvo v Rossii: istoricheskii ocherk* (St Petersburg, 1888).

Externbrink, S., 'Internationale Politik in der Frühen Neuzeit. Stand und Perspektiven der Forschung zu Diplomatie und Staatensystem', in *Geschichte der Politik: Alte und neue Wege (Historische Zeitschrift, Beiheft 44)*, ed. H.-C. Kraus, T. Nicklas (Munich, 2007), pp. 15–39.

Falcke, J., *Studien zum diplomatischen Geschenkwesen am brandenburgisch-preussischen Hof im 17. und 18. Jahrhundert* (Berlin, 2006).

Filiushkin, A. I., 'Problema genezisa Rossiiskoi imperii', in *Novaia imperskaia istoriia postsovetskogo prostranstva: Sbornik statei*, ed. I. V. Gerasimov et al. (Kazan, 2004), pp. 375–408.

Tituly russkikh gosudarei (Moscow, St Petersburg, 2006).

Fletcher, C., *Diplomacy in Renaissance Rome: the rise of the resident ambassador* (Cambridge, 2015).

Flier, M. S., 'Breaking the code: the image of the tsar in the Muscovite Palm Sunday ritual', in *Medieval Russian culture*, ed. M. S. Flier, D. B. Rowland (Berkeley, CA, 1994), pp. 213–42.

'Political ideas and rituals', in *The Cambridge history of Russia*, ed. M. Perrie, D. C. B. Lieven, R. G. Suny, 3 vols. (Cambridge, 2006), I, pp. 387–408.

Floria, B. N., *Russkoe gosudarstvo i ego zapadnye sosedi: 1655–1661 gg.* (Moscow, 2010).

Vneshnepoliticheskaia programma A. L. Ordina-Nashchokina i popytki ee osushchestvleniia (Moscow, 2013).

Franklin, S., 'Printing Moscow: significances of the Frontispiece to the 1663 Bible', *Slavonic and East European Review*, 88 (2010), 73–95.

Frey, L., Frey, M., 'The reign of the charlatans is over: the French revolutionary attack on diplomatic practice', *Journal of Modern History*, 65 (1993), 706–44.

The history of diplomatic immunity (Columbus, 1999).

Frigo, D., ed., *Politics and diplomacy in early modern Italy: the structure of diplomatic practice, 1450–1800*, trans. A. Belton (Cambridge, 2000).

Frötschner, R., Kämpfer, F., eds., *450 Jahre Sigismund von Herbersteins Rerum Moscoviticarum Commentarii: 1549–1999* (Wiesbaden, 2002).

Frühsorge, G., 'Vom Hof des Kaisers zum "Kaiserhof": Über das Ende des Ceremoniells als gesellschaftliches Ordnungsmuster', *Euphorion*, 78 (1984), 237–65.

Füssel, M., *Gelehrtenkultur als symbolische Praxis: Rang, Ritual und Konflikt an der Universität der frühen Neuzeit* (Darmstadt, 2006).

Gantet, C., *Guerre, paix et construction des états, 1618–1714* (Paris, 2003).

Garnier, C., '"Wer meinen Herrn ehrt, den ehre ich billig auch". Symbolische Kommunikationsformen bei Gesandtenempfängen am Moskauer Hof im 16. und 17. Jahrhundert', *Jahrbuch für Kommunikationsgeschichte*, 7 (2005), 27–51.

Geertz, C., *The Interpretation of Cultures* (New York, 1973, reprint, 2000).

'Local knowledge: fact and law in comparative perspective', in *Local knowledge: further essays in interpretive anthropology by Clifford Geertz* (New York, 1983), pp. 167–234.

van Gelder, M., Krstić, T., 'Cross-confessional diplomacy and diplomatic intermediaries in the early modern Mediterranean', *Journal of Early Modern History*, 19 (2015) (special issue).

Gestrich, A., *Absolutismus und Öffentlichkeit: politische Kommunikation in Deutschland zu Beginn des 18. Jahrhunderts* (Göttingen, 1994).

'Höfisches Zeremoniell und sinnliches Volk. Die Rechtfertigung des Hofzeremoniells im 17. und frühen 18. Jahrhundert', in *Zeremoniell als höfische Ästhetik in Spätmittelalter und Früher Neizeit*, ed. J. J. Berns, T. Rahn (Tübingen, 1995), 57–73.

Geyer, D., 'Peter und Petersburg', *Jahrbücher für Geschichte Osteuropas*, 10 (1962), 181–200.

Goloubeva, M., *The glorification of Emperor Leopold I in image, spectacle and text* (Mainz, 2000).

Grabar, V. E., *The history of international law in Russia, 1647–1917: a bio-bibliographical study*, trans. W. E. Butler (Oxford, 1990).

Greenblatt, S., *Marvelous possessions: the wonder of the New World* (Oxford, 1991).

Greenfeld, L., *Nationalism: five roads to modernity* (Cambridge, MA, London, 1992).

Greyerz, K. v., *England im Jahrhundert der Revolutionen 1603–1714* (Stuttgart, 1994).

Griep, W., Krahé, F., *Ausstellungskatalog 'Peter der Große in Westeuropa': die grosse Gesandtschaft 1697–1698 [Ausstellung 'Schätze aus dem Kreml – Peter der Große in Westeuropa']* (Bremen, 1991).

Grönebaum, F., *Frankreich in Ost- und Nordeuropa* (Wiesbaden, 1968).

Guerrier, V. I., *Leibniz in seinen Beziehungen zu Russland und Peter dem Grossen: eine geschichtliche Darstellung dieses Verhältnisses nebst den darauf bezüglichen Briefen und Denkschriften* (St Petersburg, Leipzig, 1873).

Gus'kov, A. G., *Velikoe Posol'stvo Petra I: Istochnikovedcheskoe issledovanie* (Moscow, 2005).

Guzevich, D. Iu., Guzevich, I. D., *Pervoe Evropeiskoe puteshestvie tsaria Petra: analiticheskaia bibliografiia za tri stoletiia, 1697–2006* (St Petersburg, 2008).

Velikoe posol'stvo: Rubezh epokh, ili Nachalo puti: 1697–1698 (St Petersburg, 2008).

Velikoe posol'stvo (St Petersburg, 2003).

Häberlein, M., Jeggle, C., eds., *Materielle Grundlagen der Diplomatie: Schenken, Sammeln und Verhandeln in Spätmittelalter und Früher Neuzeit* (Konstanz, 2013).

Habermas, J., *The structural transformation of the public sphere: an inquiry into a category of bourgeois society*, trans. T. Burger, 2nd edn. (Cambridge, 1992).

Hahn, P.-M., Schütte, U., 'Thesen zur Rekonstruktion höfischer Zeichensysteme in der Frühen Neuzeit', *Mitteilungen der Residenzen-Kommission der Akademie der Wissenschaften zu Göttingen*, 13 (2003), 19–47.

Halecki, O., 'Imperialism in Slavic and East European history', *American Slavic and East European Review*, 11 (1952), 1–26.

Halperin, C. J., 'Sixteenth-century foreign travel accounts to Muscovy: a methodological excursus', *Sixteeenth-Century Journal*, 6 (1975), 89–111.

Hampton, T., *Fictions of embassy: literature and diplomacy in early modern Europe* (Ithaca, NY, 2009).

Hartley, J. M., *Charles Whitworth: diplomat in the age of Peter the Great* (Aldershot, 2002).

'A clash of cultures? An Anglo-Russian encounter in the early eighteenth century', in *Russian society and culture and the long eighteenth century: essays in honour of Anthony G. Cross*, ed. R. P. Bartlett, L. A. J. Hughes (Münster, 2004), pp. 48–61.

Hartmann, P. C., 'Zum Gesandtschaftszeremoniell an den Höfen von München, Wien, Madrid und Versailles im 18. Jahrhundert', in *Études d'histoire européene. Mélanges offerts à René et Suzanne Pillorget* (Angers, 1990), pp. 149–57.

Hartshorne, C., Weiss, P., eds., *Collected papers of Charles Sanders Peirce*, 6 vols. (Cambridge, MA, 1974).

Hasselblat, A. T., 'Otto Pleyer, der erste förmlich accreditierte östereichische Diplomat am russischen Hofe, 1692–1719', *Russische Revue. Monatsschrift für die Kunde Rußlands*, 7 (1875), 281–435.

Haug, T., *Ungleiche Außenbeziehungen und grenzüberschreitende Patronage: die französische Krone und die geistlichen Kurfürsten (1648–1679)* (Cologne, 2015).

Haumann, H., 'Dracula und die Vampire Osteuropas. Zur Entstehung eines Mythos', *Zeitschrift für Siebenbürgische Landeskunde*, 28 (2005), 1–17.

Heal, F., *The power of gifts: gift-exchange in early modern England* (Oxford, 2014).

Hellie, R., *The economy and material culture of Russia, 1600–1725* (Chicago, London, 1999).

Hellmann, M., 'Die Friedensschlüsse von Nystad (1721) und Teschen (1779) als Etappen des Vordringens Russlands nach Europa', *Historisches Jahrbuch*, 97/98 (1978), 270–88.

Hengerer, M., 'Die Zeremonialprotokolle und weitere Quellen zum Zeremoniell des Kaiserhofes im Wiener Haus-, Hof- und Staatsarchiv', in *Quellenkunde der Habsburgermonarchie (16.–18. Jahrhundert). Ein exemplarisches Handbuch*, ed. J. Pauser, M. Scheutz, T. Winkelbauer (Vienna, Munich, 2004), pp. 76–93.

Hennings, J., 'The semiotics of diplomatic dialogue: pomp and circumstance in Tsar Peter I's visit to Vienna in 1698', *International History Review*, 30 (2008), 515–44.

'The failed gift: ceremony and gift-giving in Anglo-Russian relations (1662–1664)', in *International diplomacy. Volume I: Institutions*, ed. I. Neumann, H. Leira (London, 2013), pp. 91–110.

'Diplomacy, culture and space: the Muscovite court', in *Beyond Scylla and Charybdis. European Courts and Court Residences outside Habsburg and Valois/Bourbon Territories 1500–1700*, ed. B. B. Johannsen, K. A. Ottenheym (Odense, 2015), pp. 56–63.

'"A perfect relation of the reception, audience, and dispatch, of all ambassadors from foreign princes, sent unto the emperour of all Russia": Pristav, Master of ceremonies und die Dokumentation des frühneuzeitlichen Gesandtschaftsrituals in vergleichender Perspektive', in *Interkulturelle Ritualpraxis in der Vormoderne: Diplomatische Interaktion an den östlichen Grenzen der Fürstengesellschaft (Zeitschrift für Historische Forschung, Beiheft 52)*, ed. C. Garnier, C. Vogel (Berlin, 2016), 69–92.

Hinsley, F. H., *Power and the pursuit of peace: theory and practice in the history of relations between states* (Cambridge, 1963).

Holmes, C., 'The trial and execution of Charles I', *Historical Journal*, 53 (2010), 289–316.

Horn, D. B., 'Rank and emolument in the British diplomatic service 1689–1789', *Transactions of the Royal Historical Society*, 5th Series, 9 (1959), 19–49.

Hughes, L. A. J., 'The Moscow armoury and innovations in seventeenth-century Muscovite art', *Canadian-American Slavic Studies*, 13 (1979), 204–23.

Russia and the West: the life of a seventeenth-century westernizer, Prince Vasily Vasil'evich Golitsyn (1643–1714) (Newtonville, MA, 1984).

'V. T. Postnikov's 1687 mission to London: Anglo-Russian relations in the 1680s in British sources', *Slavonic and East European Review*, 68 (1990), 447–60.

'Russia in 1689: court politics in Foy de la Neuville's relation curieuse et nouvelle de Moscovie', in *New perspectives on Muscovite history: selected papers from the Fourth World Congress for Soviet and East European Studies, Harrogate, 1990*, ed. L. A. J. Hughes (London, 1993), 177–87.

'Matveev, Artamon Sergeevich (1625–1682)', in *Modern Encyclopedia of Russian and Soviet History*, ed. J. L. Wieczynski et al., 59 vols and supplements (Gulf Breeze, FL, 1976–1996), XXI, pp. 142–44.

'Russia: the courts of Moscow and St. Petersburg c. 1547–1725', in *The princely courts of Europe: ritual, politics and culture under the Ancient Régime 1500–1750*, ed. J. Adamson (London, 1999), pp. 295–313.

Playing games: the alternative history of Peter the Great (London, 2000).

Russia in the age of Peter the Great (New Haven, London, 2000).

Iuzefovich, L. A., 'Russkii posol'skii obychai XVI veka', *Voprosy istorii*, 8 (1977), 114–26.

'Kak v posol'skikh obychaiakh vedetsia': Russkii posol'skii obychai kontsa XV – nachala XVII v (Moscow, 1988).

Put' posla: russkii posol'skii obychai. Obikhod. Etiket. Tseremonial. Konets XV – pervaia polovina XVII v (St Petersburg, 2007).

Jacobsen, H., *Luxury and power: the material world of the Stuart diplomat, 1660–1714* (Oxford, 2012).

James, W., *The ceremonial animal: a new portrait of anthropology* (Oxford, 2003).

Jansson, M., 'Measured reciprocity: English ambassadorial gift exchange in the 17th and 18th centuries', *Journal of Early Modern History*, 9 (2005), 348–70.

Art and diplomacy: seventeenth-century decorated royal letters to Russia and the Far East (Leiden, Boston, 2015).

Jensen, C. R., Powell, J. S., '"A mess of Russian left us but of late": diplomatic blunder, literary satire, and the Muscovite ambassador's 1668 visit to Paris theatres', *Theatre Research International*, 24 (1999), 131–44.

Jensen, C. R., 'Music for the tsar: a preliminary study of the music of the Muscovite court theater', *The Musical Quarterly*, 79 (1995), 368–401.

Musical cultures in seventeenth-century Russia (Bloomington, 2009).
Jolliffe, J., 'Lord Carlisle's embassy to Moscow', *Cornhill Magazine*, 176 (1968), 217–32.
Jönsson, C., Langhorne, R., *Diplomacy*, 3 vols. (London, 2004).
Jucker, M., Kintzinger, M., Schwinges, R. C., eds., *Rechtsformen Internationaler Politik: Theorie, Norm und Praxis vom 12. bis 18. Jahrhundert* (Berlin, 2011).
Jusserand, J. J., *A French ambassador at the court of Charles the Second: le comte de Cominges* (London, 1892).
Kamenskii, A. B., *Rossiiskaia imperiia v XVIII veke: traditsii i modernizatsiia* (Moscow, 1999).
Kaminski, A. S., *Republic vs. autocracy: Poland-Lithuania and Russia, 1686–1697* (Cambridge, MA, 1993).
Kampmann, C., 'Die Balance of Europe und die Präzedenz der Englischen Krone: zur Rechtgertigung Englischer Gleichgewichtspolitik im 17. Jahrhundert', in *Imperium, Empire, Reich: ein Konzept politischer Herrschaft im deutsch-britischen Vergleich = An Anglo-German comparison of a concept of rule*, ed. F. Bosbach, H. Hiery, C. Kampmann (Munich, 1999), pp. 69–90.
Kantorowicz, E. H., *The king's two bodies: a study in mediaeval political theology* (Princeton, 1997).
Kappeler, A., *Ivan Groznyj im Spiegel der ausländischen Druckschriften seiner Zeit: ein Beitrag zur Geschichte des westlichen Russlandbildes* (Bern, 1972).
Kauz, R., Niederkorn, J. P., Rota, G., eds., *Diplomatisches Zeremoniell in Europa und im Mittleren Osten in der Frühen Neuzeit* (Vienna, 2009).
Kazakova, N. A., '"Evropeiskoi strany koroli"', in *Issledovaniia po otechestvennomu istochnikovedeniiu: sbornik statei, posviashchennykh 75-letiiu professora S. N. Valka*, ed. S. S. Volk et al. (Moscow, Leningrad, 1964), pp. 418–26.
Keenan, P., *St Petersburg and the Russian court, 1703-1761* (Basingstoke, 2013).
Keene, E., *International political thought: a historical introduction* (Cambridge, 2005).
Keay, A., *The magnificent monarch: Charles II and the ceremonies of power* (London, 2008).
Khodarkovsky, M., *Where two worlds met: the Russian state and the Kalmyk nomads, 1600–1771* (Ithaca, London 1992).
Russia's steppe frontier: the making of a colonial empire, 1500–1800 (Bloomington, IN, 2002).
Khoroshkevich, A. L., *Russkoe gosudarstvo v sisteme mezhdunarodnykh otnoshenii kontsa 'XV'-nachala 'XVI' v* (Moscow, 1980).
Russkoe gosudarstvo v sisteme mezhdunarodnykh otnoshenii serediny XVI veka (Moscow, 2003).
Kivelson, V. A., 'On words, sources, and historical method: which truth about Muscovy?', *Kritika: Explorations in Russian and Eurasian History*, 3 (2002), 487–99.
'Culture and politics, or the curious absence of Muscovite state building in current American historical writing', *Cahiers du Monde Russe*, 46 (2005), 19–28.
Cartographies of Tsardom: the land and its meanings in seventeenth-century Russia (Ithaca, NY, 2006).
Kleinschmidt, H., 'Systeme und Ordnungen in der Geschichte der internationalen Beziehungen', *Archiv für Kulturgeschichte*, 82 (2000), 433–54.

Kliuchevskii, V. O., *Kurs russkoi istorii*, 9 vols. (Moscow, 1987–1990).

Klueting, H., *Die Lehre von der Macht der Staaten: das aussenpolitische Machtproblem in der 'politischen Wissenschaft' und in der praktischen Politik im 18. Jahrhundert* (Berlin, 1986).

Klug, E., 'Das "Asiatische" Rußland. Über die Entstehung eines europäischen Vorurteils', *Historische Zeitschrift*, 245 (1987), 265–89.

Kobzareva, E. I., 'Vestfal'skaia mirnaia sistema i Rossiia', *Otechestvennaia istoriia*, 4 (1999), 146–52.

Köhler, M., *Strategie und Symbolik: Verhandeln auf dem Kongress von Nimwegen* (Cologne, Weimar, Wien, 2011).

Kollmann, N. S., 'Ritual and social drama at the Muscovite court', *Slavic Review*, 45 (1986), 486–502.

By honor bound: state and society in early modern Russia (Ithaca, NY, London, 1999).

'Comment: divides and ends – the problem of periodization', *Slavic Review*, 69 (2010), 439–47.

'A deeper early modern: a response to Paul Bushkovitch', *Kritika: Explorations in Russian and Eurasian History*, 16 (2015), 317–329.

Kolodziejczyk, D., 'Semiotics of behavior in early modern diplomacy: polish embassies in Istanbul and Bahcesaray', *Journal of Early Modern History*, 7 (2003), 245–56.

Kondakov, I., '"Poriadok" vs. "khaos": Petr I v intellektual'noi istorii Rossii', in *Petr Velikii*, ed. E. V. Anisimov (Moscow, 2007), pp. 9–33.

Konovalov, S., 'England and Russia: three embassies, 1662–1665', *Oxford Slavonic Papers*, 10 (1962), 60–104.

Kopanev, N. A., 'Knigi A. A. Matveeva iz biblioteki Mikhalkovykh', in *Knizhnye sokrovishcha. K 275-letiiu Biblioteki AN SSSR*, ed. L. I. Kiseleva, N. P. Kopaneva (Leningrad, 1990), pp. 130–37.

Korzun, S., *Heinrich von Huyssen (1666–1739): Prinzenerzieher, Diplomat und Publizist in den Diensten Zar Peters I., des Großen* (Wiesbaden, 2013).

Koselleck, R., *Vergangene Zukunft: zur Semantik geschichtlicher Zeiten* (Frankfurt a. M., 1989).

Kosheleva, O. E., *Liudi Sankt-Peterburgskogo ostrova Petrovskogo vremeni* (Moscow, 2004).

Kotilaine, J. T., Poe, M., 'Mercantilism in pre-Petrine Russia', in *Modernizing Muscovy: reform and social change in seventeenth-century Russia*, ed. J. T. Kotilaine, M. Poe (London, New York, NY, 2004), pp. 143–73.

Russia's foreign trade and economic expansion in the seventeenth century: windows on the world (Leiden, Boston, 2005).

Kozlovskii, I. P., *Pervye pochty i pervye pochtmeistery v Moskovskom gosudarstve*, 2 vols. (Warsaw, 1913).

Krauske, O., *Die Entwickelung der ständigen Diplomatie vom fünfzehnten Jahrhundert bis zu den Beschlüssen von 1815 und 1818* (Leipzig, 1885).

Krischer, A. *Reichsstädte in der Fürstengesellschaft. Zum politischen Zeichengebrauch in der Frühen Neuzeit* (Darmstadt, 2006).

'Das diplomatische Zeremoniell der Reichsstädte, oder: Was heißt Stadtfreiheit in der Fürstengesellschaft', *Historische Zeitschrift*, 281 (2007), 1–30.

'Souveränität als sozialer Status: zur Funktion des diplomatischen Zeremoniells in der Frühen Neuzeit', in *Diplomatisches Zeremoniell in Europa und dem Mittleren Osten in der Frühen Neuzeit*, ed. R. Kauz, J.-P. Niederkorn, G. Rota (Vienna, 2009), pp. 1–32.

'Das Gesandtschaftswesen und das vormoderne Völkerrecht', in *Rechtsformen Internationaler Politik. Theorie, Norm und Praxis vom 12. bis 18. Jahrhundert*, ed. M. Jucker, M. Kintzinger, R. C. Schwinges (Berlin, 2011), pp. 197–240.

Kruedener, J. F. v., *Die Rolle des Hofes im Absolutismus* (Stuttgart, 1973).

Krylova, T. K., 'Stateinye spiski petrovskikh diplomatov (1700–1714 gg.)', *Problemy Istochnikovedeniia*, 9 (1961), 163–81.

Kudriatsev, I. M., '"Izdatel'skaia" deiatel'nost' Posol'skogo prikaza (k istorii russkoi rukopisnoi knigi vo vtoroi polovine XVII veka)', *Kniga: Issledovaniia I Materialy*, 8 (1963), 179–244.

Kugeler, H., Sepp, C., Wolf, G., eds., *Internationale Beziehungen in der Frühen Neuzeit: Ansätze und Perspektiven* (Hamburg, 2006).

Kunisch, J., 'Der Aufstieg neuer Großmächte im 18. Jahrhundert und die Aufteilung der Machtspären in Ostmitteleuropa', in *Das europäische Staatensystem im Wandel. Strukturelle Bedingeungen und bewegende Kräfte seit der Frühen Neuzeit*, ed. P. Krüger (Munich, 1996), pp. 89–105.

Fürst, Gesellschaft, Krieg: Studien zur bellizistischen Disposition des absoluten Fürstenstaates (Cologne, 1992).

Lachs Phyllis, S., *The Diplomatic corps under Charles II & James II* (New Brunswick, 1965).

Lodyzhenskii, A., *Posol'stvo v Angliiu kniazia Prozorovskago, dvorianina Zheliabuzhskago i d'iaka Davydova v 1662 godu: istoricheskii ocherk po dokumentam Moskovskago Glavnago Arkhiva Ministerstva Inostrannykh del* (St Petersburg, 1880).

Lebow, R. N., *A cultural theory of international relations* (Cambridge, 2008).

Leitsch, W. *Moskau und die Politik des Kaiserhofes im 17. Jahrhundert. Teil 1* (Graz, 1960).

'Herberstein's impact on the reports about Muscovy in the sixteenth and seventeenth centuries: some choice observations on the technique of borrowing', *Forschungen zur Osteuropäischen Geschichte*, 24 (1978), 163–77.

Lentin, A., *Peter the Great: his law on the Imperial succession in Russia, 1722. The official commentary (= Pravda voli monarshei vo opredelenii naslednika derzhavy svoei (The justice of the monarch's right to appoint the heir to his throne)* (Oxford, 1996).

Lesaffer, R., '*Amicitia* in Renaissance peace and alliance treaties (1450–1530)', *Journal of the History of International Law*, 4 (2002), 77–99.

'Peace treaties from Lodi to Westphalia', in *Peace treaties and international law in European history: from the late Middle Ages to World War One*, ed. R. Lesaffer (Cambridge, 2004), pp. 9–44.

Leshkov, V., *O drevnei russkoi diplomatii* (Moscow, 1847).

Levykin, A. K., Nazarov, V. D., eds., *Representatsiia vlasti v posol'skom tseremoniale i diplomaticheskii dialog v XV – pervoi treti XVIII veka. Tret'ia mezhdunarodnaia nauchnaia konferentsiia tsikla 'Inozemtsy v Moskovskom gosudarstve', posviashchennaia 200-letiiu Muzeev Moskovskogo Kremlia. Tezisy dokladov* (Moscow, 2006).

Liechtenhan, F.-D., 'Le Russe, ennemi héréditaire de la chrétienté?: La diffusion de l'image de Moscovie en Europe occidentale au XVIe et XVIIe siècles', *Revue Historique*, 285 (1991), 77–103.

Lieven, D., *Empire: the Russian empire and its rivals* (New Haven, CT, London, 2000).

Liseitsev, D. V., *Posol'skii prikaz v epokhu smuty*, 2 vols. (Moscow, 2003).

Longworth, P., *Alexis, Tsar of all the Russias* (London, 1984).

'Muscovy and the "Antemurale Christianitatis"', in *Mesto Rossii v Evrope: materialy mezhdunarodnoi konferentsii*, ed. G. Szvák (Budapest, 1999), 82–87.

Loomie, A. J., 'The conducteur des ambassadeurs of seventeenth-century France and Spain', *Revue belge de philologie et d'histoire*, 52 (1975), 333–56.

Lossky, A., 'Moskaus Weg nach Europa: der Aufstieg Russlands zum Europäischen Machtstaat im Zeitalter Friedrich des Grossen [Review]', *American Historical Review*, 58 (1953), 920–22.

Lossky, B., 'Le séjour de Pierre le Grand en France', *Le Monde Slave*, 9 (1932), 278–303.

Lotman, Iu. M., Uspenskii, V. A., 'Echoes of the notion "Moscow as the Third Rome" in Peter the Great's Ideology', in *The semiotics of Russian culture*, ed. A. Shukman (Ann Arbor, 1984), pp. 53–67.

'Über die Semiosphäre', *Zeitschrift für Semiotik*, 12 (1990), 287–305.

Universe of the mind: a semiotic theory of culture (London, 2001).

Love, R. S., 'Rituals of majesty: France, Siam, and court spectacle in royal image-building at Versailles in 1685 and 1686', *Canadian Journal of History*, 31 (1996), 171–98.

Luard, E., *The balance of power: the system of international relations, 1648–1815* (Basingstoke, 1992).

Lubimenko, I., 'Anglo-Russian relations during the first English revolution', *Transactions of the Royal Historical Society*, fourth series, 11 (1928), 39–59.

Madariaga, I. de 'Tsar into emperor: the title of Peter the Great', in *Politics and culture in eighteenth-century Russia: collected essays by Isabel de Madariaga* (London, New York, 1998), pp. 15–39.

Ivan the Terrible: first tsar of Russia (New Haven, London, 2005).

Maier, I., 'Presseberichte am Zarenhof im 17. Jahrhundert. Ein Beitrag zur Vorgeschichte der gedruckten Zeitung in Russland', *Jahrbuch für Kommunikationsgeschichte*, 6 (2004), 103–29.

Maier, I., Waugh, D. C., 'How well was Muscovy connected with the world?', in *Imperienvergleich. Beispiele und Ansätze aus osteuropäischer Perspektive. Festschrift für Andreas Kappeler*, ed. G. Hausmann, A. Rustemeyer (Wiesbaden, 2009), pp. 17–28.

Maissen, T., *Die Geburt der Republic: Staatsverständnis und Repräsentation in der frühneuzeitlichen Eidgenossenschaft* (Göttingen, 2006).

Malettke, K., *Hegemonie – Multipolares System – Gleichgewicht: Internationale Beziehungen 1648/1659–1713/1714* (Paderborn, 2012).

Mälksoo, L., 'The history of international legal theory in Russia: a civilizational dialogue with Europe', *European Journal of International Law*, 19 (2008), 211–32.
Russian approaches to international law (Oxford, 2015).
Man'ko, A. V., *Velikikh posol'skikh del oberegatel': politicheskaia biografiia kniazia V. V. Golitsyna* (Moscow, 2007).
Manley, L., *Literature and culture in early modern London* (Cambridge, 1995).
Markel, E. H., *Die Entwicklung der diplomatischen Rangstufen* (Erlangen, 1951).
Marker, G., *Publishing, printing, and the origins of intellectual life in Russia, 1700–1800* (Princeton, NJ, 1985).
Martens, F. F., *Sovremennoe mezhdunarodnoe pravo tsivilizovannykh narodov*, 5th edn., 2 vols. (St Petersburg, 1904).
Martin, R. E., 'Gifts for the bride: dowries, diplomacy, and marriage politics in Muscovy', *Journal of Early Modern History*, 38 (2008), 119–45.
'The Petrine divide and the periodization of early modern Russian history', *Slavic Review*, 69 (2010), 410–25.
Matsuki, E., 'A diplomatic custom in Muscovy', *Mediterranean World*, 14 (1995), 17–29.
Mattingly, G., *Renaissance diplomacy* (New York, NY, 2009, originally published in 1955).
Matveyev, V., *The Karlowitz congress and the debut of Russia's multilateral diplomacy (1698–99)* (Leicester, 2000).
Mauss, M., *The gift: the form and reason for exchange in archaic societies*, trans. W. D. Hall (London, 2002).
Mckay, D., Scott, H. M., *The rise of the great powers 1648–1815* (London, 1983).
Mediger, W. *Moskaus Weg nach Europa: der Aufstieg Russlands zum europäischen Machtstaat im Zeitalter Friedrichs des Grossen* (Braunschweig, 1952).
Mecklenburg, Russland und England-Hannover 1706–1721: ein Beitrag zur Geschichte des Nordischen Krieges, 2 vols. (Hildesheim, 1967).
Meissner, B., 'Die zaristische Diplomatie. A. Der Gesandtschafts-Prikas (Posol'skij Prikas)', *Jahrbücher für Geschichte Osteuropas*, 4 (1956), 237–45.
Mervaud, M., Roberti, J.-C., *Une infinie brutalité: l'image de la Russie dans la France des XVIe et XVIIe siècles* (Paris, 1991).
Meyer, K., '"Kayserliche grossmächtigkeit". Titularfragen bei den Verhandlungen zwischen Kaiser und Zar 1661/62', in *Rossica Externa. Studien zum 15.-17. Jahrhundert. Festgabe für Paul Johansen zum 60. Geburtstag*, ed. H. Weczerka (Marburg, 1963), pp. 115–24.
Mezin, S. A., *Vzgliad iz Evropy: frantsuzskie avtory XVIII veka o Petre I* (Saratov, 2003).
Miller, D., 'Creating legitimacy: ritual, ideology, and Power in sixteenth-century Russia', *Russian History/Histoire Russe*, 21 (1994), 289–315.
Mohnhaupt, H., '"Europa" und "ius publicum" im 17. und 18. Jahrhundert', in *Aspekte europäischer Rechtsgeschichte. Festgabe für Helmut Coing zum 70. Geburtstag*, ed. C. Bergfeld (Frankfurt a. M., 1982), pp. 207–32.
Muir, E., *Ritual in early modern Europe* (Cambridge, 1997).
Müller, K., *Das kaiserliche Gesandtschaftswesen im Jahrhundert nach dem Westfälischen Frieden: (1648–1740)* (Bonn, 1976).

Mund, S., *Orbis russiarum: genèse et développement de la représentation du monde 'russe' en Occident à la Renaissance* (Geneva, 2003).

Murray, J. J., 'The Görtz-Gyllenborg arrest – a problem in diplomatic immunity', *Journal of Modern History*, 28 (1956), 325–37.

Nekrasov, G. A., 'Mezhdunarodnoe priznanie rossiiskogo velikoderzhaviia v XVII v.', in *Feodal'naia Rossiia vo vsemirno-istoricheskom protsesse: sbornik statei, posviashchennyi L. V. Cherepninu*, ed. V. T. Pashuto (Moscow, 1972), pp. 381–88.

Neumann, I. B., Welsh, J. M., 'The other in European self-definition: an addendum to the literature on international society', *Review of International Studies*, 17 (1991), 327–48.

Uses of the Other: 'the East' in European identity formation (Manchester, 1999).

Nikiforow, L. N., *Russisch-englische Beziehungen unter Peter I.*, trans. W. Müller (Weimar, 1954).

Novokhatko, O. V., *Razriad v 185 godu* (Moscow, 2007).

O'brien, C. B., 'Russian envoys at the court of Louis XIV, 1681–1687', *The Historian*, 4 (1941), 34–42.

Ocherk istorii Ministerstva inostrannykh del, 1802–1902 (St Petersburg, 1902, reprint, 2002).

Oestreich, G., *Neostoicism and the early modern state*, ed. B. Oestreich, H. G. Koenigsberger, trans. D. McLintock (Cambridge, 1982).

Opochinin, E., *Russkii teatr, ego nachalo u razvitie: istoricheskii ocherk* (Moscow, 2005).

Orlenko, S. P., *Vykhodtsy iz Zapadnoi Evropy v Rossii XVII veka. Pravovoi status i real'noe polozhenie* (Moscow, 2004).

Osborne, T., *Dynasty and diplomacy in the court of Savoy: political culture and the Thirty Years' War* (Cambridge, 2002).

'The surrogate war between the Savoys and the Medici: sovereignty and precedence in early modern Italy', *International History Review*, 29 (2007), 1–21.

Osiander, A., 'Sovereignty, international relations, and the Westphalian myth', *International Organization*, 55 (2001), 251–87.

Osterhammel, J., *Die Entzauberung Asiens: Europa und die asiatischen Reiche im 18. Jahrhundert* (Munich, 1998).

Ostrowski, D., 'The end of Muscovy: the case for circa 1800', *Slavic Review*, 69 (2010), 426–38.

Palmer, D. W., *Writing Russia in the age of Shakespeare* (Aldershot, 2004).

Paulmann, J., *Pomp und Politik: Monarchenbegegnungen in Europa zwischen Ancien Régime und Erstem Weltkrieg* (Paderborn, 2000).

Pečar, A., *Die Ökonomie der Ehre: der höfische Adel am Kaiserhof Karls VI. (1711–1740)* (Darmstadt, 2003).

Pekarskii, P. P., *Nauka i literatura v Rossii pri Petre Velikom*, 2 vols. (St Petersburg, 1862).

Pelenski, J., *Russia and Kazan: conquest and imperial ideology, 1438–1560s* (The Hague, 1974).

Pelus, M.-L., 'Un des aspects de la naissance d'une conscience européenne: la Russie vue d'Europe occidentale au XVIe siècle', in *La Conscience européenne au XVe et au XVIe siècle*, ed. Ecole Normale Supérieur de Jeunes Filles (Paris, 1982), pp. 309–28.

Perdue, P. C., *China marches West: the Qing conquest of central Eurasia* (Cambridge, MA, 2010).

Perrie, M., *The image of Ivan the Terrible in Russian folklore* (Cambridge, 1987).

Pferschy, G., ed., *Siegmund von Herberstein: Kaiserlicher Gesandter und Begründer der Russlandkunde und die europäische Diplomatie* (Graz, 1989).

Phipps, G. M., 'The Russian embassy to London of 1645–46 and the abrogation of the Muscovy Company's charter', *Slavonic and East European Review*, 68 (1990), 257–76.

Picard, B., *Das Gesandtschaftswesen Ostmitteleuropas in der frühen Neuzeit: Beiträge zur Geschichte der Diplomatie in der ersten Hälfte des sechzehnten Jahrhunderts nach den Aufzeichnungen des Freiherrn Sigmund von Herberstein* (Graz, 1967).

Pitt-Rivers, J., 'Honour and social status', in *Honour and shame: the values of Mediterranean society*, ed. J. G. Péristiany (London, 1966), pp. 21–77.

Plavsic, B., 'Seventeenth-century chanceries and their staffs', in *Russian officialdom: the bureaucratization of Russian society from the seventeenth to the twentieth century*, ed. W. M. Pintner, D. K. Rowney, H. A. Bennett (London, 1980), pp. 19–45.

Plokhy, S., *The origins of the Slavic nations: premodern identities in Russia, Ukraine, and Belarus* (Cambridge, 2006).

Pogosian, E., *Petr I – arkhitektor rossiiskoi istorii* (St Petersburg, 2001).

Poe, M., *Foreign descriptions of Muscovy: an analytic bibliography of primary and secondary sources* (Columbus, OH, 1995).

'What did Russians mean when they called themselves "slaves of the tsar"?', *Slavic Review*, 57/3 (1998), 585–608.

A people born to slavery: Russia in early modern European ethnography, 1476–1748 (Ithaca, NY, London, 2000).

'Moscow, the third Rome: the origins and transformations of a "pivotal moment"', *Jahrbücher für Geschichte Osteuropas*, 49 (2001), 412–29.

'The Truth about Muscovy', *Kritika: Explorations in Russian and Eurasian History*, 3 (2002), 473–86.

'A distant world: Russian relations with Europe before Peter the Great', in *The world engages Russia*, ed. C. Whittaker (Cambridge, MA, 2003), pp. 2–23.

The Russian moment in world history (Princeton, Oxford, 2003).

'Introduction', in *Early Explorations of Russia*, ed. M. Poe, 14 vols. (London, New York, 2003–2004), I, pp. 1–32.

Porshnev, B. F., *Muscovy and Sweden in the Thirty Years' War, 1630–1635*, trans. B. Pearce (Cambridge, 1995).

Posselt, M. C., *Der General und Admiral F. Lefort. Sein Leben und seine Zeit: ein Beitrag zur Geschichte Peter's des Grossen*, 2 vols. (Frankfurt a. M., St Petersburg, 1866).

Potemkin, V. P. et al., eds., *Istoriia diplomatii*, 2nd rev. edn., 5 vols. (Moscow, 1959–1979).

Prudovskii, P. I., 'K voprosu formirovaniia diplomaticheskogo protokola: Rossiia i Brandenburg v seredine XVII veka', *Vestnik arkhivista*, 85 (2005), 252–59.

Pustogarov, V. V., *Our Martens: F.F. Martens, international lawyer and architect of peace*, trans. W. E. Butler (London, 2000).

Queller, D. E., *The office of ambassador in the middle ages* (Princeton, NJ, 1967).

Ranke, L. v., 'Die großen Mächte', *Historisch-Politische Zeitschrift*, 2 (1833), 1–51.

Rasmussen, K., 'On the Information Level of the Muscovite Posol'skij Prikaz in the Sixteenth Century', *Forschungen zur osteuropäischen Geschichte*, 24 (1978), 88–99.

Riasanovsky, N. V., *The image of Peter the Great in Russian history and thought* (Oxford, 1985).

Riches, D., *Protestant cosmopolitanism and diplomatic culture: Brandenburg-Swedish relations in the seventeenth century* (Leiden, Boston, 2013).

Rieber, A. J., *The struggle for the Eurasian borderlands: from the rise of early modern empires to the end of the First World War* (Cambridge, 2014).

Robbins, C., 'Carlisle and Marvell', *History of Ideas Newsletter*, 3 (1957), 8–17.

Robinson, P., 'The justification of war in Russian history and philosophy', in *Just war in comparative perspective*, ed. P. Robinson (Aldershot, 2003), pp. 62–75.

Rogozhin, N. M.,*Obzor posol'skikh knig iz fondov-kollektsii, khaniashchikhsia v TsGADA (konetz XV – nachalo XVIII v.)* (Moscow, 1990).

Posol'skie knigi Rossii kontsa XV – nachala XVII vv. (Moscow, 1994).

'Mesto Rossii XVI–XVII vekov v Evrope po materialam posol'skikh knig', in *Mesto Rossii v Evrope: materialy mezhdunarodnoi konferentsii*, ed. G. Szvák (Budapest, 1999), pp. 88–96.

'Russian Richelieu: Ordin-Nashchokin', *International Affairs*, 46 (2000), 185–93.

'Obrazovanie i deiatel'nost' Posol'skogo prikaza', in *Rossiiskaia diplomatiia: Istoriia i sovremennost'. Materialy nauchno-prakticheskoi konferentsii, posviashchennoi 450-letiiu sozdaniia Posol'skogo prikaza*, ed. I. S. Ivanov et al. (Moscow, 2001), pp. 51–64.

U gosudarevykh del byt' ukazano (Moscow, 2002).

Posol'skii prikaz: kolybel' rossiiskoi diplomatii (Moscow, 2003).

Rohrschneider, M., 'Das französische Präzedenzstreben im Zeitalter Ludwigs XIV.: Diplomatische Praxis – zeitgenössische französische Publizistik – Rezeption in der frühen deutschen Zeremonialwissenschaft', *Francia. Forschungen zur westeuropäischen Geschichte*, 36 (2009), 135–79.

Roll, C., 'Hatten die Moskowiter einen Begriff vom Reich? Beobachtungen zu den Kenntnissen und Vorstellungen von der politischen Ordnung des Alten Reichs am vorpetrinischen Zarenhof', in *Imperium romanum – irregulare corpus – Teutscher Reichs-Staat. Das Alte Reich in der Wahrnehmung der Zeitgenossen und der Historiographie*, ed. M. Schnettger (Mainz, 2002), pp. 135–65.

'Europäische Gesandtschaften am Zarenhof: Zeremoniell und Politik', in *Zarensilber: Augsburger Silber aus dem Kreml*, ed. C. Emmendörffer, C. Trepesch (Munich, 2008), pp. 30–55.

'Barbaren? tabula rasa? Wie Leibniz sein neues Wissen über Russland auf den Begriff brachte. Eine Studie über die Bedeutung der Vernetzung gelehrter Korrespondenzen für die Ermöglichung aufgeklärter Diskurse', in: *Umwelt und Weltgestaltung: Leibniz' politisches Denken in seiner Zeit*, ed. F. Beiderbeck, I. Dingel, W. Li (Göttingen, 2015), pp. 307–58.

Romaniello, M. P., 'Through the filter of tobacco: the limits of global trade in the early modern world', *Comparative Studies in Society and History*, 49 (2007), 914–37.

Roosen, W. J., 'The functioning of ambassadors under Louis XIV', *French Historical Studies*, 6 (1970), 311–32.

The age of Louis XIV: the rise of modern diplomacy (Cambridge, MA, 1976).

'Early modern diplomatic ceremonial: a system's approach', *Journal of Modern History*, 52 (1980), 452–76.

Rothstein, A., *Peter the Great and Marlborough: politics and diplomacy in converging wars* (Basingstoke, 1986).

Rowland, D. B, 'Moscow – the Third Rome or the New Israel?', *Russian Review*, 55 (1996), 591–614.

'Two cultures, one throne room: secular courtiers and Orthodox culture in the Golden Hall of the Moscow Kremlin', in *Orthodox Russia: belief and practice under the tsars*, ed. R. Greene, V. Kivelson (University Park, PA, 2003), pp.33–57.

'Architecture, image, and ritual in the throne rooms of Muscovy, 1550–1650: a preliminary survey', in *Rude & barbarous kingdom revisited: essays in Russian history and culture in honor of Robert O. Crummey*, ed. C. S. L. Dunning, R. E. Martin, D. B. Rowland (Bloomington, IN, 2008), pp. 53–71.

Ruffmann, K. H., *Das Russlandbild im England Shakespeares* (Göttingen, 1952).

'England und der russische Zaren- und Kaisertitel', *Jahrbücher für Geschichte Osteuropas*, 3 (1955), 217–24.

Sagarra, E., Skrine, P. N., *A companion to German literature: from 1500 to the present* (Oxford, 1999).

Sakharov, A. N., ed., *Istoriia vneshnei politiki Rossii: konets XV v.-1917 g.*, 5 vols. (Moscow, 1995–1999).

Sanin, G. A., 'Novatsii Petra I v upravlenii vneshnepoliticheskimi delami po sravneniiu s vtoroi polovinoi XVII veka', in *Rossiiskaia diplomatiia: Istoriia i sovremennost'. Materialy nauchno-prakticheskoi konferentsii, posviashchennoi 450-letiiu sozdaniia Posol'skogo prikaza*, ed. I. S. Ivanov et al. (Moscow, 2001), pp. 148–52.

Satow, E. M., *A guide to diplomatic practice*, 4th edn. (London, 1957).

Savva, V. I., *Moskovskie tsari i vizantiiskie vasilevsy: o vliianii Vizantii na obrazovanie idei tsarskoi vlasti moskovskikh gosudarei* (Khar'kov, 1901, reprint, The Hague, Paris, 1969).

O posol'skom prikaze v XVI veke (Kharkov, 1917).

Schattenberg, S., '"Gespräch zweier Taubstummer?" Die Kultur der Außenpolitik Chruščevs und Adenauers Moskaureise 1955', *Osteuropa*, 7 (2007), 27–46.

Schaub, M.-K., 'Avoir l'oreille du roi: l'ambassade de Pierre Potemkin et Siméon Roumiantsev en France en 1668', in *Paroles de négociateurs: l'entretien dans la pratique diplomatique de la fin du Moyen âge à la fin du XIXe siècle*, ed. S. Andretta et al. (Rome, 2010), pp. 213–29.

'Comment régler des incidents protocolaires? Diplomates russes et françaises au XVIIe siècle', in *L'incident diplomatique (XVIe–XVIIIe siècle)*, ed. L. Bély, G. Poumarède (Paris, 2010), pp. 323–36.

Scheidegger, G., 'Das Eigene im Bild vom Anderen. Quellenkritische Überlegungen zur russisch-abendländischen Begegnung im 16. und 17. Jahrhundert', *Jahrbücher für Geschichte Osteuropas*, 35 (1987), 339–55.

Perverses Abendland, barbarisches Russland: Begegnungen des 16. und 17. Jahrhunderts im Schatten kultureller Missverständnisse (Zurich, 1993).

'Von alten Hüten und internationalen Staatsaffären', in *450 Jahre Sigismund von Herbersteins Rerum Moscoviticarum Commentarii 1549–1999. Jubiläumsvorträge*, ed. R. Frötschner, F. Kämpfer (Wiesbaden, 2002), pp. 263–83.

Schilling, R., 'Kommunikation und Herrschaft im Moment der Ankunft: Ein Empfang in Moskau (1603) und eine Audienz in Versailles (1686)', in *Die Ankunft des Anderen: Repräsentationen sozialer und politischer Ordnungen in Empfangszeremonien*, ed. S. Baller et al. (Frankfurt a. M., 2008), 135–51.

Schlögl, R., 'Kommunikation und Vergesellschaftung unter Anwesenden: Formen des Sozialen und ihre Transformation in der Frühen Neuzeit', *Geschichte und Gesellschaft*, 34 (2008), 155–224.

'Politik beobachten. Öffentlichkeit und Medien in der Frühen Neuzeit', *Zeitschrift für Historische Forschung*, 25 (2008), 581–616.

Schlöss, E., 'Über die Begegnung des Zaren Peter I mit dem Kaiser Leopold I', *Wiener Geschichtsblätter*, 49 (1994), 149–62.

Baugeschichte des Theresianums in Wien (Wien, 1998).

'Zar Peter der Grosse in Wien: Übertragung der Blätter 411 bis 452 der Ceremonialprotocolle 1698 (ZA Prot. 5) in die Schrift unserer Zeit wort- und zeilengetreu', *Mitteilungen des Österreichischen Staatsarchivs*, 51 (2004), 375–546.

Schmale, W., *Geschichte und Zukunft der europäischen Identität* (Stuttgart, 2008).

Schnakenbourg, É., *La France, le Nord et l'Europe au début du XVIIIe siècle* (Paris, 2008).

Schnitzer, C., *Höfische Maskeraden: Funktion und Ausstattung von Verkleidungsdivertissements an deutschen Höfen der Frühen Neuzeit* (Tübingen, 1999).

Schroeder, P. W., *The transformation of European Politics, 1763–1848* (Oxford, 1994).

Schulze-Wessel, M., 'Systembegriff und Europapolitik der russischen Diplomatie im 18. Jahrhundert', *Historische Zeitschrift*, 266 (1998), 649–69.

Schwarcz, I., 'Velikoe posol'stvo i Venskii dvor: K voprosu o prebyvanii Velikogo Posol'stva v Vene', in *Tsentral'naia Evropa v novoe i noveishee vremia: sbornik k 70-letiiu T.M. Islamova*, ed. A. S. Stykalin (Moscow, 1998), pp. 55–68.

'Diplomatisches Zeremoniell in Europa und im Mittleren Osten in der frühen Neuzeit', in *Diplomatisches Zeremoniell in Europa und im Mittleren Osten in der frühen Neuzeit*, ed. R. Kauz, J.-P. Niederkorn, G. Rota (Vienna, 2009), pp. 265–86.

Scott, H. M., 'Russia as a European great power', in *Russia in the age of enlightenment: essays in honour of Isabel de Madariaga*, ed. R. P. Bartlett, J. M. Hartley, J. M. (Basinstoke, 1990), pp. 7–39.

The European nobilities in the seventeenth and eighteenth centuries, 2 vols. (London, New York, 1995).

The emergence of the Eastern powers, 1756–1775 (Cambridge, 2001).

The birth of a great power system, 1740–1815 (Harlow, 2006).

'Diplomatic culture in Old Regime Europe', in *Cultures of power in Europe during the long eighteenth century: essays in honour of T. C. W. Blanning*, ed. H. M. Scott, B. Simms (Cambridge, 2007), pp. 58–85.

Sedov, P. V., *Zakat Moskovskogo tsarstva: tsarskii dvor kontsa XVII veka* (St Petersburg, 2006).

Seed, P., *Ceremonies of possession in Europe's conquest of the New World, 1492–1640* (Cambridge, 1995).

Semenov, I., *U istokov kremlevskogo protokola: istoriia vozniknoveniia rossiiskogo posol'skogo tseremoniala i nravy Kremlia v XV-XVII vekakh* (Moscow, 2005).

Sen, B., *A diplomat's handbook of international law and practice*, 3rd edn. (Dordrecht, 1988).

Sergeev, F. P., *Russkaia diplomaticheskaia terminologiia XI–XVII vv.* (Kishinev, 1971).

Formirovanie russkogo diplomaticheskogo iazyka (L'vov, 1978).

Serov, D. O., *Administratsiia Petra I* (Moscow, 2007).

Shepelev, L. E., *Chinovnyi mir Rossii: XVIII-nachalo XX v.* (St Petersburg, 1999).

Shmidt, S. O., ed., *Opisi Tsarskogo arkhiva XVI veka i arkhiva Posol'skogo prikaza 1614 goda* (Moscow, 1960).

ed., *Opis' arkhiva Posol'skogo prikaza 1626 goda*, 2 vols. (Moscow, 1977).

ed., *Opis' arkhiva Posol'kogo prikaza 1673 goda* (Moscow, 1990).

Shmurlo, E., 'Kriticheskie zametki po istorii Petra Velikago', *Zhurnal Ministerstva Narodnogo Prosveshcheniia*, 329 (1900), 54–95.

Siegelberg, J., Schlichte, K., eds., *Strukturwandel internationaler Beziehungen: zum Verhältnis von Staat und internationalem System seit dem Westfälischen Frieden* (Wiesbaden, 2000).

Sienell, S., *Die geheime Konferenz unter Kaiser Leopold I.: personelle Strukturen und Methoden zur politischen Entscheidungsfindung am Wiener Hof* (Frankfurt a. M., 2001).

Singer, J. D., Small, M., 'The composition and status ordering of the international system: 1815–1940', *World Politics*, 18 (1966), 236–82.

Sizeranne, Robert de la, *Beatrice d'Este and her court*, trans. N. Fleming (London, 1924).

Sofsky, W., Paris, R., *Figurationen sozialer Macht: Autorität, Stellvertretung, Koalition* (Frankfurt a. M., 1994).

Solov'ev, S. M., *Istoriia Rossii s drevneishikh vremen*, 15 vols. (Moscow, 1959–1966, originally published 1851–1879).

Soloviev, S. M., *History of Russia, vol. 25: rebellion and reform. Fedor and Sophia, 1682–1689*, trans. L. A. J. Hughes (Gulf Breeze, FL, 1989).

History of Russia, vol. 26: Peter the Great. A reign begins, 1689–1703, trans. L. A. J. Hughes (Gulf Breeze, FL, 1994).

Sowerby, T. A., '"A memorial and a pledge of faith": portraiture and early modern diplomatic culture', *English Historical Review*, 129 (2014), 296–331.

'Approaches to early modern diplomacy', *History Compass* (2016, forthcoming).

Spielman, J. P., *Leopold I of Austria* (London, 1977).

Staubach, N., 'Honor Dei' oder "Bapsts Gepreng" Zur Reorganisation des Papstzeremoniells in der Renaissance', in *Rom und das Reich vor der Reformation*, ed. N. Staubach (Frankfurt a.M., 2004), 91–136.

Steppan, C., *Akteure am fremden Hof: Politische Kommunikation und Repräsentation kaiserlicher Gesandter im Jahrzehnt des Wandels am russischen Hof (1720–1730)* (Göttingen, 2015).

Steiger, H., 'Concrete peace and general order: the legal meaning of the treaties of 24 October 1648', in *1648: war an peace in Europe. Exhibition catalogue*, ed. H. Schilling, K. Bussmann, 3 vols. (Münster, Osnabrück, 1998), I, 437–45.

Steinberg, R. H., 'Who is sovereign?', *Stanford Journal of International Law*, 40 (2004), 329–49.

Stenzig, P., *Botschafterzeremoniell am Papsthof der Renaissance: Der Tractatus de oratoribus des Paris de Grassi – Edition und Kommentar*, 2 vols. (Frankfurt a. M., 2014).

'Nunquam antea in usu. Das diplomatische Protokoll an der Kurie', in *Das Ursprüngliche und das Neue: Zur Dynamik ritueller Prozesse in Geschichte und Gegenwart*, ed. B. Dücker, G. Schwedler (Münster, 2008), 207–25.

Sternberg, G., 'Manipulating information in the Ancien Régime: ceremonial records, aristocratic strategies, and the limits of the state perspective', *Journal of Modern History*, 85 (2013), 239–79.

Status interaction during the reign of Louis XIV (Oxford, 2014).

Stevens, C. B., *Russia's wars of emergence, 1460–1730* (Harlow, 2007).

Stewart, F. H., *Honor* (Chicago, London, 1994).

Stökl, G., 'Rußland und Europa vor Peter dem Großen', *Historische Zeitschrift*, 184 (1957), 531–54.

'Imperium und imperiale Ideologie: Erfahrungen am Beispiel des vorpetrinischen Russland', in *Vom Staat des ancien Regime zum modernen Parteienstaat: Festschrift für Theodor Schieder zu seinem 70. Geburtstag*, ed. H. Berding et al. (Munich, Vienna, 1978), pp. 27–39.

Stollberg-Rilinger, B., *Der Staat als Maschine: zur politischen Metaphorik des absoluten Fürstenstaats* (Berlin, 1986).

'Höfische Öffentlichkeit: zur zeremoniellen Selbstdarstellung des brandenburgischen Hofes vor dem Europäischen Publikum', *Forschungen zur Brandenburgischen und Preussischen Geschichte*, NF 7 (1997), 145–76.

'Zeremoniell als politisches Verfahren: Rangordnung und Rangstreit als Strukturmerkmale des frühneuzeitlichen Reichstages', in *Neue Studien zur Frühneuzeitlichen Reichsgeschichte (Zeitschrift für Historische Forschung, Beiheft 19)*, ed. J. Kunisch (Berlin, 1997), 91–132.

'Zeremoniell, Ritual, Symbol: neue Forschungen zur symbolischen Kommunikation in Spätmittelalter und Früher Neuzeit', *Zeitschrift für Historische Forschung*, 27 (2000), 389–405.

'Honores Regii: die Königswürde im zeremoniellen Zeichensystem der Frühen Neuzeit', in *Dreihundert Jahre preussische Königskrönung: eine Tagungsdokumentation*, ed. J. Kunisch (Berlin, 2002), pp. 1–26.

'Die Wissenschaft der feinen Unterschiede: das Präzedenzrecht und die europäischen Monarchien vom 16. bis zum 18. Jahhundert', *Majestas*, 10 (2002), 1–26.

'Die zeremonielle Inszenierung des Reiches, oder: Was leistet der kulturalistische Ansatz für die Reichsverfassungsgeschichte?', in *Imperium Romanum – irregulare corpus – Teutscher Reichs-Staat: das Alte Reich im Verständnis der Zeitgenossen und der Historiographie*, ed. M. Schnettger (Mainz, 2002), pp. 233–46.

'Symbolische Kommunikation in der Vormoderne: Begriffe – Forschungsperspektiven – Thesen', *Zeitschrift für Historische Forschung*, 31 (2004), 489–527.

'Herrschaftszeremoniell', in *Enzyklopädie der Neuzeit*, 5 vols., ed. F. Jaeger (Stuttgart, Weimar, 2007), pp. 416–24.

'Völkerrechtlicher Status und zeremonielle Praxis auf dem Westfälischen Friedenskongreß', in *Rechtsformen internationaler Politik. Theorie, Norm und Praxis vom 12. bis zum 18. Jahrhundert*, ed. M. Kintzinger, M. Jucker (Berlin, 2011), pp. 147–64.

Rituale (Frankfurt a. M., 2013).

The emperor's old clothes: constitutional history and the symbolic language of the Holy Roman Empire, trans. T. Dunlap (New York, Oxford, 2015).

Stolleis, M., *Geschichte des öffentlichen Rechts in Deutschland*, 3 vols. (München, 1988).

Subrahmanyam, S., *Courtly encounters: translating courtliness and violence in early modern Eurasia* (Cambridge, MA, 2012).

Sunderland, W., *Taming the wild field: colonization and empire on the Russian steppe* (Ithaca, London, 2004).

Szeftel, M., 'The title of the Muscovite monarch up to the end of the seventeenth century', *Canadian American Slavic Studies*, 13 (1979), 59–81.

Teschke, B., 'Theorizing the Westphalian system of states: international relations from absolutism to capitalism', *European Journal of International Relations*, 8 (2002), 5–48.

Thiessen, H. v., 'Diplomatie vom type ancien. Überlegungen zu einem Idealtypus des frühneuzeitlichen Gesandtschaftswesens', in *Akteure der Aussenbeziehungen: Netzwerke und Interkulturalität im historischen Wandel*, ed. *H. v. Thiessen, C. Windler* (Cologne, 2010), pp. 471–503.

Thiessen, H. v., Windler, C., eds., *Akteure der Aussenbeziehungen: Netzwerke und Interkulturalität im historischen Wandel* (Cologne, 2010).

Tiukhmeneva, E. A., *Iskusstvo triumfal'nykh vrat v Rossii pervoi poloviny XVIII veka* (Moscow, 2005).

Tomsinskii, S. M., *Pervaia pechatnaia gazeta Rossii (1702–1727)* (Perm, 1959).

Torke, H.-J., ed., *Von Moskau nach St. Petersburg: das russische Reich im 17. Jahrhundert* (Wiesbaden, 2000).

Turilova, S. L., *Istoriia vneshnepoliticheskogo vedomstva Rossii (1720–1832)* (Moscow, 2000).

Uspenskii, B. A., *Tsar' i imperator: pomazanie na tsarstvo i semantika monarshikh titulov* (Moscow, 2000).
Ustrialov, N. G., *Istoriia tsarstvovaniia Petra Velikago*, 6 vols. (St Petersburg, 1858–1863).
Vásáry, I., 'Why was Muscovite Russia considered "Barbarian" by contemporary Europe?', in *Mesto Rossii v Evrope: materialy mezhdunarodnoi konferentsii*, ed. G. Szvák (Budapest, 1999), pp. 97–102.
Vaudin, E., *Notice sur Antoine Benoist de Joigny peintre et sculpteur en cire de Louis XIV* (Paris, 1887).
Vec, M., 'Zeremonialrecht', in *Handwörterbuch zur deutschen Rechtsgeschichte*, ed. A. Erler, E. Kaufmann, 5 vols. (Berlin, 1998), V, pp. 1673–77.
Zeremonialwissenschaft im Fürstenstaat: Studien zur juristischen und politischen Theorie absolutistischer Herrschaftsrepräsentation (Frankfurt a. M., 1998).
Vermeer-Künzli, A., 'As if: the legal fiction in diplomatic protection', *European Journal of International Law*, 18 (2007), 37–68.
Veselovskii, N. I., 'Tatarskoe vliianie na russkii posol'skii tseremonial v moskovskii period russkoi istorii', in *Otchet o sostoianii i deiatel'nosti Imperatorskogo S.-Peterburgskogo univerziteta za 1910*, ed. I. S. Ivanovskii (St Petersburg, 1911), pp. 1–19.
Watkins, J., 'Toward a new diplomatic history of medieval and early modern Europe', *Journal of Medieval and Early Modern Studies*, 38 (2008), 1–14.
Watson, A., 'Russia and the European states system', in *The expansion of international society*, ed. H. Bull, A. Watson (Oxford, New York, 1984), 61–74.
Weber, M., *Economy and society: an outline of interpretive sociology*, trans. G. Roth, C. Wittich, 2 vols. (Berkeley, 1978).
Welch, E., 'Between Italy and Moscow: cultural crossoads and cultural exchange', in *Cultural exchange in early modern Europe, Volume IV: forging European identities 1400–1700*, ed. H. Roodenburg (Cambridge, 2007), pp. 59–99.
Welke, M., 'Rußland in der deutschen Publizistik des 17. Jahrhunderts (1613–89)', *Forschungen zur osteuropäischen Geschichte*, 23 (1976), 105–276.
Weller, T., *Theatrum Praecedentiae: zeremonieller Rang und gesellschaftliche Ordnung in der frühneuzeitlichen Stadt, Leipzig 1500–1800* (Darmstadt, 2006).
Wieczynski, J. L., ed., *The modern encyclopedia of Russian and Soviet history*, 56 vols. (Gulf Breeze, FL, 1976–).
Wieland, C., *Fürsten, Freunde, Diplomaten: die römisch-florentinischen Beziehungen unter Paul V. (1605–1621)* (Cologne, 2004).
Willan, T. S., *The early history of the Russia Company 1553–1603* (Manchester, 1956).
Wilson, P. H., 'Bolstering the prestige of the Habsburg: the end of the Holy Roman Empire in 1806', *International History Review*, 28 (2006), 709–36.
Europe's tragedy: a new history of the Thirty Years War (London, 2010).
Wilson, R., 'Visible bullets: Tamburlaine the Great and Ivan the Terrible', *English Literary History*, 62 (1995), 47–68.
Windler, C., 'Diplomatic history as a field for cultural analysis: Muslim-Christian relations in Tunis, 1700–1840', *Historical Journal*, 44 (2001), 79–106.
La Diplomatie comme expérience de l'Autre: consuls français au Maghreb (1700–1840) (Geneva, 2002).
Winter, E., *Russland und das Papsttum*, 3 vols. (Berlin, 1960–1972).

Winterling, A., *Der Hof der Kurfürsten von Köln, 1688–1794: eine Fallstudie zur Bedeutung 'absolutistischer' Hofhaltung* (Bonn, 1986).

Wittram, R., 'Peters des Großen erste Reise in den Westen. Herrmann Aubin zum 23. Dezember 1955', *Jahrbücher für Geschichte Osteuropas*, 3 (1955), 373–403.

Peter I. Czar und Kaiser: zur Geschichte Peters des Großen in seiner Zeit, 2 vols. (Göttingen, 1964).

Wolf, A., 'Geographie und Jurisprudenz – Historia und Genealogie. Zum "Theatrum praetensionum . . . in Europa"', *Ius Commune*, 14 (1987), 225–45.

Wolff, L., 'A duel for ceremonial precedence the Papal Nuncio versus the Russian Ambassador at Warsaw, 1775–1785', *International History Review*, 7 (1985), 235–44.

Inventing Eastern Europe: the map of civilization on the mind of the Enlightenment (Stanford, CA, 1994).

Wood, J. R., Serres, J., *Diplomatic ceremonial and protocol: principles, procedures and practices* (London, 1970).

Wortman, R., *Scenarios of power: myth and ceremony in Russian monarchy*, 2 vols. (Princeton, NJ, 1995–2000).

'Ceremony and empire in the evolution of Russian monarchy', in *Visual texts, ceremonial texts, texts of exploration: collected articles on the representation of Russian monarchy* (Boston, 2014), pp. 27–46.

Zakharine, D., *Von Angesicht zu Angesicht: der Wandel direkter Kommunikation in der ost- und westeuropäischen Neuzeit* (Konstanz, 2005).

Zernack, K., 'Das Zeitalter der nordischen Kriege von 1558 bis 1809 als frühneuzeitliche Geschichtsepoche', *Zeitschrift für Historische Forschung*, 1 (1974), 55–79.

Zitser, E. A. *The transfigured kingdom: sacred parody and charismatic authority at the court of Peter the Great* (Ithaca, NY, 2004).

'Post-Soviet Peter: new histories of the late Muscovite and early imperial Russian court', *Kritika: Explorations in Russian and Eurasian History*, 6 (2005), 375–92.

Zonova, T. V., 'Komparativnyi analiz stanovleniia rossiiskoi i evropeiskoi professional'noi diplomaticheskoi sluzhby', in *Rossiiskaia diplomatiia: istoriia i sovremennost'. Materialy nauchno-prakticheskoi konferentsii, posviashchennoi 450-letiiu sozdaniia Posol'skogo prikaza, 29 oktiabria 1990 goda*, ed. I. S. Ivanov et al. (Moscow, 2001), pp. 93–109.

Unpublished Theses

Beliakov, A. V., 'Sluzhashchie Posol'skogo prikaza vtoroi treti XVII veka' (unpublished doctoral dissertation, Russian Academy of Sciences, Moscow, 2002).

Clayton, R., 'Diplomats and diplomacy in London, 1667–1672' (unpublished DPhil dissertation, University of Oxford, 1995).

Kugeler, H., '"Le parfait ambassadeur." The theory and practice of diplomacy in the century following the Peace of Westphalia' (unpublished DPhil dissertation, University of Oxford, 2006).

Taylor, D. J., 'Russian foreign policy 1725–1739: the Politics of stability and opportunity' (unpublished PhD thesis, University of East Anglia, 1983).

Unkovskaya, M. V., 'Anglo-Russian diplomatic relations, 1580–1696' (unpublished DPhil dissertation, University of Oxford, 1992).

Electronic Resources

Acta Pacis Westphalicae, available from www.pax-westphalica.de/. Last access 6 February 2016.

Allgemeine Deutsche Biographie, 56 vols. (1875–1912, reprint, 1967–1971), available from www.deutsche-biographie.de. Last access 6 February 2016.

A collection of the state papers of John Thurloe, volume 3: December 1654 – August 1655, available from www.british-history.ac.uk/report.aspx?compid=55367#s14. Last access on 6 February 2016.

Bödeker, H. E., '"Europe" in the discourse of the sciences of state in 18th century Germany', *Cromohs*, 8 (2003), 1–14, available from www.cromohs.unifi.it/8_2003/bodeker.html. Last access 6 February 2016.

Calendar of State Papers Relating to English Affairs in the Archives of Venice, Volume 33: 1661–1664 (1932), available from www.british-history.ac.uk/report.aspx?compid=90112. Last access 6 February 2016.

Clayton, R., 'Cotterell, Sir Charles (1615–1701)', *Oxford Dictionary of National Biography* (Oxford 2004), available from www.oxforddnb.com/view/article/6397. Last access 6 February 2016.

Goodwin, G., Kelsey, S., 'Howard, Charles, first earl of Carlisle (1628–1685)', in *Oxford Dictionary of National Biography* (Oxford, online edn., 2009), available from www.oxforddnb.com/view/article/13886. Last access 6 February 2016.

Hartley, J. M., 'Poltavskaia bitva i anglo-rossiiskie otnosheniia', *Voprosy istorii i kul'tury severnykh stran i territorii*, 3 (2009), available from www.hcpncr.com/journ709/journ709hartley.html. Last access 6 February 2016.

Henry, C., 'Le séjour de Pierre le Grand à Paris: contribution à l'histoire de la formation du cabinet de Saint-Pétersbourg', *Publications du Groupe Histoire Architecture Mentalités Urbaines*, available from www.ghamu.org/IMG/pdf/Pierre1er-txt-def-20-04-2011.pdf. Last access 6 February 2015.

Journal of the House of Commons: volume 4: 1644–1646, available from www.british-history.ac.uk/report.aspx?compid=23716. Last access 6 February 2016.

Journal of the House of Lords: volume 8: 1645–1647, available from www.british-history.ac.uk/report.aspx?compid=34049. Last access 6 February 2016.

Journal of the House of Lords: volume 7: 1645, available from www.british-history.ac.uk/report.aspx?compid=33443. Last access 6 February 2016.

Krischer, A., 'Können Rituale gesammelt werden? Vormoderne Aufschreibesysteme für symbolisches Handeln in außereuropäischen Gesellschaften', *TRANS. Internet-Zeitschrift für Kulturwissenschaften*, 15 (2004), available from www.inst.at/trans/15Nr/06_2/krischer15.htm. Last access 6 February 2016.

Larminie, V., 'Miege, Guy (bap. 1644, d. in or after 1718)', *Oxford Dictionary of National Biography* (Oxford, online edn., 2004), available from www.oxforddnb.com/view/article/18687. Last access 6 February 2016.

Le service du Protocole, French Ministry of Foreign Affairs and International Development, available from www.diplomatie.gouv.fr/fr/le-ministere-et-son-reseau/organigramme-de-l-administration/article/le-service-du-protocole. Last access 6 February 2016.

Peskova, G. N., '"Zamysly nashi, mozhet byt', velikie . . .": K 300-letiiu Velikogo posol'stva Petra I', *Mezhdunarodnaia Zhizn'*, 11–12 (1997), 140–49, available from www.idd.mid.ru/letopis_dip_sluzhby_05.html. Last access 6 February 2016.

Poe, M., *Foreign descriptions of Muscovy: an analytic bibliography of primary and secondary sources,* available from *Iowa Research Online* http://ir.uiowa.edu/cgi/viewcontent.cgi?article=1008&context=history_pubs. Last accessed 6 February 2016.

Rauschenbach, S., 'Albert Heidenfeld: Asiatischer Schauplatz', *Welt und Wissen auf der Bühne: Theatrum-Literatur der Frühen Neuzeit,* available from www.theatra.de/repertorium/ed000094.pdf. Last access 6 February 2016.

Rogozhin, N. M., Boguslavskii, A. A., 'Posol'skie knigi kontsa XV – nachala XVIII vv.', *Vostochnaia literatura: srednevekovye istoricheskie istochniki vostoka i zapada,* available from www.vostlit.info/Texts/Dokumenty/Russ/XVI/Posolbook/PosolBook.html. Last access 6 February 2016.

Seaward, P., 'Hyde, Edward, first earl of Clarendon (1609–1674)', *Oxford Dictionary of National Biography* (Oxford, online edn., 2008), available from www.oxforddnb.com/view/article/14328. Last access 6 February 2016.

Smith, D. L., 'Colepeper, John, first Baron Colepeper (bap. 1600, d. 1660)', *Oxford Dictionary of National Biography* (Oxford, online edn., 2005), available from www.oxforddnb.com/view/article/5876. Last access 6 February 2016.

Thumfart, J., 'Zurzeit liegt Osteuropa im Orient', *Zeit Online,* 22 September 2010, available from www.zeit.de/kultur/literatur/2010-09/literaturfestival-berlin-osteuropa. Last access 6 February 2016.

Venning, T., 'Prideaux, William (1604/5–1660)', *Oxford Dictionary of National Biography* (Oxford, online edn., 2008), available from www.oxforddnb.com/view/article/66273. Last access 6 February 2016.

Vulpius, R., 'Das Imperium als Thema der Russischen Geschichte: Tendenzen und Perspektiven der jüngeren Forschung', *Zeitenblicke,* 6 (2007), available from www.zeitenblicke.de/2007/2/vulpius/index_html. Last accessed 6 February 2016.

Weller, T., '*Kein Schauplatz* der Eitelkeiten: das frühneuzeitliche *Theatrum Praecedentiae* zwischen gelehrtem Diskurs und sozialer Praxis', *Metaphorik.de,* 14 (2008), 379–403, esp. p. 406, available from www.metaphorik.de/sites/www.metaphorik.de/files/journal-pdf/14_2008_weller.pdf. Last access 6 February 2016.

Audio Visual Materials

Petrov, V. M., *Petr Pervyi* (Lenfil'm, 1937–1938).

Index